D0146574

WHEN A COMMUNITY WEEPS

WHEN A COMMUNITY WEEPS:
Case Studies in Group Survivorship

Edited by

Ellen S. Zinner, Psy.D.
Mary Beth Williams, Ph.D.

BRUNNER/MAZEL
Taylor & Francis Group

USA	Publishing Office:	BRUNNER/MAZEL
		A member of the Taylor & Francis Group
		325 Chestnut Street, Suite 800
		Philadelphia, PA 19106
		Tel: (215) 625-8900
		Fax: (215) 625-2940
	Distribution Center:	BRUNNER/MAZEL
		A member of the Taylor & Francis Group
		47 Runway Road, Suite G
		Levittown, PA 19057-4700
		Tel: (215) 269-0400
		Fax: (215) 269-0363
UK		BRUNNER/MAZEL
		A member of the Taylor & Francis Group
		1 Gunpowder Square
		London EC4A 3DE
		Tel: 171 583 0490
		Fax: 171 583 0581

WHEN A COMMUNITY WEEPS: Case Studies in Group Survivorship

1 2 3 4 5 6 7 8 9 0

Printed by Edwards Brothers, Ann Arbor, MI, 1998.

A CIP catalog record for this book is available from the British Library.
∞ The paper in this publication meets the requirements of the ANSI Standard Z39.48-1984 (Permanence of Paper)

Library of Congress Cataloging-in-Publication Data

Zinner, Ellen
    When a community weeps: case studies in group survivorship / Ellen S. Zinner, Mary Beth Williams.
        p. cm. — (Series in trauma and loss)
    Includes bibliographical references and index.

    1. Social psychology. 2. Collective behavior. 3. Community psychology.
4. Psychic trauma—Social aspects. 5. Disasters—Social aspects. 6. Disasters—Psychological aspects. 7. Bereavement—Social aspects. I. Williams, Mary Beth.
II. Title. III. Series.
HM251.Z553 1998
    320—dc21   98-25989
                                                                                                              CIP

ISBN: 0-87630-953-8 (case)

*To my father, Louis Jack Scheiner (1921–1998),
to make him proud—E.S.Z.*

*To John Calvin Little and Elizabeth Kerr Little, my parents,
whose caring for others and the belief "It Can Be Done" guide me;
And to George Oravec Kemeny and Esther Kemeny,
my surrogate parents and Holocaust survivors,
who began me on my path of helping the traumatized—M.B.W.*

*To the victims and survivors past, present, and future
whose resilience and courage inspire us all.*

Contents

INTRODUCTION

PART ONE   HUMANMADE AND NATURAL DISASTERS

SYNOPSIS

Contributors

ELLEN S. ZINNER, Psy.D., is a certified grief therapist and death educator and a licensed psychologist who has taught, counseled, and published in the area of grief and loss for over 25 years. She is past president of the Association for Death Education and Counseling and cochaired the International Conference on Grief and Bereavement held in Washington, DC, in 1997. Her numerous publications have spanned the topics of death education, adolescent suicide, death and loss on college campuses, and loss support groups within assisted living centers. In 1996, she established and coordinated the Bereavement and Hospice Support Netline (www.ubalt.edu/www/bereavement), a national web resource of support groups across the United States. Dr. Zinner is Assistant Provost at the University of Baltimore and currently serves as president of the Maryland Psychological Association.

MARY BETH WILLIAMS, Ph.D., LCSW, CTS, is the author, coauthor, and editor of numerous publications about trauma. Dr. Williams is a board member of the International Society for Trauma and Stress Studies and the President of the Association of Traumatic Stress Specialists. She is a consultant to the Police College of Finland in Espoo, Finland, and is a Diplomate member of the American Academy of Police Psychologists. Dr. Williams has also been a school social worker for the Falls Church City School System for over two decades. She is director of the Trauma Recovery Education and Counseling Center, a private practice in Warrenton, Virginia. A Phi Beta Kappa graduate of the College of Wooster (Ohio), she received her M.S.W. degree from Syracuse and later earned her Ph.D. in Human Development and Organizational Systems Development from the Fielding Institute.

Contributors

G. ROBERT "BOB" BAKER, M.S.W., Ph.D., psychologist, social worker, certified alcohol counselor, and certified trauma specialist, is a founding board member of the International Association of Trauma Counseling. Known to kids as "Dr. Bear," he led development of "Bearaby," a technique using Teddy Bears to help traumatized children through role playing, coping skills development, and storytelling. A disabled combat Marine who served in Vietnam, Dr. Baker spent nearly 20 years working with other veterans through the U.S. Veterans Administration, primarily at the National Center for Post-Traumatic Stress Disorder and as a Vet Center Director. A former patrolman and police chief, he has also counseled, debriefed, and crisis-trained members of law enforcement and various emergency services in the United States and overseas. He has worked worldwide with survivors of natural and manmade disasters and violent crime by providing trauma counseling and training.

DAVID BOLTON, CQSW, CCETSW, is the Community Health and Social Services Manager and Executive Director of Social Work with the Sperrin Lakeland HPSS Trust in the Fermanagh District of Northern Ireland. His work in trauma support arose from the Remembrance Day Bombing in Enniskillen in November, 1987. A year later, he was asked to assist with the repatriation of passengers and their families following the Kegworth aircrash. In 1991, Mr. Bolton began providing a training series to support civil services managers dealing with Northern Ireland bombings. He continues to provide counseling for people who have experienced trauma. Through conference presentations and publications, he has contributed to the development of a relatively new area of social work response to individual and community adjustment to violence.

RICHARD R. ELLIS, Ed.D., is an Associate Professor of Applied Psychology, Department of Applied Psychology, in the School of Education at New York University. For 31 years, he has taught in the Programs of Counseling (M.A. degree) and Counseling Psychology (Ph.D. degree) and, in 1985, founded the first M.A. degree program specializing in grief and loss counseling. Prior to his NYU post, Dr. Ellis was the supervisory coordinator of the Institute for Developmental Studies, designers of the blueprint for the National Head Start Program. He is a long-standing member of the Association for Death Education and Counseling (ADEC) and is ADEC-certified as a Professional Death Educator and Grief Counselor. He frequently works with Ph.D. students researching death-related topics.

ROBIN H. GURWITCH, Ph.D., a clinical psychologist, is an Assistant Professor in the Department of Pediatrics at the University of Oklahoma Health Sciences Center. Dr. Gurwitch is involved in service, training, and research focusing on child and family issues. Since the bombing in Oklahoma City, she has been an active participant in the assessment and treatment of families affected by this disaster. In conjunction with colleagues both from the Health Sciences Center and around the country, Dr. Gurwitch is conducting several projects to aid in our understanding of how manmade disasters may impact young children. She shares her experiences and finding with professionals at state and national meetings.

LYNDA HARRELL became a freelance writer after a 15-year career in human resource management in Dallas, Texas. She writes for a variety of business and general audience journals and works on commercial projects. Mrs. Harrell and her husband, Jackson, lost their only child in 1994. Leslie Michelle Harrell was murdered at the age of 21. The crime remains unsolved. At the time of Leslie's death, the Harrells challenged Dallas' standard ruling against organ donation in homicide cases. Their effort saved lives and helped them accept their loss. Mrs. Harrell has remained active with her local donor family community since her daughter's death and organ donation.

ANIE SANENTZ KALAYJIAN, R.N.C., Ph.D., D.D.L., is an educator, international trauma expert, logotherapeutic psychotherapist, registered professional nurse, researcher, and consultant. She has over 10 years of experience in disaster management and mass-trauma intervention and over 15 years of clinical and teaching experience. She is the author of *Disaster & Mass Trauma: Global Perspectives on Post Disasters Mental Health Management.* For the past three years, Dr. Sanentz Kalayjian has been actively involved at the United Nations, pursuing the human rights of children, survivors, women, and refugees. She is the World Federation for Mental Health representative for the United Nations and currently serves as cochair of its Human Rights Committee. Dr. Sanentz Kalayjian is founder and President of the Armenian American Society for Studies on Stress and Genocide and cofounder of the Mental Health Outreach Program to the Republic of Armenia.

AMIA LIEBLICH, Ph.D., is a full professor of psychology at the Hebrew University in Jerusalem, Israel, specializing in psychological issues of the Israeli society: the effects of military service, gender differences in Israel, and the Kibbutz. She has been a visiting professor in several American universities, including University of Michigan (Ann Arbor) and the University of California (Berkeley). Dr. Lieblich has published numerous articles in professional journals as well as several books in Hebrew and English. Dr. Lieblich's books include *Transition to Adulthood During Military Service (1989)* and *Seasons of Captivity* (1994).

RUTH MALKINSON, Ph.D., teaches at the Bob Shapell School of Social Work, Tel Aviv University. She is the immediate past president of the Israeli Association for Family and Marital Therapy and coordinator of the Bereavement

Fund based at the School of Social Work. Dr. Malkinson specializes in Cognitive Therapy, especially Rational Emotive Behavior Therapy (REBT) and its application to grief, and combines it in her research, therapy, and teaching. She has lectured and published in Israel and abroad in the area of loss, trauma, and bereavement. She is coeditor, along with Eliezer Witztum and Simon S. Rubin, of the forthcoming text, *Traumatic and Non-Traumatic Loss and Bereavement: Clinical Theory and Research* (International Universities Press).

LASSE NURMI, M.A., Doctoral Candidate, is senior lecturer at the Police College of Finland and is a member of the Finnish Disaster Victims Identification Team. He is a consultant in Critical Incident Stress Management and debriefing and hostage negotiation assistance, working with various organizations including FinnAir, hospitals, and governmental departments. From 1979–1986, he served as a military psychologist. Mr. Nurmi has written extensively in the field of traumatic stress and is coauthor of *Death of a Co-Worker* and the forthcoming *Creating a Comprehensive Trauma Center: Choices and Challenges* (Plenum). Mr. Nurmi is a founding member of the Finnish Folk Band Kyläpelimannit.

KAREN A. SITTERLE, Ph.D., is a Clinical Associate Professor of Psychology at the University of Texas Southwestern Medical Center, Dallas, Texas, and is in private practice. She specializes in the treatment of trauma-related disorders and bereavement in children and adults and provides debriefing, training, and consultation to individuals, organizations, and communities experiencing traumatic and violent events. She has responded to numerous disasters including several plane crashes, hurricanes, shootings, and the Oklahoma City bombing. She has authored many publications, consulted on three ABC specials entitled *I Survived a Disaster,* and codirected the video, *Hope and Recovery: Ritual and Remembrance.* Dr. Sitterle is also on the APA Disaster Response Network National Task Force and is a coauthor of the American Psychological Association's Report on *The Mental Health Response to the Oklahoma City Bombing.*

ROD WATTS, Ph.D., M.S.W., is the manager of Rehab Plus, a rehabilitation facility in Auckland, New Zealand, with inpatient, outpatient, and community-based programs. Preceding this position, he worked in rehabilitation in Australia, as a consultant in trauma management, and as a trainer in debriefing for the New South Wales Institute of Psychiatry. Dr. Watts completed a Ph.D. in the field of psychiatry, examining the impact of large-scale bus accidents and associated benefits of psychological follow-up. His Masters of Social Work thesis was based on a longitudinal study of the levels of distress of people with cancer. Dr. Watts has had several publications in the area of trauma. He is particularly interested in how to ease the imprint and consequences of trauma on the psyche.

TOM WILLIAMS, Psy.D., attended the U.S. Naval Academy and served in the Marine Corps, including two years in Vietnam. He received his Doctor of Psychology degree from the University of Denver. As a clinical psychologist, he has specialized in emotional recovery from traumatic events. He is a founding board member of the *Journal of Traumatic Stress* and has edited two textbooks on posttraumatic stress disorder. He lives in Bellingham, Washington, and is a consultant to Crisis Management International in Atlanta, Georgia.

MARISE WILSON, B.Soc.Studs., completed her social work education at Sydney University in 1973. Her early career was spent in Sydney, Australia, with the state child welfare department before moving to the town of Kempsey in northern New South Wales. She identifies her appointment to the then embryonic mental health team as the beginning of a period of great personal and professional growth. As Acting Coordinator (Community Health) in December 1979, she managed the team response to Australia's worst road accident, the Kempsey Bus Disaster. Out of this event, she has developed a deep empathy for victims of trauma and their helpers and honed skills in group debriefings and individual counseling. Mrs. Wilson now lives in the city of Newcastle, where she teaches community welfare and maintains a private practice.

ELIEZER WITZTUM, M.D., is Professor in the Division of Psychiatry, Faculty of the Health Sciences, at Ben Gurion University of the Negev, and Director of Psychotherapy Supervision, Mental Health Center, Beer Sheva, Israel. He also serves as Senior Psychiatrist at the Jerusalem Mental Health Center where he established a Cultural and Religion Consultation Unit providing culturally sensitive psychiatry services to religious patients. Dr. Witztum is well known for his work in the fields of medical psychology, forensic and cultural psychiatry, and dissociation and posttraumatic stress disorder in relation to the Arab–Israeli wars. His book, *Traumatic and Non-Traumatic Loss and Bereavement: Clinical Theory and Practice*, edited with Ruth Malkinson and Simon S. Rubin, will be published next year by International Universities Press.

Foreword

Up until the time my father died when I was 17 years old, I had witnessed tears in his eyes on only two occasions. The second was during a time of life-threat to one of our family members. It reflected the well-known dynamics that operate when one confronts the possibility of the death of a dearly beloved other with whom a deep and personally meaningful and reciprocal attachment has been sustained, and when that loss specifically threatens the very structure, stability, and continued existence of one's intimate family group. Countless publications have been devoted to the analysis of this experience, informing the wider mental health community in general and the disciplines of thanatology and traumatology specifically. There have been many concepts and terms to describe what my father underwent.

In contrast, the first occurrence manifested a phenomenon that heretofore has not received even the smallest fraction of the attention accorded to individual responses to threatened and actual loss. It was in reaction to the death of someone my father did not personally know, yet experienced by him as a significant enough event to generate the type of public sorrowful behavior that I was to observe only once more in his lifetime. This initial incident was the funeral of the assassinated President John F. Kennedy in 1963. My father's response was, I now know in retrospect, the first and, for me, one of the most potent examples of group survivorship. Up until now, there has been insufficient conceptualization and an absent lexicon to describe what I observed with him. The process simply has not been the subject of concerted investigation and in-depth examination. Thanks to Ellen Zinner and Mary Beth Williams, this oversight has been corrected with *When A Community Weeps: Case Studies in Group Survivorship.*

The phenomenon of group survivorship involves a fascinating interplay of factors specific to the individual and to his/her community, which operate as the individual contends with the death of one or more members of the group. Given the requisite experience of death loss, concepts of trauma are necessarily relevant in group survivorship. This is true even following deaths that are not unexpected, violent, horrific, preventable, or that personally expose one to life threat or grotesquerie. This is because postdeath acute grief, even that which is relatively benign, can be legitimately viewed as a form of traumatic stress reaction (Rando, In press). Arguments for this revolve around each of these two processes having inherent involvement with loss, being significantly associated with anxiety, and sharing six broad areas of similarity. For both acute grief and traumatic stress—whether or not criteria are met for diagnosis of posttraumatic stress disorder, acute stress disorder, or any other mental disorder recognized in the American Psychiatric Association's *Diagnostic and Statistical Manual of Mental Disorders, Fourth Edition* (DSM-IV, 1994)—two tasks are presented to the affected individual: trauma mastery and loss accommodation (i.e., healthy mourning).

For both individuals and groups (construed herein, as in systems theory, to be more than merely the sum of the members), a trauma can be considered to be any experience generating intense anxiety too powerful to be assimilated or dealt with in typical fashion, overwhelming the individual or group and engendering feelings of loss of control, helplessness, and other flooding affects. Frequently, it is accompanied by the shattering of fundamental assumptions on which life has been predicated (Janoff-Bulman, 1992). In instances of traumatic bereavement, these coincide with other violations of the mourner's assumptive world pertaining either to specific assumptions about the deceased or to global assumptions about the self, others, life, or the world in general (Rando, 1993). Such violated assumptions comprise some of the many psychosocial "secondary losses" (Rando, 1984) that develop consequent to a death and create additional loss and trauma for the mourner.

It is fair to say, theretofore, that in all trauma there is loss, and that in most loss there are at least some dimensions of trauma. This means that group survivorship inherently incorporates both experiences of loss and traumatization. These experiences—and their ensuant grief/mourning and traumatic stress—depend upon the unique constellation of dozens of specific factors operating to influence the situation, the individuals, and the group. It may also involve the experience of vicarious bereavement, which alone or in combination with other processes adds to the interesting complexion of group survivorship.

As a social phenomenon, one of the ways in which group survivorship can be analyzed is according to whether or not the deceased member(s) was personally known by the surviving members. Elsewhere I have written about the concept of *vicarious bereavement* (Rando, 1997). I address it here because of its strong relevance in many cases of group survivorship. As I had conceptualized it, vicarious bereavement refers to the experience of loss and consequent grief and mourning that occur following the deaths of others *not* personally known by the mourner. The three psychological processes necessary for its development are empathy, sympathy, and identification.

Two types of vicarious bereavement exist. In Type I, losses to the mourner are exclusively vicarious, and are mildly to moderately identified with what is being experienced by the actual mourner (e.g., the vicarious mourner feels that this is what it must be like to be in the actual mourner's position). In Type II, in addition to the vicarious losses being identified with, there are personally experienced losses. These develop as a consequence of (a) relatively intense reactions to the actual mourner's loss (e.g., the vicarious mourner feels quite personally shocked, shaken, and adversely impacted in response to the actual mourner's experiencing the traumatic death of a loved one), and/or (b) any assumptive world violations sustained by the vicarious mourner. These violations may occur either because of heightened identification with the actual mourner (e.g., the vicarious mourner so identifies with the actual mourner that he/she experiences a shattering of his/her own sense of parental control when the actual mourner's child is killed) and/or traumatization of the vicarious mourner secondary to the circumstances of the death under which the actual mourner had lost the loved one (e.g., the vicarious mourner becomes traumatized by the violent and mutilating death of the actual mourner's loved one, and consequently experiences personal assumptive world violations, such as a loss of security). Although the term vicarious bereavement may seem a little bit of a misnomer because personal bereavement is stimulated in this case, it is retained because it is useful in focusing attention on the fact that bereavement initially can be stimulated by losses not personally experienced.

In those situations where the death of the group member has not severed a reciprocal personal relationship, vicarious bereavement probably partially explains some group survivors' responses. There may be at least two additional factors. First, a variation of vicarious bereavement might be stimulated in an individual who survives a traumatic event that takes the lives of others. Although these others may be personally unknown, the experience of being in the same event that took their lives may be sufficient to create a sense of communality or identification with the victims, or enough survivor guilt, to bring grief over their deaths. As well, heightened senses of empathy and sympathy for, and identification with, the victims' survivors can create vicarious bereavement as described above.

An additional factor, and one particularly evidenced in the wake of Princess Diana's tragic death in 1997, may be the mourner's getting caught up in the responses of others. In other words, the group survivor's responses are not just to the actual death and the loss it signifies, but as well are a response to others' responses. In this regard, witnessing the grieving behaviors of other survivors (e.g., seeing others overwhelmed, crying, and leaving flowers in reaction to Princess Diana's car crash) can catalyze grief responses in that witness. Depending upon the person and circumstances, this can be the result of the observed reactions of others: (1) inviting imitation, (2) disinhibiting one's grief, (3) providing implicit legitimization of certain feelings and/or permission to engage in particular behaviors, (4) stimulating unfinished business about other losses or important issues in one's past or present life, (5) eliciting a contagion response, or (6) creating a sense of community via commonly shared experiences. It is in this last course of action that one can see how a kinship can be specifically formed with others via one's responses to trauma, death, and loss.

Survivor groups can be created prior to the event (e.g., family, local community), during it (e.g., emergency services workers, crisis interveners), or after it concludes (e.g., mental health professionals, loved ones of the victims). They may be strongly, narrowly, or rigidly defined. Group membership may be formally designated or self-assigned. Among other traits, survivor groups may be transitory or permanent, naturally developed or officially created, inclusive or exclusionary, facilitative of or inhibitory to healthy mourning and adaptation. The point so well made by this book is that there is a unique constellation of influencing variables, along with personal and psychosocial contextual issues, that go into the creation of these survivor groups. In turn, the groups both affect and are affected by the individual member's responses to the loss and trauma experienced. Effective interventions on either the individual or group level requires being appropriately informed about both, and realizing that questions about the meanings and impacts of losses of people not personally known must be asked.

While people have been experiencing group survivorship since the dawn of time, it appears there are a number of changes that have intensified the group survivorship phenomenon in recent years. Among other changes, two prominent ones need to be mentioned here. The first is that there is a greater probability of death today to be sudden and unexpected, and associated with traumatic circumstances. This is because technological advances have decreased the proportion of natural death and increased the proportion of unnatural death (i.e., accidents, suicide, and homicide). While biomedical technology helps people survive illnesses that previously would have killed them, it leaves them alive longer to be susceptible to unnatural death, through greater exposure to potentially dangerous technology such as motor vehicles, mass-transport vehicles (e.g., airplanes, ferries, trains) that can take the lives of a larger number of people if there is mishap, weapons of mass destruction, and toxic chemicals. To add to the increased chance of sudden, traumatic death, recent sociocultural trends have culminated in significant increases in political and societal violence, acts of terrorism, and homicide rates.

Thus, human-induced mass disasters and terrorist actions are particularly relevant to the creation of survivor groups, especially those that are significantly traumatized due to the nature of these types of deaths. They tend to embody a number of high-risk factors identified to make any death circumstance traumatic. As adapted from Rando (1994), these include: (1) suddenness and lack of anticipation; (2) violence, mutilation, and destruction, (3) preventability and/or randomness; (4) loss of a child; (5) multiple death; and (6) the mourner's personal encounter with death secondary to either (a) a significant threat to survival, or (b) a massive and/or shocking confrontation with the death and mutilation of others. Certainly, one readily can see how these factors are present as well in natural disasters, and are vividly exemplified in the case examples within this volume.

The second critical change intensifying the experience of group survivorship is the role of the media. Here is found an example of the "double-edged sword" effect *par excellence.* On the one hand, as illustrated so well in the majority of these chapters, the media can be a positive, therapeutic agent. It can disseminate necessary and accurate information about the event. It can provide acknowledgment of precisely what has happened, and be the vehicle by which healing can be promoted, even early on, if it is effectively utilized by leaders who convey messages that enable and provide direction for healthy grief. It can illustrate the fact that others are impacted too, and that there are concerned individuals, communities, and nations that care about the survivor's losses and traumatization and share the survivor's sorrow and the often accompanying feelings, such as shock, confusion, outrage, and so forth. Media can be the conduit for telling one's story, connecting individuals to others, and reducing disenfranchisement (see Doka, 1989). Media can help—through the repetitious recounting of events, presentation of images, and the analysis provided by experts—to facilitate the beginning of cognitively grasping what has occurred, and therefore enable the beginnings of mourning and, ultimately, the composition of the narrative of the event. These processes can also be a way of coping with the emotions that have been generated, and they can implicitly and explicitly provide the legitimization and permission to appropriately engage in grief and self-care after trauma. The psychoeducational information media transmits can eliminate or ameliorate problems, as can its encouraging self-referral to professionals if necessary.

However, the other side of the double-edged sword slices. In this case, it can increase the suffering of actual mourners, and actually create vicarious mourners, by the confrontation of the public with graphic images of and horrifying information about traumatic events and the responses of others to them. These can perpetuate one's already-existing traumatization, or can create it through the arousal of great anxiety, an internal sense of terror and helplessness, frightening perceptions, and other traumatic sequelae. Secondary traumatic stress (Figley, 1995) is spawned. Additional problems occur when secondary victimization (Remer & Elliot, 1988a, 1988b) takes place because of the media's insensitivity or intrusion, or when it is perceived to fail to acknowledge certain realities about given individuals or groups.

Perhaps there has been no other agent that has been as valued and as vilified in contemporary events creating group survivorship, and in impacting upon so many of the dynamics of that very survivorship, as the media.

Although thanatologists and traumatologists have long noted that death and trauma occur in a social context, this book, moreso than any other, clarifies and explores this reality to which so many authors have merely given lip-service in their inclusion of the dimension among lists of factors identified to influence response. Like it or not, the human being is embedded in a sociocultural fabric that is an important determinant of one's personal reactions and that, in itself, becomes colored by those reactions. Social "ripples" after death have been mentioned, but their clinical impacts upon survivor groups have never been this carefully probed. Zinner and Williams have orchestrated a resource that has clearly identified a phenomenon, richly illustrated it with cases that give it life, delineated critical therapeutic conclusions that are, in many cases, generalizable to numerous other situations, and, in lucid, practical terms, provided the specifics for effective intervention with survivors on the individual and group levels.

Whether one is interested in group survivorship from an individual, group, systems, ethnocultural, national, or international perspective; regardless if he/she is concerned about policy, planning, or intervention; and irrespective of focus upon directly affected family members, communities, or emergency services personnel, or upon vicarious mourners of any kind, *When A Community Weeps: Case Studies in Group Survivorship* addresses relevant concerns. In the Introduction, Williams, Zinner, and Ellis put forth the conceptual integration of grief and trauma, concluding with a series of questions to assist the reader in examining how actual communities responded to the problem of coping with nodal traumatic events that took the lives of one or more members, and offering some preliminary thoughts as to how communities begin to heal. In the Summary, Zinner and Williams delineate a reference frame for community recovery and restoration. This, one of the highlights of the book, should be in the armamentarium of *every* thanatologist, traumatologist, sociologist, and community and disaster planner, along with those having *anything* to do with such areas.

In between these two chapters are ten that examine specific traumas resulting from the death of one or more community members. Each is remarkable in its own right, poignantly portraying one or more grieving survivor groups and identifying concrete strategies for coping with the trauma and the death, loss, and traumatic stress encountered. There are gems to be found in all. While space prevents me from synopsizing the chapters, let me identify one of the nuggets from each.

In Zinner's discussion of the *Challenger* disaster (Chapter 2), the reader finds an excellent specification of the four levels of survivor groups and an enumeration of the social rights and obligations of these groups. In Chapter 3, a discussion of the *Estonia* disaster, Nurmi provides a candid and critical look at what to do and, more importantly, what not to do with rescue workers and other emergency services personnel. In their discussion of an Australian bus crash in Chapter 4, Watts and Wilson present quite interesting information about the long-term effects of rescue work and its impact, not only among those who were at the scene, but upon those subsequently hired to the disaster-response team years after the event.

Analyzing the community response to the earthquake in Armenia (Chapter 5), Kalayjian asserts that concepts of logotherapy, or existential analysis, are especially helpful in enabling survivors to cope with disaster—given that when all else has been taken away by trauma the individual is left with the "ultimate freedom" to choose one's attitude in even the worst circumstances. Williams, Baker, and Williams, in their examination of the Kobe, Japan earthquake (Chapter 6), address how, unfortunately, a country's cultural mandates can prohibit acceptance of greatly needed assistance and interfere with emotional self-care in the survivors.

Turning to the topic of the loss of leaders and heroes, Witztum and Malkinson address the assassination of Israeli Prime Minister Yitzhak Rabin (Chapter 7). The authors compare and contrast individual bereavement with that of social-collective grief, observing that differing needs at differing times can lead to responses that serve one group at the expense of the other. In Chapter 8, exploring the legacy of Mickey Mantle following the death of the newly reborn hero, Harnell demonstrates that groups can recover in part by taking action to restore balance after a loss, turning their grief into positive undertakings.

Sitterle and Gurwitch offer detailed and extremely useful information regarding mental health operations after disasters based upon their work after the Oklahoma City terrorist bombing (Chapter 9). Another bombing, this time in Enniskillen, Northern Ireland (Chapter 10), is the focus for Bolton's compelling analysis of the impacts upon and interventions required for community belonging and communality that is attacked by terrorism springing from decades of political conflict. In Chapter 11, Lieblich beautifully weaves together the three developmental processes—covering the personal, social, and national levels—that both influence and are influenced by the unexpected death of a 30-year-old member of an Israeli kibbutz, as the community struggles with the confusion and uncertainty of its continued existence.

While I have intuitively "known" for many years the issues about my father's grief over the death of John F. Kennedy, I very much appreciate Ellen Zinner and Mary Beth Williams for providing me with the conceptual framework, the language, and the clinical information enabling me to understand, speak about, and appreciate these issues so much more today.

Therese A. Rando, Ph.D.
The Institute for the Study and Treatment of Loss
Warwick, Rhode Island

REFERENCES

American Psychiatric Association. (1994). *Diagnostic and statistical manual of mental disorders.* (Fourth Edition). Washington, DC: Author.

Doka, K. (Ed.). (1989). *Disenfranchised grief: Recognizing hidden sorrow.* Lexington, MA: Lexington.

Figley, C. (Ed.). (1995). *Compassion fatigue: Coping with secondary traumatic stress disorder in those who treat the traumatized.* New York: Brunner/Mazel.

Janoff-Bulman, R. (1992). *Shattered assumptions: Towards a new psychology of trauma.* New York: The Free Press.

Rando, T. A. (1984). *Grief, dying, and death: Clinical interventions for caregivers.* Champaign, IL: Research Press.

Rando, T. A. (1993). *Treatment of complicated mourning.* Champaign, IL: Research Press.

Rando, T. A. (1994). Complications in mourning traumatic death. In I. Corless, B. Germino, & M. Pittman (Eds.), *Dying, death, and bereavement: Theoretical perspectives and other ways of knowing.* Boston: Jones and Bartlett Publishers.

Rando, T. A. (1997). Vicarious bereavement. In S. Strack (Ed.), *Death and the quest for meaning.* Northvale, NJ: Jason Aronson.

Rando, T. A. (In Press). On the experience of traumatic stress and anticipatory and postdeath grief and mourning. In T. A. Rando (Ed.), *Clinical dimensions of anticipatory mourning: Theory and practice in working with the dying, their loved ones, and caregivers.* Champaign, IL: Research Press.

Remer, R., & Elliot, J. (1988a). Characteristics of secondary victims of sexual assault. *International Journal of Family Psychiatry, 9*(4), 373–387.

Remer, R., & Elliot, J. (1988b). Management of secondary victims of sexual assaults. *International Journal of Family Psychiatry, 9*(4), 389–401.

Preface

This book on group survivorship has been a long time in coming. I am not referring to the time involved with the publishing process: creating a proposal, soliciting authors, and putting experiences and insights onto hard copy. I write, instead, of the earliest threads of interest or awareness in society's need to cope with sudden change and loss.

I was a 17-year-old freshman at a women's college outside Baltimore when John F. Kennedy was assassinated. The news of his having been shot moved quickly round the campus that November Friday. While many afternoon classes were cancelled, my 2:30 PM English class was not—my professor believed that routine should not be disrupted despite the enormity of the event. Her decision angered me at the time; it still does. Even then I believed that the everyday activities of people must pause in acknowledgment of life-altering occurrences.

That weekend, perhaps it was Saturday night or Sunday morning, I joined a friend in journeying to Washington, DC, just an hour away, to pay our respects to the slain president lying in state in the Capitol Rotunda. We went late, planning our arrival for a time when few others would be there. But, despite the hour, the line of quietly crying people wended its way out of the government building, down the east portico steps, and across First Avenue. I was amazed. I had never expected to be part of such a community outpouring of emotions. I had never before felt myself so much a part of a larger community.

My career as a death educator started but 5 years later. My interest, then as a sociologist and later as a clinical psychologist, and always as an active member of the Association for Death Education and Counseling, has predominantly been with the ways individuals cope with loss. But always I have been fascinated by and drawn to the larger scale of bereavement, believing then, as now, that the group psyche requires attention when wounded and that members of a wounded group cannot readily recover as separate and isolated elements of the whole. The *Challenger* explosion in 1986 reaffirmed my involvement personally and professionally in group survivorship, and the chapter that appears in this text on the *Challenger* disaster has been one that I have wanted to explore since my first hearing of that loss to our space program and to the American nation.

But the idea of examining community disasters across nations, time, and type required more energy and ideas than I alone possessed. Mary Beth Williams, a trauma counselor and traumatologist who had been involved early in the trauma field, made the difference in moving this idea to reality.

Ellen S. Zinner

The year was 1994; the place, Stockholm, Sweden. After the conference chair for the succeeding 1997 International Conference on Grief and Bereavement in Contemporary Society was announced, I made my way up to her—Ellen Zinner—to introduce myself as a neighboring colleague in the Greater Washington, DC area and to offer my help. From that meeting has developed a close friendship and, hopefully, a series of grief- and trauma-related books yet to come.

My journey into the world of group survivorship also includes a flashbulb memory of the death of President Kennedy. I, too, was a freshman, then at the College of Wooster in Ohio. Unlike Ellen's experience, our college stopped. What I remember most were the church bells tolling. Everyone went to the nearest church to pray. For days, I was engulfed by the grief and wedded to any television set I could find.

But my awareness of group survivorship goes back much further—to my first 8 years in Wellsville, Ohio and my days and nights with my parents' best friends and my surrogate parents, George and Esther Kemeny—Holocaust survivors who introduced me to the world of survivorship, resilience, and continuity. And, as a daughter of a Presbyterian minister/state police officer, I was, perhaps, predestined to find a path toward trauma work. It was through my association with the International Society for Trauma and Stress Studies that I put a name to the work I was doing. It is through the Association for Trauma and Stress Specialists that I try to bring voice to the sufferings of survivors in as many arenas as I can.

Mary Beth Williams

Our mutual efforts paralleled the coming together in 1996 of two professionals whose reputations in the grief and trauma fields, respectively, are known and highly regarded throughout the world. Therese Rando and Charles Figley were working with the Taylor & Francis Group to create a book series that might bring together the field of grief and bereavement with that of trauma and crisis intervention. While clearly overlapping in many areas, these two fields have developed independently, and relatively few professionals published or shared their work across both areas. This historic separation denied ready exposure to the predominant theoretical models and clinical techniques of both camps. The new book series, *Trauma and Loss,* was designed to emphasize and blend areas of mutual interest and concern. We are very proud to be editing an early volume in this series.

When we contacted the chapter authors for this text, we asked each to tell the story of the crisis in which they had been involved either vicariously or directly. What we wanted was for the reader to get a true flavor of the event, its preceding history and cultural context, its statistical and existential dimensions, and the response mustered by the community involved and those surrounding the affected group. We asked the authors to tell "the story," not only because this would be more inherently interesting but also because an understanding of intervention efforts is not solely or even largely an academic pursuit. Only after they had the story laid out were the authors to assess what was helpful or harmful to the survivors of these communal disasters.

Each author has fulfilled these requests. From Japan to Armenia, the United States to Israel, Australia to Northern Ireland to Finland, the reader is invited to review the events that shook a community or communities and the efforts to respond to the immediate and longer range needs of crisis victims. The summary section of this text is a synthesis of the issues, strategies, and goals addressed in each of the chapters. It is an effort to bring together in one place, across a time line from the beginning of a trauma until its general physical and emotional resolution, a reference framework that can direct future intervenors in their work. We do not present a causative model here. Instead, we highlight issues that must be addressed within the context of the particular crisis, in a particular culture, under particular social, political, and historical circumstances. Sensitizing concepts that each of the authors have identified and found to be especially relevant to the incidents they describe are noted in the hopes that these may serve as signposts to guide others in the future.

When a Community Weeps: Case Studies in Group Survivorship is a collegial effort of professionals, deeply involved in trauma, loss, and grief, to assist communities and other social groups to recover when the fabric of social networks has been torn by crisis. We salute them, their colleagues, and those they serve.

Ellen S. Zinner and
Mary Beth Williams

Acknowledgments

An edited work is, by definition, the contribution of many. The editors would like to begin by thanking each other for bringing unique talents and temperaments to what turned out to be a larger task than we first realized. Our chapter authors, however, lightened our labor by providing us with fascinating and remarkable accounts of difficulties experienced and challenges endured in many areas of the globe. Their expertise in assessing and/or responding to these crises and their patience in participating with us in bringing together these experiences into one contributory whole is greatly appreciated. Futhermore, our series editors, Drs. Therese Rando and Charles Figley, are to be congratulated for their efforts to create a series, with the Taylor & Francis Group, designed to bridge the fields of grief counseling and traumatology. The good ideas of both these clinical and academic fields are better served working in tandem to support those who are responding to loss. We would like to thank, too, the efforts of our manuscript editors at Brunner/Mazel for bringing consistency and graphic style to the text.

While this book focuses its spotlight on community crises, it was never far from our minds, no matter how widespread and dramatic the calamity described, that the essence of tragedy is the suffering of the individuals whose lives have been permanently changed by forces outside of their control. We wish to acknowledge those thousands of people whose stories have been described in these chapters but whose names must go unwritten, as well as the courage of the professional responders who are willing to support them.

Introduction

Chapter 1

The Connection Between Grief and Trauma: An Overview

Mary Beth Williams, Ellen S. Zinner, and Richard R. Ellis

It is a warm, still summer evening. Peaceful quiet sits hand in hand with humidity. The air hangs heavily outside the window as a concerted effort is made to create an introductory chapter linking the unquiet, disruptive worlds of the gemini of chaotic sorrow: grief and trauma. Professionals in each of these domains, up until a short few years ago, spoke their own languages and failed to see the commonalities of their approaches, foci, and even their goals. Traumatologists looked at the enduring effect of crises and critical incidents on the individuals, families, groups, and communities who experienced them. Researchers of post-traumatic stress disorder (PTSD) studied those factors that might lead to more intense reactions, particularly aspects related to the traumatic stressor. Meanwhile, professionals working in the grief and bereavement fields, thanatologists (from the Greek *thanatos,* god of death), directed their attention toward loss, particularly losses due to death, and the repercussions of those losses upon their clients, students, and research participants. The sequelae of traumatic events, however, also include loss of property, home, a known and comfortable world view, innocence, and community. It is the last of these losses, or perhaps all of them played out on a larger social stage, which is the focus of this book.

Just as each chapter in this volume begins with the story of the traumatic event or events leading to community bereavement, grief, loss, adaptation, and change, so does this introductory chapter begin with a story of far-reaching trauma. Not long after the initial conception of this first chapter, TWA Flight 800 exploded in midair in July 1996. Over 230 persons met their deaths. Sixteen of the victims were teenagers from Montoursville, Pennsylvania, members of their high school French Club on their way to Paris for an extended field trip.

The community of Montoursville still weeps deeply for these children and for the five adults who accompanied them. Persons who are regular travelers on international flights might recognize that at the time of the explosion the passengers were just settling in. Those in first and business class seating perhaps had had their first glass of champagne, orange juice, or a mimosa. Those in tourist class were probably adjusting seats, checking out the movie selection, and thinking of the exciting adventures ahead. It is doubtful that those 16 teens would have gotten much sleep on their transatlantic flight. It is more likely that their excitement, youth, and vitality would have carried them through the 7+-hour flight with enough energy to greet Paris with astonishment and joy. Instead, their parents and others waited in hotels in New York for word of the coroner's report, each person thinking about the words but resisting the question: Was the latest body found and identified my loved one?

And what of the community those teens left behind? During the first few days after the disaster, many Montoursville citizens appeared on television. The high school principal and guidance counselor talked of debriefings, availability of counselors, memorial services, and loss. Media people placed classmates in front of cameras and asked intrusive questions: "___ was your date at the prom. How do you feel?" or "How do you feel now that ___ is dead?" Soon a new school year began. Sixteen desks remained empty. Families who were to have celebrated homecomings and the beginning of a new school year for their children, instead, grieved and mourned.

That was the summer of 1996. Today, at the time of writing this paragraph, it is December 1997. The agony from TWA Flight 800 continues as new hearings begin about what caused the explosion. The report from Redmond (1989), a family and grief counselor who works with survivors of loved ones who were murdered, provides what seems to be a parallel with the family members of those who died on Flight 800. Homicide cases can take up to 7 years to litigate. Families reexperience an acute grief reaction each time the case arises in court. The survivors report that they have to put their grief "on hold" because dealing with each court proceeding takes more emotional energy than they have. Perhaps the family survivors of Flight 800 find themselves in similar positions. There have been numerous hearings, reports, and television "documentaries," and now, 17 months later, a new round of hearings has begun. When and how can the wounds of grief heal?

THE CONTEXT OF TRAGEDY

Janoff-Bulman (1992) and others, in describing the impact of traumatic events, recognize that such events shatter the survivor's world view. When a tragedy such as that of TWA 800 occurs, nothing makes sense. A community, as well as the individual members of that community, recoils in shock and anguish. Questions are asked over and over: "Why?" "How could this have happened?" "What was the purpose?" The answers are slow to come, if they come at all. Trauma destroys life's long-held meanings; daily living is no longer predictable or safe; those directly affected no longer see themselves as invulnerable to harm. If the comforting belief that "bad things happen only to bad people" can no longer be sustained, then what or who controls destiny? How can justice exist and be meted out? We see, far too frequently, that bad things do happen to good people, and to individuals, families, and groups. Communities must face the impact and consequences of tragedies in their lives and in their social networks.

It is the task of this chapter to examine the theoretical framework of grief and loss, trauma, and healing as it affects groups of individuals. This is the essence of group survivorship. This book examines how communities that are in existence prior to a traumatic event or are created during or in response to an event react and respond, recoil or recoup. Each chapter examines a specific traumatic event or series of events. Some of these events are natural in origin (e.g., the Kobe and Armenian earthquakes). Others are of manmade origin (the *Estonia* ferry disaster, a bombing in Ireland, a bus crash in Australia). Still other chapters focus on the loss of an individual life whose death touches many in the broader community (the assassination of Prime Minister Rabin or the death of Mickey Mantle). The groups associated with these events may be geographical (Kobe, Japan), temporal (passengers on the *Estonia*; rescue workers brought together to respond to the sinking of the ferry), recreational or social (baseball lovers), national (residents of Israel), or organizational (employees of NASA; a small Israeli kibbutz). Their responses may also vary in time perspective, ranging from short-lived rescue interventions to the creation of long-term family support communities. Some of the communities have natural support systems that are ready to respond to a crisis. In other instances, support systems become the community itself.

KEY DEFINITIONS

Several terms appearing in this and other chapters require definition. Some terms will be expanded in other sections. *Bereavement* is the state of deprivation or loss (Switzer, 1970). *Loss* is the separation of an individual or group of individuals from a loved or prized object; the object may be, for example, a person or group of persons, a job, social position or status, an ideal or fantasy, or a body part. *Grief* is the set of responses to a real, perceived, or anticipated loss (Kastenbaum & Kastenbaum, 1989); responses usually include physical, emotional, cognitive, and psychological components (see Rando, 1984). *Mourning* is the cultural response to grief (Rando, 1984). *Trauma*, according to various dictionaries, is serious injury, wound, or shock to the body or to the mind, often resulting in psychological and behavioral disorders. *Posttraumatic stress disorder* [American Psychiatric Association (APA), 1994] results from personal "exposure to an extreme traumatic stressor" (p. 424) including, for example, actual or threatened harm or death to oneself; witnessing a death, injury, or threat to another; or learning about a death, injury, or threat to another.

Existing communities can experience traumas and grieve. Trauma and loss may lead community members to create new communities of grievers in response to those events. Further, those in existing communities who did not personally sustain a loss resulting from the traumatic event but who resonate sufficiently to the traumas and losses of others can become members of the newly created communities. Trauma does not necessarily accompany bereavement; bereavement does not necessarily produce trauma. These statements pertain to both the individual and the community. However, when bereavement and trauma coincide, the individual and/or the community situation often becomes quite complicated.

Trauma often occurs within an emergency situation. An emergency, by definition, is a serious situation or occurrence; it usually happens unexpectedly, but sometimes it can be anticipated; it also demands immediate attention. Each of these three dimensions is strong in its impact upon people. Taken together, these dimensions exert a powerful force which propels people into fear, disorientation, uncontrollable behavior, or immobility. Psychological trauma may or may not reveal itself immediately. When in does occur, trauma—physical or mental or spiritual—impedes grieving.

A natural bridge between the two fields of grief and trauma is that of group survivorship. Large-scale social disasters have been of clinical and research interest to traumatologists, many of whom came to their field of work via their interactions with Vietnam veterans. Social disasters bring with them thousands of individual tragedies that are the focus of the work of grief counselors and grief researchers. A parallel set of questions addresses issues of appropriate intervention from both perspectives.

Group survivorship is a concept that encompasses the behavioral and emotional reactions of a defined, socially recognizable group experiencing the loss of one or more group members. The question of group survivorship could also arise for organized groups experiencing significant changes that pose a challenge to group identity and structure. For the purposes of this book, member loss focuses upon significant losses incurred due to the deaths of individual group members, be they expected or unanticipated and/or from natural or human agent causes.

The significance and meaning of a loss depend upon the survivor's valuing of the object (person, place, thing, idea, etc.). One's loss and concomitant grief are unique. This applies in large measure to a community. Those who would intervene in the trauma and loss of an individual or community can take their preformed formulas, tightly held assumptions, or references to the most recent person or group they have helped and place those ideas aside, not near the person or group in need of help now. Education, training, and information can be instructive and guiding; but they are not necessarily prescriptive. Effective helpers allow those they help to instruct them about what or who was lost and the meaning of the loss. Effective helpers learn from their observations of the scene of crisis and from those affected by the crisis what interventions may be helpful for the moment. Our assumptions can easily seduce us away from the requisite path.

Outsiders to a community who come in, by invitation or intrusion, to assist those affected may rush survivors to overcompensate and to normalize too quickly; outsiders may urge community members to return to predictable routines that are not appropriate for the circumstances (Garrison, 1996). Other outsiders may prematurely emphasize discussions of feelings, thereby disrupting the survivors' abilities to function on the job, in their family unit, or within that community. Still others speak "about" the event in a manner of false knowledge, alienating survivors who can speak knowledgeably "from" the event. Effective intervention comes in part from the science of human behavior and in part from the art of interacting therapeutically with others.

WHAT IS A COMMUNITY?

Communities may be natural or transitory. Natural communities are bonded together through time and any number of characteristics, for example, geography or profession. Transitory communities are bound together situationally and only at one point in time (Young, 1994). Whatever their origin or purpose, members of a community have a common focus which brings them together. Within this context, a traumatic event may threaten the community's existence, purpose, focus, or goal. If the event is one around which the community measures time—for example, anniversaries or centennials—it takes on a symbolic meaning of its own. An event may increase or lessen community connectedness and bonding. If the scale of the event is particularly large, it may have exceptionally widespread and long-lasting effects.

Traumatic events within communities can lead to different outcomes. Some communities rise in anger following tragedy; others collapse in grief. Still others may become almost catatonic out of fear of confronting the event and its outcome. But what phoenix may rise from the ashes of a community's grief? What new roads are explored and what new meanings found? Consequences realized in the wake of a community trauma depend upon whether the community's caretakers can provide the leadership necessary to direct physical and emotional recovery efforts. This leadership is impossible if caretakers themselves have been injured, violated, or traumatized. If their world has also been compromised or challenged, order as it previously existed may not be possible (Garrison, 1996).

According to the DSM-IIIR (APA, 1987), a traumatic event occurs out of the range of usual human experience and is markedly distressing to almost anyone. The most serious reaction may be persistently reexperiencing the event in one of a variety of ways, including recollections, dreams, flashbacks, and sensitivity to cues. The event survivor has persistent symptoms of heightened arousal, including anger outbursts, concentration difficulties, hypervigilance, and sleep difficulties. The DSM-IV (APA, 1994) changed the definition of a traumatic event to involve a response of fear, helplessness, or horror, and to include the importance of a victim's perception and appraisal in that response. There is no listing of what constitutes trauma in the DSM-IV; generic trauma is discussed under the rubric of PTSD.

Green (1996) proposed eight aspects of a stressor event that may be perceived as contributing to the assessment of an event as traumatic. These included: (a) threat to life or bodily integrity; (b) severe physical harm or injury; (c) intentional injury; (d) exposure to grotesqueness; (e) witnessing or learning of violence to loved ones; (f) learning of exposure to a noxious agent; (g) causing death to another; and (h) causing severe harm to another. Other factors include lack of preparedness for the occurrence of the event, lack of controllability of the event, lack of warning, greater lack of chaos accompanying evacuation efforts, cumulation of trauma losses, duration of the trauma, and the greater number of unresolved past traumas (Green, 1996). Only recently have researchers recognized that these aspects are similar to those that researchers report as leading to a more prolonged grief reaction and complicated bereavement. Parkes (1985) identified sudden or unexpected or untimely death as factors placing the griever at significant risk of complicated grief. Knapp (1987) added the death of a child to the above factors as generating increased risk. He also noted that grief after a homicide is frequently delayed. The research of Lehman, Wortman, and Williams (1987) found grief the unexpected loss of a child or spouse continuing 4–7 years after the death. These factors are quite similar to those risk factors noted in traumatic events.

Community tragedies frequently involve the death of a member or many members of that community. If the extent of the loss is large and involves a large number of dead and/or injured, the tragedy will most likely affect a larger segment of the community (Young, 1994). If the tragedy involves massive dislocation or relocation, long-term unemployment, and/or widespread property destruction, the catastrophe may challenge the identity and even the structure of that community. As in the case of an individual trauma or grief reaction, the more unexpected and unanticipated the loss, the more serious the consequences and the challenge to coping abilities. Other community risk factors leading to more intense grief and/or traumatic reactions include prolonged exposure to traumatic events, repetitive events, intentionality of traumatic events, events that are physically damaging or threatening to life and physical integrity, and events damaging to the community support system (Kulka et al., 1989). However, communal perception of the stressor event as being traumatic to the group is also necessary for that event to have severe impact (APA, 1994). As Young (1994) noted, "if this is the worst thing" that has happened to the community and there "have been no pre-existing disasters, it may be perceived as a legitimate 'end of the world'" (p. 152).

The grief a community experiences after a traumatic event may become either a developmental crisis or opportunity for that community. It may stagnate a community's future development or propel a community into new areas of growth. The crisis may be one of attachment and identity as it disrupts stability and structure. The first task of healing after a crisis is to acknowledge what has happened to the fullest extent possible. The second task is to try to restore community equilibrium. This latter task has many parts in meeting its goal, including experiencing group loss and finding meaning. Only over time will the crisis become interwoven into the history of the community to become a part of that community's narrative record. With time, perhaps depending on its attributed significance, the event may evolve as a pivotal event in the life and world view of the group.

As community members seek to restore functioning, they must transform themselves and their relationships with community organizations, neighbors, political structures, and other groups as they try to find a functional and socially acceptable meaning in what has occurred and in an altered community identity. The community itself, depending upon the level of pain and disruption, may or may not be able to respond in a supportive manner during the attempts to regain homeostasis or a steady state. However, if and when homeostasis is achieved, it may include a new community definition of stability and a new normal state.

In addition, community intervention may differ depending upon how the community defines the event: as a challenge needing intervention or as a traumatic crisis best handled by avoidance, denial, or escape. Eventually the goal of the community within the context of group survivorship is to intervene in acceptable ways that are supportive and functional to the community as a whole.

Shapiro (1994) noted that communities have a variety of social supports available to them. Social networks may be based on kinship, religious practices and beliefs, sociopolitical systems, mutual interests, and cultural practices. The meaning of the traumatic event is frequently influenced by the social context in which it occurs. If leaders or the general membership view support as soothing and as a means of regaining footing, then the support will be more accepted and more effective. If the event becomes a catalyst for social change and the community takes adaptive action, healing may occur more quickly and pervasively. However, if communities do not move past intracommunity struggle and blaming and cannot find positive meaning in catastrophic events, stagnation or regression may occur. Communities and individuals want life to be predictable and orderly (McFarlane & van der Kolk, 1996). Finding a way to reestablish these cherished attributes is the goal of successful group survivorship.

MODELS OF BEREAVEMENT AND GRIEF

Bowlby's (1973) model of grief examines interactional factors of attachment fractured by loss or by significant life changes engendered by a traumatic event. Throughout life, individuals attach to others for survival. Disasters and other types of traumatic events cause severe disequilibrium for individuals and communities by severing those attachments. Bowlby's description of grief responses includes times of protest, despair, detachment, and personality reorganization. Parkes and Weiss (1983) noted that loss causes childlike fears of loss of attachment while individuals and communities try to regain a sense of personal and

environmental safety. Thus, recovery is both an intrapsychic and an environmental process of resecuring attachment. Initially, communities may feel a sense
of numbness and blunting before they begin to pine for lost persons, possessions, and meanings. Once the pain sets in, however, communities, too, may
experience despair and disorganization. Reorganization may occur more slowly
within communities in which large numbers of individuals were affected or felt
vulnerable to traumatic circumstances.

Early bereavement paradigms offered stage models which provided macro
descriptions of dominant emotional and cognitive characteristics of responses
over time. Parkes (1985) postulated stages of denial/shock; protest (searching/
seeking); disorganization/despair/disorientation/suffering; and resolution/reinte-
gration/transformation/adaptation. Elizabeth Kubler-Ross (1969) was an early
writer about death and dying who formulated five stages of dying. Unfortunately many practitioners mistakenly believed she wrote about grieving and not
dying. Therapeutic goals for a dying person are quite different from those of a
grieving person. Worden (1991) identified four necessary tasks of the griever
for achieving resolution of the grief: I. accept the reality of the loss; II. work
through the pain of grief; III. adjust to an environment in which the deceased is
missing; IV. emotionally relocate the deceased and move on with life. Worden's
model seems to emphasize the considerable overlap and linearity of bereavement efforts. However, he states that grievers do not necessarily proceed in tidy
steps.

Rando (1993, 1996) was among the first clinicians to summarize and organize the theories of various researchers and to write in detail about types of
complicated grief. Complicated grief might include avoidance response, chronic
grief, and repressed grief. Patterns of complicated grief frequently are similar to
the various aspect of PTSD. Avoidance responses and repressed reactions to
grief parallel the avoidance phase of PTSD. Chronic unresolved grief may include intrusive thoughts and/or physiological reactivity, similar to the symptomatology describing PTSD (van der Kolk, McFarlane, & Weisaeth, 1996).

In addition to the above models, there are many others. Those cast in *stages*
are frequently misinterpreted to be linear. This probably occurs because the
printed page is only two-dimensional, and any attempts to show real life movement could result in a jumble of crossing lines and arrows. In real life, grievers
and sufferers of trauma do not move toward resolution in a linear fashion.
Anyone observing nature must eventually realize that, during development, all
growing people (individuals and groups) and things experience some regression,
retreat, or pauses on a plateau. Many models do not directly acknowledge secondary losses (for example, property, home, schools, neighborhoods) which occur
following a disaster and may even occur after incidents have been resolved.
Most do not acknowledge the impact of variables of culture, gender, religion,
social support, past experiences with loss and death, prior history of trauma, and
other variables. Additional and unrelated losses occurring during the bereavement period complicated recovery and are never addressed in theoretical models.

For the community and the individual, resolution of grief is a process that may be conceptualized from a variety of theoretical models which look at attachment, loss, and coping. Grief, as well as resolution of trauma, occurs within a sociocultural context fashioned, in part, by the community's general conceptualization and specific assessment of loss and trauma. Communities and individuals have personalities affecting their grief and the intrapsychic process of the resolution of grief.

Community grief may take months to years to resolve fully, even though public expression of mourning through ceremony and ritual may be limited to a few days, weeks, and/or special anniversary dates (Cook & Dworkin, 1992). Only when community grief is resolved does the acceptance of the loss become a cognitive and emotional reality within the community's identity. The loss is then recognized as permanent, and accommodations are made. Certainly, community memory of the loss may continue to involve pain, but, conversely, the event may become part of the communal history shared by all group members (Wolfelt, 1987), an event that may become an important source of pride and positive group identity, if only in the surviving of catastrophe.

PTSD AND TRAUMATIC EVENTS

The core of PTSD often is unresolved grief stemming from repressed emotions (Widdison & Salisbury, 1990). PTSD in one sense is a form of grief reaction. Redmond (1989) was the first grief counselor to link PTSD with mourning in families of murder victims. In recent conversations on the Internet between members of the Traumatic Stress Forum, the question was posed as to what constitutes a traumatic event. Brisk dialog included comments that "Events are either traumatic or they are not . . . ; we cannot add up non-traumas to make traumatic damage . . . ; [trauma] . . . falls within the perceived context of the individual" (Dennert, August 8, 9, 1996). "Both the duration and the intensity (of the event) are factors that go into the mix" (Gottschalk, August 9, 1996). An additional comment was that any event "must pass through perceptual filters. The word trauma can be used to describe an event and the consequences of an event" (Dalenberg, August 13, 1996) and trauma "always hurts and it always scars" (Michaels, August 13, 1996).

To what extent factors predictive of a particular PTSD outcome vary depending upon the type of exposure, type of event, and the cultural context of the event is not known (Marsella, Friedman, Gerrity, & Scurfield, 1996). The definition of what constitutes a traumatic event as well as symptoms of trauma may change among individuals, families, groups, communities, and cultures. Issues of timing of assessments of traumatic impact, identity of target populations, dosage of exposure, and vulnerability (for example, due to socioeconomic conditions), are still in need of examination. Cultures and communities within cultures interpret trauma and loss differently.

The impact of a traumatic event is even greater when the loss is the result of an individual or group hostile action; for example, the assassination of Rabin and the Oklahoma City bombing. The impact may also increase if the event had been preventable and preventive measures were not taken, for example; if the *Estonia* ferry been going slower in the rough seas or if better safety checks had been done. Further, when the event kills large numbers (as in the *Estonia* sinking), destroys massive amounts of property (the Armenian earthquake), involves prolonged suffering (the *Challenger* astronauts who are now thought by some to have stayed alive until their capsule hit the ocean; earthquake survivors who died slowly in the rubble of Kobe), or happened suddenly without warning (the Oklahoma City bombing, the explosion of TWA 800), the reactions of the community (whether natural or temporal) may be greater (Doka, 1996; Williams & Nurmi, 1994).

As the chapters in this book demonstrate, if a traumatic event suddenly destroys property and life (Kobe), rips apart an entire community by taking away its livelihood (Armenia), or shows how quickly and unpredictably life can be extinguished even in a moment of glory (the *Challenger* disaster), it becomes more difficult to find meaning.

HEALING WITHIN A COMMUNITY

Different types of traumatic events may lead to differing types of reactions and patterns of community healing. The social context of an event, the community perception and conceptualization of the meaning of that event, and the method of community coping (cognitive or affective) can influence outcomes.

The various authors in this book look at community response to tragedy from a variety of perspectives and chart various courses of healing. Do community members seek to suppress/repress or avoid grief and the impacts of trauma, trying to act as if nothing happened? Do they seek to live with the impact of the event, allowing grief, anxiety, and traumatic impact to take over, but without open expression or acknowledgment? Do members live the trauma fully, expressing pain and grief without reservation through a variety of means and rituals in order to move on (as in Oklahoma City)? Or, do members seek to transform their pain, shock, anger, and depression into a cause (for example, increased organ donation awareness as in the case of family and friends of Mickey Mantle; Grant, 1995)?

While many community members may have both acute and long-term stress reactions or eventually suffer from PTSD, the majority are often resilient. Learned resourcefulness rather than learned helplessness marks their recoveries. Communities and individuals who are resilient are able to delay gratification as they rebuild, use more problem-focused coping skills and strategies, and are more able to self-regulate. Antonovsky (1990) referred to a learned resourcefulness model of healing as a salutogenic model based on a sense of coherence. The coherent community has made sense of what has happened and has found comprehensibility in the traumatic event. Interventions after the event have contributed to making the event manageable; and resources for recovery are sufficient to the need. In addition, the community has found, or is trying to find, meaningfulness by transforming or reframing the event into a challenge.

Within communities, different groups and individuals may coexist and recover at different levels of healing. Groups may be cohesive or may split apart into fragments. Groups may offer focused services to those most affected, while other groups or individuals victimize those weaker than themselves. Community and group leaders may use power wisely or may misuse power to further themselves.

Many models for healing exist. The majority of these are based on healing within individuals; however, it is possible to apply them to communities as well. Some of these were described earlier. Everly (1995, 1996) designed a model that he terms the SAFE-R model. The first step in this model helps individuals in charge of the community to *s*tep back from the scene of the traumatic event and take a visual break. This break may occur at a command center outside the perimeter of the event, at a retreat center, or at a debriefing center. Community leaders then need to *a*cknowledge the crisis event by giving information to the public. This information provides a cognitive framework, helping to calm the community and encourages appropriate emotional expression. Community members also need *f*acts that are presented openly and honestly. A community's ability to "come through" a traumatic event can be facilitated when the community receives accurate explanations that can be tapped directly into community resources. Responsible media coverage, appropriate debriefings by trained persons, community meetings, and organization interventions can be used to encourage controlled ventilation.

Community leaders next *f*acilitate an understanding of symptoms of acute stress that frequently appear within the community. However, the identity of "trusted providers of information" varies among communities. Is the source of information the media? The police? A governing body? A business organization? The medical community? Media spots, on-site interventions (e.g., defusings and individual counseling by trained and certified professionals and peers), walk-in clinics, and hotlines can all assist in the healing.

Help can be more effectively given if help-giving mechanisms and structures are in place prior to a traumatic event. Then, procedures can be activated more easily and follow-through can be ensured. These explanations and interventions are employed to normalize and to explain crisis and stress, develop plans for intervention within the salutogenic framework of resilience, and help to *r*estore at least minimal functioning within the community as members stabilize. Triage can also occur at this stage to identify persons and organizations needing more intensive intervention. Support groups may also form to promote a new sense of community among survivors, helping them to find meaning in what happened.

Kalayjian (1996) presents a seven-stage model of community healing that may be applicable to many of the events described in this book. Preassessment prior to intervention involves investigating the nature, extent, and dynamics of the community. In other words, what event occurred and to whom? Who are the survivors and what is the economic, political, sociocultural climate of the community? Were members prepared for the event or was it a shock?

On-site assessment occurs next (Kalayjian, 1996). Community leaders, intervention teams, response teams, and others begin to collect data. Analysis of data and identification of community strengths, deficits, resources, motivation, phenomenology of symptoms, and readiness for change occur next. Questions asked at this stage are: What meaning does the community place on the event? Has responsibility for the event's occurrence been given, assumed, or assigned? This step is followed by an analysis of the community's response to the event and community planning for needed service delivery. A comprehensive plan with centralized leadership, perhaps through a local comprehensive trauma center, can be indispensable at this point (Williams & Nurmi, in press). The plan would prioritize service delivery to meet acute and long-term community needs, organize resources, request outside assistance if necessary, and determine how to achieve those goals.

The sixth stage (Kalayjian, 1996), implementation, puts the crisis plan into effect. The seventh stage evaluates the interventions, quality of care provided, changes that have occurred in the community, and future needs. Recommendations for additional clinical, educational, political, philanthropic, and other interventions are included in this stage. The final stage, remodification, reevaluates and reprioritizes problems and interventions.

Having a plan of action can empower a community. Offering enough information to community members so they can understand what happened and can evaluate possible alternatives for action lessens the impact of traumatic events. Supportive messages from community leaders need to convey information reframing what happened, providing instruction, reassuring verbally and nonverbally, and suggesting how to ventilate (Albrecht & Adelman, 1987a). As Miller and Steinberg (1975) noted, having options, a plan of action, or a knowledge of how to cope gives strength to an otherwise traumatized community.

Many supports that a community offers come in the form of "weak ties" (Adelman, Parks, & Albrecht, 1987). Weak ties are supportive groups and individuals found beyond the family and close friends. They may number in the hundreds and offer help to individuals who do not have or cannot develop close, intimate relationships. Weak ties also may offer support when stronger ties are disrupted by trauma. Exchanges between weak ties tend to be more instrumental, as means to ends, and may have interactions limited to specific geographical locations, for example, a debriefing group, a hotline staff, or a support group. The cognitive functions of support are to provide interpretations of events, to reduce uncertainty, and to provide a sense of control or mastery over events that have occurred (Albrecht & Adelman, 1987b).

As the reader assesses how the communities described in this book met the challenge of traumatic events, it will be helpful to reflect on the following questions:

- Has the community had a history of similar losses?
- What was the history of the community?
- What losses did the event entail?
- What secondary losses (hopes, dreams, property) occurred?
- How did the community perceive the event and losses involved?
- What relationship did the community and its members have to those losses?
- What expectations for resolution did the community have?
- How was the event normalized?
- What impact did the event have on the community?
- What conditions of the event made it unique? Generalizable?
- What community-based interventions worked or did not work?
- What was the extent of community support?
- What cultural practices, beliefs, rituals, and customs helped or interfered with healing?
- What legacy of loss has remained within the community?
- How has the community grown and/or found positive meaning from the event?

CONCLUSIONS

One major goal of this book is to examine actual community responses and strategies for coping with traumatic events. Chapters investigate how various communities responded cognitively (through discussion, planning, and education), physically (action rituals, rest periods), emotionally (through rituals, expression of feelings), spiritually (through funeral ceremonies), creatively (through the arts), and practically (through legal action, relocation, and physical resource development).

Another goal of this book is to explore how communities rebound, reflect, and recover from the events they have experienced. Communities are never "the same" after catastrophic events. Advocacy for airline safety and better bomb detection do not bring back the hundreds of victims killed. Uprooted members whose homes have been destroyed by earthquake or flood may never return to their neighborhoods. Yet, by joining together, by developing rituals and ceremonies, and by talking about the event over and over and thereby finding a forum for pain, survivors and their communities begin to heal (Lord, 1996; Wortman, 1983). As many of the authors in this volume demonstrate, rituals are frequently used to create a context and container for the expression of community feelings and to provide a focus on community healing. Rituals also provide a way for communities to bring closure.

To return to the disaster identified at the beginning of the chapter, now in the chill of December 1997, the "official" word continues to be that no one yet knows for certain what happened to TWA Flight 800. Most of the bodies have been recovered. The grief and mourning continues; questions go unanswered.

Cliches say "only time will tell" or "patience is a virtue." But as the community of families of the dead of TWA Flight 800 know and as neighborhoods and communities directly touched by this one trauma will tell you, the pain is only beginning. It is up to them, the family and community survivors, to acknowledge their deep loss, pose their questions of how and why, create strategies and rituals for coping, and try to heal. Perhaps, in time, they will.

REFERENCES

Adelman, M. B., Parks, M. R., & Albrecht, T. L. (1987). Beyond close relationships: Support in weak ties. In T. L. Albrecht & M. B. Adelman (Eds.), *Communicating social support* (pp. 126–147). Newbury Park, CA: Sage.

Albrecht, T. L., & Adelman, M. B. (1987a). Communicating social support: A theoretical perspective. In T. L. Albrecht & M. B. Adelman (Eds.), *Communicating social support* (pp. 18–39). Newbury Park, CA: Sage.

Albrecht, T. L., & Adelman, M. B. (1987b). Measurement issues in the study of support. In T. L. Albrecht & M. B. Adelman (Eds.), *Communicating social support* (pp. 64–75). Newbury, Park: CA: Sage.

American Psychiatric Association (1987). *Diagnostic and statistical manual of mental disorders* (3rd ed., Revised). Washington, DC: Author.

American Psychiatric Association (1994). *Diagnostic and statistical manual of mental disorders* (4th ed.). Washington, DC: Author.

Antonovsky, A. (1990). Pathways leading to successful coping and health. In M. Rosenbaum (Ed.), *Learned resourcefulness: On coping skills, self control, and adaptive behavior* (pp. 31–63). New York: Springer-Verlag.

Bowlby, J. (1973). *Attachment and loss: Separation* (Vol. II). New York: Basic Books.

Cook, A. S., & Dworkin, D. S. (1992). *Helping the bereaved: Therapeutic interventions for children, adolescents, and adults.* New York: Harper/Collins.

Doka, K. J. (Ed.). (1996). *Living with grief after sudden loss: Suicide, homicide, accident, heart attack, stroke.* Washington, DC: Hospice Foundation of America.

Everly, G. S., Jr. (Ed.). (1995). *Innovations in disaster and trauma psychology, Vol I: Applications in emergency services and disaster response.* Ellicott City, MD: Chevron.

Everly, G. S., Jr. (1996). A rapid crisis intervention technique for law enforcement, the SAFE-R model. In J. T. Reese & R. M. Solomon (Eds.), *Organizational issues in law enforcement* (pp. 183–191). Washington, DC: U.S. Government Printing Office.

Garrison, W. (1996). Organizational triage: Restoring the state of the organization altered by trauma. In J. T. Reese & R. M. Solomon (Eds.), *Organizational issues in law enforcement* (pp. 193–205). Washington, DC: U.S. Government Printing Office.

Grant, A. C. (1995). *The healing journey: Manual for a grief support group.* Long Branch, NJ: Vista.

Green, B. L. (1996). Cross-national and ethnocultural issues in disaster research. In A. J. Marsella, M. J. Friedman, E. T. Gerrity, & R. M. Scurfield (Eds.), *Ethnocultural aspects of post-traumatic stress disorder* (pp. 341–362). Washington, DC: American Psychological Association.

Janoff-Bulman, R. (1992). *Shattered assumptions: Towards a new psychology of trauma.* New York: The Free Press.

Kalayjian, A. S. (1996). *Disaster and mass trauma: Global perspectives on post disaster mental health management.* Long Branch, NJ: Vista.

Kastenbaum, R., and Kastenbaum, B. (1989). *Encyclopedia of death.* Phoenix, AZ: Orgx Press.

Knapp, R. J. (1987). When a child dies. *Psychology Today, 21*(7), 60–63, 66–67.

Kubler-Ross, E. (1969). *On death and dying.* New York: Macmillan.

Kulka, B. A., Schlenger, W. E., Fairbank, J. A., Hough, R. L., Jordan, B. K., Marmar, C. R., & Weiss, D. A. (1989). *Trauma and the Vietnam war generation: Report of findings from the National Vietnam Veterans Readjustment Study.* New York: Brunner/Mazel.

Lehman, D. R., Wortman, C. B., Williams, A. F. (1987). Long-term effects of losing a spouse or child in a motor vehicle crash. *Journal of Personality & Social Psychology, 52*(1), 218–231.

Lord, J. H. (1996). America's number one killer: Vehicular crashes. In K. J. Doka (Ed.), *Living with grief after sudden loss* (pp. 91–102). Washington, DC: Hospice Foundation of America.

Marsella, A. J., Friedman, M. J., Gerrity, E. T., & Scurfield, R. M. (1996). *Ethnocultural aspects of posttraumatic stress disorder: Issues, research and clinical applications.* Washington, DC: American Psychological Association.

McFarlane, A. C., & van der Kolk, B. A. (1996). Trauma and its challenge to society. In B. A. van der Kolk, A. C. McFarlane, & L. Weisaeth (Eds.), *Traumatic stress: The effects of overwhelming experience on mind, body and society* (pp. 24–46). New York: Guilford Press.

Miller, G. R., & Steinberg, M. (1975). *Between people: A new analysis of interpersonal communication.* Chicago: Science Research Associates.

Parkes, C. M. (1985). Bereavement. *British Journal of Psychiatry, 146,* 11–17.

Parkes, C. M., & Weiss, R. S. (1983). *Recovery from bereavement.* New York: Basic Books.

Rando, T. (1993). *Treatment of complicated mourning.* Champaign, IL: Research Press.

Rando, T. (1996). Complications in mourning traumatic death. In K. Doka (Ed.), *Living with grief after sudden loss* (pp. 139–160). Washington, DC: Hospice Foundation of America.

Redmond, L. M. (1989). *Surviving when someone you love was murdered: Professional's guide to group grief therapy for families and friends of murder victims.* Clearwater, FL: Psychological Consultation and Education Services.

Shapiro, E. R. (1994). *Grief as a family process: A developmental approach to clinical practice.* New York: Guilford Press

Switzer, D. (1970). *The dynamics of grief.* Nashville, TN: Abington Press.

van der Kolk, B. A., McFarlane, A. C., & Weisaeth, L. (1996). *Traumatic stress: The effects of overwhelming experience on mind, body and society.* New York: Guilford Press.

Widdison, H. A., & Salisbury, H. G. (1990). The delayed stress syndrome: A pathological delayed grief reaction? *Omega, 20*(4), 293–306.

Williams, M. B., & Nurmi, L. A. (1994). *Death of a co-worker: Personal and institutional responses.* Helsinki, Finland: Poliisin Oppikirjasarja.

Williams, M. B., & Nurmi, L. A. (in press). *Creating a comprehensive trauma center: Choices and challenges.* New York: Guilford Press.

Wolfelt, A. D. (1987). Resolution vs. reconciliation: The importance of semantics. *Thanatos (Winter),* 10–13.

Worden, J. W. (1991). *Grief counseling and therapy* (2nd ed). New York: Springer-Verlag.

Wortman, C. B. (1983). Coping with victimization: Conclusions and implications for future research. *Journal of Social Issues, 39*(2), 195–221.

Young, M. A. (1995). Crisis response teams in the aftermath of disasters. In A. R. Roberts (Ed.), *Crisis intervention and time-limited cognitive treatment* (pp. 151–187). Thousand Oaks, CA: Sage.

Part One

Humanmade and Natural Disasters

Disasters that occur by dint of human miscalculation or through violent acts of nature can be traumatic for many reasons. In four of the five chapters included in this section of the book—the *Challenger* explosion, the sinking of the ferry *Estonia*, a dual bus crash in Australia, and the earthquakes in Armenia and in Japan—loss of life was extensive. Countless numbers of individuals suffered severe injury and physical harm. Survivors and rescuers alike were exposed to death, perilous conditions, and grotesque scenes. Events were unexpected. While predisaster training was in place prior to some of these disasters, no one was prepared for the specific crisis that occurred, and no one had clear control over the outcome. In Kobe, Japan, for example, massive dislocation and relocation accompanied widespread destruction of property and contributed to the enormous breadth of the disaster. Yet cultural norms and mores prevented outward expression of grief, led to rejection of outside help, and delayed the onset of crisis intervention.

In Chapter 2, Ellen Zinner, a certified grief therapist and death educator and college administrator at the University of Baltimore, in Baltimore, Maryland, describes the events of January 26, 1986, that are burned into the memory of millions of children and adults who were watching the explosion of the *Challenger* Space Shuttle on television from their homes and schools. In contrast to the Armenian and Great Hanshin earthquakes described in later chapters, loss of life was relatively small. Yet the event became a nodal loss for many in the United States. The shared sense of national mourning was facilitated by wide television coverage and immediate political response. How that loss and subsequent bereavement were expressed and resolved is the central point of her chapter. An important focus is the role of initial and even decade-later memorializations, including the creation of the *Challenger* Centers for Space Science Education. This chapter also addresses the various aggregates of individuals who composed survivor groups in the wake of the *Challenger* loss.

Lassi Nurmi, Senior Lecturer at the Finnish Police Academy in Espoo, Finland, and psychologist on the Disaster Victim Identification Team, describes in Chapter 3 the sudden sinking of the *HMS Estonia* in September 1994, and the frantic attempts to rescue hypothermic survivors in rough seas. A major focus is the response of national disaster teams and effectiveness of later critical incident stress debriefings. The impact of the sinking of the ferry on Finland as a nation, on rescuers, and on the author himself was extensive. No longer was ferry travel seen to be free from danger. Rescuers who did not receive debriefing (such as the nurses at Turku Hospital) appeared to suffer more than others. Nurmi himself changed his philosophy of life and lost his ability to believe in a nondisappointing God. The chapter concludes with the lessons learned from this rescue effort.

Rod Watts and Marise Wilson, both involved with their local Community Health Team in Australia, chronicle in Chapter 4 the response of community rescuers to a holiday bus crash near Kempsey, New South Wales, Australia. After the collision of two coaches in late December, 1989, over 360 persons responded in some fashion to the disaster. Assessment results of State Emergency Service workers at 1, 3, and 12 months postaccident demonstrate the emotional repercussions that interventions efforts can have even upon trained professionals. Over 50% of the workers who responded to the accident were moderately negatively affected even a year later. The chapter also describes the changes that occurred both to the town of Kempsey and to the emergency service teams following this nationally significant event.

In Chapter 5, Dr. Anie Kalayjian, a noted traumatologist and logotherapy psychotherapist in New York, describes the community response to the Armenian earthquake of December 7, 1988. The quake, measuring 6.9 on the Richter scale, left 500,000 children orphaned and over 500,000 homeless. In contrast to the Kobe earthquake which occurred 7 years later, goods, food, and services quickly poured into Armenia from various governments around the world. Kalayjian describes the nation's and citizenry's responses to the earthquake in light of the culture and history of Armenia. She also looks in detail at psychosocial responses during the acute and chronic phases of this immense disaster.

The final chapter in this section speaks to the Great Hanshin (Kobe) earthquake and the culturally based responses (and lack of responses) to that disaster. Initially, this chapter was written by Dr. Tom Williams. However, when he was unable to finish it, Dr. G. Robert Baker came to the "rescue" to try his turn at relating the events that occurred following the massive destruction of Kobe. He, too, found that vicarious traumatization takes its toll, and the task of completing the chapter passed to their colleague, coeditor Mary Beth Williams.

Writing about a disaster that has left such a personal toll on those who witnessed the aftermath was a powerful experience, even at a distance. The chapter attempts to do justice to the contributions of the two original authors and the work that they did in training the Japanese in critical incident responses and in implementing Dr. Baker's innovative "bearapy."

Figure 2.1 *Challenger* memorial in Arlington National Cemetery (Sec. 46), one of hundreds erected nationwide to honor the crew of the ill-fated spacecraft. Plaque on front shows the faces of the seven astronauts and mission specialists on board and reads "In Grateful and Loving Tribute to the Brave Crew of the United States Shuttle, *Challenger*, 28 January, 1986." Note cards at base of memorial are messages left by anonymous visitors. One writes: "We wish you to rest in peace and thank you for your courage." (Personal photo of author.)

Chapter 2

The *Challenger* Disaster: Group Survivorship on a National Landscape

Ellen S. Zinner

Few events are of such consequence as to affect the memory of a nation. In the history of the United States over the last half-century, only the Kennedy assassination equals that of the *Challenger* explosion in having made an indelible impression on all those who lived through the tragedy and its aftermath. For the generation of Americans born in the 1970s, the tragedy of the *Challenger* shuttle and its crew, witnessed live on television (as it was by an estimated 40% of late elementary and secondary students; Clymer, 1986), holds special significance as a primary national loss.

When the *Challenger* exploded 73 seconds after launch on January 28, 1986, where were you? Most people can readily answer that question. The *Challenger* explosion not only was a genuine tragedy in the loss of life of its seven crew members and posed a real threat to the future of the U.S. manned space program, but it was also "one of those rare events that sear the nation's soul" (Cook, 1996, p. 11). On the one hand, the accident represents a failure of technology and of organizational communications, according to the findings of the Rogers Commission established by then-President Reagan to investigate and report on the cause of the explosion. Of significance, too, however, is that the loss of the *Challenger* shuttle generated a prime example of group survivorship on a broad scale. How and why the *Challenger* disaster became a nodal loss for many Americans and how bereavement was addressed within many diverse survivorship groups is the focus of this chapter.

THE SHUTTLE *CHALLENGER*: MISSION 51-L

NASA's Shuttle Program   The National Aeronautical and Space Administration (NASA), created to respond to Russian space accomplishments in the

1950s, was in its 28th year at the time of the launching of *Challenger* in January 1986. Mission 51-L marked the 25th time that a reusable manned shuttle had been employed and the 10th launching of the *Challenger* ship. *Challenger*, first launched in 1981, and its sister ships, *Columbia, Discovery*, and *Atlantis,* were considered the "most advanced space transportation technology in the world. No other nation had achieved a reusable spaceship that could maneuver inside and outside the atmosphere and lift payloads with an earth weight of 32 tons" (Lewis, 1988, pp. 2–3).

Mission 51-L   The mission of *Challenger* that January was to have lasted for approximately 7 days, with a return landing at the Kennedy Space Center scheduled for a little more than 144 hours after launch. On board were the Haley's Comet Experiment Deployable, a satellite designed to observe the fly-by of Haley's Comet; a shuttle-controlled astronomy tool; fluid dynamics experiments to be carried out by a civilian engineer employed by the Hughes Aircraft Company; and three student-designed experiments. Additionally, a set of lessons designed for the Teacher-in-Space Program to be delivered in a live broadcast from space by the first ever teacher/astronaut heightened public interest in this particular fight. Two lessons were planned: "The Ultimate Field Trip," a description of life aboard a space shuttle, and a second exercise explaining ways of exploring space and manufacturing new products utilizing zero gravity.

Two aspects of Mission 51-L made it unprecedented. The first was the inclusion of Sharon Christa McAulliffe, the "teachernaut," listed as the *Challenger*'s Payload Specialist 2. Generally known by her middle name, Christa was a high school social science teacher from Concord, New Hampshire, who had been among the 10,000 teachers who had applied for the Teacher-in-Space Program first announced by President Reagan. Described by reporters as articulate and personable, she had been in training for the mission for over 5 months.

The second special feature of this mission was the diversity of the entire *Challenger* crew for Mission 51-L. Dubbed the "all-American" crew, the seven-member crew was composed of five men and two women and included African-American, Asian-American, and Jewish astronauts who seemed to "represent Everybody's America" (Wolfe, 1986, p. 40). Crew members consisted of the shuttle commander, Francis R. Scobee, an Air Force test pilot; the shuttle pilot, Michael J. Smith, a Navy-trained test pilot; Mission Specialist 1, Ellison S. Onizuko, the first American astronaut of Japanese descent; Mission Specialist 2, Judith A. Resnik, the second woman to have flown in space; Mission Specialist 3, Ronald E. McNair, the second African-American astronaut; Payload Specialist 1, Gregory Jarvis, a civilian engineer; and Christa McAuliffe, representing the Teacher-in-Space Program.

Mission Delays   Originally scheduled for a late December 1995 launching, 51-L had been delayed or scrubbed a total of five times before actual launch. Delays in the previous *Columbia* mission had pushed the launch date into January. Poor weather conditions, both at the Kennedy Center or at alternative emergency landing sites in Africa, had forced further delays. The Sunday, January 26th postponement permitted some of the crew members to watch the SuperBowl match-up between the New England Patriots (McAuliffe's home team) and the Chicago Bears that night (Broad, 1986). On Monday, January 27th, an exterior handle on the crew compartment door could not be properly latched and had to be cut away, but only after several hours delay while a replacement battery for the handheld saw was located. The series of delays was reported with some frustration and annoyance by the press. Vice President Bush, on hand for the Monday launch, could not stay for the rescheduled Tuesday take-off. Although denied by the White House, some still believe there was political pressure to press for a launch by Tuesday to allow President Reagan to use its success in his State of the Union address scheduled for Tuesday evening. Moreover, there was some concern that further postponements might interfere with the 15 other shuttle missions planned for 1986 and a planned May launching of *Challenger* that depended on the position of the planet Jupiter for its mission success (Lewis, 1988).

Launch Day   Tuesday, January 28th was clear and cold with acceptable wind conditions for launching. Overnight temperatures had fallen to the low 20s, causing icicles to form on the mobile launch platform and chunks of ice to cluster in the overpressure water troughs below the platform. The seven crew members were in place aboard the *Challenger* an hour before a set 9:36 a.m. launch, but Mission Control ordered a 2-hour hold to allow rising temperatures to melt some of the ice. When an ice inspection team reported favorable conditions, the countdown was continued. Temperature at launch had risen to 36° Fahrenheit (Lewis, 1988).

At 11:38 a.m., *Challenger*, attached to its external fuel tank and twin solid rocket boosters, was launched. According to initial telemetry data received in Houston and from the view of cameras and those watching from reviewing stands on the ground, all appeared to be normal. But, at 70 seconds into launch, a NASA camera recorded an orange glow that expanded into a yellow-orange flame on one side of the external fuel tank. Within seconds, a huge fireball engulfed the shuttle, the fuel tank, and both solid fuel rocket boosters. At T plus 1:13, 73 seconds into launch, the last recorded words from a *Challenger* crew member, Pilot Michael Smith, were heard: "uhh . . . oh."

From the ground, the fireball and its gray-white vapor trails were clearly visible to the 1,000 VIPs, family members, and guests who had been invited to witness the event from the reviewing stands situated almost 4 miles from the launch pad (Magnuson, 1986a). The solid rocket boosters flew away from each other, leaving a ragged Y-trail in the sky. Dark smoke clouds filled the sky and falling debris was visible on monitoring cameras. Clearly visible moments later, too, was a single parachute drifting slowly downward, leading many in the stands and on TV to believe that the crew may have been spared. But the parachute was only part of the recovery system for the solid rocket boosters which had been destroyed by Mission Control when they went out of control. For a moment, the voice of Stephen Nesbitt, Public Affairs Officer, was silent. Nesbitt then reported over the loudspeaker system to all those witnessing the event: "Flight controllers are looking very carefully at the situation. Obviously a major malfunction. We have no downlink. We have a report from the flight dynamics officer that the vehicle has exploded" (Lewis, 1988, p. 21).

Recovery efforts were begun immediately by Naval and Coast Guard ships which had been in place for the planned recovery of the twin solid rocket boosters. Ultimately, 31 ships, 52 aircrafts, and 6,000 workers would be employed in recovery efforts over the next 4 months (Dowling, 1996). It would become the "largest salvage operation in world maritime history" (Lewis, 1988, p. 142); about one third of the entire shuttle would be recovered. Christa McAuliffe's lesson plans, intact and dry within a plastic bag, were recovered within the first few days, the crew compartment and bodies, 2 months later (Thomas, 1986).

Investigation Into Cause   Within 3 days of the explosion, information gleaned from close review of film and telemetry data turned the focus of NASA's investigation toward a defective field joint on the right solid rocket booster. The field joint was part of the assembly, completed at the Kennedy Space Center, of the 149.5' rocket booster following manufacture of the solid rocket fuel and four motor segments in Utah by Morton Thiokol Inc. Reagan appointed The Presidential Commission on the Space Shuttle *Challenger* Accident on February 3. Led by William P. Rogers, former Secretary of State under Nixon, and popularly known as the Rogers Commission, it moved control of the investigation away from NASA and pledged to make all information about the explosion available to the public. Televised public hearings began within days. From internal NASA documents leaked to the press and examined publicly by the Commission panel soon thereafter, it quickly became apparent that NASA had noted problems with the rubber O-rings in the solid rocket booster joints as early as 1981, 5 years before the explosion.

The Rogers Commission ultimately determined that, within the first second of launching, hot gas at a temperature of 5,600°F had escaped past a lower O-ring of the right solid rocket booster, quickly melting or severing the attachment brace between the booster and the external liquid fuel tanks. Based on visual inspection of the recovered parts of the right booster, it was determined that over 6 square feet of joint had been burned away. Freed from its brace, the end of the booster had rotated outward, smashing its nose into the external tank, which then ruptured. Escaping liquid propellant ignited into a fireball. The Commission also reported that the low temperatures prior to and at the time of launch, which made the O-rings less resilient and less able to contain gases as designed, contributed to the malfunction (Lewis, 1988).

The Commission concluded that the explosion was the result of a flawed design unacceptably susceptible to a number of factors including outside temperature, deterioration following multiple usage, and probable water seepage at the joint. *Challenger* had been on the launch pad for over 37 days while a total of 7 inches of rain fell. The report found Morton Thiokol Inc. blameworthy of poor engineering and lack of verification of design specifications and pointed critically to the lack of specific safety monitoring within NASA. Further, the Rogers Commission pointed out what it termed "managerial rashness" for NASA to have set up an overly demanding launch schedule for 1986 which only served to increase scheduling pressures and to decrease prudent decision making. "The committee is not assured that NASA had adequate technical and scientific expertise to conduct the space shuttle program properly" was a final Commission censure (Lewis, 1988, p. 232).

Immediate Responses to the *Challenger* Disaster

News media coverage of the *Challenger* disaster was extensive, focusing both on the technological failure and on its emotional impact. But from the beginning, the failure of the *Challenger* was recognized as having a broad and serious impact on the nation as a whole and numerous related subgroups. Wrote one reporter, "The shuttle explosion left a psychological wake that ripples from those closest to the astronauts and NASA to our entire American people" (Goleman, 1986, A11). Both at the time of the explosion and in 10th anniversary remembrances, many Americans likened the event to their experience of the assassination of President John Kennedy in 1963. People across the country noted a silence that immediately overcame workplaces and schoolrooms of children, and the stopping of classes or regular routines. Many talked about being in stunned disbelief. The public's strong need to know the cause and to have an explanation of why the unthinkable could happen was explained by one trauma researcher as a way to "assuage such insecurities" arising from an unexpected disaster (Goleman, 1986, A11).

   Next-of-Kin   Family members who witnessed the explosion in the reviewing stands at the Kennedy Space Center were quickly removed from the view of cameras and reporters' questions and put on waiting buses. They were some time later taken back to hotel rooms. None of the articles reviewed mentioned whether these families received a formal debriefing or not. Vice President Bush, at the request of President Reagan, returned to Cape Canaveral to speak with the families of the crew. He was joined by two U.S. Senators, John Glenn of Ohio and Jake Garn of Utah, both of whom had previously flown in space, and the acting Administrator of NASA, William Graham (Boyd, 1986). Within days, NASA flew family members back to their homes, each family accompanied by an astronaut who would be on hand to answer their questions, assist with immediate arrangements, and handle the inpouring of mail and requests for interviews. Thousands of cards and letters were sent to immediate family members of the crew. Within a week, memorial funds were established across the country for the 11 children of crew members.

National Response   At the national level, President Reagan addressed the country by TV late Tuesday afternoon, within hours of the explosion. In a brief statement, Reagan set the tone for national mourning. He identified each of the crew members by name and praised their courage. He acknowledged the grief of immediate family members but added that "we mourn their loss as a nation together," and spoke directly "to the school children of America who were watching the live coverage of the shuttle's takeoff" ("President Expresses," 1986, p. A9). Reagan affirmed that the nation had become complacent about NASA successes and so had been taken by surprise, but he pledged a continuation of the space program in saying that "the *Challenger* crew was pulling us into the future, and we'll continue to follow them" ("President Expresses," 1986, p. A9). Reagan postponed the annually delivered State of the Union address scheduled for that night. Speaker Tip O'Neill recessed the House of Representatives on Capitol Hill.

Across the country, recognition of the loss of the *Challenger* was immediate and diverse, and many ritual observances occurred. Common was the lowering of flags to half-staff and shared moments of silence (Rimer, 1986). In Atlanta, daytime motorists turned on their headlights. In Los Angeles, the Olympic torch was relit. The Governor of Illinois asked his citizens to turn on their porchlights as a tribute to the lost crew. In New York City, the outside lighting of the Empire State Building was dimmed. Along the Florida coast, over 20,000 citizens shone flashlights into the sky on Friday night (Magnuson, 1986a).

In communities and within institutions that had special connections with individual crew members, special ceremonies and memorial services were held within the first few days. At Framingham State College in Massachusetts, from which Christa McAuliffe received her undergraduate degree, a service of over 1,000 people was addressed by the state Governor and concluded with the release of seven black balloons. The Governor of Ohio spoke at services held in the temple attended by the Resnik family. At North Carolina Agricultural and Technical State University in Greensboro, Rev. Jesse Jackson addressed a memorial service for its alumnus, Ron McNair. The National Education Association announced that it would seek memorial funds to underwrite a special projects program in McAuliffe's honor

Concord High School, where Christa McAulliffe had taught, and, indeed, the entire town of Concord, received particular attention. Even though reporters, who had been assigned to cover student reactions to the launch at McAulliffe's high school, had been immediately asked to leave following the explosion, interviews with Concord students and McAuliffe neighbors were frequently reported (Wald, 1986a). Students tied black ribbons to a tree outside Concord High. Hundreds of floral wreaths lined the school halls. President Reagan sent a letter of condolence to the high school which was read at a special assembly held on that Friday, January 31st ("President's Letter to Concord," 1986). The mayor of Concord, who led a memorial service held at the Statehouse Plaza in Concord, accepted hundreds of letters, poems, artwork, and cards on behalf of the town (Wald, 1986c).

The major national memorial service was held in Houston at the Johnson Space Center late on Friday morning, January 31st. President and Mrs. Reagan, along with over 90 members of the U.S. Congress, attended the ceremony. The President and his wife met with family members of the deceased crew before the service and escorted them to the front rows of the outdoor seating. Witnessed by an estimated 6,000 NASA employees and 4,000 family members and guests at the service itself and by millions of Americans via live television broadcast, President Reagan's presentation echoed themes he had drawn in his initial response on the day of the explosion (Weintraub, 1986). On behalf of the nation, he expressed his sorrow to the families and noted "the brave sacrifice of those you loved and we so admired." He emphasized the national sense of grief, generated and expressed through public media: "Last night, I listened to a call-in program on the radio. People of every age spoke of their sadness. ... Across America, we are reaching out, holding hands and finding comfort in one another." Reagan also drew strong analogies to the pioneering history of America and the new frontiers of space, promising the lost crew that "their dream lives on; that the future they worked so hard to build will become a reality" ("Transcript," 1986, A11). Following Reagan's address, NASA T-38 jets flew in missing man formation over the audience while an Air Force band played "God Bless America" (Weintraub, 1986).

NASA Response   Both President Reagan and Vice President Bush recognized NASA as a group particularly affected by the shuttle misfortune. Reagan addressed the agency directly in his immediate response to the nation on Tuesday, when he said that he wished he "could talk to every man and woman who works for NASA or who worked on this mission" and tell them that both their past professionalism and present pain were recognized ("President Expresses," 1986, A9). Bush talked with about 200 NASA workers at the Kennedy Center following his visit with the families of crew members late on the afternoon of the explosion (Boyd, 1986). Schoolchildren in numerous classrooms took time to send sympathy notes to the agency. So, too, did Soviet cosmonauts (Magnuson, 1986a). A memorial service was conducted within view of the *Challenger* launch pad on the Sunday following the explosion at the Kennedy Space Center. Over 3,000 NASA employees and family members were in attendance as the Director of the Center, Richard G. Smith, pledged to honor the *Challenger* crew with a minute of silence every January 28th at 11:39 a.m. At the appointed time, taps were played for those in the reviewing stands and a large floral wreath was dropped by helicopter 2 miles out to sea (Schmidt, 1986).

Outside Response   International response reflected world recognition of the significance of the *Challenger* accident for the United States. Numerous international leaders sent letters of condolences to the White House. One newspaper in the Soviet Union wrote that "America is frozen in shock. It seems that the flow of time in this country has been broken for several days. As Americans themselves say, at no time since the assassination of President Kennedy in 1963 has the country been so tragically benumbed" (Schmemann, 1986, p. 16). On Sunday, the Soviet Union announced that it would name two of the craters on Venus after Judith Resnick and Christa McAulliffe. In Vatican City, Pope John Paul II led thousands in prayer for the astronauts. In Japan, national TV news was expanded and devoted to the explosion coverage.

Later Memorialization

The immediate response to a major crisis is not always the truest measure of its significance. The magnitude of an event can be measured and, at the same time, enhanced by the creation of more permanent memorializations. Many occurred in the weeks and months that followed the explosion of the *Challenger*.

Next-of-Kin   In an effort led by June Scobee, widow of the *Challenger* commander, family members of the crew founded and continue to help direct a foundation that promotes *Challenger* Centers for Space Science Education. The Centers, designed to serve as "living memorials" to the crew, offers hands-on education to schoolchildren, allowing them to participate in simulated space missions and space science experiments (Dowling, 1996). The original $30 million dollar fundraising effort was started with contributions from Morton Thiokol Inc. and other space-related private companies. The first *Challenger* Center was opened in 1988 in Houston, Texas, at the Museum of Natural Science. As of 1995, 25 centers had been opened across the United States and Canada, with another half-dozen centers in the planning stage. Serving as center educators are many of the 114 finalists in the Teacher-in-Space Program. One of the earliest centers was located at Framingham State College, McAuliffe's alma mater.

Grace Corrigan, mother of Christa McAuliffe, raises money for the *Challenger* Centers through hundreds of lectures and from profits from her 1993 book, *A Journal for Christa* (Dowling, 1996) The brothers of Ronald McNair manage a nonprofit foundation in his name aimed at increasing children's exposure to science (Swarns, 1996). The parents of Gregory Jarvis are involved with the Astronaut Memorial Foundation at the Kennedy Space Center near where they live.

National Response   Across the country, especially in the communities of individual astronauts, buildings and community sites were named after the crew. The name of *Challenger* was given to dozens of elementary and middle schools built in the ensuing years. There is the Michael J. Smith Airport in Beaufort, North Carolina. In Lake City, South Carolina, in addition to the Ronald McNair

Junior High School, there is a McNair Memorial and a McNair Boulevard (Swarns, 1996). In California, the Air Force named their satellite control center in Sunnyvale after Mission Specialist Ellison S. Onizuko. In Florida, fees from commemorative automotive license plates raised the $16 million needed to establish the Astronauts Memorial Foundation which financed a granite monument to all 16 Americans who have died while working on space projects and an educational center as well. Both are located at the Kennedy Space Center at Cape Canaveral ("We Remember," 1996). Another national monument was erected at Arlington National Cemetery, near the Capital in Washington, DC. In mid-1987, the U.S. Geological Survey Board on Geographic Names approved a request to name a high ridge of the Kit Carson Mountain in Colorado "*Challenger* Point." A plaque was laid on the ridge, "In Memory of the Crew of Shuttle *Challenger*," a few months later (Eberhard, 1994).

In the city of Concord, The Christa McAulliffe Planetarium offers free admission and special workshops for teachers and their families ("Christa McAulliffe Remembered," 1996). The Christa Corrigan McAulliffe Center for Education and Teaching Excellence, also in Concord, supports innovations in science teaching.

10th-Anniversary Commemorations

While brief tributes were held annually to mark the date of the *Challenger* explosion, particularly at the *Challenger* Space Centers and at NASA space facilities, the 10th anniversary was commemorated by numerous special ceremonies to mark the occasion of the loss. Speaking the day before the decade anniversary, January 27, 1996, President Bill Clinton, in his regular Saturday radio broadcast, asked Americans "to remember together a tragedy . . . that tore at our nation's heart" ("Clinton Remembers," 1996). He spoke of the sacrifice of the *Challenger* crew "not in the name of personal gain, but in the pursuit of knowledge that would lead to the common good." Mrs. Corrigan, Christa's mother, made herself available to the public in a chatroom that evening on an international on-line service, saying that this was "the type of thing Christa herself would do" ("Christa McAuliffe's Mom," 1996).

Memorial ceremonies were held at 11:39 a.m. Sunday morning at the Johnson Space Center in Houston and at Kennedy Space Center in Cape Canaveral, where Gregory Jarvis's father was the keynote speaker. Seventy-three seconds of silence were observed at both sites. In Florida, a wreath was again dropped into the Atlantic off-shore, this time by James Harrington, a NASA manager who had worked on the *Challenger* 51-L mission. ("Media Coverage," 1996). In Houston, at a NASA observance closed to the general public, seven bells tolled for the crew, flags were at half-staff, and family members left flowers around a central flagpole. Watched by millions of Americans on TV, a special tribute was held just prior to SuperBowl XXX in Tempe, Arizona, when Air Force F-16 fighters flew over the stadium in missing man formation. Captain

Rich Scobee, son of the *Challenger* shuttle commander, piloted the lead plane. Events and exhibits dedicated to individual crew members were held in various parts of the country.

At Christa McAuliffe's grave in Concord, New Hampshire, visitors left flowers, gifts, and apples. Students at Concord High walked the mile from their school to the Capital Center for the Arts to hear a presentation by a Concord alumna who had been a news reporter covering the launch 10 years before. A new exhibit on the life of McAuliffe was unveiled at the planetarium in Concord ("Christa McAuliffe Remembered," 1996).

Much attention was paid to how the families of the crew had fared over the ensuing decade. Lengthy articles appeared in magazines and newspapers describing remarriages of spouses and current interests of their children (Dowling, 1996; "Their Families Today," 1996). And, according to a list of anniversary events maintained on the internet by the Ontario *Challenger* Centre, the families made themselves available to the public, appearing on over a dozen TV news shows and granting interviews for national and local newspapers ("Media Coverage," 1996).

GROUP SURVIVORSHIP AND THE LOSS OF *CHALLENGER*

"The nation came together yesterday in a moment of disaster and loss," wrote one New York Times reporter the day after the explosion (Rimer, 1986). For younger Americans, the *Challenger* explosion was seen as a national event that took away innocence and faith and brought in a heavy dose of reality. On the 10th anniversary, the *Houston Chronicle* invited its readers and *Houston Chronicle* Interactive internet service users to share their memories of the *Challenger* explosion. Amy Chen, a graduate student at University of California at Berkeley, wrote:

> Many people consider the assassination of President John F. Kennedy as the one moment in history that they will never forget. Since I was not even born at that time, I could never truly understand the emotions and memories of that tragedy, until the *Challenger* accident. For me, *Challenger* will always be the one defining moment in history that I will remember. ("We Remember," 1996)

What factors contributed to this tragedy becoming such a notable marker in recent American history? This section of the chapter will examine why the *Challenger* explosion was such a significant historic event and will analyze how the reactions of diverse groups of survivors are reflected by one model of group survivorship.

A NODAL LOSS FOR THE UNITED STATES

Trust in NASA and in Space Technology   NASA's solid reputation, built on a string of well-publicized successful missions, contributed to the shock and disbelief engendered by the news of the *Challenger* failure. NASA had been known as an organization that exemplified open communications and nonhierarchical organization, allowing for the free flow of innovative ideas so necessary to the building of a cutting-edge space program (Schwartz, 1987). Under its administration, NASA had made the wonders of space travel commonplace. Even the near disaster in April 1970 of Apollo 13, whose moon-bound mission was brought safely back to earth despite the explosion of oxygen tanks on board, only served to increase belief in NASA know-how (Wainwright, 1986).

The *Challenger* disaster marked the first time that an astronaut had died while in flight, although other space employees had died while working in the space program. Most publicly known were the deaths of Apollo I astronauts Gus Grissom, Ed White, and Roger Chaffee in a 1967 fire while in a training session on the launch pad at the Kennedy Space Center. But school-age children had no memory of this early tragedy, occurring as it did just 9 months before the assassination of Robert Kennedy.

Shuttle flights had become routine. Even the word shuttle implied a certain ordinariness. No longer considering shuttle technology to be experimental, NASA had declared the shuttle "operational" in July 1982, following the fourth test flight of the space shuttle *Columbia* (Lewis, 1988). Not surprisingly, the launch of Mission 51-L drew relatively limited coverage despite the publicity over its teacher crew member, with only CNN and NBC's Today Show, in its West Coast early morning broadcast, providing live coverage of the launch (Wright, Kunkel, Pinon, & Huston, 1989). The shuttle was both an impressive accomplishment of American technology and something relegated to the inside pages of the nation's newspapers.

Special Attributes of the Crew   Despite the fact that the shuttle flights had become somewhat routine, Americans developed a special connectedness and identification with Mission 51-L and its crew members. NASA had created the idea of a "citizen observer-participant" who would be chosen to fly into space as a shuttle crew member, with the clear aim of building public support for space program funding. President Reagan was credited with insisting that the first "ordinary person" selected for space be a teacher (Magnuson, 1986a). Christa McAuliffe became "the national focus of the last *Challenger* mission— the apple-cheeked schoolteacher who was going to teach a lesson from space. If people cannot remember any other name from the crew, they do remember hers" (Cobb, 1996, p. 1). She was called "a public relations natural" (Magnuson, 1986a), and, indeed, media attention to the flight was greatly increased. Over 800 reporters, five times the usual number, were at the Kennedy Space Center on launch day. That number increased to 1,200 within hours after the explosion (Murphy, 1986a).

The rest of the crew became much more widely known from media coverage following the explosion. The seven-person crew was shown to be made up of broadly talented, dedicated professionals, six married, five with children, who had a love of science and space exploration. The crew was seen as "good people" whose untimely death was especially unjust (Goleman, 1986). The racial and gender diversity of the Mission 51-L crew offered role models for almost every group in America.

Multiple Group Ownership of the *Challenger* Mission and Crew   The popularity of the crew and the awareness and interest of the public, all fueled by broad media coverage following the explosion, resulted in many groups feeling that they were actively involved in the mission, the crew, and their destruction. The interest of no group was more frequently recognized than American schoolchildren. Both Reagan and Bush had directed comments to America's schoolchildren in their initial addresses to the nation. Part of the success of the Teacher-in-Space Program was in eliciting youth participation and enthusiasm about the mission. This was the "schoolchildren's shuttle." Science classrooms across the country were provided with special teaching plans related to Mission 51-L in preparation for Christa McAuliffe's two live broadcasts from space, which were to be carried by the educational broadcasting system (Wald, 1986a).

Millions of schoolchildren were witnesses to the explosion. Later studies showed that most children experienced "substantial emotional distress" following the loss of *Challenger*. A New York Times/CBS News Poll of over 200 children, ages 9–17, 2–3 days after the accident found 52% of teens and 30% of late elementary schoolchildren reporting being upset "a lot" by the accident. The majority of students in both groups reported knowing that a teacher was on board Mission 51-L, and the majority felt that the teacher was much like their own. A smaller majority reported that their school had discussed the accident in class (Clymer, 1986). As for older students, a study on the impact of the explosion on college students conducted soon after the disaster revealed that the *Challenger* explosion was named as the "most shocking" major news story in their lives. Seventy-eight percent of those interviewed reported "strong" or "very strong" emotional reaction to the tragedy; almost 90% predicted that they would never forget where they were when they heard about it (Kubey & Peluso, 1990). Follow-up studies over a year later revealed that the memories of the event were still clear in the minds of both young and older students (Terr et al., 1996). The majority of students interviewed could recall where they were and how they came to learn about the explosion. However, almost a third of those students interviewed had retained false details based on initial misconceptions about the event.

The emotional impact of the crew death was magnified for students of all ages by McAuliffe's presence. Said one teacher finalist, "A teacher in space becomes your teacher. Do you know an astronaut? Everyone knows a teacher" (Magnuson, 1986a, p. 30). But it seemed that groups everywhere knew someone on the crew. Hometowns, home states, high schools, undergraduate and graduate schools, times seven, could and did claim strong connection to the "heroes" of Mission 51-L. More so than at the time of the Kennedy assassination, a diverse array of survivor groups mourned the loss of "their" astronaut. Moreover, that loss was uncontaminated by the feelings of revenge that may accompany a terrorist act or any divisions of race, religion, nationality, or political beliefs, as have followed other U.S. disasters and tragedies (Morrow, 1986).

A "shared sense of mourning" was the situation described in many news articles in the days following the explosion, and this communality was significantly enhanced by the media. *The New York Times* devoted an unprecedented 10 full pages, including the entire front page, to the disaster. *The Miami Herald* produced a special 8-page section that needed to be added to the already printed daily edition of January 28th. All 67,000 copies of an extra edition of Denver's *Rocky Mountain News* sold out; no other extra edition had been printed by the *Rocky Mountain News* since V-J day, more than 4 decades before (Murphy, 1986a).

But it was television that would provide the most vivid coverage of the explosion and the impact of the loss by showing the faces of those who witnessed it. A survey conducted by the National Science Foundation determined that 95% of Americans had viewed some of the *Challenger* explosion coverage by the end of the day of the loss (cited in Wright et al., 1989). All three network channels were on-air with coverage within 6 minutes of the explosion, and they provided continuous reporting for more than 5 hours. Each offered special evening broadcasts. The blow-up of the *Challenger* was repeated hundreds of times, in regular speed, slow motion, and stop action. ABC's news anchor, Peter Jennings, recalled, "We all shared in this experience in an instantaneous way because of television. I can't recall any time or crisis in history when television has had such an impact" (Murphy, 1986a, p. 42). Jennings received over 10,000 letters thanking him for his coverage during such a difficult time (Kaye, 1989). The role television played in both intensifying reactions to the disaster and in providing a surrogate grief processing group has been the topic of discussion of mass communication professionals (see Kubey & Peluso, 1990). It is clear that television furnished the American public with pictures of the loss itself, cues to emotional reactions and interpretation of the event through interviews and commentaries, and front-row seats to memorial ceremonies and investigative hearings—all "up front and personal."

The Survivor Groups

The idea of *group survivorship* permits the examination of the impact of a death on aggregates of individuals beyond the family and friends of the deceased and promotes the explorations of ways to help groups respond positively to the death. A positive response would be one that assists members in acknowledging the loss as a group and serves to facilitate adjustment to the loss. A model outlining rights and obligations of survivor groups will be described in greater detail later in the chapter. But even a cursory review of the events that took place following the *Challenger* disaster reveals that many groups, from the United States as a nation to the crew members' families as a unit, were identified and identified themselves as distinct aggregations of people uniquely touched by the loss of *Challenger*. That so many groups would want to claim a connection to the disaster is not surprising in light of the high profile of the event that resonated so much with America's image of itself and its history. Moreover, President Reagan provided an immediate and powerful guide at the national level that could be readily copied by those community and state leaders who wished to express their special connection to individual astronauts.

Following the death of a member within a typical organization, such as a school or business, some group members or classes, departments, or sections of the organization will be more directly affected by the member's death than others. The degree of connectedness of a particular group or subgroup to a crisis often determines the need for group response or the consequence for group members if such commemorative responses are not undertaken. This is the idea and impetus of the concept of *levels of survivorship* (Zinner, 1985).

At the primary level of survivorship are the family members and intimates of the deceased. But anyone who identifies strongly with the deceased may experience the grief ordinarily ascribed to family members. Secondary-level survivors are those individuals who have intermediate-level knowledge and interaction with the deceased through work or neighborhood association. Friends and acquaintances might readily be considered secondary-level survivors. Their grief level might be anticipated to be more moderate than that of primary survivors, but there may be some expectation of their taking part in postdeath ceremonies or, at least, directly contacting family members of the deceased.

Tertiary survivors are those who share a significant social characteristic with the deceased, such as occupational or recreational activity or geographic or ethnic identity, but who may have had little or no interaction with the deceased. These "socially ascribed" survivors may experience strong but relatively temporary feelings of loss because someone "like" them has died. Finally, quartenary or fourth-level survivors are those individuals who share one particularly broad and general characteristic, again, such as geographic or ethnic identification. Such groups of survivors may or may not feel connected to the deceased and may or may not be or wish to be incorporated into postloss activities.

Identification of specific survivor groups and their degree of connectedness to the loss of *Challenger* is a complex undertaking given the number and size of so many self-identified groups and the high emotional involvement of so many of their members. The cultural nodality of the explosion, no doubt, also impelled some groups to want to be associated with this historic event. The following groups and subgroups may be seen as survivor groups spanning all levels of survivorship.

Next-of-Kin   Over time, the private grief of family members became the subject of numerous newspaper and magazine articles (Dowling, 1996; Swarns, 1996). Although crew spouses continued to be publicly supportive of NASA, and all families were represented on the board of the *Challenger* Centers for Space Education, family members reported the continued difficulty they experienced with the repeated showings of the *Challenger* explosion. Pilot Michael Smith's younger brother explained, "On any given moment, on any given day, I can turn on the television and see my bother and the shuttle crew die." The frequent ceremonies held in honor of crew members brought mixed feelings to some. "Every new year brings another anniversary of the disaster, another flurry of publicity and another wave of what [Gregory] Jarvis' stepmother, Ellen, describes as 'dreadful, shattering pain'" (Swarns, 1996) (p. 21). In Beaufort, North Carolina, the Michael Smith family requested that the annual ceremony honoring their son be called off. In this instance, at least, a conflict seemed to have developed between the larger social group's need to identify with the loss of a heroic member and the family's need to put the public aspects of the event behind them.

NASA   At first, NASA received many expressions of sympathy from outsiders who recognized the personal and professional effort represented by the shuttle and the impact of the loss on the organization. NASA, second only to the families in level of intimacy with the crew, was mourning the loss of its own. But the Rogers Commission blamed NASA and its management style for allowing what the Commission saw as an avoidable accident. The strong conflict of feelings among NASA employees and between subgroups within NASA became known through news articles and interviews. "'There's more outrage here than in the public because of what might have been seen but not acted on,' one unidentified source close to the Johnson Space Center in Houston was quoted as saying a month after the accident" (Martz, 1986, p. 19). Although both the Johnson Space Center in Houston and the Kennedy Space Center in Cape Canaveral held private ceremonies following the explosion and both continue to carry out annual rituals in memory of the crew and mission, NASA itself was on trial during the Commission hearings, and this fact, along with the complex bureaucractic divisions and multigeographic locations, could be expected to complicate the grief process of the organization and its employees.

In addition to NASA, other groups closely associated with the space program and with the shuttle missions, such as the private contracting companies, tended to see themselves as survivor groups as well. Also affected were the communities of Florida's Space Coast, such as Titusville, Cocoa, Rockledge, and Palm Bay, towns in which space talk is common, and every fast-food restaurant displays shuttle pictures.

Concord   The town of Concord, New Hampshire, the smallest state capitol in the nation and the home of Christa McAuliffe, clearly identified itself as a "close" survivor group. When she was alive, the city newspaper, the *Monitor*, called McAuliffe "this city's shining example" (Wald, 1986c, p. 17). She was asked to serve as grand marshall in Concord's 1986 New Year's Day parade. It was the town's big send-off for its most famous citizen. After the disaster, the editor of the *Monitor*, Mike Pride, wrote a piece for *Newsweek* magazine (Pride, 1986) which he entitled, "There had been a death in the family." He described his joy and civic pride when the crew member to represent the Teacher-in-Space Program had been selected from his home town. He wrote that "Christa made Concord proud. The people in our city saw in her the best that we have to offer" (Pride, 1986, p. 42). Said the Rev. Daniel Messier, at a Catholic service for McAuliffe the morning following the explosion: "She was Concord. When she stepped on that shuttle, Concord stepped on that shuttle" (Wald, 1986b).

All of Concord—McAuliffe's students, her fellow teachers, her neighbors, and members of her church—took her death quite hard. Newspaper articles described a town that had closed ranks against outside reporters and any interference with the McAuliffe family's privacy. "The state memorialized McAuliffe by building a planetarium and space museum. But many locals say they've never been there. Some say they prefer to remember McAuliffe as a friend or a teacher, not as a subject of media hoopla" (Larrabee, 1996). Ten years later, no streets have been renamed in her honor and no plaques honoring McAuliffe hang in Concord city buildings (Larrabee, 1996).

Other Survivor Groups   Other identifiable groups of individuals who could be seen as connected to the loss of the shuttle were American schoolchildren; primary and secondary school teachers, especially science teachers; the hometown and universities of all of the astronauts; and the United States as a nation. Whether any or all of these groups responded positively as a survivor group depended greatly on whether group leaders existed and acted in a way that clearly identified the link between the group and Mission 51-L. The largest of the survivor groups mentioned, the United States, benefited from the leadership provided by President Reagan in his two public addresses. In his speeches on the afternoon of the explosion and at the national memorial service on the following Friday, Reagan acted as "chief national mourner" (Adler, 1986, p. 26). He offered words of consolation to family members both privately and publicly. He invoked the image of pioneers in describing the bravery and courage of the astronauts. He pledged to continue their "dream" and to continue the idea of "ordinary citizens" being a part of the manned space program. In doing so, he provided affirmation of the shared pain and offered direction for finding meaning in the loss. Reagan was acknowledged as a "healer" in the media (Apple, 1986).

A Model of Group Survivorship

Postdeath rituals focused on the next-of-kin serve many purposes. Primary aims of such rituals are the necessary disposal of the body in a culturally prescribed manner designed to show respect for the body, affirmation of the loss and the subsequent pain for the survivors, and, often, a community-focused expression of support for the bereaved. Postdeath rituals also provide direction for immediate and longer term behavior of family survivors. Condolence rituals, such as the sending of flowers and sympathy notes and the printing of obituaries, often acknowledge the significance of the deceased to the family and community in general and offer salutary explanations of the meaning of life and death. In sum, postdeath rituals are designed to propel and facilitate the bereavement process. The structure of culturally sanctioned postdeath rituals is fairly universal because the need for the family to grieve and to adjust is universal following the loss of a member.

Bereaved groups of individuals, beyond the family unit, often have a similar need for directed response and adjustment when the group organization is disrupted by the loss of a significant member. Unfortunately, norms for group survivorship are not as culturally established, nor are their purpose as intentionally described. But not to consider and encourage a response from a group following the death of a member is to give a public indication of the minor impact of the loss and, by extension, the minimal worth of the absent member *or* of any other member.

An articulated model of group survivorship would serve as a sensitizing paradigm to alert group members, particularly group leaders, to those actions and needs that would facilitate group adjustment in times of significant loss. It could also guide policy planning for organizations such as schools, where deaths of group members must be anticipated and planned for, given the unfortunate frequency of their occurrence. Such a model, too, would be useful in assessing the appropriateness and completeness of those actions that are taken following a group loss so as to better prepare for any future circumstances.

One theoretical model of group survivorship, described by Zinner (1985), proposes that survivor groups have certain social rights and obligations, analogous to those afforded family survivors. While groups differ in size and cohesiveness and even in awareness of their being (e.g., a temporary grouping of football fans at a stadium), recognition of the rights and obligations of members who experience a crisis *as a group* is hypothesized to facilitate the immediate, as well as long-term, well-being of all those associated with the loss. Conversely, if no coordinated response to a member's death is forthcoming, the lack of group response suggests a lack of leadership or awareness of group needs— a common occurrence in this society.

Social Rights (SR) of Survivor Groups   A survivor group can be seen as having certain social rights conferred on it, ideally, by those outside the group.

(SR/1) The first right is *to be acknowledged and recognized as a survivor, as having suffered a significant loss*. When outsiders react to group members as a group that has endured a loss through a member's death, it serves as public affirmation that the deceased was not just any isolated individual but, indeed, a member of that group. Following the explosion of *Challenger*, social condolences were directed to a number of survivor groups. Certainly, spouses and parents of the crew received many expressions of concern and sympathy, but social condolences were also clearly bestowed upon the United States, NASA, Concord High School, and the town of Concord. These groups were perceived as secondary-level survivor groups or perhaps as symbolic secondary-level survivors in the case of the American nation. Others saw these groups as being especially distressed by the crew loss and responded accordingly. This right did not appear to be extended to other communities or universities historically associated with the crew.

(SR/2) A survivor group has the right *to be informed of facts concerning the death and subsequent actions taken*. This claim is fairly obvious and presupposed in the instance of family survivors. When a family member dies, close relatives expect to be fully informed as to the cause of death and to be permitted to participate in any postdeath ritual. Not to be so treated would be a breach of cultural expectations and would be received with bewilderment and anger in most cases. In instances of terrorist acts, this may create conflict when issues related to national security prevent full disclosure to relatives of the deceased. Indeed, one of the earliest issues typically addressed by survivors is the question of how and why a death took place.

Initially, NASA approached the issue of the cause of the *Challenger* explosion with much public reticence, refusing during the first few days following the explosion even to release information on the temperature at the launch pad (Marbach, 1986b). Within the first week of the investigation, *The New York Times* had disclosed internal NASA documents that had warned about problems with the O-rings of the solid rocket boosters. After only 7 days of hearings before the Roger Commission, evidence emerged that pointed to problems in the O-ring of the right solid rocket booster. But NASA publicly ignored leaks to the press about its prior knowledge of such problems and the evidence that was mounting before the Commission. Commission Chair Rogers found sufficient NASA dereliction in the decision-making process for him to excuse all NASA officials involved in the mission launch from participating in the investigation (Murphy, 1986b)

Over the months of the Commission's investigation, no NASA employee who appeared before the Rogers Commission conceded that he would have altered his decision to launch, given the same set of circumstances (Magnuson, 1986c). Lawrence Mulloy, manager of the solid rocket booster project and seen by many as bearing a significant amount of responsibility for the accident, had been alerted the night before the launch of serious reservations on the part of Morton Thiokol engineers who only reluctantly signed off on the go-ahead for launch. Before the Commission, Mulloy stated, "I regret the accident, but I don't feel guilty about it. In hindsight, it was a very bad decision to launch. Wish we hadn't done that. But . . . given the same data, given the same history and following the same rules, one would have to make the same decision again"

(Burkey, 1997, p. 2). Mulloy maintained that everyone, from astronauts to top managers, was aware of the problems related to the O-rings; all had accepted what would be considered a calculated risk.

Where an apology can do little in reality to make up for a disaster, the lack of an apology will outrage those most affected by a tragedy. Even the corps of astronauts, a survivor group about which little was written following the disaster, expressed disillusionment and anger. John Young, chief astronaut, sent a strongly worded letter berating NASA for allowing internal and external pressures to lower safety standards, putting the ship and lives at serious risk (Marbach, 1986a). Christa McAuliffe's mother remembered her husband being most upset because "no one ever said they were sorry" (Cobb, 1996, p. 1).

NASA's reputation was further damaged by revelations that Rockwell International also had objected to the *Challenger* launch because of the presence of ice on the launch pad structure. Their reservations were also ignored by NASA officials although, in fact, the ice proved not to be contributory to the accident (Magnuson, 1986c). Public confidence in NASA in 1986 was further eroded when, in April, a Titan 34-D rocket carrying a military reconnaissance satellite for an Air Force mission not related to NASA and, in May, a Delta 3920 rocket carrying a weather satellite, both exploded soon after launching (Lewis, 1988). The Delta rocket was struck by lightning and destroyed by NASA seconds after being launched during a severe rain storm. It would be almost 3 years before the shuttle program would resume flights.

A second issue of fact that proved troublesome to the public had to do with the timing and cause of the crew members' deaths. From the beginning, NASA had maintained that the crew had died instantly in the explosion. Given a projected force of 20-Gs occurring when the cockpit section separated from the orbiter after the explosion, it does seem unlikely that anyone would be conscious after experiencing this type of shock. What is more, the cockpit section continued upward to an altitude of 80,000 feet after separation, and the cabin would have experienced explosive decompression that would have proved lethal to the crew members who were not wearing pressure suits.

Still, NASA was not to be believed on this point by many Americans. This alleged deception is explained by some to not only have been undertaken to protect the feelings of next-of-kin but also as a political maneuver to keep the public from learning that the crew most probably survived the explosion only to die in the subsequent fall of the shuttle into the ocean. Several news agencies sued in court, under The Freedom of Information Act, for access to the tape recordings of cabin conversation in order to verify the transcript released by NASA. A federal appeals court sided with NASA's contention that voice records would be a serious invasion of the privacy of the families ("*Challenger*: The final words," 1990). When the crew compartment was discovered within a month of the disaster, NASA would not confirm or deny the find (Magnuson, 1986b).

Eventually, a NASA official did report to the Rogers Commission that the "crew survived the fireball and the breakup of the orbiter and perished of either decompression shortly thereafter or impact with the water" (Lewis, 1988, p. 175). Three of the four individual crew member air packs found in the recovery effort had been manually turned on. But because of extensive damage to the bodies of the crew members, the cause of death could not be determined. No discussion appears in the Commission report on the bodies of the astronauts and no forensic evidence was ever given to the public. Even the request from the *Journal of the American Medical Association* to examine the autopsy report was denied by NASA, which cited Exemption 6 of the 1977 Freedom of Information Act, a clause permitting government agencies to withhold information which would represent an unnecessary invasion of privacy (Lewis, 1988). Whether the pubic had a "right" to know the disturbing details of the crew's deaths is reasonably debatable; that the public wanted to have full knowledge of the details in order to comprehend fully what had occurred is clear. The review of the *Challenger* tragedy shows that it is this aspect of this particular model of group survivorship that appears most seriously violated.

(SR/3) A final right of a survivor group is *to be allowed to participate in traditional or in creative leave-taking ceremonies.* Funeral rites exist universally to give direction to the bereaved in their efforts to acknowledge and cope with loss. In western society, many occupational groups who experience high mortality rates (such as law enforcement agencies, fire departments, military organizations) and male-dominated groups in general (such as adult fraternal organizations and sports associations) have developed traditional observances which are carried out when a member dies. Funeral rituals that are either attended by a survivor group or its representatives or created by and for the survivor group offer confirmation of the group's association with the deceased and an opportunity for surviving group members to "pay their respects."

Live television coverage of the memorial services on Friday, January 31, provided an opportunity for Americans to attend the national tribute to the astronauts and mission payload specialists of the shuttle *Challenger*. With the President at the podium, all Americans were duly represented. Group survivors from NASA, from Concord, from Concord High School, and from the crew's home states and universities all were able to be a part of commemorative efforts that spoke of both the courage of the crew members and the relationship of each of these survivor groups with Mission 51-L.

Social Obligations (SO) of Survivor Groups   While survivor groups may be afforded certain social rights by those outside the group in recognition of their bereavement status, survivor groups are also required to respond in particular ways. Thus, specific social obligations coexist with the social rights previously described.

(SO/1) An important social obligation is for the group *to acknowledge publicly the group's survivorship status.* Without an outward display to indicate that a loss has occurred, others cannot know or respond to a group's loss. On an individual level, the American society has abandoned many of its earlier symbols of bereavement such as the draping of a home with black materials or the wearing of a black arm band or widow's weeds. However, it is not uncommon to find a sports team wearing black arm bands, or a police station flying a flag at half-mast, or high school students tying ribbons to a tree in recognition of another student's death. These actions alert all who see them that the group has suffered a significant hurt. Indeed, when no externally directed action is taken by a group or subgroup within a larger organization, a business-as-usual impression is created which is increasingly perceived as heartless as opposed to stoic.

Almost all of the survivor groups previously discussed in relation to the *Challenger* explosion reacted in a manner that alerted others (and their own members as well) that they had been directly affected by the death of *Challenger*'s crew members. There are two notable exceptions. One is the group composed of American schoolchildren. This group might be seen at first to be merely an aggregation of individuals based on a given age range and occupational similarity of sorts. An organized response perhaps could not really be expected. But an organized response was created on behalf of the American people. Flags were lowered at all government buildings; national memorial services were arranged; a national marker was erected at Arlington Cemetery. NASA did receive small donations of money from many schoolchildren who hoped to contribute to the rebuilding of the shuttle (Magnuson, 1986a). The difference between the survivor group of American children and the survivor group of the America people was one of leadership. There was no leadership structure in place or assumed (for example, by a national council of PTAs, scouting organizations, or even a fast-food chain) which might have served to guide a response symbolizing the impact of Christa McAuliffe's death, in particular, on school-aged children. Students across the country might have been encouraged to wear an apple-red ribbon on the day of the Friday national service or to have "their" representative speak at the service itself or to have the front doors of all primary and secondary schools trimmed in some appropriate manner by student leaders; but none of these was done.

The other group which did not outwardly identify itself as a survivor group was the corps of astronauts who may well be considered a near primary-level survivor group, both in their personal association with the astronauts and payload specialists who died and in their identification of the tragedy with their own professional role. It may be that, like the family members of the crew, their group behavior and personal grief was kept as private as possible. There was little mention of the astronaut corps in the public documents examined for this chapter.

(SO/2) A second obligation connected to a survivor group is *to make a tangible response to the defined immediate/family survivors on behalf of the group*. It is assumed that the next-of-kin are most bereft following a death and are in most need of consolation. A show of support of the family through the sending of sympathy cards, attendance at the funeral, or the establishing of memorials to the deceased by the group and/or its representatives is a traditional mechanism used by groups to pay due respect to the next-of-kin and to show attachment. Clearly, family members were recognized by many in an outpouring of written words of sympathy received by all families of the *Challenger* crew, both from individual Americans and from recognized groups.

An obstacle to adequately meeting this social obligation arises frequently when group leaders express their commiseration to family members on behalf of the group but overlook the need to inform their own group members of such actions. Any action taken in the name of a survivor group which is generally unknown to group members does not serve the bereavement needs of the whole.

(SO/3) Finally, a survivor group is obliged *to make a tangible response within the group to benefit group members*. The deceased member is known to the group in ways distinct from how the family or other associated groups know the deceased. Group-centered ceremonies or memorials can be created in a way that honors this idiosyncratic relationship and that simultaneously reflects the special attributes, goals, or achievements of the group. Typical in our culture is the naming of a government building after an influential leader or creating a memorial playground in honor of a student who has died. These are ways in which members of an affiliated group can signify their special remembrance of a member. Often, these unique commemorations also provide a way of formulating a meaningful interpretation of the loss.

The founding of *Challenger* Centers for Space Science Education by the families of the Mission 51-L crew not only provided an educational benefit to schoolchildren but, just as importantly, created a living tribute which could give purpose and meaning to the loss of the crew. So, too, special projects and memorials established by NASA via the Astronaut Memorial Foundation, by the National Education Association, and by the state of New Hampshire, to name a few, lent poignant expression to the examination of the meaning of the *Challenger* tragedy.

PERSONAL WORD AND SUMMARY

It is an interesting exercise to research and write about the *Challenger* explosion and its aftermath given that I, too, am a group survivor, an American who witnessed the events being described. Friends and colleagues who were aware of my professional interest in constructing this piece seemed compelled to tell me where they were when they first heard about the accident. And I felt the same compulsion to confess that I had been sequestered that momentous day, assisting in a neuropsychological assessment of a sailor at the Portsmouth Naval Base, and felt as if the world had somehow changed when I learned, hours later, that the *Challenger* and its crew had been lost. My interest in the issues of supporting bereaved groups of individuals preceded the tragedy but was always somewhat influenced by it.

The academic and clinical fields of grief and bereavement and of trauma are only now coming together after years of investigation in both areas. The *Challenger* disaster serves as but one broad example of how the deaths of individuals can affect the identity and emotions of organized groups of people. The *Challenger* explosion stands out in American history as an event that captured the attention and heart of a diverse number of groups. Clearly, the conduct of many of *Challenger*'s survivor groups met the social rights and obligations noted by the model of group survivorship that was presented. Whether actions taken on behalf of these groups over the intervening 10 years successfully met the needs of their many members is not answerable based on public documents. But observing the model applied, even in a particularly broad-scale instance, may assist intervenors and group leaders in directing responses in new situations of group loss and in evaluating the efficacy of those responses.

"The Shuttle Explodes," ran the banner headline of *The New York Times* on January 28, 1986. Clearly, the images of that explosion endure in the American psyche a decade later.

REFERENCES

Adler, J. (1986, February 10). We mourn seven heroes. *Newsweek*, 26.

Apple, R. W., Jr. (1986, January 29). President as healer. *The New York Times*, p. A7.

Boyd, G. M. (1986, January 29). Bush offers his solace and urges nation to 'press on' with exploration of space. *The New York Times*, p. A9.

Broad, W. J. (1986, January 27). Shuttle launching delayed again over weather fears. *The New York Times*, p. A14.

Burkey, M. (1997, June 10). *"I was playing by the rules."* [On-line]. Available: http://www.htimes.com/today/*Challenger*/part2.htlm

Challenger: The final words. (1990, December 24). *Time*, 15.

Christa McAuliffe remembered by hometown. (1996). Associated Press [On-line]. *Remembering Challenger Index*. Available: http://www.infoseek.com

Christa McAuliffe's mom speaks out on *Challenger* disaster to Prodigy members. (1996, January 26). *Prodigy Services Company* [On-line]. Available: http://pages.prodigy.com:8987/mservice/pn012696.xbm

Clinton remembers 'explorers' of *Challenger* crew. (1996, January 27). *Nando.Net* [On-line]. Available: http://www.nando.net/newsroom/netn/nation/012796/national12-24463.html

Clymer, A. (1986, February 2). Poll finds children still enthusiastic about space. *The New York Times*, pp. A1, A16.

Cobb, K. (1996, January 27). *Challenger* families wrestled with loss shared by the world. *Houston Chronicle*, p. 1ff.

Cook, W. J. (1996, January 29). Shuttling cautiously ahead, 10 years later. *U.S. News & World Report*, 11.

Dowling, C. G. (1996, February). Ten years ago seven brave Americans died as they reached for the stars. *Life*, 38-40, 42-43.

Eberhard, J. (1994, January). *Challenger Point, 14080', memorial plaque* [On-line]. Trip report. Newsgroups: rec.aviation.stories, rec.aviation.misc.

Goleman, D. (1986, February 1). Anger, confusion, and fear in the nation's grief. *The New York Times*, p. A11.

Kaye, E. (1989, September). Peter Jennings. *Esquire*, 158-176.

Kubey, R. W., & Peluso, T. (1990). Emotional response as a cause of interpersonal news diffusion: The case of the space shuttle tragedy. *Journal of Broadcasting and Electronic Media*, *34*(1), 69-76.

Larrabee, J. (1996, January 26). For New Hampshire students, a difficult memory. *USA Today*, p. 3A.

Lewis, R. S. (1988). *Challenger: The final voyage*. New York: Columbia University Press.

Magnuson, E. (1986a, February 10). They slipped the surly bonds of earth to touch the face of God. *Time*, 24–31.

Magnuson, E. (1986b, February 17). A cold soak, a plume, a fireball. *Time*, 25.

Magnuson, E. (1986c, March 10). A serious deficiency. *Time*, pp. 38–39, 42.

Marbach, W. D. (1986a, March 24). No cheers for NASA. *Newsweek*, 18–19.

Marbach, W. D. (1986b, February 24). Closing in on calamity. *Newsweek*, 58–59.

Martz, L. (1986, March 3). Days of decision: A countdown. *Newsweek*, 16–19.

Media coverage of *Challenger* 10th observance. (1996, January 23). *Challenger Learning Centre* [on-line]. Available: http://www.osc.on.ca

Morrow, L. (1986, February 10). A nation mourns. *Time*, 22–23.

Murphy, J. (1986a, February 10). Covering the awful unexpected. *Time*, 42–43.

Murphy, J. (1986b, February 24). Zeroing in on the O rings. *Time*, 58.

President expresses his sorrow at the astronauts' deaths. (1986, February 29). *The New York Times*, p. A9.

President's letter to Concord High School. (1986, February 1). *The New York Times*, p. A11.

Pride, M. (1986, February 10). There had been a death in the family. *Newsweek*, 42.

Rimer, S. (1986, January 29). After the shock, a need to share grief and loss. *The New York Times*, pp. A1, A3.

Schmemann, S. (1986, February 2). Soviet Union to name 2 Venus craters for shuttle's women. *The New York Times*, p. A16.

Schmidt, W. E. (1986, February 2). Memorial wreath dropped into the sea. *The New York Times*, p. A16.

Schwartz, H. S. (1987, Spring). On the psychodynamics of organization disaster: The case of the space shuttle *Challenger*. *Columbia Journal of World Business*, 59-67.

Swarns, R. L. (1996, January 28). *Challenger* disaster 10-year anniversary. *The New York Times*, p. 21.

Terr, L. C., Bloch, D. A., Michel, B. A., Shi, H., Reinhardt, S. A., & Metayer, S. (1996). Children's memories in the wake of *Challenger*. *American Journal of Psychiatry*, *153*(5), 618–625.

Their families today. (1996, January). *Houston Chronicle* [On-line]. Available: http://www.chron.com/content/interactive/special/*Challenger*

Transcript of the President's eulogy for the seven *Challenger* astronauts. (1986, February 1). *The New York Times*, p. A11.

Wainwright, L. (1986, March). After 25 years, an end to innocence. *Life*, 15ff.

Wald, M. L. (1986a, January 29). Cheers turn to numbness as Concord High School mourns one of its own. *The New York Times*, p. A3.

Wald, M. L. (1986b, January 29). In Concord, McAuliffe's neighbors mourn loss of a 'shining example.' *The New York Times*, p. A17.

Wald, M. L. (1986c, January 31). A day of grief and praise for McAuliffe. *The New York Times*, p. A15.

Weintraub, B. (1986, February 1). Reagan pays tribute to 'our 7 *Challenger* heroes.' *The New York Times*, pp. A1, A11.

We remember. (1996). *Houston Chronicle Interactive* [On-line]. Available: http:www.chron.com/content/interactive/special/*Challenger*/response/response.html

Wolfe, T. (1986, February 10). Everyman vs. Astropower. *Newsweek*, 40–41.

Wright, J. C., Kunkel, D., Pinon, M., & Huston, A. C. (1989). How children reacted to televised coverage of the space shuttle disaster. *Journal of Communication, 39*(2), 27–45.

Zinner, E. S. (1985). Group survivorship: A model and case study application. In E. S. Zinner (Ed.), *Coping with death on campus* (pp. 51–68). New Directions for Student Services, No. 31. San Francisco: Jossey-Bass.

Figure 3.1 The roll-on, roll-off passenger ferry, *Estonia,* which went down in rough seas, September 28, 1994. Over 850 people died, making the accident the worst peacetime sea disaster in Scandinavian history. Shown here docked in Helsinki, a year before the disaster. (Photo taken by Mary Beth Williams, co-editor.)

Chapter 3

The *Estonia* Disaster: National Interventions, Outcomes, and Personal Impacts

Lasse Nurmi

The Republic of Estonia lies south of Finland between Scandinavia and Russia. This Eastern European country is small and has approximately 1,500,000 inhabitants. When the Soviets introduced glasnost, Estonia sought its independence from Russia. It was re-recognized as an independent nation in 1991, and the first free elections in Estonia were held in 1992. Estonia has chosen to model itself after its closest capitalistic neighbor, Finland, and travel between the two nations is frequent, both by air and by sea. One major means of travel is by passenger ferry. Both Finns and Estonians speak unique languages that are similar and rooted in the far eastern Ural Mountains of Russia.

Finland, a member of the European Union since 1995, is one of the northernmost countries in the world. Finland, too, has a history of warring with the Russian Empire and lost part of its territory to the Soviet Union at the close of World War II. Finland has a population of 5 million; much of the Finnish economy is based upon its rich forests.

The *HMS Estonia*, a ro-ro (roll on, roll off) passenger ferry, had a long career of transporting individuals between Scandinavian countries. The ferry was built in Germany in 1980 with a capacity of 1,500 passengers and 460 vehicles. It was launched July 5, 1980, as the *Viking Sally* on its maiden voyage between Turku, Finland, and Stockholm, Sweden. Between 1990 and 1992, it was owned by the Silja Line and registered as the *Silja Star* and was then part of the Wasa Line, registered as the *Wasa King*. In 1992, it was purchased by Estline, a joint venture between the Nordstrom and Thulin Shipping Company of Stockholm (which owned 47% of the line), the Estonian State (which owned 50% of the line), and an unnamed Swiss citizen (who owned 3%). Officially, the ship was owned by the Estonian Shipping Company out of Cyprus.

The *Estonia* began its run between Tallinn, the capital of Estonia, and Stockholm on January 1, 1993. At the time of its registry as an Estline vessel, this 157-meter (approximately 480') passenger ferry was the only one to traverse the route. The ship was equipped to hold over 1,500 passengers, the majority of whom slept in small cabins near the car decks for the overnight journey.

On September 27, 1994, the ship was commanded by Arvo Andersson; a second Estline captain, Avo Piht, was on board as a passenger. The majority of the 189 crew members (27 of whom were dancers and singers employed to entertain the passengers on their overnight journey) were Estonian and had received instruction or education in Sweden. The *Estonia* was licensed by Sweden and had undergone an official inspection by Swedish authorities prior to this trip. The inspection revealed that the rubber seals around the hatch were slightly damaged. However, the inspectors did not believe that the seals were a threat to the integrity of the ship. The inspectors also found that three of the rope bands used to secure the trucks in the car deck were slightly damaged.

THE DISASTER OF SEPTEMBER 28, 1994

On the evening of September 27, 1994, into the morning hours of September 28, 1994, after passengers, vehicles, and cargo were loaded on board and the bow port was securely closed and inspected, the *Estonia* left Tallinn and sailed into the Baltic Sea. Because bad weather (with gale force winds of 60 miles per hour) was expected, cargo marshals double checked all vehicles to make sure that they were securely tied down prior to departure; in addition, they rechecked them every half-hour during the journey. As usual, the ship left in the late evening for its overnight trip to the capital of Sweden.

This evening, passengers and crew totaled at least 989. On board were persons of various nationalities and ethnic backgrounds, although the majority were Swedes (at least 552) and Estonians (163). For many of these individuals, riding across the Baltic was a reward for hard work, a short vacation, a means to return home, or time to relax, party, and "get away."

As the ship crossed the Baltic Sea, Captain Andersson changed course from a westerly to a more southerly route to sail more with the wind and decreased his speed to 8 knots from 15 or 16 knots due to rough seas. The Uto Fort Radar Station observed these changes. A crew fireman made his hourly check of the boat, including the car deck, and had nothing out of the ordinary to report. Before 1:00 a.m., the speed of the ship decreased to 5 knots, according to radar observations. The fireman reported later that the car deck was still dry at this time. This evening, it held 32 cars and trucks, a house trailer, two busses, and four caravan cars, according to a 23-year-old passenger, Dutchman Stefan Duyndam.

Shortly after 1:00 a.m., third engineer Narcys Treu heard loud noises from the bow area and felt the recoil of two heavy blows to the bow that shook the whole ship. Engineer Treu heard the deck crew report to the bridge that water was coming into the car deck. The captain sent Treu down to check on the noises; he was met by people rushing up from the lower decks.

By 1:10 a.m., the Captain began to turn the ship to the right, to the wind, perhaps to return to Tallinn and to make sailing easier. However, the ship was not particularly responsive. As the ship turned sideways, the waves and wind drove water into the car deck on the right side, and the ship began to list heavily. By 1:24 a.m., the list was between 20° and 30°. At this point, it became impossible to use the ballast tanks to balance the ship because those on the left side were already airborne. Thus the ship continued to list more and more. Soon the main engines stopped, and the reserve power engines on the eighth deck were turned on.

Treu attempted to restart the port (left-side) engines but was not successful. By now, the list was 60 degrees, and Engineer Treu had to run on the walls of the engine room to get out. At 1:30 a.m., the bridge issued a general alarm. The auxiliary engines stopped, but emergency batteries and diesel generators continued to work; there was never a blackout on board. Surviving passenger Jaan Stern recalled that he heard strong waves beating against the ship shortly before the alarm was sounded. He noted that water was already appearing on the floor of his first-deck cabin.

At 23:24 Greenwich Mean Time (GMT) or 1:24 a.m. local time, when the *Estonia* sent a mayday call, the weather was extremely rough on the Baltic. Some waves were reportedly several apartment stories high; winds were at gale force of 95 kilometers (60 miles) per hour and the temperature of the sea was approximately 8–10°C (50°F) (Eesti Ringvaade, 1994).

The first mayday, sent by a portable radio, was barely heard by the *Silja Europa* ferry traveling in the Baltic and was not heard in Turku, Finland. The distress call did not indicate that the ship was sinking, just that there was some trouble. The crew then appeared to change radios from the hand-held set which had no high-gain antennas or high transmit power. The mayday call at 1:24 a.m. used a proper emergency radio. The last clear call said, "It seems really bad here," and a later transmission of location could hardly be understood. Within relatively few minutes after listing, the ship sank in international waters 59 23' and 21 42', 20 miles south west of Uto, in Finnish territorial responsibility, at a depth of approximately 90 meters (300 feet).

When the call was heard at the Finnish rescue center in Turku, the operator alerted the Finnish Frontier (Coast) Guard. Their priority was to get rescue vehicles airborne before deciding which other organizations needed to be involved. This decision is in agreement with what Mitchell (1996a) calls the first

priorities in a disaster. These priorities include accessing the survivors and res-
cuing (if possible) trapped survivors; establishing emergency medical triage
and treatment with transportation and hospitalization; initiating law enforcement
activities (e.g., setting up phone lines, establishing a command post, interrogat-
ing survivors as soon as is possible); providing for communications and sectori-
zation of the incident; activating resource assessment (what do we need and
what do we have?); acquiring resources (including notification of other countries); and logistical managing of rescue efforts (including all the helicopters,
ferries, and other ships).

Weeks later, the investigation into why VHF emergency transmissions
either were not sent or were not picked up by monitoring frequencies (e.g.,
in Sweden) determined that a Russian military naval base located about 300
kilometers (180 miles) east of the site of the disaster on Suursaari Island (Great
Island or Gogland) was either jamming the VHF frequency or had failed to
break transmissions using the proper push-to-talk switch. The Finnish organization monitoring the use of frequencies, the Telehallin-tokeskus, had reported
this failure to the Russian authorities many times. The problem was periodically
corrected and would then reappear. Investigators determined that the failure
was due to negligence, not sabotage. In other words, a radio on the island
transmitted continuously on channel 16 and blocked other transmissions. Thus,
the Swedish Rescue Center could not have heard any transmissions from the
Estonia. Furthermore, even if the frequency had been open, the list of the ship
was so great that the transmission range would probably have been limited to
40–60 kilometers (24–36 miles). The conversation between the *Estonia* and the
Silja Europa was heard in Turku because Finnish relay links were designed to
convey even very weak emergency signals. The Swedish Rescue Center received notification perhaps 15 minutes later than if it had come from the ship or
from Turku.

At 1:35 a.m. Finnish time, the *M/S Mariella*, steaming to the scene, was
able to see the *Estonia*'s lights. However, she sank at 1:48 a.m., and the Uto
Radar Station (located in Finnish territory) lost contact. According to survivors, the ferry sank within 15–20 minutes after the alarm sounded. The *Mariella* did not reach the scene until 2:30 a.m., when her crew began rescue operations.

The Extent of the Disaster

The sinking of the *Estonia,* in which 852 people perished, was the worst peacetime sea disaster in Scandinavian history and the worst disaster in Swedish
history since the 1809 war against Russia, when more than 500 Swedes were
killed. Other Scandinavian sea disasters with extensive loss of life occurred
during wartime. For example, on January 30, 1945, a Russian submarine sank
the German transport *Wilhelm Gustloff,* a 25,484-ton ship that held troops and
civilian refugees; thousands died.

Prior peacetime sea disasters in that area of the globe did not have as devastating a number of casualties. In 1990, the *Scandinavian Star* caught fire while sailing between Norway and Denmark; 150 persons died. In January 1993, the Polish freighter *Jan Hevelius* sank while enroute to Sweden; 50 persons died. In March 1994, the *Sally Albatross*, a large passenger ferry sailing from Helsinki, Finland, to Tallinn, Estonia, ran aground in the ice during daylight hours. However, a potential disaster was averted because passengers were not sleeping in their cabins. A sister ship rescued all passengers and crew and returned them to Helsinki, where Finnish psychologists waited to provide educational information about stress, acute stress, and posttraumatic stress as well as to hold debriefings. (This author was not among those debriefers, although he provided information and support to those who went to the terminals.) The *Sally Albatross* was eventually salvaged after water from the hold was pumped out.

The sinking of the *Estonia* was a disaster of especially great magnitude. Because the onset of the disaster was extremely rapid, the number of casualties (852), in contrast to the number of rescued persons (137), was very high. No one was prepared for a disaster of this magnitude. The Disaster Victim Identification Team in Finland had been organized only a relatively short time before the disaster (1991) and practice scenarios had not included a sea disaster, let alone one of this magnitude.

There were also immediate questions about the locus of cause for the disaster. Was it due to bad weather conditions? Was it due to mechanical failure from improperly constructed equipment or from improperly maintained equipment? Who was at fault, if anyone?

Rescue Operations

Under the leadership of Commodore Raimo Tiilikainen, commander of the Archipelago Area Sea Rescue organization, rescue operations were well coordinated and effective. Both the weather conditions and the nighttime occurrence of the disaster limited visibility and placed extreme pressure on the rescuers. The rescue attempts began in the middle of the night and employed a total of 15 helicopters. The Finns believed that using more would be too risky.

The Swedish Rescue Center got the alarm at 0.55 a.m. Swedish time (1.55 a.m. Finnish time), and their first helicopter was airborne by 1:35 a.m. (2:35 a.m.), 1 hour postdisaster. However, three of the nine Swedish Vertol helicopters that responded developed malfunctions in their hauling mechanisms and winches (e.g., ropes broke) and had to return to base to be repaired before returning to action. These malfunctions occurred, perhaps, because of the high wind (at its highest, a velocity of 25–30 meters per second, or 80–100 miles per hour). Three Swedish surface rescue haulers also developed some problems; their crews reported that the weather conditions were among the worst they had ever experienced.

At the time the helicopters were launched, winds were between 20 and 27 meters per second (or 70–85 miles per hour) and the water in the sea, at the most, was 10°C (50°F). At this temperature, a male could survive in the sea for perhaps 30 minutes before hypothermia led to death. Women might survive slightly longer because of their additional layer of body fat.

The degree of exposure to trauma was high for these rescue workers. The physical conditions, as have been noted, were extremely treacherous. Rescuers were exposed to mass death and scores of bodies, primarily in the lifeboats. They knew they had only a limited amount of time to save any individuals and, therefore, the rescuers put themselves at risk in the face of hostile elements of nature. They had to cover an immense area of sea quickly while making sure that helicopters did not collide with one another as the winds tossed them through the air. Their actual involvement in the disaster was rather short; rescues took place within a 6–7 hour window of time.

Finnish helicopters were also used in rescue operations. One helicopter, while attempting to deposit rescue workers on the deck of the local command ship, had little reserve power to gain altitude because of the bad weather conditions. As this operation occurred, a wave raised the ship to within a half meter of the helicopter, almost causing another disaster! The first rescue helicopter, containing five survivors, landed on the deck of the *Silja Symphony* at 4:10 a.m.; five more survivors landed 2 hours later, and eleven survivors and one deceased victim landed at 7:57 a.m. Two of the rescued were women; the rest, men.

As the ship listed, passengers and crew on deck threw life rafts in the water. Some landed upside down. Passengers and crew then threw themselves into the water and tried to get into or onto those rafts. Investigation showed that the life rafts from the *Estonia* were poorly designed. Many of them tipped over in the heavy seas and floated upside down. Survivors were repeatedly washed overboard, particularly from the overturned rafts, or were swamped by waves. Some survivors had to cling to the top of these overturned rafts to survive. Also, because rafts did not have numerical markings, helicopter crews found it difficult to keep track of which ones had been checked for survivors. In some instances, crews made triple checks of the same raft.

Some ships who came to the rescue found that they were unable to raise their own rescue boats after they had been lowered because the seas were so rough (Downing, 1995). The Viking Line and Silja Line ferries that were in the vicinity did not have proper equipment to aide in the rescue of passengers. For example, the *Viking Mariella* sent down rubber floats and a steward in a diving suit. Over 7,000 persons traveling on the four Finnish car ferries and the one Swedish car ferry, as well as over 1,000 crew members, witnessed these attempted rescue scenes. In many instances, there was little to be done as the rescue ferries' lifeboats were crushed by heavy waves against the sides of their mother ferries (Saari, Lindeman, Verkasalo, & Pryta, 1996). (Many of the crew on one Finnish ferry reported initial symptoms of acute stress during the first week after the disaster. The majority of males were symptom-free 8 months after the disaster, although 24% of the women still suffered from general traumatic symptoms (Saari, Lindeman, Verkasalo, & Pryta, 1996).

IMMEDIATE RESPONSES TO THE DISASTER

The Media

The first news report "hit the air waves" at 6:07 GMT. The magnitude of the disaster made it an international event with high drama (auf der Heide, 1989), and the media were quick to note the scope of the tragedy. For example, approximately 13 hours after the ship sank (allowing for a 7-hour time difference), news footage brought the disaster to the American public. Media were given limited access to the military island upon which the rescue command post was created as the nearest point of land to the disaster. Members of the media also helped Finnish police officials by disseminating information, including lists of names of survivors.

The members of the Union of Finnish Psychologists worked with the media to keep them well informed and to protect survivors from intense media exposure. Their interventions protected the privacy of the survivors. The broadcasts of the media, in general, were done without extensive gruesomeness, avoiding detailed descriptions of the numbers and conditions of the dead. (As Young, 1994, noted, the media often broadcast photographs that show gory details of a tragedy or sensationalize stories of rescue or tragedy. Media personnel who have some knowledge of trauma and traumatic stress reactions are more concerned with dissemination of accurate information, not speculative conclusions. In any crisis, let alone a crisis of this magnitude, media personnel seek information. In this crisis, assigning persons to provide factual information through designated spokespersons helped to quench the thirst for details.)

The present author, as psychologist member of the Disaster Victim Identification Team, shuttled back and forth among teams of law enforcement officials, psychologists, and others and provided information to a variety of sources. With extensive media experience, I was aware of the need to include information about the impact of a crisis on the victims, families, rescue workers, and others in my interviews.

The Victims: Initial Reflections

Exactly 989 persons were on board the ship; 137 persons were rescued, resulting in a loss of 852 passengers and crew. Five hundred thirty-nine Swedes were among the missing, and 38 of the 93 bodies brought to Finland were Swedes. One body was sent to Sweden. Two additional bodies were found later (one, months later). A total of 95 persons were eventually identified (The Estonia Disaster, 1994).

The victims were from a wide range of localities and occupations but many shared a common factor. For example, 68 members of the Stockholm Police Department and 22 mothers from the municipality of Lindesberg, Sweden, died. Many of the Swedish victims were pensioners: 56 were from Norkorpping and 44 were from Borlange. Lundin (1994) noted that hardly a person in Sweden, a country with a population of approximately 9 million inhabitants, was untouched personally by the disaster.

Two hundred fifty or more Estonian families lost one or both bread winners in the disaster, and at least 1,000 persons suddenly became dependent on out-side support for survival. Fifty-five of the recovered bodies of victims were crew members. Most of them, as crew, had earned rather small salaries and did not have pensions. One Estonian factory had sent an entire department (mostly wives and mothers) on a short vacation on the ship. They all perished. Another Estonian town lost the personnel of its entire governmental organization. Very few of the victims were Finns (12 of 15 Finns on board died), since this ferry originated in Tallinn, Estonia, rather than Helsinki, Finland. All 11 of the children under 12 years of age known to be on board perished. Twenty-three of the 27 children aged 12 to 18 also were victims. Fifty-three women and 42 men were found dead; 340 men and 417 women were among the missing.

The Survivors

One hundred thirty-seven persons survived the disaster; an additional survivor died later in the hospital. Ninety-seven of the 137 survivors were initially res-cued by helicopter; 40, by ferries. Fifty-four of the 137 survivors were Swedes, 28 of whom were taken to Stockholm. Swedish policeman Tom Jonsson was the only one of the officers returning from attending a law enforcement confer-ence in Estonia who survived. Most of the survivors were relatively fit, young males who made their way out of the lounges, cabins, and bars. The majority of these survivors initially suffered from hypothermia but recovered fairly quickly. Huddart (1994) reported via Reuter News Service in an Internet Dispatch that "only the young and strong could have made their way out of the lounges and cabins and up sharply sloping decks as the ship listed suddenly and catastrophi-cally." In addition, bars and restaurants on the upper decks tended to have younger persons present in the early morning hours. Of the passengers, 80 males and 14 females survived.

One fourth of the survivors were women, and the youngest survivor of the four children was a 14-year-old Norwegian boy who managed to get out from below the main deck. Forty-three (31 men, 12 women) of the 162 crew mem-bers were survivors; the most senior crew member among them was second engineer P. Tuur. The visiting captain also survived (Ministry of Foreign Af-fairs, 1994).

Some survivors and many bodies were brought to the military island, Utö; 99 survivors eventually were taken by car ferries (including some deposited on ferries by helicopters as well as those rescued by ferries) to hospitals at Turku, Mariehamn, Tammisaari, and Hanko, Finland. Although it was necessary to interview survivors as quickly as possible before they returned to their countries of origin in order to get as much specific information about the circumstances of the disaster while the information was fresh in survivors' minds, nurses in Turku believed the police were too intrusive in their questioning and were angry that such interrogations were necessary. The police, on the other hand, acted in their official capacity in order to determine as quickly as possible what had happened in the disaster.

Thirty-eight survivors went to the hospital in Helsinki, where they were treated, observed, and then transferred to a hotel to be debriefed and counseled by three psychologists speaking six languages (Saari, Lindeman, Verkasalo, & Pryta, 1996). By the third day after the disaster, 55 of the survivors had returned to Estonia.

Initially, Russian submarine designer Anatoly Kuteinikov of St. Petersburg stated that hundreds of survivors could have survived inside the hull in air cushions for at least a week. However, Swedish and Danish experts refuted that theory, noting that water pressure at a depth of 90 meters would make survivors mentally unstable very quickly, and the temperature of 10–12°C (45–50°F) would make survival impossible (Baltic News Service, 1994a).

What made this disaster particularly traumatizing for survivors? The situation they faced, once they abandoned the ship, was extremely dangerous. The seas were very treacherous, and survivors were in danger of drowning if not dying from hypothermia. Many of them huddled together for hours in or on life rafts that were thrown from the ship as it sank. Many of the rafts were upside down and could not provide shelter.

Roles of the Intervention Teams

In many disasters, too much psychological "help" comes to the rescue. Mitchell (1996a) terms this onslaught of professionals "mass convergency." However, this "help" is frequently not helpful at all. Survivors need some time to process what has happened; rescue workers need time to do their jobs. The priorities that were listed earlier must take precedence. Therefore, the roles of psychologists in the initial stages of the disaster included providing support only to those individuals who were significantly at risk, providing advice to command staff, and giving immediate assistance to the survivors, their families, families of the dead, bystanders on the ships, and other nonemergency personnel on the scene (crews of the other ships). Their role was not to offer treatment to these survivors or to families and friends of survivors and the dead. In his foundation newsletter, Mitchell (1996a) wrote that "people are not ready to manage their stress reactions when they are caught up in disaster operations. . . . They suppress their emotions in order to keep their mental and physical stamina up so they can complete the various tasks assigned to them during the disaster" (p. 2).

It is important to let functioning people do what they have to do as rescuers until the disaster operations are completed.

In Finland, the postdisaster work was, in essence, a national effort as the national disaster response teams mobilized. The largest groups involved were the DVI (a law enforcement team), the 20-person emergency group, and the 20-person reserve group from the Union of Finnish Psychologists. The Union team members had had various kinds of training in trauma and disaster management. Members of all teams were released from their normal duties within 24 hours of the disaster and, in conjunction with the Finnish Red Cross, responded to the disaster in a number of ways (Eränen, 1994). The majority of the psychologists worked in Helsinki, although six members went to Tallin for a week to organize local crisis teams, train Estonian responders, counsel families of survivors, and participate in joint interventions with the Estonian Red Cross and the Ministry for Social Affairs and Health (Saari, Lindeman, Verkasalo, & Pryta, 1996). Over a 10-day span, team members held over 250 debriefings and clocked over 2,400 working hours.

Psychologists helped with the emergency work with rescuers, survivors, onlookers, families of victims (particularly in Estonia), and ferry crews. They also coordinated local groups who responded, including the Hanko Emergency group, Parainen Emergency Group, and the University of Turku Central Hospital Group.

Work with the 7,000 passengers and 1,200 crew who observed the rescue operations from one Swedish and four Finnish ferries (including the *Silja Europe, Silja Symphony,* and *Viking Mariella*) as well as a number of freighters included a variety of interventions. Materials about crisis reactions, acute stress reactions, and posttraumatic stress disorder were distributed in six languages to passengers on Finnish ferries when they disembarked at the Port of Helsinki. Pamphlets also included a hotline number. Phone contacts were made and debriefings were offered as well to these persons.

Many of the survivors with whom the teams worked experienced crisis reactions or acute stress reactions. In other words, they felt anxiety, shock, disbelief, anger, and other emotions. Burgess and Roberts (1995) noted that survivors are often most willing to seek help during this period. Therefore, the members of the teams who were available to debrief survivors and do other activities that helped with the information processing of what happened did so at an opportune time for intervention (Hartman & Burgess, 1988).

Crisis intervention groups were also immediately organized in Stockholm at Police Headquarters and the Estline Terminal. The Estonian government offered 24-hour counseling through the weekend, and information about financial assistance was distributed to the families of the victims. Staff from counseling centers in Estonia were asked by Finnish psychologists and police officers to help with families and friends of victims; many went over to assist Estonian efforts through direct service and training.

Work with Rescuers

Rescue workers do not escape the emotional impact of their jobs. Disaster scenes and interventions may task the limits of human coping, particularly if rescue workers are not prepared for the magnitude of the traumatic event (Dunning, 1990). Ideally, immediate, brief interventions for rescue workers during and after a disaster help mitigate the stress of the impact. However, it is not always possible to provide such interventions. In fact, many rescue workers may seek to distance themselves from the event as soon as possible in order to maintain the ability to do their jobs.

One way to offer help to rescue workers postdisaster is through a structured debriefing, whether educational and informational or psychological. The goal of debriefing is to help the rescue worker integrate the disaster into his or her life history. Paton and Stephens (1996) note that debriefing is "a non-threatening education on reactions to trauma and coping strategies . . . delivered in everyday language to normalize predictable reactions" (p. 179). They conclude that "debriefing is a helping process" (p. 195).

Critical incident stress debriefing is a standardized approach to providing short-term assistance to persons involved in crisis situations or disaster. It may be offered or ordered to persons involved in rescue efforts, depending on the nature of the incident, the policies of the organization, and the needs of the rescuers. Debriefing sessions held with team members foster natural connections among teams and help rescuers to provide witness to what they have experienced, felt, and need to know (Dunning, 1988; Dunning, 1996). One aspect of debriefing is storytelling, set within limits in order to prevent overload and retraumatization. Debriefings must be done sensitively and skillfully to provide relief to rescuers who are stressed and to strengthen their hardiness so that they can go on with the job at hand and not succumb to fatigue and the horrors that they have experienced. Dunning (1996) noted that debriefing needs to be conducted within a philosophical atmosphere of wellness, increasing rescuers' sense of control, cohesion, communication, commitment, and sense of challenge. Thus the major roles of debriefing are to provide clarification and to help rescuers recognize that they are experts concerning the disaster itself, not further victims. Debriefing provides an opportunity for emotional disclosure in a supportive environment (Pennebaker, 1992).

The basic model used for debriefing in Finland is the Mitchell Model (Mitchell, 1983; Mitchell, 1988; Mitchell, 1996b; Mitchell & Everly, 1993). This model has seven stages identified as the introductory phase, fact phase, thought phase (cognitions), reaction phase (individual disclosure of emotions), symptom phase, teaching phase (education about posttraumatic stress response syndromes), and re-entry phase (winddown and reassurance that reactions are normal and triaged help is accessible). Secondary goals of debriefing include exploration of the literal and symbolic meanings of the disaster, cognitive restructuring, skill building, building of group/team support, and initiation of the grief process (Dunning, 1990).

The majority of rescue workers recover from working with critical events without long-term traumatic effects even without debriefing. However, those who were debriefed appear to have fared somewhat better than the nurses at Turku Hospital who did not receive debriefing (Nurmi, in press). Saari, Lindeman, Verkasalo, and Pryta (1996) write that, ideally, debriefing occurs shortly after a disaster, before the human mind can close down. The goals of debriefing are to "confront the participants with reality . . . [and] what actually happened . . ."; to process reactions by allowing victims "to talk through their experiences, impressions, feelings and thoughts"; to help prepare participants for future reactions and symptoms, should they occur, normalizing their appearance to increase tolerance of them; to strengthen coping mechanisms through mental exercise or later direct action; and to "enhance feelings of affinity" among persons who share the disaster experience (p. 136).

Many of the Finnish rescuers were debriefed either by the present author, as psychologist with the Disaster Victim Identification Team (DVI), or by members of the Red Cross-sponsored teams from the Union of Finnish Psychologists. During debriefings conducted by this author, rescue personnel and police personnel talked to one another and shared experiences about multiple-death disasters. Debriefings occurred when the time allowed or suited them to occur; in truth, reality dictates the opportunities one has for debriefing.

Rescue workers, including this author, felt a sense of death overload. I was especially impacted when I first saw all the bodies lined up on the ship which transported them from the military island of Utö and the temporary morgue to the mainland. I and my partner debriefed the body handlers who worked at the military island evacuation center and who had placed the bodies in temporary coffins, working for long hours over a 2-day period and suffering extreme exhaustion. These body handlers were police officers from the Turku Police Department sent to the island by the various rescue services. The large number of dead in this temporary morgue was stressful to them. It was also their job to photograph and document the victims before preparing the bodies for the return to the mainland. Body handlers were debriefed 2 days after they finished their work, either at the Turku Police Department or with their units of the Frontier Guard. Also debriefed were police officers who interrogated survivors in Turku University Hospital.

I remained in Turku until Saturday (2 days after the sinking), when I returned with the bodies to Helsinki. I also served as liaison officer between the DVI team and Red Cross crisis intervention teams in Finland and Finnish delegations in Estonia. I gave up-to-date information to each team about the status of body identification, including when and where bodies could be seen, and I also debriefed and counseled police investigators who worked with families of the dead in Estonia.

The scope and enormity of an event and the exposure of rescue workers to the injury, mutilation, and death of victims are very important variables that can lead to severe reactions. In addition, when rescue workers have to operate under adverse conditions, more demands are then placed on them (Hartsough & Myers, 1985; McCammon, 1996). In this disaster, the weather conditions were horrible, and workers were put at risk due to the high winds, rough seas, and cold water temperature. The workers were also operating under a serious time pressure to minimize hypothermia in victims. As it was, many survivors died because of the weather conditions as well as poor equipment.

Rescue workers as well as others involved often seek to find meaning in the disasters they face. Reverend Kaj Engström, chaplain and debriefer for the DVI team, spontaneously initiated religious rituals when the bodies were brought from the military island to Turku. Rituals can provide social support and help rescue workers integrate the experience into the past. Several emergency room nurses worked at the military island and participated in these rituals. However, most rescue workers were not available when the bodies returned to the main-land of Finland and, therefore, did not have the benefit of participation.

Work With the Dead and Families of the Dead

Interpol requires the staffing and organization of a DVI team. Its mandates are to help in the identification of the dead when disasters occur within its territory and to go to foreign countries to help in identification of the dead who are its country's citizens. In Finland, the DVI team was organized under the auspices of the Central Criminal Police and mobilized December 20, 1991.

The majority of members of the team are police officials. The actual team has about 20 members and includes a debriefing team consisting of myself (a police psychologist) and a clergyman. The DVI team conducted two airline disaster training scenarios annually prior to the *Estonia* disaster but was not prepared for an event of its magnitude.

The *Estonia* disaster introduced the DVI team to the world. The team mo-bilized before noon on September 28, 1994, and contacted trained officers from local police units all over Finland to assist in the disaster victim identification. Initially, as has been noted, most bodies were taken to Hanko and to Utö mili-tary Island, where body collection was extremely stressful, before the latter bodies were sent to Turku.

The work of the DVI team lasted 5 weeks, 93 victims were identified in the Search Center organized at the University of Helsinki. The center was respon-sible for conducting autopsies, fingerprinting the bodies, identifying dental structures, and conducting post-mortem forensic pathology activities. When a match was made between antemortem and postmortem data, a commission of a forensic doctor, forensic dentist, and police officer officially determined the final identity of the body and signed the identification certificate. The Identifi-cation Center (also in Helsinki) was responsible for technical and tactical inves-tigations as well as working with the property of victims. According to Finnish law, investigation of the cause of death (in a disaster as well) belongs to the police and, in this instance, to DVI-recruited doctors. It was necessary to conduct an autopsy on each of the 93 bodies brought to Finland to help in the identification. The autopsies revealed that the majority of the victims died of drowning or hypothermia.

Some members of the team went to Estonia to help gather information from victims' families. These officers brought pictures of the dead with them. Also, two Finnish police officers trained Estonian colleagues to fill out the antemortem form that had been translated into Estonian. Many of the police officers who were sent to Estonia to meet with the families of the dead needed individual support sessions after they participated in debriefings 2–3 weeks after the disaster.

The team instituted numerous self-care measures during its time together. Technical debriefings, psychological defusings (a shorter form of debriefing), work hours that did not extend past 5 p.m., trips to the sauna in the evenings, and a final dinner that included colleagues from Sweden, Estonia, and Norway who had worked with the team helped members withstand stress and combat vicarious traumatization. The more informal defusings were conducted by myself in a supportive manner at the end of the work day, particularly with members of the autopsy team. Defusings were also conducted with officers who worked with the deceased victims' belongings. Team members worked under the constant watchfulness of the media as well as international forensic experts. In general, members of the team were resilient and defined the event in understandable terms. They used their personal emotional resources, interpersonal resources, and cognitive resources to cope with the disaster's aftermath.

Members of the Finnish National Crisis Team cooperated across international boundaries with relatives of the dead in Estonia as well. Team members went to Estonia to conduct debriefings and offer psychosocial support.

MEMORIALS, INVESTIGATIONS, AND CONCLUSIONS

The Finnish Perception of Death

The Finnish people, in general, have a Lutheran conception of death, although they are not very religious in outward practice. Finns believe in God and salvation. Death is final and definite, and therefore most Finns do not believe in reincarnation. To the Finnish people, it would be an appropriate and fitting decision to let victims of the disaster lie in the ocean. Finns have been astonished, therefore, that the Swedes have had such extensive discussions about reclaiming the bodies so they could go to their home areas. On April 18, 1996, Swedish Prime Minister Goran Persson decided to reexamine the decision to cover the ferry with a concrete shell, just days before the first stones were to be poured to make the resting place of the ferry a permanent grave site at a depth of between 180 and 270 feet, approximately 60 miles off the southwest coast of Finland.

The disaster was a national tragedy to the Finns but not a tragedy in the same sense as it was for the Swedes or Estonians. Very few victims (reports vary from 10 to 12) were Finns by citizenship. Between 50 and 100 had Finnish surnames/family names and were of Finnish origin; at the time of the disaster, however, they were Swedish citizens who had emigrated to Sweden.

When news of the disaster became public early in the morning of September 28, 1994, Finland, as a nation, was shocked and reacted very strongly. However, the first question asked was "Which boat went down?" When the first newscast at 5 a.m. revealed that the boat was not from Turku or Helsinki, Finland, but from Tallin, Estonia, there was relief that it was not a Finnish ship full of Finns.

Memorials and Rituals

Rituals which are culturally sensitive provide a sense of group identity and give guidance for healing. They offer a way for survivors and families of the dead to share their grief and give one another mutual support. Rituals, commemorations, and memorials reassure survivors and families that the dead are remembered and, at the same time, provide a sense of closure to the disaster. Some memorials and rituals occur within the context and frame of religion; others, within the context of other avenues of commemoration (Meichenbaum, 1994). Jay (1994) also notes that prayer (as ritual) is a way to bind an individual's loss to the losses of a community or group (or nation).

Finland has had an established system of national mourning for some time. National mourning takes place when a major accident or air crash occurs and 10 or more persons die (e.g., a previous air crash in which 17 politicians died was responded to with national mourning). The scale of disaster that results in national mourning, because of the size of Finland as a country of approximately 5 million population, is much smaller than in other countries.

After the disaster, the President and Prime Minister immediately expressed the deep concern of the Finnish State and offered condolences to Estonia and Sweden in particular. Flags immediately were flown at half-mast, and the same official day of mourning was adopted by all three countries.

In Sweden, one of the first symbolic communal responses to the tragedy was that of Prime Minster Carl Bildt ordering all state flags to be flown at half-mast. He then went to Turku to meet with and thank members of the rescue teams. A state of mourning was also declared in Estonia, and Estonian national radio immediately changed programming from rock and roll to more somber music.

Reverend Kaj Engström, a member of the DVI team, used culturally sensitive, religiously based rituals during the rescue operations to help Finnish rescue workers deal with their experiences and to honor the dead. These rituals served as a way for Finns present to share the grief. When approximately 60 bodies were brought in temporary coffins to Turku by boat, Reverend Engström conducted a short religious ceremony at 2 a.m. While filming of the transportation of the bodies from the boat was not permitted for the general media, the Finnish Police filmed those services and incorporated them into the official police video. Seeing those 60 bodies in their temporary coffins en masse was a very moving experience for myself as well. When the visor of the boat bringing the bodies to Turku opened and the coffins were exposed in their rows, deep sadness was experienced.

On the night of October 8, 1994, the bodies of 93 identified individuals were placed in funeral clothes and were then transported from the University of Helsinki to a temporary mortuary by a cortège of hearses. Again, only the Finnish police filmed the cortège. Eventually, these identified victims were transported from the mortuary to their home countries.

Religious rituals instituted weeks later when these identified victims were returned to their homelands brought a degree of closure to Finland's role in the tragedy. For example, 60 Swedish victims were transported by truck from Helsinki to Turku in a daylight procession. Finnish citizens lined the roads and held flowers to show their respect for these unfortunate individuals. The bodies were then sent by boat to Stockholm. Religious ceremonies also were conducted by Reverend Engström when Estonian victims were sent by boat. The rituals were designed to help those working on the body collection and identification jobs with our own coping and mental health. They also were organized, as the bodies were sent back home, as a symbolic way to show relatives that the victims were being honored and handled with respect. The body handling and transport also gave the families of the deceased a positive view of the Finnish Police.

The exact number of dead will never be known because of the incomplete passenger lists. By the first anniversary of the disaster, in spite of protests from the survivors' group and others, the governments of Sweden, Estonia, and Finland decided to turn the resting place of the ship into a gravesite, covering it with stones or cement to prevent entry by divers.

The Final Report

According to the Washington Post Internet Report of August 30, 1996, poor maintenance caused the door of the *Estonia* to rip open and kill the 800+ individuals who remained on board. Hinges on the door, according to the attorney for the Meyer-Werft Ship Company, which built the ferry, were "in disastrous condition." Estline supposedly knew about this problem, although the owners have denied any fault. Initially, the International Commission organized to investigate the disaster (with representatives from Sweden, Estonia, and Finland) blamed the shipbuilders and stated that the cargo door locks were not strong enough to withstand the intensity of the Baltic storm that occurred (Joint Accident Commission, 1994a, 1994b; Karpinnen, 1994; Rikken, 1994). A British military expert, viewing a Swedish videotape of the ferry made a few days before the disaster, utilized reconnaissance photography techniques to evaluate the hinges. His investigation said that the interior cargo door's hinges had deteriorated. Thus, when the ship turned and the waves hit it sidewise, the cargo door ripped off. The attorney also added that "the ship was not seaworthy. . . . They knew about the decisive point, the leaky ramp seal. . . . It was gross negligence by the shipping company." The bow visor was leaky and the interior vehicle ramp that folded to form the additional barrier was also leaky because it had a broken hinge. The gap from the break was stuffed with rags. According to the investigation, water flooded in through these leaks and made the ferry unstable. As it began to list, and as the *Estonia* turned sideways, waves ripped off the cargo door.

The Final Report (1997) indicates that the bow locking devices failed due to wave-induced impact loads creating opening moments about the hinges. Thus, large amounts of water ran into the deck and the vessel capsized (Estonia Final Report, 1997). One group of survivors is suing the German company that built the boat; the German company is suing the Finnish shipping line because the line originally accepted the boat from the German firm when the boat sailed between Turku and Stockholm. This suit is against the Finnish State and is being defended by an American attorney. Other legal battles involve attorneys and experts from Germany, France, Sweden, and Norway as well as the United States (Estonian News Agency, 1994). Conclusions were that weather conditions, technical defects in the doors, high speed of the boat and delays in issuing evacuation orders led to the enormity of the disaster (Estonia Final Report, 1997).

DVI team members also met several times postdisaster to process their interventions and debrief themselves. During these meetings, team members affirmed their shared values, including the commitment to aid families of victims of other disasters in the least painful manner through identification of victims as quickly as possible. In October 1995, the team conducted a special seminar to examine its work and to make recommendations for future disaster response.

CONCLUSIONS AND IMPACT

The sinking of the *Estonia* was a transport disaster of significant consequence; it had an impact on whole nations as well as on numerous smaller communities and organizations. It underscored the necessity for broadly based crisis interventions involving multiple agencies and multiple levels of interventions, crossing international boundaries as well as multinational teams (auf der Heide, 1989; Williams & Nurmi, in press).

Interventions both during and after a disaster can lead to new behaviors, can teach lessons to those who were involved, and can provide ways of learning new coping skills. In other words, disasters also offer opportunities for growth (Kalayjian, 1996). One such opportunity was afforded to the DVI team. The team's capability to respond and cope with a major disaster were tested and later analyzed. The consensus is that the team did an admirable job without forewarning or drills for a disaster of this magnitude.

Although there were no comprehensive trauma centers in existence in either Turku or Helsinki, Finland was fortunate to have a DVI team in place, in contrast to Sweden and Estonia. The DVI team became a working entity because of this disaster. Members of the team, and the team as a whole, had not been prepared for this type of disaster or its breadth. The call came, the team mobilized, and the work continued for weeks. When the last body was identified and the trucks departed to return the victims to their home countries, DVI members were able to return to their "normal" jobs. However, the impact of the disaster on these individuals continued. Personal philosophies of life changed. Workers needed some time off to rejuvenate or to reenter into families, jobs, shift work, commitments, and communities. Members found it very difficult to change roles and become "just another regular fellow" after they had faced such a disaster.

Instead, the DVI team had become a community of its own. Not only did members work together during and after the disaster, but they had to take a supportive role in disaster intervention. They offered debriefings to most rescue groups and sent teams to Estonia as well. The teams were flexible; members took time off from their regular, daily jobs to go where they were needed. Teams were collaborative and worked well with other organizations and debriefers, including myself, who served as liaison between the various teams and the authorities and rescue workers. In Finland, private practitioners and noninvited agencies did not swarm to the scene of any component of the disaster because, culturally, that response would not have been appropriate. (This is in contrast to the Oklahoma City disaster in which professional groups, professionals as individuals, and others swarmed upon that scene to offer help, debriefing, defusing, and any other type of intervention.)

Personal Reactions

As the psychologist on the DVI team, I continue to experience a personal impact from the *Estonia* disaster. The work was intense and demanding; I have become content with less in my material world and want to live quietly and peacefully. The level of exposure to real pain and sorrow has shown me just how insignificant one individual is in the scope of things. I and other members of the DVI team received a "baptism by fire" for which we had not been prepared. I acknowledge that my job was to serve my team. I did not talk with relatives but did talk with police who were talking with relatives. I prepared, with my partner Rev. Engström, to meet the relatives; he did, I did not. I was there with all the bodies and faces in pictures, but the relatives did not come when I was there.

The work has had an impact on my philosophy of life; disaster and my work (as police psychologist) have made an impact on me. Earlier, I found it easier to believe in God and life after death. However, I have seen so much tragedy in the last 5 years that I have started to disbelieve. On the other hand, I want to believe in a Higher Power—let's call him/her/it God—that is common for all of us. I respect religion and Lutheranism and won't divorce myself from the Church. I have not lost my belief in rituals; on the contrary, my experiences reinforce the importance of religious rituals for me. Rituals are important for the living, not for the dead. They are important for us who are mourning the dead. This is in conflict with my earlier beliefs. This disaster has enforced my belief in religion as a formal process. On the other hand, it leads to a disappointment in God. I am constantly confronted with the question of where God is when something like this happens.

National Community Reactions

The Finnish people, as a nation, are resilient. This tragedy challenged their response resources and the belief of emergency services and the government that the greatest disaster the nation would face would be an airline disaster. No one expected a ferry disaster to occur. Thus, the DVI team, prepared to face a disaster on a smaller scale, was called upon to perform and deal with massive death in a different mode. The tragedy itself was quick; the rescue and recovery process took only a few hours. Some responses were informal (e.g., Finns lining the roads with flowers in hand as they paid homage to the coffins that were being taken to the ships); others were formal, including funerals, memorials, and a National Day of Mourning.

The sinking of the *Estonia* led to changes in attitudes and assumptions about the safety of travel by ferry. No longer is the Baltic Sea seen to be benevolent and kind to its travelers. Hundreds of persons now lie entombed on its murky bottom. Schemas about safety have been challenged (Janoff-Bulman, 1992), and the belief that a similar disaster may recur is strong among the Finnish people. Still, ferry travel increases yearly as more and more people traverse the Baltic and the Gulf of Finland (Popeski, 1994).

Lessons Learned

The most important conclusion from work with the *Estonia* rescuers, survivors, and families is that this disaster has underlined the importance and purposeful-ness of stress management interventions and rituals (Hiley-Young & Gerrity, 1994; Hodgkinson & Stewart, 1991; Paton, 1996). Critical incident stress man-agement interventions and the development of appropriate rituals are very im-portant for healing of rescue workers and other disaster helpers. However, one intervention alone (e.g., a defusing or a debriefing) is not enough. Multiple methods of intervention are needed to help those affected to heal: Group ses-sions, individual consultations with psychologists, defusings, and other inter-ventions are necessary. The entire range of critical incident stress management interventions is necessary in a disaster of this consequence.

A second realization gained from both observation and research is that workers in a disaster as great as this one can see the stress in one another's faces and doings. However, they do not necessarily recognize the same level of stress in themselves. For this reason, it is important that more than one professional helper be available to check on how the personnel involved in disaster rescue and disaster work behave and think. These persons need to be flexible and careful when approaching and working with disaster workers. It is not possible to apply, systematically, only one set method with all workers. Any person who works with and debriefs rescue workers needs to be sensitive enough to find the right method for the right situation.

Establishing a schedule for debriefings is not always the way to provide support. For example, doing defusings (short, immediate interventions) with police officers who were answering phone calls from the thousands of concerned relatives and friends of potential deceased individuals turned out to be a very effective intervention. Doing one-on-one sessions with officers who went to Tallinn, Estonia to work with the relatives of the deceased or with those officers who worked on the military island was also the right choice of intervention. However, these individuals did not need therapy and would not have responded to persons who utilized the language of therapy in their interventions. However, relying only on the two members of the DVI team (myself and my partner) to do these one-on-one sessions was not satisfactory. In the future, it is important to have more than two persons available for such sessions.

A third lesson learned is that it is better to wait to give help to helpers until after they are removed from the "throes" of the disaster (Williams & Nurmi, 1994). Initially, rescuers want to do their jobs and then sleep and eat. These activities are more critical than debriefing. Interventions scheduled for the first day of a disaster or even the first day after a disaster are not ideal. The helicopter crews and winchmen needed to be debriefed after their missions were concluded, a couple of days after the disaster rather than during the height of their involvement.

A final lesson that has been learned through a disaster of this magnitude is that different teams, different agencies, and different groups of professionals are exposed to different types of stress. In spite of training and education, professionals do not appear to have been prepared for exposure to the prolonged stress that came with the sinking of this ferry. Rescue workers, for example, generally expect a rescue operation to take a few hours of time. In this instance, rescue operations took over 2 days for helicopter pilots and crews and weeks for members of the DVI team who were identifying and autopsying the 93 decomposing bodies, answering the thousands of phone calls, and working with the relatives of the deceased.

This level of prolonged stress has to be taken into account when interventions are being organized. Critical incident stress management interventions with these helpers cannot be limited to just one debriefing or one defusing. Rules for practice need to be established (Robinson & Mitchell, 1993). Rescuers, police officers, and others must decide the length of work time and when to close the work day. These individuals cannot be driven so hard that they lose energy, because they cannot be replaced. For this reason, the DVI team lived together at a hotel, finished the work day at 5:00 p.m., and then went to the sauna to ventilate and debrief.

In conclusion, the sinking of the *Estonia* has had a major impact on the country of Finland. It has underlined the importance of having established, prepared crisis teams at numerous levels of intervention, ranging from the governmentally sponsored DVI team to teams organized by the Union of Finnish Psychologists. It has affected me in many ways and has changed me dramatically. It is the hope and prayer of all Finns that such a disaster will never repeat itself. In this instance, the majority of survivors and victims were not of Finnish origin and, therefore, the cultural impact on the nation was not as great. However, the whole of Scandinavia is still reeling from the impact of this disaster and the recognition that travel across the Baltic can never be fully safe and secure.

REFERENCES

auf der Heide, E. (1989). *Disaster response: Principles of preparation and coordination.* St. Louis, MO: Mosby.

Burgess, A., W., & Roberts, A. R. (1995). Levels of stress and crisis precipitants: The stress-crisis continuum. *Crisis Intervention, 2,* 31–47.

Downing, J. (1995, September 28). *The Estonia disaster: One year on.* Radio Sweden Broadcast.

Dunning, C. (1988). Intervention strategies for emergency workers. In M. Lystad (Ed.), *Mental health response to mass emergencies: Theory and practice.* New York: Brunner/Mazel.

Dunning, C. (1990). Mental health sequelae in disaster workers: Prevention and intervention. *International Journal of Mental Health, 19*(2), 91–103.

Dunning, C. (1996, June). *The salutogenic model of crisis debriefing.* Paper presented at the Second World Congress of Traumatic Stress, Jerusalem, Israel.

Eränen, L. (1994, November). *The Finnish role in the Estonia disaster: An informational presentation.* Paper presented at the 10th Annual Meeting of the International Society for Traumatic Stress Studies, Chicago, IL.

Eesti Ringvaade, Internet Edition (1994, September 26–28). *A weekly review of "Estonian News,"* 4(39), p. 1.

Estonia Commission (Joint Accident Commission of Estonia, Finland, and Sweden). (1997). Final report of the M/S Estonia disaster of 28 September 1994. Helsinki, Finland: Edita Ltd.

Estonian News Agency (1994, October 18). News reports on the Estonia.

Hartman, C. R., & Burgess, A. W. (1988). Information processing of trauma: Case application of a model. *Journal of Interpersonal Violence, 3*(4), 443–457.

Hartsough, D. M., & Myers, D. G. (1985). *Disaster work and mental health: Prevention and control of stress among workers.* Rockville, MD: National Institute of Mental Health.

Hiley-Young, B., & Gerrity, E. T. (1994). Critical incident stress debriefing (CISD): Value and limitations in disaster response. *Clinical Quarterly, 4*(2), 17–19.

Hodgkinson, P. E., & Stewart, M. (1991). *Coping with catastrophe: A handbook of disaster management.* London: Routledge.

Huddart, A. (1994, October 2). Statistics of survival: Ferry survivors mainly young males, doctors say [On-line]. CBI@news report.

Infoosakond, Information Division, MFA of the Republic of Estonia. (1995, January 5). Wire Services News Reports.

Janoff-Bulman, R. (1992). *Shattered assumptions: Towards a new psychology of trauma.* New York: The Free Press.

Jay, J. (1994, May–June). Walls for wailing. *Common Boundary,* 30–35.

Joint Accident Investigation Commission. (1994a, October 4). Preliminary report.

Joint Accident Investigation Commission. (1994b, October 17). Second interim report.

Kalayjian, A. (1996). *Disaster and mass trauma: Global perspectives on post disaster mental health management.* Long Branch, NJ: Vista.

Karpinnen, T. (1994, November 21). *Commission report.* Helsinki, Finland: Reuters Press.

Lundin, T. (1994, November). *The Swedish role in the Estonia disaster: An informational presentation.* Paper presented at the 10th Annual Meeting of the International Society for Traumatic Stress Studies, Chicago, IL.

McCammon, S. L. (1996). Emergency medical service workers: Occupational stress and traumatic stress. In D. Paton & J. M. Violanti (Eds), *Traumatic stress in critical occupations: Recognition, consequences, and treatment* (pp. 58–86). Springfield, IL: Charles Thomas.

Meichenbaum, D. (1994). *A clinical handbook/practical therapist manual for assessing and treating adults with post-traumatic stress disorder (PTSD).* Waterloo, ON, Canada: Institute Press.

Ministry of Foreign Affairs, Republic of Estonia (1994, September 30). "Press Release."

Mitchell, J. T. (1983). When disaster strikes: The critical incident debriefing process. *Journal of Emergency Medical Services, 8,* 36–39.

Mitchell, J. T. (1988). The history, status, and future of critical incident stress debriefings. *Journal of Emergency Medical Services, 11,* 47–52.

Mitchell, J. T. (1996a, Spring). A short course in disaster response. *Life Net, 7*(1), 1–3.

Mitchell, J. T. (1996b, May). *Responses to criticisms of CISD* [On-line]. Traumatic-StressForum.

Mitchell, J. T. (1996c, Summer). Some guidelines for managing CISM critics. *Life Net, 7*(2), 1.

Mitchell, J. T., & Everly, G. S. (1993). *Critical incident stress debriefing.* Ellicott City, MD: Shevron.

Nurmi, L. (In press). *CISD and Estonia Rescue Workers.* Espoo, Finland: Police College of Finland.

Nurmi, L., & Williams, M. B. (1996). The Finnish experience of a major sea disaster: Functions of the police organization and its mass casualty disaster victim identification team—strategies of investigation and debriefing. In J. T. Reese & R. M. Solomon (Eds.), *Organizational issues in law enforcement* (pp. 223–240). Washington, DC: U.S. Government Printing Office.

Paton, D. (1996). Traumatic stress in critical occupations: Current status and future issues. In D. Paton & J. Violanti (Eds.), *Traumatic stress in critical occupations: Recognition, consequences, and treatment* (pp. 206–225). Springfield, IL: Charles Thomas.

Paton, D., & Stephens, C. (1996). Training and support for emergency responders. In D. Paton & J. M. Violanti (Eds.), *Traumatic stress in critical occupations: Recognition, consequences, and treatment* (pp. 173–205). Springfield, IL: Charles Thomas.

Pennebaker, J. W. (1992). Inhibition as the linchpin of health. In H. S. Friedman (Ed.), *Hostility, coping and health.* Washington, DC: American Psychological Association.

Popeski, R. (1994, October 2). *Finns pour into Estonia.* Tallin, Estonia: Reuters News Press.

Rikken, M. (1994, October 17). *The Baltic ferry disaster: Second interim report.*

Robinson, R. C., & Mitchell, J. T. (1993). Evaluation of psychological debriefings. *Journal of Traumatic Stress, 6*(3), 367–382.

Saari, S., Lindeman, M., Verkasalo, M., & Pryta, H. (1996). The Estonia disaster: A description of the crisis intervention in Finland. *European Psychologist, 1*(2), 135–139.

The *Estonia* disaster. *Helsingen Sanomat.* (1994, October 15).

Tedeschi, R. G., & Calhoun, L. G. (1995). *Trauma and transformation: Growing in the aftermath of suffering.* Thousand Oaks, CA: Sage Publications.

Williams, M. B., & Nurmi, L. A. (1994). *Death of a co-worker: Personal and institutional responses.* Helsinki, Finland: Poliisin Oppikirjasarja.

Williams, M. B., & Nurmi, L. A. (in press). *Creating a comprehensive trauma center: Choices and challenges.* New York: Plenum Press.

Young, M. A. (1994). *Responding to communities in crisis: The training manual of the NOVA Crisis Response Team.* Dubuque, IA: Kendall/Hunt.

Figure 4.1 Marise Wilson, Acting Coordinator of the Community Mental Health Team, is reflected in the polished stone surface of the memorial plaque erected in the Memorial Garden adjacent to the scene of the Kempsey Bus Disaster. (Personal photo of the author.)

Chapter 4

The Kempsey Bus Disaster: The Effects on Australian Community Rescuers

Rod Watts and Marise Wilson

Australia has not escaped disasters. The Granville Rail Crash, which had a death toll of 83, was the first to systematically provide psychological first aid alongside rescue, retrieval, and acute medical treatment (Raphael, 1979/1980). Other disasters include the Ash Wednesday Bush Fires (Clayer, Bookless-Pratz, & McFarlane, 1985), the Queen Street shooting (Creamer, Burgess, Buckingham, & Pattison, 1989), and the Newcastle Earthquake (Webster, Lewin, & Carr, 1991). The Port Arthur Massacre, in which 35 people died in April 1996, was the most recent disaster.

In 1989, two large-scale road crashes occurred in the State of New South Wales. The first, near Grafton, claimed the lives of 21 people; the other, near Kempsey, killed 35 and injured 41. This chapter focuses on the second accident, the Kempsey Bus Disaster, Australia's largest fatal road accident. Two main sources of information are utilized to examine how this tragedy affected a group of emergency workers, a Community Health Team, and the general community surrounding the accident site. One source is a study by Griffiths and the first author (Griffiths & Watts, 1992) that included 1-, 3-, and 12-month postcrash assessments of the Kempsey State Emergency Service (SES). A second is focus group meetings with two groups of community health staff (those involved in the recovery operation and those who have subsequently joined the service) conducted by the second author approximately 6 years postcrash. The chapter also includes professional and personal reflections of the second author, who lived in the community of Kempsey for 16 years, and perceptions gleaned by examining the local newspaper publications for the 12-month period after the crash.

THE KEMPSEY BUS DISASTER

On the 22nd of December, 1989, two interstate passenger coaches collided head-on, at approximately 3:30 in the morning, 15 kilometers north of Kempsey, New South Wales. Both the southbound coach (traveling from Brisbane to Sydney) and the northbound coach (Sydney to Brisbane) were traveling at approximately 100 km per hour (60 mph) at the time of impact. The front sections of the coaches concertinaed together on impact, leaving all contents, including passengers, squashed into the front six rows of seats. The coaches collided with such force that items in the luggage bays were catapulted from one coach into the other. It took the Kempsey police 4 days to finalize identification of the personal effects. Rescue personnel, surrounded by screams of pain and pleas for help from many of the survivors, cut holes in the sides of the coaches to gain access. An estimated 360 personnel, consisting of ambulance and fire officers, state emergency service and volunteer road rescue crews, police, medical teams, ministers of religion, salvation army workers, and health department staff, were involved in the initial response.

The survivors, once freed from their entanglement, were maneuvered down ladders in Stokes Litters and taken to the triage area established at the roadside. The enmeshment of the injured with the deceased and the seats in addition to the confined space of the coaches made recovery difficult. It took 5 hours before the last of the survivors was finally released. After initial identification of the deceased was completed, the bodies were transported to a temporary mortuary established in a refrigeration room at a nearby dairy processing plant. The last four bodies were so embedded in the wreckage that it was only after two large cranes separated the coaches that they could be removed. This was completed by 4:00 in the afternoon. The site was finally cleared an hour later, some 13½ hours after the family who lived opposite the site was awakened by the horrendous crash of impact.

The town of Kempsey, situated midway on the main coastal highway between the capital cities of Sydney and Brisbane, was highly involved with the accident. Located just south of the crash site, it provided the majority of rescue personnel and received and cared for a large number of the survivors. It was through Kempsey that the final tangled mass of both coaches was towed in the late afternoon on a shopping day, just 3 days before Christmas. It was upon Kempsey that media and politicians converged and where major memorial services were held. The town's close involvement in and identification with what occurred are reflected in the fact that the accident is now commonly referred to as the Kempsey Bus Disaster.

The Kempsey SES Workers

The SES is an Australia-wide organization of volunteers trained in rescue and recovery. These SES workers consequently attend motor vehicle accidents; assist during droughts, floods, fires, and other natural disasters; search for missing persons (or body retrieval) following mishap; and provide emergency services after damage to homes (e.g., placing tarpaulins over damaged roofs). The service is administered on a state basis although crews are organized locally. Usually, a subgroup in each local unit is trained as a road rescue crew. Thus, the Kempsey SES was at the forefront of the response following the Kempsey Bus Disaster.

The Kempsey SES crew undertook a wide range of duties in this response, including retrieving the deceased, removing the injured from the coaches and transferring them to the triage area, assisting in the tagging and identification of bodies, removing seats and other contents from the coaches, and clearing the site. Those based at the SES headquarters were engaged in communication; organizing backup workers, equipment, and supplies; and supporting fellow crew members as they returned. It was about 5:00 p.m. when the last crew returned to headquarters, almost 14 hours after being called out. In addition to being exhausted, some seemed dazed and numb; others were highly emotional. Research conducted during the following year revealed that many were traumatized by their involvement, some sustained significant psychological harm, and many subsequently left the SES.

This community of SES workers was assessed at 1, 3, and 12 months postaccident. Assessments included the completion of the Impact of Event Scale (IES; Horowitz, Wilner, & Alvarez, 1979) and the 28-item General Health Questionnaire (GHQ 28; Goldberg & Hillier, 1979). The IES has two subscales and quantifies the levels of intrusion and avoidance phenomena, which are well recognized as fundamental reactions to trauma (Figley, Scrignor, & Smith, 1988). The intrusion subscale measures the degree of intrusively experienced ideas, images, feelings, and bad dreams; the avoidance subscale measures the degree of consciously recognized avoidance of thoughts, feelings, or situations which are reminders of the incident. The GHQ 28, in addition to detecting likely cases of psychiatric disorder, consists of four subscales measuring somatic symptoms, anxiety and insomnia, social dysfunction, and severe depression. The GHQ 28 is unable to identify specific types of disorder.

Thirty workers from the Kempsey SES crew were assessed by questionnaire and interview at 1 month; 28 at 3 months, and 24 at 12 months. Seventyone percent of those interviewed at 1 month reported having distressing intrusive phenomena during the first week. These consisted of:

- *Visual reminders*, such as the condition of the coaches, bodies hanging out of the bus, bodies laid out on the side of the road, a decapitated and/or mutilated body, the blood that seemed to be everywhere, parts of the rescue that were gruesome, remembering particular victims, and the media with their cameras.
- *Olfactory reminders*, such as the smell of death, the smell of blood mixed with diesel fuel and foam.
- *Auditory reminders*, such as people moaning or crying out for help, the sound of the generators, something a victim may have said, a particular sound of rescue (e.g., the head of a body bumping on the ground).

The extent to which this disaster affected personnel over the first year is reported in detail elsewhere (Griffiths & Watts, 1992; Watts & Walkden, 1994), but a summary of the key results is as follows:

Likely psychiatric disorder. Forty-three percent of the Kempsey SES workers assessed were likely to have had a psychiatric disorder at 1 month postaccident, 18% at 3 months, and 17% at 12 months. Forty-seven percent were likely to have had a psychiatric disorder at some time during the course of the first year.

Intrusion and avoidance phenomena. At 1 month, 87% had at least moderate levels of intrusion or avoidance phenomena, including 53% who had high levels of one or the other. At 3 months, 48% had at least moderate levels of intrusion and 32% had avoidance; 14% had high levels of either. Fifty-four percent had moderate to severe levels of intrusion at 12 months, 42%, moderate to severe levels of avoidance. Twenty-nine percent had high levels of either intrusion or avoidance, including 8% who had both.

The proportions affected according to severity ranges on the three measures are presented in Table 4.1.

Course of reactions over the first year. A significant reduction in somatic symptoms and intrusion and avoidance phenomena occurred between 1 and 3 months, but not between 3 and 12 months. There were no significant changes in the prevalence of likely disorder, anxiety and insomnia, social dysfunction, and severe depression. However, there were small increases in the incidence of intrusion, social dysfunction, and depression between 3 and 12 months. These increases may have been due to the anniversary effect or may have indicated that the reactions of some personnel were becoming worse. In addition, symptoms that persisted among personnel included flashbacks, nightmares, sleep disturbances, excessive fatigue, mood swings, irritability, outbursts of anger or

Table 4.1   Scores on the GHQ 28 and the IES for Kempsey SES Workers by Severity Range at Three Times-Since-Accident Intervals

Measure	Range	Time since accident		
		1 Month	3 Months	12 Months
GHQ 28	0–4 (non)	57%	83%	83%
	5+ (case)	43%	18%	17%
IESI	0–8 (low)	20%	54%	46%
	9–19 (mod)	27%	39%	31%
	20+ (sev)	50%	7%	23%
IESA	0–8 (low)	40%	68%	58%
	9–19 (mod)	33%	18%	31%
	20+ (sev)	27%	14%	11%
	Total	*N* = 30	*N* = 28	*N* = 24

tears, withdrawing from others, feelings of inadequacy, diminished concentration, reduction in short-term memory, and loss of interest at work.

The longitudinal study documented that 85% of the Kempsey SES crew were at least moderately affected during the first month, and 50% were severely so. Just over 50% remained moderately affected at 12 months, including 29% who remained severely affected. These results are likely to be a conservative estimate of the extent to which involvement in the disaster response negatively affected personnel. Therefore, the prevalence of psychological difficulties among all those involved in the response to the Kempsey Bus Disaster may likely be higher than that found in the study because rescue personnel prefer the image of being "tough" and are likely to minimize their reactions (Ersland, Weisaeth, & Sund, 1989). While not examined, it can be presumed from other disaster studies that the families of these personnel, including children, would also have been negatively affected (McFarlane, 1987; Wraith, 1994). This reflects one dimension of the ripple effect of trauma.

These summarized findings describe a group in which the majority membership is substantially distressed at the same time. Ninety-three percent of those assessed at 1 month postcrash reported the Kempsey Bus Disaster as the most distressing of any of their previous emergency work experience; while, for 32%, it was the most distressing experience of their entire lives. As there was little evidence that these reactions reduced significantly over the first year, we can only speculate as to the possible effects of this shared and pervasive distress on individual and group functioning as well as related work performance. The fact that all but two of the 14 crew who worked in the coaches have since left the service is significant and suggests an impact of disasters that needs further investigation.

The Kempsey Community Health Team

At the time of the Kempsey Bus Disaster, a multidisciplinary team of 23 professionals and support staff worked in the Community Health Centre, located on the grounds of the Kempsey District Hospital. The Centre offered a range of community-based healthcare services, including nursing, psychology, social work, speech pathology, aboriginal services, and dentistry. The second author was the acting coordinator of the Centre when the Disaster Plan was implemented at approximately 3:50 a.m., after authorities were alerted to the coach crash. She also maintained her usual role as Team Leader (Mental Health). The long-standing Chief Executive Officer of the hospital was on leave at the time, and the position was being filled in an acting capacity.

The Community Health Team's primary role, defined by the Disaster Plan, was to provide nonmedical support services to survivors and their families. Ensuring access to and availability of food, clothing, shelter, finances, and transport, plus providing information and psychological support were priorities. Involvement during the first day varied. The community nurses on the team worked alongside other nursing and medical staff in the direct care of victims. Several worked in the hospital's recovery area to determine support needs of survivors. The nonnursing staff involved in this activity found it quite distressing, perhaps due to their lack of prior exposure to the sights and sounds of large numbers of injured persons. Some members of the team were assigned to a designated area to await the relatives of the survivors and/or the deceased. However, after 2–3 hours, it became apparent that none of the passengers on the coaches were from nearby areas, and their families would be unlikely to arrive at the hospital for some hours. Consequently, these staff, frustrated by their inactivity while knowing their colleagues were frantically busy, were redeployed.

During the first day, demand on services was extremely high, and tasks were performed under extreme pressure. For example, between 6:00 a.m. and 4:00 p.m., there were over 600 telephone inquiries. Staff informed families of any available information about their injured family members, assisted them in making travel plans, organized accommodations, and provided emotional support. Two members of the team also received and organized the large number of offers of voluntary help made by members of the Kempsey community. In addition, staff organized psychological support and debriefing for the SES crew and health personnel.

During the first week, staff provided ongoing psychological support to survivors who remained in hospital, their families, hospital staff, the Kempsey-based personnel, and any other members of the community who became distressed. This response continues even at the time of writing this chapter, over 6 years later, as individuals present occasionally with mental health problems associated with their exposure to the coach crash. The community Health Team staff have also not escaped the impact. Assessments 12 months postevent of a large number of personnel involved in the Kempsey coach crash identified that support staff were as significantly affected as rescue and recovery personnel (Griffiths & Watts, 1992). With 21% at risk of psychiatric problems at 12 months posttrauma (as identified by the case score on the 12-item General Health Questionnaire), it is apparent that regular and prolonged exposure to the distress of others about a specific event presents an occupational health risk.

Evidence also suggests that involvement changes the dynamics of the community. The nature and extent of comraderie, for example, can alter when a group shares a traumatic experience. Walkden (Watts & Walkden, 1994) intimated that, among the crew of Kempsey SES workers, one of the changes was the way they talked with each other. They were, perhaps, prepared to talk to one another in a more personal way than before their involvement in the bus crash. The trauma they shared had likely broken down some of the communication barriers and altered what they were prepared to discuss among themselves. To examine the nature of this change among a community of health workers, two focus groups were held in May 1996, some 6½ years postcrash. These groups consisted of (a) a response group, consisting of five of the seven staff involved in the response effort who remain employed at the Community Health Centre;

and (b) a nonresponse group, consisting of seven of the staff who have been employed at the Centre since the crash. All but two are members of the Mental Health Team. Both groups were asked about their perception of the crash, its place in the history of the organization, the perceived effect on relationships within the team, and any persistent changes.

The response group described the team precrash as having a high level of cohesion. Commitment to the philosophy of community health was common and a strong sense of ownership existed. Members of the team were included in decision making and had regular contact during their day-to-day professional functions. Regular interaction was facilitated by team size (23 at the time) and location, being housed in a building that necessitated close contact. Members felt that the sense of connection encouraged by the participatory model of management and a shared philosophy were equally significant in this cohesion. The change in leadership at the time of the crash was regarded as an opportunity for new challenges and was thus embraced rather than resisted. Relationships between the team and the adjacent hospital service were perceived as generally less comfortable, with community health staff perceived as the less serious side of the health coin.

Memories of December 22, 1989, remain vivid for members of this group. It was the team's first experience in responding to a state-declared disaster. While many critical incidents have occurred since, none have been on such a large scale. It thus serves as a significant reference point in individuals' professional lives. Additionally, as residents of a small town, they shared the shock of the general community as they dealt with the fact that Australia's worst road accident had occurred in their territory, on a highway used by all. Exposure was heightened for some because their partners were also involved in the response effort. The significance of the devastation and loss occurring during the Christmas season was also not lost on the workers. Family life at that holiday time was invaded, not just by the regular and explicit media reporting, but also by the shock and numbing experienced by the staff who had spent hours tending the wounded and bereaved. This was a personally and professionally momentous event for all staff involved.

All members of the response group expressed the recognition that caring for and supporting each other were key features of their team effort. This care and support remains. Their response was described by several as being like a "well-oiled machine." The capacity to pull together was regarded as resulting from the strength of leadership at the time and the maturity of both the individuals and the team as a whole. The organizing of a critical incident stress debriefing for the team and hospital staff at the completion of the first day of response was interpreted as a significant statement of support by management. Attendance by the Acting Executive Officer reinforced this sense of recognition, and the community health/hospital divide evaporated as both services pulled together in the response effort.

Community health staff were also involved in the planning and delivery of ongoing interventions that targeted primary victims and general community.

These interventions included case management meetings, attendance at community debriefings, and preparation of educational material for local publication and distribution. A "buddy" system was encouraged within the team, and support for open discussion of the incident became the group norm. This ongoing provision of support, even when directed to those outside of the team, very likely validated their own reactions as well as encouraged them to undertake the same self-care they were prescribing for others.

Some less positive responses included the suggestion that staff, particularly nurses, should be able to cope without debriefing and support because they had been exposed to injuries before. One nursing team member was unavailable for the debriefing. As a consequence, she was distressed and felt excluded from the group response. The cohesion of the team reduced during the first weeks after the crash as members attended to personal emotional pain and recovery and withdrew from the intensity of the group's recovery operation. However, a lasting bond and a new level of group functioning, which then included a sense of mutual pride and respect for a job well done, were outcomes. One member described this bond as identifying with others as a "bus crash person."

As the response group discussed changes in the size of the team since the Kempsey Bus Disaster (now a team of 45) and relocation into larger premises with separate subteams, members identified a feeling of loss of the old connectedness, sharing, and bonding. However, they continue to seek each other out in times of distress in their working life or when new critical incidents occur, whether they be local or elsewhere in Australia. When learning of nonlocal disasters, their immediate thoughts are for the workers who would be engaged in the recovery operation and ongoing care. Two of the response group, who are members of the Mental Health Team, are increasingly involved in responding to critical incidents in the local community. The extent of their involvement is regarded by many of their peers as being excessive. Some perceive them as too eager to respond and too prepared to do so. The two workers themselves claim it is due to a greater appreciation of the need for and possible benefit of responding.

In summary, the response group recognized the existence of an "invisible thread" from the Kempsey coach crash connecting them, particularly in the face of new critical incidents. However, this thread was not woven purely from the fabric of the crash; it was also part of the pretrauma group experience. Although strengthened by participation in the recovery, the thread tightened the existing private and public cohesion. It also included an empathic link with personnel, particularly support staff, who respond to other major critical incidents.

In their separate meeting, the nonresponse group, whose members joined the team at points 3 months to 6 years after the crash, confirmed many of the reflections of the response group. All persons but one were aware of the team's general involvement in the recovery within a short time of taking up their employment. Becoming informed was not a component of any official orientation; it occurred during general discussions with existing staff or via intake processes within the Mental Health Team. Recall by those involved was kept vivid for

Mental Health Team members by their regular exposure to critical incidents within the local community. This continued involvement seemingly reinforced the impact and psychological aftermath of the Kempsey Bus Disaster.

Members of the nonresponse group recognized the thread of connectedness between longer serving members of the team and regarded it as emanating from the coach crash. They were also aware of the "romantic" recollections of a "golden era" in the history of Community Health. This period of time, identified as existing prior to and for 2 years after the coach crash, was viewed as being one of a high degree of team cohesion and participation in decision making. However, the crash was also a reference point from which cohesion within the group and greater community recognition developed. The nonresponse group did not feel excluded by this connectedness and recognized a general openness and support freely given within the service. Newer members felt safe in knowing that the response group would lead the way and provide a nurturing response should a major incident occur. Their one concern was for the well-being of the response group who were regarded as being in danger of taking on too much and being burdened by the long-term impact of the Kempsey Bus Disaster.

Several of the nonresponse group spoke of the hypervigilance of members of the response group when any local critical incidents occurred. While some regarded this as a protective stance (it being better to be overprepared than ill-prepared), others thought it indicated a legacy of ongoing personal and professional vulnerability. They also reported that, while ongoing critical incidents had a unifying effect, they also had a capacity to fracture the larger team. The exclusion phenomena was identified as a potential problem in this regard. Thus, there was always the potential for fragmentation of the team on the basis of who had been involved in the response following the bus crash. In fact, several staff who had been involved in the Kempsey Bus Disaster no longer belonged to the Mental Health Team who responded to smaller incidents (e.g., murder-suicide, bank holdups, fatal car crashes). This exclusion could lead to tension within the wider team.

The nonresponse group was aware that increased size, changes in accommodation, and structural adjustments at an organizational level at least contributed to, if not caused, a reduction in team cohesion. However, they acknowledged positive outcomes of these changes and expressed some frustration that the "old guard" continued to mourn for what was and, thereby, resisted change. This old guard was not confined to the response group but included those members of the nonresponse group with the longest periods of service. When this change was examined, it became apparent that it was not just about size and location but included issues of participation in and ownership of the change. These are themes reminiscent of the precrash era and up to 2 years postcrash. Significantly, leadership during that period was appointed from within existing Community Health personnel: individuals who shared a philosophy and who worked with the team in its disaster response. Coordinators appointed after this period had no shared history on either level.

The General Community of Kempsey

Of all the towns along the section of the highway involved, Kempsey, a regular stopover point for travelers, was the most closely associated with the bus crash. As with the assassination of John F. Kennedy in the United States, people in Kempsey remember where they were and what they were doing on the day of the bus crash. The streets were packed, with just 3 shopping days to go until Christmas. After the crash, however, there was an eerie quiet at a time when there is usually much noise and celebration. People went about their business aware that, just a few kilometers away, members of their own community were involved in Australia's worst road crash. The scale of death, destruction, and injury was sobering and particularly poignant at a time of year when families are supposed to come together, not be ripped apart.

The general community was directly exposed to the disaster via rescue, medical, and welfare personnel. More indirectly, the impact was felt by the families of recovery personnel; by staff at the local airport and motels who met the bereaved and families of survivors; by "vulnerable others" who had previous personal exposure to trauma; and by those who felt "it could have been me or mine." This latter group included not only those who had relatives traveling by road at the time, but almost anyone who has traveled by road at Christmas to be with family.

The offers of assistance and flow of gifts and flowers to survivors in the local hospital reflected Kempsey's spirit of connection and generosity. At the memorial service held in Kempsey within a week of the disaster (*Macleay Argus*, 1989), local ministers and politicians expressed the "state of despair and shock" in the town whose "heart" was torn by the horrific accident. The community had a common focus, and the sense of connection continued after all the survivors had left the hospital. Human error, induced by either poor road construction and surface, or driver fatigue and impossible schedules, emerged as the dominant explanation. This were later supported by the coroner's report. As both drivers were killed in the crash, the community humanely directed their energy elsewhere. Anger soon replaced shock and, within 5 days of the crash, had galvanized into strong demands for upgrading the highway from a 2-lane road to a 4-lane dual carriageway. Within a month, a Community Action Force formed to fight for this change and was supported by other communities along the highway.

Other evidence of the affects on the general community of Kempsey included, for example, the fact that 54 of the 156 publications of the local paper during the first year carried headlines and articles in its first 5 pages on the bus crash or related issues. The Community Action Force dominated headlines for many months. Included in these early publications were articles submitted by the community health service providing information about critical incident stress and helpful coping strategies as well as contacts for professional support and details about a community debriefing. This information was replicated in radio broadcasts. Only a handful of individuals attended the community meeting, however, and requests for counseling were minimal. Traumatic phenomena associated with the incident have been evident in other presentations for counseling in the months and years following the crash.

A memorial garden was erected at the side of the road where the crash occurred, organized and funded by the Kempsey Lions Club. Club members raised the necessary funds by a well-publicized walk from Sydney to the crash site, a distance of over 400 kilometers (245 miles). Further, 500 people attended the first anniversary commemorative service, held at the memorial garden. This garden includes a plaque listing all those killed and provides a quiet and contemplative environment in which visitors are invited to remember all who were involved. According to reports, many travelers stop to visit, reflecting the continued interest in the Kempsey Bus Disaster.

REFLECTING ON A GROUP CRISIS

Kempsey has been indelibly marked by the coach crash that occurred just 15 kilometers (a little more than 9 miles) north of the town. It was caught up in the wake of aftermath as the focus of national attention for weeks. Just less than a year later, another large-scale bus accident killed 11 elderly folk and provided a reason to replay footage of the Kempsey Bus Disaster on both State and National News Bulletins. The trauma of the Kempsey coach accident was, at least momentarily, reawakened. Six years after the disaster, there are no outwardly obvious signs of the town remaining affected. However, beneath the surface, there may well lurk continued vulnerability and community reaction. The Kempsey-based crews and health teams are no longer the same. Certainly, a number of these personnel experience residual emotional pain, particularly when the memories are rekindled. No doubt so do their families.

Recollections by a group of community health responders 6 years after their involvement, supported by the observations of their colleagues, places the Kempsey Bus Disaster as a significant reference point in the group's history. Transitional periods in group life, as members deal with new arrangements of roles and status and develop new working norms, are often accompanied by regressions to earlier stages of group development. A critical event at such a time has the potential to fracture a group. In the case of the Community Health Team, however, the incident served to increase rather than decrease existing cohesion.

The disaster occurred at a time when the team was dealing with a change in leadership, with an existing member temporarily serving as the Acting Coordinator. The Acting Coordinator knew the team well. There was mutual respect and trust. The shared history of participatory management informed the leader's response alongside the necessity to implement directive crisis management strategies. Had a new and little known coordinator been in place, the "well-oiled machine" referred to may have experienced some malfunction. Thus, exposure to a common threat can, with the right leadership, pull people together, and the recollection of cooperation and support can also promote individual and group maturity.

Several mechanisms were put in place to acknowledge the distress experienced by team members as they responded to the bus disaster. The team culture was supportive at both professional and personal levels. Members attended the local memorial service, and some became involved in the community action focused on upgrading the highway. Interestingly, only the formal debriefing session was referred to during the focus group meeting. The recollection was connected not to the process but to the fact that it was initiated and attended by management personnel. Members valued this as recognition of their needs and validation of their involvement. Validation was heightened by receipt of a facsimile of support from a team in another state who had assisted in a disaster and a visit from a member of the SES coordinating body.

Given the maturity and supportive milieu of the Community Health Team, it is interesting that members still connect personally and collectively with the crash and carry with them an alertness to critical incidents. This alertness is perceived by several other members of the team as overly vigilant. Perhaps the significance lies in the reality that, as members of the affected community, they responded at both a professional and personal level. Their distress could not be left at work and, in some instances, was heightened at home as they talked with partners who had similarly been involved in the recovery. On the positive side, there was also the sense of pride associated with doing their best in response to the worst road crash in Australian history. Pain and pride served to embed this experience in their collective psyche. The potential impact of such an incident on a less mature team is of some concern. For the Kempsey team, any more assistance may have been perceived as gratuitous or intrusive, while another group may have required and welcomed more specific and ongoing attention to psychological sequelae. Knowledge of preincident group functioning is of value in determining what and how much assistance is appropriate.

Despite the many real and potential victims in the community, few made use of offers of professional assistance at the time. What isn't known is how many found support in the educative media releases and pamphlets. Hundreds attended the local memorial service, and, as the days passed, outrage and grief galvanized into action against the only feasible common enemy: the state of the highway. Not being relatives or friends of the deceased reduced the numbing effect of shock and facilitated a quick shift into recovery mode. This action was sustained for several months and later included development of the memorial garden site. The "growth-promoting potential" of crisis was evident (Rapoport, 1970, p. 287). These community actions demonstrated efforts to reestablish a sense of control in the face of human disaster, reminding us of the resilience of humankind. By their very spontaneity, they demonstrate the return to autonomous functioning desirable after a crisis and suggest that, at least at the community level, no further interventions were required.

Direct victims, the survivors, would of course be of greatest risk for long-term psychological harm, as would their families and the families of the deceased. If people injured in the bus crash and/or those killed were from the local community, it is probable that the general community would have incurred a more profound psychic scar. Such was not the case. However, there have been long-term, if not permanent, casualties.

There have also been positive changes, such as greater connectedness among team members and preparedness to support and help one another. Conducting focus groups to gather material for this chapter about the effects on responders as a group revealed the potential benefit of facilitating discussion among team members, even years postinvolvement. The groups provided an opportunity to address any persisting negative changes as well as to ensure that new members are not impeded in becoming integrated into the team. If not addressed, this could have led to fragmentation of teams, tension, and inefficiencies. Thus, how best to reduce the prevalence and persistence of negative consequences and promote positive changes remains a pressing question after examining the long-lasting effects of the Kempsey Bus Disaster on the communities involved.

REFERENCES

Clayer, J., Bookless-Pratz, C., & McFarlane, A. C. (1985*). The health and social impact of the Ash Wednesday Bushfires*. Adelaide, AU: Mental Health Research and Evaluation Centre, South Australian Health Commission.

Creamer, M., Burgess, P., Buckingham, W., & Pattison, P. (1989). *The psychological aftermath of the Queen Street shootings*. Melbourne, Australia: University of Melbourne.

Ersland, S., Weisaeth, L., & Sund, A. (1989). The stress upon rescuers involved in an oil rig disaster, "Alexander L. Kielland." *Acta Psychiatrica Scandinavica, 80* (Suppl. 355), 38–49.

Figley, C., Scrignor, C., & Smith, W. (1988). PTSD: The aftershocks of trauma. *Patient Care, 5,* 111–127.

Griffiths, J., & Watts, R. (1992). *The Kempsey and Grafton bus crashes: The aftermath*. Lismore, Australia: Instructional Design Solutions, University of New England.

Goldberg, D., & Hillier, V. (1979). A scale version of the General Health Questionnaire. *Psychological Medicine, 9,* 21–29.

Horowitz, M., Wilner, N., & Alvarez, W. (1979). Impact of Event Scale: A measure of subjective stress. *Psychosomatic Medicine, 41,* 209–218.

Macleay Argus. (1989). Sydney: Regional Press.

McFarlane, A. (1987). Posttraumatic phenomena in a longitudinal study of children following a natural disaster. *Journal of American Academy Child and Adolescent Psychiatry, 26*(5), 764–769.

Raphael, B. (1979/1980). A primary prevention action programme: Psychiatric involvement following a major rail disaster. *Omega, 10*(3), 211–226.

Rapoport, L. (1970). Crisis intervention as a mode of treatment. In W. Roberts & R. Nee (Eds.), *Theories of social casework*. Chicago: University of Chicago Press.

Watts, R., & Walkden, R. (1994). Trauma: The initial impact and consequences for rescue personnel. *Journal of Mental Health, 3,* 123–129.

Webster, R., Lewin, T., & Carr, V. (1991). The psychosocial impact of the Newcastle earthquake: Levels of exposure and morbidity. In *Proceedings of the UCLA International Conference*, Los Angeles, CA.

Wraith, R. (1994). The impact of major events on children. In R. Watts and D. Horne (Eds.), *Coping with trauma: The victim and the helper* (pp. 101–120). Brisbane, AU: Australian Academic Press.

Figure 5.1 The author, Anie Kalayjian, in a classroom set up in an army tent, assisting Armenian adolescents in expressing their experiences and feelings following displacement from the earthquake. (Personal photo of the author, taken in Leninakan, now Gurnei, Armenia, January 1989.)

Chapter 5

Coping Through Meaning: The Community Response to the Earthquake in Armenia

Anie Kalayjian

Bereavement is the reaction to the death of a loved one; collective bereavement, therefore, is the reaction of the community to a massive loss. This chapter describes the collective bereavement and coping of a community in the Republic of Armenia after the devastating earthquake of 1988. It reviews bereavement patterns and systematic responses to the disaster, discusses research, and presents logotherapeutic perspectives as therapeutic modalities.

THE DAY THE LAND MOVED: DECEMBER 7, 1988

On Wednesday, December 7, 1988, at 11:41 a.m., a devastating earthquake shook the Republic of Armenia (Soviet Armenia at that time) for 40 seconds. This catastrophic destruction occurred in a zone where several plates of the earth's surface converge. The quake did not come as a total surprise to American and Soviet experts in the field, according to the Director of the Geological Institute in Frankfurt (Sullivan, 1988). But, due to gross unpreparedness and lack of emergency and evacuation plans, the Armenian community experienced the quake as a total nightmare.

Measuring 6.9 on the Richter scale, the 1988 quake occurred in an area highly vulnerable to seismic activity. It destroyed two thirds of Leninakan, Armenia's second-largest city (now Gumri, population about 300,000) and half of Kirovakan (population 150,000), and heavily damaged some 56 of 150 villages and towns in the northwest corner of Armenia, near the Turkish border. Spitak, a town of about 30,000, lay at the epicenter of the quake and was obliterated.

Earthquakes have been part of Armenian history. In 893 AD, a quake in the same general area of Armenia caused 20,000 deaths. In 1667, another earthquake in that general region claimed 80,000 lives, and, in the late 1800s, yet another devastating quake had taken place in the same general vicinity (Sullivan, 1988). The 1988 earthquake, however, was an order of magnitude beyond these tragedies. "I have Chernobyl behind me, but I have never seen anything like this," Yevgeny I. Chazov, the Soviet Health Minister, told the government newspaper *Izvestia* after visiting the scene with fellow physicians (Fein, 1988, p. 23).

Initial reports of casualties spoke of "thousands," which then became "tens of thousands" and went on to climb day-by-day to 130,000, even though the official death toll was announced as 25,000. In the end, there were approximatley 500,000 people handicapped, approximately 500,000 children orphaned, and over 500,000 (one sixth of Armenia's population) left homeless. A more accurate count of human loss was very difficult to determine for several reasons: the uncertain number of refugees from the February 1988 massacres in the Azeri cities of Baku and Sumgait; the poor record-keeping procedures; and, finally, the Soviet government's covert style of operation. Therefore, the above estimates, or any estimates from this incident, are only provisional. Proportional losses in the United States would have amounted to six million dead and 40 million homeless. The physical damage was estimated at $20 billion (U.S.) (Kalayjian, 1995).

All hospitals, schools, churches, and community centers were severely damaged or destroyed, unlike the Mexican quake of 1986, the San Francisco quake of 1989, and the Los Angeles quake of 1994. Survivors were forced to head for the capital, Yerevan, 90 miles southeast of the epicenter, to receive emergency medical care. This meant traveling 4 to 6 hours, instead of the usual 2 hours, due to the extremely crowded conditions and roads that were partially destroyed by the quake. The delay caused additional casualties. "My only brother, 10 years old, died in my arms in the car going to Yerevan," stated Nayiri, a 16-year-old female Armenian survivor from Spitak.

In the earthquake region, survivors had no services or buildings left intact in their community in which to seek support or refuge. In turn, this made relocation for all survivors a necessity and created additional stress and trauma. Further trauma was caused by the Soviet government when it decided to relocate women and children to Yerevan and other Soviet Republics while keeping the traumatized men in the earthquake zone to help "clean up" (Kalayjian, 1995). According to Terr (1989), families cope better if they remain together after a trauma. Therefore, these relocations and separations further aggravated the trauma by shattering and displacing family units.

Assistance from all over the world poured into Armenia. Within the first 10 days, $50 million worth of goods, food, and supplies were delivered to Yerevan's airport from around the world, overwhelming the damaged distribution system. This airlift marked the first time since World War II that the Soviet government had accepted disaster assistance from the United States. In all, the

American government spent about $4 million, and U.S. Air Force and National Guard planes were used to fly in the relief supplies. Private contributions from Americans in the first 4 weeks following the earthquake reached about $34 million. The grand total given by all countries outside the Soviet Union reached $106 million (Simon, 1989). According to U.S. Senator Paul Simon, what the United States did as a nation was not that impressive in view of the fact that the United States represents 20% of the world's economy. However, aid sent by the U.S. government to the Soviet Union and the Soviets' acceptance of it were unprecedented. When the Marshall Plan was announced in 1948, the Soviets would accept no American aid whatsoever. Therefore, the fact that aid was given and received was a healthy sign of collaboration (Simon).

THE REPUBLIC OF ARMENIA

Survivor Characteristics in Armenia

Who were the survivors of the 1988 earthquake in Armenia? They were intelligent, hard-working, peaceful, religious, family-oriented, and hospitable people (Jordan, 1978). The Republic of Armenia is geographically the smallest of the former Soviet Republics (11,500 sq. mi.), with a population of approximately 4 million, and is the most entrepreneurial and the economically fastest-growing republic (Walker, 1991). An Armenian presence in the general region of Asia Minor and the Caucasus dates back over three millennia (Ishkanian, 1989). Armenia's history through the centuries is one of enduring oppression, war, relocation, and survival. From the end of the 14th century until 1991, Armenia had only 2 years of independence (1918–1920); yet its people, culture, and language survived. On September 23, 1991, Armenia once again declared independence. For the first time in 71 years, the Armenian people freely elected a president and representatives to the Republic's Parliament, the Supreme Soviet, from a slate of candidates representing a variety of political movements and organizations.

In discussing their history, Armenians mention three things: their religion, language, and survival. Religion is a point of great pride since Armenia became the first nation to adopt Christianity as its national religion in 301 AD. The Armenian language is a distinct branch of the Indo-European family of languages, with a unique 38-character alphabet. Lastly, they mention their survival of the Ottoman-Turkish Genocide. From 1895 to 1923, the Armenian nation was brought to the brink of annihilation as almost 2 million Armenians, more than half the Armenian population, were massacred by the Ottoman-Turkish rulers. To this day, the Genocide is denied by the current Turkish government. This denial causes tremendous anger and resentment, with no reparation or resolution in sight (Kalayjian, Shahinian, Gergerian, & Saraydarian, 1996).

During World War II and for over 70 years under Communism, Armenians experienced yet more pain and suffering. The Soviet system relied on the oppression of individual needs for the sake of the party, and any attempt at independence could lead to one's disappearance (Kalayjian, in press-b). Pain and suffering continued in the postindependence era, due to territorial conflict with Azerbaijan (East of Armenia) over Nagorno-Karabagh, a 4,000-square kilometer enclave (at the southeast border) mostly populated by Armenians and locally ruled by Armenians until 1923, when Josef Stalin gave it to Soviet Azerbaijan. Adding to the suffering has been the Azeri blockade of Armenia. This blockade began in 1988, preventing 80% of goods destined to Armenia from entering that country. As of late 1996, this crippling blockade had yet to be lifted.

The literacy rate is comparatively high in Armenia. Virtually all Armenian children attend school for 8–10 years from age 6 to 16. People are industrious yet poor, as the economy has been decimated by decades of Soviet rule, further exacerbated by the Azeri blockade. As in many third world countries, an insurance industry is nonexistent. Per Soviet design, healthcare is free in Armenia, but the quality and availability vary greatly.

Sociopolitical and Economic Climate at the Time of the Disaster

During the 10 months preceding the quake, Armenia was experiencing sociopolitical tension and was economically drained. This was due to the conflict with neighboring Azerbaijan over Nagorno-Karabagh, a historically Armenian area, given to Soviet Azerbaijan by Stalin to ensure instability in the region. For over 50 years, Armenians in Nagorno-Karabagh were oppressed by the Azeris: they were forbidden to speak their mother tongue or practice their religion, and were forced to adhere to Azeri Muslim traditions. In early 1988, Armenia challenged Gorbachev and put "Glasnost" and "Perestroika" to their first true test; the challenge failed. As a result, in 1988, over 200,000 Armenian refugees from Azerbaijan came to already overcrowded Armenia. In February 1988, there was a yet another massacre in Sumgait, Azerbaijan, where dozens of Armenians were killed, houses were burned, and women were raped and set on fire (Kalayjian, 1991b).

Seismologists described the quake area as a "structural knot," engendered by the interaction of several rigid plates (Sullivan, 1988). Ironically, this paralleled the sociopolitical and emotional situation: political agitation, tension, anger, resentment, disappointment, and mistrust, due, at least partly, to rigid attitudes.

DISASTER THEORY AND RESPONSE

Bereavement

In the early 1930s, researchers began to describe stages of the bereavement process (Parkes, 1975; Pollack, 1961). Later, researchers distinguished the differing affects and intensities of feelings in each phase (Erikson, 1976; Glick, Weiss, & Parkes, 1974; Smith, 1971). In light of research in three countries following natural disasters, this author found more similarities than differences across cultures in the sequential nature and symptomatology of the bereavement process (Kalayjian, in press-a). The two generally accepted phases are the acute and the chronic. The acute phase includes the following stages: the initial feeling of shock, fear, numbness, disbelief, and denial; followed by sadness, weeping, generalized anxiety, helplessness, frustration, emptiness, and meaninglessness. Unique to the earthquake in Armenia were expressions of feelings of anger. The chronic phase may include attempts toward reintegration, moving towards acceptance of the loss, and finding meaning in trauma and bereavement.

These phases do not prescribe how a community *should* respond to a massive loss; instead, they attempt to summarize and organize the reactions often observed by mental health professionals. They attempt to shed some light onto the dynamics of massive loss. Coping and adaptation to massive, often unexpected natural disasters (e.g., an earthquake) are complex emotional phenomena. The conceptual framework presented in this chapter is only a guide for professionals, the community leaders, and the surviving community in their attempt to make sense of the chaotic and to manage the unmanageable.

General Systems Theory

Natural disasters, no matter what the degree, intensity, or kind, subject the surviving community to a wide range of disruptions and stressors. It is useful to look at the impact of a natural disaster on a community from a general systems perspective, that is, to view the general science of "wholeness" irrespective of the nature of the entities. Part of this view includes seeing the community as an "open system," a living organism that maintains itself in a continuous inflow and outflow, in a building up and breaking down of components (von Bertalanffy, 1968).

Disasters and mass trauma affect an existing community social system, with its unique historical background, predisaster characteristics and experiences, traditional rituals, cultural practices, religious beliefs, and psychosocial responses. Any event that affects one part of the system will affect the whole system, directly or indirectly. One system influences the other and is in turn influenced by it. The parts of a living system cooperate not just with each other but with the whole, and are homeotelic, seeking order and stability (Goldsmith, 1993). Therefore, although two thirds of the Republic of Armenia were directly affected by the earthquake, the entire country was affected to some degree.

Disaster Research

Scientists often place emphasis and focus their research and discussions on the here and now, on the disaster itself and its immediate impact on the community. It is as if the disaster has occurred in a vacuum, as if the clock stopped at the time of the disaster, as if the community did not have a past or future. According to Bolin (1989), however, predisaster characteristics are important in determining the degree of vulnerability to the trauma as well as the impact and the psychosocial response to it.

Predisaster characteristics, socioeconomic climate, and psychosocial responses to any disaster are important areas to assess. According to Quarantelli (1985), distinguishing between disaster-produced stress and response-generated demands is essential in gauging the types of mental health services necessary to assist the surviving community. Bolin (1985) suggests that survivor characteristics, event characteristics, and psychosocial responses are the three categories for preassessment of the community. But three additional categories are necessary (Kalayjian, 1995): issues during the disaster relief; sociopolitical and economic climate before, during, and after the disaster; and resistance to change.

Current disaster research suggests that traumatic experiences may result in posttraumatic stress disorder (PTSD) in survivors. According to DSM-IV (American Psychiatric Association, 1994), PTSD is categorized as an anxiety disorder with the following symptoms experienced for over 1 month of duration following exposure to a traumatic event: persistent reexperiencing of the event, persistent avoidance of the stimuli associated with the trauma, and clinically significant decrease in the individual's ability to function.

Not all traumas cause psychopathology, and not all psychopathology resulting from a massive trauma can be diagnosed as PTSD. Expert clinicians are necessary to make the differential diagnoses and to meet the mental health needs of a community following disasters.

Logotheory

Logotheory is based on spiritual and existential principles, placing emphasis on meanings instead of feelings as a means of understanding and resolving spiritual conflicts. Logotherapy, as a form of individual and group psychotherapy, was introduced by Frankl (1969). Logotherapy is the third Viennese school of psychotherapy, the predecessors being the Freudian and Adlerian schools.

There is wide misconception that Frankl introduced his theory as a long-time prisoner of the Nazi concentration camps; in fact, he had introduced the core concepts of logotherapy before his imprisonment. But, in the concentration camps, he was first able to put his theory to use. Although his entire family except his sister died in the camps, Frankl was not only able to find meaning in his suffering, he was able to help many other prisoners to exercise their will to freedom. When all is taken away, due to humanmade or natural disasters, Frankl tells us to focus on "the last of human freedoms—the ability to choose one's attitude in a given set of circumstances" (1969, p. 73). This ultimate freedom is what we can exercise in any given situation, even in the worst conceivable one.

Frankl is well known as the author of *Man's Search for Meaning* (1962/ 1984), which outlines his pioneering work pertaining to treatment of PTSD and other existential crises. In logotherapy, or existential analysis, the human will to give meaning is the core for most behavior. In his writings, Frankl (1969, 1978) consistently points out that human beings readily sacrifice safety, security, and sexual needs for things that are meaningful to them. According to Frankl (1978), being human means being always directed and pointed to something or some-one other than oneself: to a meaning to fulfill or another human being to en-counter, a cause to serve or a person to love. Only to the extent that one is living out this self-transcendence of human existence is one truly human.

For Frankl (1978), each life situation is unique, and therefore the meaning of each situation must be unique. He asserts that therapists can never define what is or is not meaningful for individuals; meaning is often found in a self-transcendent encounter with the world. Just as people differ in their perceptions of trauma and in the ways that they cope with it, they also differ in the mean-ings they attribute to the same situation. Frankl (1962/1984) points out that meanings and meaning potentials are reactive to trauma and thus can be clouded, covered, and/or repressed. Such meaning repression will ultimately lead to a meaning vacuum or existential vacuum. This vacuum is then filled by the devel-opment of anxiety, depression, phobias, compulsive sexual behavior, or self-medicating practices, as in the case of substance abuse.

Frankl was the first psychiatrist to recognize the positive outcomes from traumatic situations. The role of the therapist within logotherapy is to help the trauma survivor discover a unique personal meaning, thereby transforming the trauma-related pain and suffering into meaningful awareness or a rediscovery of meaning in one's own existence.

Several other theorists have expressed ideas on meaning. Jung (1972) stated that finding meaning in life was a difficult task, and he believed that most of us were not forced to answer the extraordinary question of the meaning of life. Adler (1980) stated that every human being had assigned a meaning to life by the age of 5 and that this meaning, although unconscious, objectively existed.

Frankl (1962/1984) maintained that, as long as we are breathing, our life has meaning, whether we believe it or not, whether we have discovered it or not, and whether we admit it or not. Tolstoy, in his book *My Confession,* rein-forced Frankl's assertion that life has meaning and that we must have the mental capacity to understand it (Leontiev, 1992). Traumas, whether humanmade or natural, have the ability to challenge previously held assumptions about the meaning of life and to force the discovery or rediscovery of a new meaning, one that incorporates the new experience and the the trauma and that integrates one's personal perception.

PSYCHOSOCIAL RESPONSE
OF THE ARMENIAN COMMUNITY

The Acute Phase

Four to 6 weeks after the earthquake, I interviewed survivors at five shelters located in Soviet Armenia ($N = 60$). Survivors in this study ranged from 22 to

65 years of age, with a majority (75%) being between the ages of 30 and 60. Half of all respondents were male. A majority (68%) were college educated (which is consistent with the general population). Over 62% were married. The overwhelming majority (98%) had lost their jobs as a result of the earthquake and had been forced to relocate. All had incurred physical and monetary losses (Kalayjian, 1996).

In this initial phase, immediately after the trauma, the following stages were detected:

1 *Feelings of intense fear, shock, numbness, and disbelief.* Several different subpopulations of the community were observed in their natural environments, for example, school-age children and adolescents in their classrooms and during recess, in hospitals, shelters, or in their homes. Adults and older adults were observed at their workplaces (if they were still employed), in hospitals, at government shelters, or in their homes.

Feelings of fear (98%), shock (98%), disbelief (62%), and numbness (58%) were often expressed. This was consistent with research findings in bereavement as well as in disaster research. Survivors repeatedly stated: "I am really scared; I try not to think about it (the quake), but it is still in front of my eyes." "I can't believe this, I am in shock," and "If they had told me that there was a horror movie such as this (quake), I would not have believed it." There were piles of steel, chunks of concrete, leveled buildings, and the stench of corpses everywhere. People wearing inadequate clothing wandered about, their eyes filled with tears of sadness, shock, and disbelief. This was compounded by the terror of impending aftershocks and the decreasing hope of finding loved ones.

In this acute phase, it is essential for mental health caregivers to assess the community's psychosocial needs effectively, focusing on target groups. The most vulnerable groups affected by the earthquake as well as any other natural disasters are: the very young, adolescents, and the very old, due to their concurrent developmental challenges. Other vulnerable groups, due to the weight of responsibilities in key positions are: governmental officers, administrators, clergy, media, educators, disaster relief workers, and healthcare providers.

2 *Sadness and generalized anxiety.* These feelings generally followed for the majority of survivors once feelings of disbelief and denial were, as survivors later reported, found to be ineffective. A deep, enduring sadness prevailed in Armenia as a whole, even in areas that were not directly affected by the earthquake, i.e., where there were no physical damages, nor any financial losses or casualties. It was a collective sadness, connected to their identity as Armenians and how they felt about their country and their land.

This was inconsistent with the feelings expressed to this author by American survivors of the 1994 earthquake in Southern California and Hurricane Andrew in Southern Florida. Earthquake survivors in Armenia talked about their land as "holy," "unique," and "one and only." They expressed spiritual and emotional connectedness to "Mother Armenia," unlike survivors of Hurricane Andrew or the 1994 earthquake in California, who expressed plans to move to another state or another part of the country, with little emotional difficulty expressed.

3   *Uncertainty*. In addition to fear, uncertainty pertaining to their connectedness to the earth, to the "Motherland," was expressed frequently (by 75% of respondents). Violent aftershocks continued for 2 months after the initial quake, and, with each aftershock, the sense of uncertainty was exacerbated. Every bulldozer or truck passing by caused a minor tremor that would jolt survivors, disconnecting them from their beliefs regarding the safety and security of the Motherland. But the majority of the survivors expressed in a heroic manner: "This is the land of our great-great-great-grandparents; our roots are here." "We have been here for over three millennia, we're not going to leave no matter what" (Kalayjian, 1994).

Other uncertainties caused by the quake and by the Soviet regime overwhelmed many survivors. "What's going to happen to my home?" "Are they [the Soviet government] going to provide us with food?" asked survivors, focusing on their basic needs for shelter and food. Some survivors were more pessimistic and fatalistic in their expressions: "Nothing is certain when the earth itself moves under your feet" and "If this quake could destroy our country in 40 seconds, what is the use of all the everyday planning we do in life—all for nothing!"

Uncertainty coupled with fear overwhelmed many survivors and influenced all aspects of their lives as well as their decision making. In a previous research study conducted by the present author with spouses of cancer patients, uncertainty was also one of the major coping difficulties expressed (Kalayjian, 1989). Cancer, as a chronic illness, caused the spouses to anticipate the loss, prepare for grieving, and raise issues concerning their mortality. Earthquake survivors also challenged their feelings of immortality and experienced emotional uncertainties regarding the self, death, and dying. They feared the death of loved ones (62%); they reported that they behaved more protectively (58%).

4   *Anger*. Anger was expressed very frequently. This is contrary to previous research in this area, where natural disasters are referred to as "acts of God," a label that automatically eliminated human involvement and left no clear target of resentment and anger (Sorensen et al., 1987). Feelings of anger coexisted with the previously mentioned feelings of sadness and uncertainty.

Anger was expressed toward others: the Azeris and the Turks (87%), the Soviet regime (85%), the builders and the engineers (83%), the Soviet Armenian caregivers and "doctors" (80%), the Soviet Government (76%), "our bad luck and fate" (70%), and God or the Creator (11%).

Anger at oneself was also expressed in the form of feelings of guilt. There was guilt for surviving (61%): "They're lucky and fortunate [those who died in the quake]"; guilt for not being able to rescue a loved one (28%): "I could hear him yelling for help, and I couldn't do anything about it, I can still hear him today"; and guilt for expressing anger toward the Creator (6%), for this challenged their religious beliefs. Anger toward the deceased, which is a common phenomenon in Western research in death and dying, was not expressed because this is culturally unacceptable. Survivors talked about the deceased as being perfect, placing them on a pedestal. The deceased boys were "the smartest, top of their class"; meanwhile the deceased girls were "the most beautiful, kind, caring and sensitive, living saints." This is indicative of cultural, traditional, gender-specific values. Anger toward the deceased was displaced onto other survivors: siblings, friends, and neighbors. As Levinson (1989) has pointed out, the deceased are usually stripped of their human and sometimes imperfect qualities, thus inhibiting the grief process.

5 *Helplessness and frustration.* Feelings of helplessness were expressed over 50% of the time. Survivors repeatedly stated, "There is nothing I can do," especially referring to the Soviet regime, the hierarchy of the decision making, and the constant pressure from Moscow. Some survivors did not even feel that they could make decisions and take actions regarding personal issues such as housing, food, and other family matters because all the decisions had to be made in Moscow.

6 *Emptiness and meaninglessness.* Although Frankl asserted that meaning is available under any condition, even the worst conceivable one, it was very difficult for most Armenians to find meaning immediately after such a devastating earthquake. It was enlightening, therefore, to see that one fifth of those interviewed had discovered positive meanings in their traumatic experiences.

Survivors were asked an open-ended question to elicit the meaning they had attributed to the earthquake. Twenty percent attributed a positive value and meaning to their experiences surrounding the disaster (Kalayjian, 1991b). This is congruent with Quarantelli's (1985) notion and with Frankl's central assertion that disaster survivors are primarily attempting to cope with the meaning of the trauma. This observation is somewhat contrary to Figley's (1985) belief that one of the fundamental questions a victim needs to answer in order to become a survivor is "Why did it happen?" This type of question forces a survivor to remain in the past, in the role of a victim, a dependent, without a rational and satisfactory answer. It also leaves the survivor filled with feelings of self-induced guilt and, therefore, trapped in a cycle of destructive behavior. Frankl labeled this type of "why" question as the "wrong question" (personal communication, June 29, 1989). Any question that begins with a "why" has a built-in presumption that there is someone responsible for the incident or that there is a particular predetermined reason for the event.

Those survivors who were preoccupied with "why did this happen?" were dissatisfied with the scientific answer that the plates moved, pressure built up, and finally the tension was released. They continued maintaining, "But why? Why us? Why me?" One "why" question led to yet another "why," like a vicious circle, moving the survivor around and around without a satisfactory end. These "why" questions implied that trauma and disaster happen to bad, sinful, or unworthy people, attributing a negative meaning to the disaster experience. In addition, these questions helped maintain an external focus, in comparison with questions such as: "What can I do about it now?" or "How can I deal with my experiences?" This latter type of question focuses on our internal powers and keeps us engaged and active, instead of feeling passive and reactive to external forces. Armenian survivors who were preoccupied with the questions of "why?" remained helpless, more depressed, and showed higher scores on the PTSD Reaction Index Scale (Frederick, 1977).

Survivors who attributed a positive meaning to the trauma focused instead on the present moment and the meaningful experiences they had gained by helping or receiving help from one another and from the world. As one survivor stated, "Look at how the world has come to help us [the Armenians], the closed Soviet system has opened its doors, there is more communication, caring, and sharing." It should be noted, however, that Frankl (1969) emphasizes the importance of trauma survivors expressing sadness, terror and rage, and going through these stages of grief and bereavement before prematurely becoming involved in a self-transcendence activity to find a positive meaning in their trauma experiences.

Therapeutic interventions utilized by mental health volunteers in Armenia in this acute phase included: art therapy, group therapy, play therapy, biofeedback and stress inoculation training, expressive art training, eye movement desensitization and reprocessing, symbolic expressive theory, pharmacotherapy, and psychotherapy. No single clinical intervention alone would have been successful to treat the surviving community and all postdisaster symptomatology (Kalayjian, 1995).

The Chronic Phase

The chronic phase immediately follows the acute phase. This phase involves the long-term rehabilitation of the community. The chronic phase includes the following stages: integration of loss into the psyche, acceptance of loss, and finding meaning in trauma experiences. Education is essential to help the community through these stages. Community education is not only the responsibility of educators, but of mental health professionals as well. Educators in Armenia, being survivors themselves, experienced difficulties in simultaneously going through their own bereavement and being sympathetic to their pupils' experiences. Mental health volunteers, as part of the program called *Mental Health Outreach for Armenia*, cofounded and coordinated by the present author, were extremely instrumental in helping educators, parents, and government leaders in this arena. Through television and radio programs and through written materials, mental health volunteers were able to educate the community regarding the phases and stages of bereavement, signs of PTSD, and other symptomatology requiring further professional interventions.

Media experts, journalists, and government leaders also have a responsibility to help the community by collaborating with mental health professionals and volunteers. This collaboration can result in a community that can grieve appropriately and move beyond grief toward acceptance, integration, and meaning.

The chronic phase also includes finding meaning in this massive loss. Principles of logotherapy are very useful in helping the community integrate trauma psychically and noogenically and in discovering or recovering a new meaning in bereavement experiences. There are two levels of bereavement. The first level is the personal level: bereavement over one's own personal losses. These losses could be human losses, material losses, and losses of social and economic status (Kalayjian et al., 1996). The second level is the collective loss: loss of community, land, and collective identity as well the loss of the sense of safety, security, and certainty (Kalayjian, 1995). Mental health professionals need to assess the type of loss and the reaction to it in order to assist the surviving community toward integration and resolution.

In Armenia, 20% of those interviewed were able to achieve a positive meaning in their disaster experiences through what Frankl (1986) has called "dereflection." Dereflection means turning one's attention away from self and one's own particular situation, as opposed to hyperreflection, which directs focus toward oneself. According to Goldsmith (1993), dereflective behavior requires the involvement of our instincts, emotions, and values, all of which must be mediated at the primitive level.

This 20% attributed meaning to reaching beyond themselves and volunteering to work with and help other survivors. They revealed that caring and ministering to others and helping one another were the real meanings they had attributed to the quake. They not only expressed valuing what they had learned from their experiences, but using this insight to help other survivors. These respondents also found meaning through acceptance of what was beyond their control: "We could not have prevented it [the quake]." They then went on to modify their attitudes: "I am changing the way I look at things; although I've lost everything, everything material, I have myself and I have this moment with you on this Earth; no one or no disaster can take that away from me" and "We live in a mountainous region, where seismic activity is not uncommon. If you read our history, you'll notice that a devastating quake had struck this area some 100 years ago; we rebuilt then and we'll do the same now—even better!"

They also reiterated convictions such as: "I am stronger now" and "We [the Armenians] are an indomitable nation; we dealt with the Ottoman-Turkish Genocide when over 2 million Armenians were killed; we dealt with the 70 years of Stalinist regime, losing many more lives; we dealt with the Azeri blockade and more massacres and oppression, yet losing more lives—and now we deal with this devastation. We can deal with anything!" (Kalayjian, 1996).

They were convinced that they were indomitable, echoing the words of Nietzsche (1956), who said, "That which does not kill me makes me stronger."

CONCLUSION

According to systems theory, a community is more than the sum of its parts. Therefore, although we can assess individual survivor responses, it is a challenge to evaluate effectively the community response and to address the community needs after a devastating natural disaster. Expeditious, careful, and comprehensive assessment of several layers of the community is essential to diagnose and meet the bereaved community's needs.

Disasters create enormous tensions in a community: physical, psychological, and spiritual, on one level, and social, political, and economic on the other. These tensions can create challenges in the soma, psyche, and spirit of community members, in addition to sociopolitical and economic challenges. Although there are unique individual responses to any massive loss, we need to recognize also the many similarities in the grieving process.

The community response is influenced by several factors, among which are: event and survivor characteristics; the sociopolitical and economic climate before, during, and after; rescue efforts, and leadership and media attitudes and practices. The role of media and government leadership is very important in helping the community grieve effectively, moving them away from victimhood and dependence to acceptance, empowerment, and positive meaning. Because media experts and many leaders were unable to recognize the importance of their role in the community's grieving process, mental health professionals took the initiative to instruct, guide, and empower them.

Mental health professionals are in key positions to empower individual leaders and, therefore, the entire community by helping them uncover, discover, or recover their responsibility. We can empower them and help them become free but yet connected to their emotions, environment, and soul. We can help them build skills to help free themselves from moral conflicts, guilt, and self-destructive behaviors, and from conflicts of conscience which, according to Frankl, can lead to an existential neurosis.

Pain and suffering caused by massive losses after natural or human-induced disasters may cause a fruitful tension, making the community aware of what could be, appreciate what it is, and prevent what ought not to be. These tensions may help the community to come together and act responsibly and collectively. Massive traumatic losses not only create a crisis in the community; they create opportunities for survivors to understand their obligations to one another and to the earth, and also help the community *feel* such obligation. Above all, crises carry the potential to help community members care for each other and exhibit this caring in a humanistic way. It may well be a paradox that traumatic disasters that disrupt the way of life of a community may lead to spiritual evolution as long as the community can learn from and find positive meaning in a communal crisis.

REFERENCES

Adler, A. (1980). *What life should mean to you.* London: Oxford University Press. (Original work published 1932)

American Psychiatric Association. (1994). *Diagnostic and statistical manual for mental disorders* (4th ed.). Washington, DC: Author.

Bolin, R. (1985). Disaster characteristics and psychosocial impacts. In B. Sowder (Ed.), *Disaster and mental health: Selected contemporary perspectives* (DHHS Publication No. 854-1421, pp. 3–28). Washington, DC: U.S. Government Printing Office.

Bolin, R. (1989). Natural disasters. In R. Gist & B. Lubin (Eds.), *Psychosocial aspects of disaster* (pp. 61–85). New York: Wiley.

Erikson, K. (1976). *Everything in its path.* New York: Simon & Schuster.

Fein, E. (1988, December 9). Toll out on tens of thousands from quake in Soviet Armenia. *New York Times*, p. 23.

Figley, C. R. (1985). *Trauma and its wake.* New York: Brunner/Mazel.

Frankl, V. E. (1962/1984). *Man's search for meaning.* New York: Simon & Schuster.

Frankl, V. E. (1969). *The will to meaning.* New York: New American Library.

Frankl, V. E. (1978). *The unheard cry for meaning.* New York: Simon & Schuster.

Frankl, V. E. (1986). *The doctor and the soul.* New York: Vintage Books.

Frederick, C. J. (1977). Current thinking about crises and psychological interventions in United States disasters. *Mass Emergencies, 2*, 43–50.

Glick, I., Weiss, R., & Parkes, C. (1974). *The first year of bereavement.* New York: Wiley.

Goldsmith, E. (1993). *The way: An ecologic world-view.* Boston: Shambhala.

Ishkanian, R. (1989). *Badgerazart badmoutioun hayotz* [A pictorial history of Armenians.] Armenian SSR: Yerevan, Armenia, Arevig Press.

Jung, C. (1972). Vom werden der personlichkeit. In D. Leontiev, The meaning crisis in Russia today. *The International Forum for Logotherapy, 15*(1), 41–45.

Jordan, R. P. (1978). The proud Armenians. *National Geographic, 153*, 846–873.

Kalayjian, A. S. (1989). Coping with cancer: The spouse's perspective. *Archives of Psychiatric Nursing, III*(3), 166-172.

Kalayjian, A. S. (1991a, October). *Genocide, earthquake, and ethnic turmoil: Multiple traumas of a nation.* Paper presented at the 7th Annual Convention of the International Society for Traumatic Stress Studies, Washington, DC.

Kalayjian, A. S. (1991b, November). *Meaning in trauma: Impact of the earthquake in Soviet Armenia.* Paper presented at the VIII World Congress of Logotherapy, San Jose, CA.

Kalayjian, A. S. (1994). Emotional and environmental connections: Impact of the Armenian earthquake. In E. A. Schuster & C.L. Brown (Eds.), *Exploring our environmental connections.* New York: National League for Nursing Press.

Kalayjian, A. S. (1995). *Disaster and mass trauma: Global perspectives on post disaster mental health management.* Long Branch, NJ: Vista.

Kalayjian, A. S. (1996). Armenian relief uses nursing process. *Reflections, 22*(1), 14–15.

Kalayjian, A. S. (in press-a). Cultural specificity, cultural diversity, and cultural sensitivity post disaster: A new challenge. In R. Gist & B. Lubin (Eds.), *Psychosocial aspects of disaster.* New York: Wiley.

Kalayjian, A. S. (in press-b). Psychotherapist experiences working in Soviet Armenia after the 1988 earthquake. In J. Lindy & R. J. Lifton, (Eds.), *Invisible walls—Legacy of Soviet trauma victims and their therapists.* New Haven, CT: Yale University Press.

Kalayjian, A. S., Shahinian, S. P., Gergerian, E. L., & Saraydarian, L. (1996). Coping with Ottoman-Turkish Genocide. The experiences of Armenian survivors. *Journal of Traumatic Stress, 9*(1), 87–97.

Leontiev, D. (1992). The meaning of crisis in Russia today. *The International Forum for Logotherapy, 15*(1), 41–45.

Levinson, J. (1989). Existential vacuum in grieving widows. *International Forum for Logotherapy, 12*(2), 48–51.

Nietzsche, F. (1956). *Birth of tragedy and other genealogy of morals* (F. Golffing, Transl.). New York: Doubleday.

Parkes, C. M. (1975). Unexpected and untimely bereavement: A statistical study of young Boston widows and widowers. In B. Schoenberg, I. Gerber, A. Weiner, A. Kutscher,

D. Peretz, & A. Carr (Eds.), *Bereavement: Its psychosocial aspects* (pp. 119–138). New York: Columbia University Press.

Pollack, G. (1961). Mourning and adaptation. *International Journal of Psychoanalysis, 42,* 341–361.

Simon, P. (1989). US Government should do more to help Armenia rebuild. *Journal of Armenian Assembly of America, 16,* 3–4.

Smith, J. (1971). Identificatory styles in depression and grief. *International Journal of Psychoanalysis, 52,* 259–266.

Sorensen, J. M. et al. (1987). *The impact of hazardous technology: The psycho-social effects of restarting TMI-I.* New York: SUNY Press.

Sullivan, W. (1988, December). Pressing rock masses mark center of quake. *The New York Times,* p. 6.

Terr, L. C. (1989). Family anxiety after traumatic events. *Journal of Clinical Psychiatry, 50*(11), 15–19.

Quarantelli, E. L. (1985). An assessment of conflict views on mental health: The consequences of traumatic events. In C. R. Figley (Ed.), *Trauma and its wake* (pp. 173–215). New York: Brunner/Mazel.

von Bertalanffy, L. V. (1968). *General system theory.* New York: George Braziller.

Walker, B. (Producer). (1991, April 5). *Armenia at crossroads.* Los Angeles: CBS News.

Figure 6.1 Bob Baker surrounded by children (and his teddy bears) in a kindergarten on Awajii Island, where the earthquake began. In back row is Yoshiko Luscombe, Bob's main interpreter. (Pesonal photo of author.)

Chapter 6

The Great Hanshin-Awaji Earthquake: Adapted Strategies for Survival

Mary Beth Williams, G. Robert Baker, and Tom Williams

Once upon a time, in San Francisco, California, there lived a teddy bear. He loved sleeping and didn't like walking around. But, one morning, when he was in bed, he was awoken by a tremendous shaking. The bed shook, the house shook; books and glasses and plates fell all around him. There was a huge noise. He was so frightened. He got out of bed and rushed outside. He saw that trees had fallen down; houses and apartment buildings had collapsed and were burning; schools were broken up and there were cracks in the ground. The sky was gray with smoke and dust. There was a horrid smell. The teddy bear got scared and wanted to run away.

But he decided to stay in San Francisco and help rebuild the city. He rescued injured people, put out the fires, cleared up the rubble from broken buildings and mended the roads. He was so busy helping people. After the clearing up was finished, he built new houses and apartments, schools, and hospitals. He planted trees and flowers, and sunshine returned to San Francisco.

The teddy bear has many faces. He is a policeman, nurse, teacher, fireman, doctor, volunteer, builder, truck driver, psychologist, social worker, mother, grandmother, father, grandfather. As he worked, he helped peace return to the city. It became clean and beautiful again. People began to be happy again and the teddy bear smiled and went back to his favorite pastime—sleeping. He knew that children, grownups, and the elderly know how scary an earthquake is but it is not the end. After an earthquake can come a new future (Baker, 1995).

When an earthquake struck Kobe, Japan, a densely urban community of commercial establishments, residential facilities, and industry, in 1995, Dr. Robert Baker, a Vietnam veteran and former clinical consultant at the National Center for Post-Traumatic Stress Disorder in Palo Alto, California, wanted to do something to help the young victims. He and his wife collected 10,000 teddy bears to give to the children of Kobe. Two months after the disaster, Dr. Baker, his wife, son, and other concerned Americans were flown to Kobe by United Airlines. An adapted version of the children's story related above was used by Yoshiko Luscombe and Andrew Luscombe, coordinators of the Mental Health Support Team, to accompany the bears when they were given to children at a sports club and other sites. The bears became a symbol of love, support, and hope for the Japanese children as well as for the adults who cared for them. Based on the San Francisco earthquake, the tale told children what happened, helped them focus on working together to rebuild what was broken or destroyed and look toward a happy future. Along with the stuffed bears came efforts at normalization and validation of the children's behavior after their tragic experience in the quake. Mental health support team managers helped over 2,000 children, their parents, other family members, and teachers over a 2-week period. Dr. Baker returned to Kobe several times. The presentations of bears and the accompanying attempt at normalization and validation of children's behavior after their tragic experience in the quake helped to train the Japanese about trauma response and disaster reactions (Baker, 1996).

THE DISASTER STRIKES

On the morning of January 17, 1995, at 5:46 a.m., the city of Kobe, Japan, was sleeping. Suddenly, an earthquake hit the area. The epicenter was on the Northern part of Awaji Island (N 34.6, E 135.0) at a depth of 14 kilometers (8.7 miles), registering a force of 7.2 on the Richter scale and 6 or 7 on the Japanese scale (Japan Meterological Association, 1995). It struck the southern Hoygo Prefecture and lasted 22 seconds, creating both vertical and horizontal movement that liquefied the landfill sections of the Kobe harbor facilities and much of the city itself. The devastation extended through central Japan, traversing an area 69 kilometers long (42.9 miles) and 3–9 kilometers wide (1.9–5.6 miles; Great Hanshin Earthquake Statistics, 1996; "The Quakes," 1995). Prior to the devastation, Kobe was considered one of the most earthquake-prepared cities in Japan ("Up From the Ashes," 1995). That belief proved to be very wrong.

When the disaster statistics were gathered officially some 6 weeks later on March 9, 6,269 persons were reported dead, 1 missing, and 14,679 injured. Approximately 1,000 children lost one or both parents. Almost half of the deaths were among the elderly: older persons tended to sleep on the ground floors of the multiple-story family homes and therefore were killed when the buildings collapsed upon them [International Psycho-Oncology Society (IPOS), 1995]. The massive extent of destruction also meant that many thousands lost relatives and friends as well as their financial livelihood, community, and a feeling of belonging.

Of the total 472,160 houses standing before the quake, 54,949 were fully destroyed and 31,783 were partially destroyed. Only 3% of the homes had earthquake insurance. Rebuilding would therefore mean large mortgage payments on limited land ("Up From the Ashes," 1995). Many of these houses in Old Kobe were constructed with thin wooden supports and stucco. They collapsed as if they were houses of cards. The lower levels of many buildings pancaked as the quake caused vertical lifting and dropping.

> "I can still hear my daughter cry for help," murmurs an anguished father. The fifth grader was trapped when the roof of their home collapsed. She died in front of him. . . . Another resident . . . and his wife were sleeping side by side when their house fell on them. The old man managed to grab onto his wife's hand, but, as they waited to be rescued, he felt it grow cold and still. ("Up From the Ashes," 1995)

One physician reported treating 10 patients with crush injuries whom he eventually released. Nine of the 10 returned to the ruins of their homes and committed suicide. Property damage was over $8 billion. Port facilities were 90% destroyed.

One hundred seventy-six fires raged, and an area of 65.85 hectares (163 acres) burned to the ground. There were 7,046 fully burned and 331 partially burned buildings. Many of these fires were caused by knocked-over gas stoves; others, by sparks from damaged electrical wires. These fires continued for 3 days. Fighting them was difficult because broken water mains could not supply water to the hydrants. (Later, the head of the water department committed suicide.) The air became smoke-filled and the thick haze darkened the daylight hours. Survivors helped one another out of the rubble, gathering meager personal possessions if possible. Others tried to rescue trapped persons as the firestorms raged.

Elevated expressways collapsed in a way similar to the collapse of the I-80 Cypress Street Expressway in Oakland, California, in the 1991 Loma Prieta/ San Francisco earthquake. The quake twisted railroad tracks as if they were ribbons; it destroyed the monorail for the Bullet Train. Almost all of the 116 kilometers (72 miles) of waterfront was damaged; only 9 of the 239 berths escaped damage. One hundred six berths were restored by March 16, but the entire rehabilitation was expected to take 2 years.

Thirty-five schools were completely destroyed and 38 others were seriously damaged. Almost two thirds of all schools sustained some damage. Most were reopened by March 6. Two of three municipal hospitals were damaged. Three of the 112 total hospitals in Kobe were totally destroyed, 9 were half-destroyed, and 88 were slightly damaged. Of the 192 member companies of the Shoe Federation, 158 were seriously damaged. Twenty-one of 31 breweries were seriously damaged as well.

Four hundred forty-one temporary shelters housed those who survived. As of 1 week after the quake, 232,403 persons were residing in them; 6 weeks later, 114,679 people still remained.

The Stories of Kobe

The stories of Kobe are many. One story describes the agony of a gas service control point worker as he decided to turn off the gas supply to the city without proper authorization. His quick thinking saved many lives and averted immeasurable property damage. Cultural norms in Japan, as well as organizational procedures, required him to contact a supervisor before terminating natural gas services to millions of customers. If he made an independent, wrong decision, his act would cost millions of dollars to reestablish gas service to the entire area. The worker had seconds to decide to violate procedure, go against cultural tradition, and assume personal responsibility. However, through his action, he became known as the "hero of Kobe" although he was given no official recognition by the press.

Because many of the survivors were elderly, they had also survived the bombs and fires of World War II. They remembered March 14, 1945, when, at 2:20 a.m., American planes bombed Kobe, destroying 30% of the city and killing over 250,000 persons. One older woman, standing at the steps of her temporary housing unit, wondered out loud and asked "is this worse than the bombs and fires of WWII?" Thus, the history of the community was one of "planes from the sea, fire from the sky, . . . flames (leaping) more than 300 feet in the hot air, exploding gas tanks" that blew house apart, firestorms, and a quivering fireball sky (Thomas, 1994, p. ??).

Thomas (1994) continues that the devastation "looked like a no man's land. Brick chimneys stood like stark tombstones over mounds of ashes and smoking rubble. The stench of death permeated the air. . . ." This quote was made by an American in Kobe in 1945. In this instance, though, the elderly seemed to universally agree that the 1995 earthquake was worse because of the lack of warning and the inability of citizens to seek shelter and to protect themselves, their loved ones, and their possessions.

The Helpers: Initial Responses

The initial response from government and community agencies was to provide food, water, and shelter, to conduct search and rescue operations, and to prevent disease. Perhaps hundreds more could have been saved had rescue operations started immediately after the quake rather than 4 days later. It took the Self-Defense Force 4 days to send 30,000 men into the most devastated areas. The Kobe City Earthquake Relief Headquarters was established at 7:00 a.m. on January 17, 1995. The over 61,000 rescue personnel consisted of 16,000 police officers, 3,400 fire officials, 14,200 fire volunteers, 25,700 self-defense forces, 1,520 medical staff, and 1,000 maritime safety agency personnel. Dr. Shinfuku Naotaka, M.D., Ph.D., in charge of the mental and physical care aspects of the operation, loosely supervised the Hyogo Prefectural Mental Health Welfare Center.

Sixty-four organizations and governments from 22 countries sent relief supplies to Kobe by March 14, 1995. However, supplies were often kept in customs quarantine for weeks (T. Larson, personal communication with the head of the Hanshin Team, Tokyo, February 9, 1995). Six foreign rescue teams of 106 persons and eight foreign medical teams of 75 persons also assisted in the rescue efforts. Even the Yamaguchigumi, Japan's largest crime syndicate, provided food, water, blankets, and umbrellas ("Japanese Gangsters," 1995).

Electrical service was reestablished within a few weeks and drinking water became available at distribution sites in about a month. It took months longer for sewer and tap water as well as gas service to be reinstated. Gas was 90.5% restored by March 24, and water was 99.9% restored by March 25.

One week after the earthquake, Western mental health professionals living in or near Kobe and professional and paraprofessional Japanese volunteers formed the Mental Health Support Team (MHST). The objective of MHST was "to provide an organization which would bring together experts in the field of mental health, crisis intervention, and disaster psychology who would teach and train those who would be caring for the survivors and their care givers" (K. Lemmon-Kiski, personal communication with President of the Kansai International Association of Counselors and Psychotherapist, February 2, 1995). Professor Naotaka took this organization under his wing as well and invited a training team from the National Organization for Victim Assistance (NOVA) in Washington, DC to provide 2½ days of training and consultation to over 200 MHST volunteers and other mental health professionals ("Counselors Due," 1995). Dr. Tom Williams (one of the coauthors of this chapter) was a member of the NOVA team. At the close of the team's stay, he remained in Kobe as a consultant to volunteers working in the shelters.

The Hyogo Prefecture government, for the first time in Japanese history, put counselors in all usable public schools to offer psychological stress counseling ("Next Step Dealing," 1995). In addition, elementary and special education teachers were taught to use the teddy bears provided by Dr. Robert Baker in a clinical approach dubbed "bearapy." Kyoto University's Research Center for Disaster Systems and Disaster Prevention Research Institute added a mental health component to disaster research and planning with the help of visiting professor, Dr. Glen Edwards.

MENTAL HEALTH NEEDS

Once the safety needs and immediate environmental needs had begun to be addressed, officials began to recognize the apparent need to deal with the emotional aftermath of the earthquake. What did volunteers and professionals see? Children sat in the shelters in near catatonic states; workers dropped dead from pushing themselves beyond their physical limits. The culture of Japan demands such worker dedication and devotion and, if that level of dedication cannot be met or if self- and cultural expectations fail to come up to what is expected, then seppuku (ritual suicide) may become an accepted act. There were reports, largely unconfirmed, of seppuku following the earthquake.

In spite of this initial awareness of emotional needs, there was no system in place to provide the needed emotional support. The Japanese government, furthermore, refused to accept foreign aide unless it was given by a nongovernmental agency (NGO), and then only if an official invitation was given. The U.S. Department of Veterans Affairs (VA) and the Australian Department of Veterans Affairs had to wait for invitations, even though teams were ready to assist immediately after the quake. Because of the cultural mores of not accepting help from other governments, the teams were not invited. Individuals, instead, came to help. One such individual was Australian certified trauma specialist Glen Edwards who trained, offered support and consultation, and coordinated the work by international trauma specialists with MHST. Edwards remained in Kobe about 4 months.

Furthermore, the Japanese culture prescribes a stoic, private response to crisis situations. The mental health system in Japan, therefore, is not as formalized as it is in many western countries. There is no system of licensure for psychiatrists, psychologists, or social workers, and those professionals who have been trained in the United States, as is the case for Americans as well, have had little education in the fields of bereavement, disaster, and trauma. The Japanese caregivers had had almost no appropriate trauma-related training; in addition, many were exhausted; some were even living in shelters themselves; and many were vicariously traumatized as well.

The NOVA training team was among the first to teach the process of group debriefing. Sharing one's emotional responses in a group format, as noted earlier, was not culturally acceptable. Yet the training provided was designed to give volunteers in shelters and professionals a road map of trauma responses of shock, impact, and resolution and intervention techniques. This training addressed the need to: (a) provide for or ensure safety and security; (b) provide a mechanism to allow survivors to ventilate feelings; (c) enable validations of feelings individually or with others, if possible; (d) predict general patterns of crisis reactions over time; (e) prepare survivors for future possible reactions; and (f) provide referral sources (NOVA, 1994).

Trained teams began their work at shelters on a twice-weekly basis only after receiving an invitation from a shelter manager. Ideally, the team consisted of a mental health professional, a university student, and two or three volunteers. Initially, the team helped at the food line or with individual needs (e.g., assisting a family to recover personal possessions from a destroyed home or arranging a visit by a public health nurse). After teams became known to and accepted by managers and refugees, they began to help survivors deal with emotional needs in the most acceptable manner possible. Team members played with children and provided lessons in knitting, music, art, and other areas while talking to parents about emotional aspects of survival. Soon, refugees were more than willing to start to discuss their emotional turmoil.

During the first 3 months after the earthquake, Dr. Shigeo Tatsuki organized the Kwansei Gakuin University Relief Volunteer Center and managed that Center's crisis response activities. In June 1995, the Center, with help from the American Jewish World Service, organized a workshop on posttraumatic stress management for 24 helping professionals. The workshop featured Dr. Robert J.

Lifton and others and taught critical incident stress debriefing, relaxation techniques, bibliotherapy, and other interventions. Dr. Tatsuki then participated in community-based debriefing group work projects between November 1995 and March 1996 with mothers of preschool children. The project's team of social worker, clinical psychologist, and psychiatrist provided outreach services to local preschools under the auspices of the Kobe City Child Guidance Clinic. The Kobe Mother-Child Stress-Coping Research Project was conducted during the same period and looked at the impact of the earthquake on preschool children and their mothers as well as their coping styles. The project examined 438 questionnaires. Results of the questionnaires indicated that the majority of respondents had experienced major daily hardships after the earthquake (Tatsuki, 1997b).

A structural equation model of variables of postquake hardship, mothers' stress, children's stress, mothers' preferred coping resources, and family cohesion and adaptability identified the following results:

1   Hardships caused by earthquake damage caused an increase in mothers' psychological stress that, in turn, caused higher stress reactions among their children.

2   Mothers used internal and external resources to alleviate their children's stress levels.

3   Family cohesion increased as a response to hardship stressors, but did not act as a coping resource to lessen stress levels in children or mothers.

4   Mothers who joined debriefing groups expressed their own emotions and lessened their own stress levels. They were taught that it was acceptable to express stress and that it was important that they, themselves, receive stress care.

The *jichihai,* or "neighborhood organizations," with the assistance of the police, maintain records as to who lives at each residence and the location of distant family members. The government therefore knows where everyone in Kobe lives, and people also know their neighbors. In some instances, neighbors were assigned to shelters by neighborhoods. When this was possible, the relocation helped with natural recovery from loss and grief.

However, in many instances, it was not possible. The elderly and handicapped were given first priority for housing and were placed in temporary housing often far from their original neighborhoods. The death rate of these individuals, subsequently, was high. Over 70 of these "lonely deaths" due to alcoholism, dehydration, slips, falls, and natural causes had been reported by 1996 (Japanese Organization for Crisis Response, 1996). Many elderly have become isolated, discouraged, and hopeless. Neighbors who do not know them do not check on them because, culturally, they have been taught not to intrude. These elderly often say that they have lost everything. Meanwhile, those remaining in the shelters report that their bodies are getting weaker as they wait to return to their homes (IPOS, 1995).

DEALING WITH DEATH: INTERRUPTION
OF NORMAL RITUALS

Persons who have experienced the multiple deaths of family and friends are particularly vulnerable to "bereavement overload" in Western culture (Kastenbaum, 1969). However, the religious beliefs of the Japanese more frequently follow Buddhist and Shinto beliefs and practices. Shinto beliefs rule the lives of the Japanese while Buddhism focuses on the death and afterlife (Pikin, 1989). The apparent attitude toward life that accompanies these beliefs is *shoganai*: "It can't be helped." Thus, after the earthquake, some persons wept but were ignored by others out of respect and a desire to provide them with privacy. The general populace showed no hysteria, and grief was private and muted ("The Quakes," 1995). Mourners exhibited self-control in following the cultural injunction that states "do not burden others with your sorrow," an injunction that was in conflict with the process and goals of critical incident stress debriefing and emotional self-care (Haberstein, 1963).

In addition, it was not possible for families and friends of the dead to complete traditional religious practices before and after cremations of the mass casualties. These practices would have allowed a formal, culturally specific mourning process to occur. The lack of crematoriums and absence of natural gas necessitated nontraditional funeral practices. The *otsuya*, the all-night vigil with the body, was not generally possible. During this vigil, in the Buddhist, Shinto, and Christian customs, family and friends stayed up all night eating, drinking, praying, and discussing the deceased individual's virtues. In the Buddhist tradition, a priest led the sutras and prayers, burned incense, and helped attendees express sorrow, pray for the salvation of the soul, and show respect to for the departed. The body would then be cremated the day following the death.

The *kaiso,* or funeral reception, also was not generally possible. This reception traditionally occurred after the body was cremated or placed in a coffin, and took place in the home of the deceased at the family altar. In Kobe, after the quake, there was generally no time for such a reception, no food, and often no home in which to hold it. Another practice which had to be modified was the "honorable bone gathering" of the cremains. In this ceremony, the family, in a stylized format, pick the bone shards from the cremains and pass them from person to person. Many of the dead were incinerated in firestorms or trapped under collapsed buildings, their bodies were not available for quick ceremony. In contrast, services had to be held in large auditoriums of mourners and lasted only a few minutes instead of the usual day and night time period (K. Lemmon-Kiski, personal communication with President of the Kansai International Association of Counselors and Psychotherapists, February 2, 1995).

On the 49th day following the Kobe earthquake, the *shinjunichi* ceremony was to occur. During this ceremony, the *kami,* or spirit of the deceased, was to be installed in the family's home shrine and given a new posthumous name. While this day was officially recognized and celebrated by many families, thousands and thousands of others were still living in shelters and, thus, they were unable to observe this ceremony in a proper fashion.

The *Obon* festival (Bon festival), a Buddhist/Shinto ceremony, is held every summer to welcome back the souls of the deceased to their homes for 2 days (Pikin, 1989). This national celebration was recognized in Kobe but, as was the case with the other ceremonies, could not be conducted in the family homes by the many who, even by this time, were still living in temporary housing and shelters.

The circumstances of the earthquake and the direction of the government therefore led to the suspension of normal funeral practices. In many cultures, the people would have expressed hostility toward that government as well as anger because of the slow emergency response. In Kobe, too, anger was apparent 1 year postdisaster. Yet this anger was often hidden and indirectly expressed because displeasure and confrontation are not generally expressed directly in the Japanese culture.

Dr. Williams, as he walked through a destroyed part of town on his way to lecture on grief and recovery, met an elderly man in street clothes who wanted to know where he came from. The man and the woman accompanying him were Buddhist priests who invited Dr. Williams to their damaged temple. The priest told Dr. Williams that God was everywhere and anywhere and did not need a temple; God was in the air. This priest, Sato Nichirin of the Hokke Sect, Satosensei, explained to Dr. Williams, using sumi ink and calligraphy to supplement the translation provided by Dr. Williams' translator, the cultural and religious aspects of dealing with refugees. He said:

- You must have heart and teach from the spirit. You can look through 10,000 pieces of metal before you can find one diamond, one real teacher.
- You must recognize bad spirit in everyone, not just see the good. You must accept the bad with the good. If you are wise you can see the bad side so you can be whole.
- You should have anger toward the injustice done to others; if you expect anger from others, you will get it.
- You must have the power to endure. Teaching takes effort and patience.
- You must have life, have humanity, and be a natural person. If you live properly and be yourself, you are a natural person. A wise man knows he is stupid; a stupid man thinks he is smart. Don't be afraid to be stupid. Life is difficult; deal with the hardships, do not hide from them. As with the drum, don't hit life hard.
- You must study. Life is a study until you die. To understand takes time; this is very important.
- You can achieve peace by completing your mission.

Death is a release from the drudgery of human existence, he explained. The spirit continues through the cycle of life, death, and rebirth. Thus, Satosensei ventured the opinion that the quake was a result of humanity's not respecting the earth.

One year after the quake, Dr. Williams again asked Satosensei about the affect on families of their inability to complete the traditional services in a proper manner. He and his lessor priest said that they were still finding kami that had not been properly dispatched and had been quite occupied in sending them off. He was more concerned with the spirits of the dead than the remaining families and had been finding spirits from the samurai days to assist with helping the kami to go beyond.

COMMUNITY OUTCOMES

The Kyoto University Disaster Research Center is developing a national plan for crisis response that includes a mental health component. The program is also providing training and education and is creating a training manual that is more culturally appropriate than those available from western countries (Japanese Organization for Crisis Response, 1996).

When Tom Williams wrote the first draft of this chapter in 1996, Kobe had not yet been rebuilt. Buildings were still being torn down and new building had not yet commenced because the new master plan had not yet been approved. Government planners were seeking to recapture Kobe's charm through a 10-year plan of rebuilding that intersperses residential areas, commercial enterprises, and nature.

The Japanese national and local governments, including emergency services, have publicly accepted that the disaster response to Kobe was poorly handled. Services that could have been offered were denied because they were not from NGOs or because formal capabilities were not available. Officials are now taking steps to have a response system in place prior to the next disaster.

As Tatsuki (1997a) noted, Kobe residents historically have been rather conservative in expectations about gender role performance. The dominant lifestyle for most urban females in Kobe is to remain in the home until children are in their teens. Mothers traditionally have used their own resources to lessen their children's stress rather than to handle their own stress. The media also promoted the role of mother as "protector of children" after the quake, while companies expected fathers to return to the workplace almost immediately. Only through education and outreach did mothers learn to use their resources to lessen personal stress rather than to direct all their energies toward helping the children. This finding is extremely important for future policy planning in disaster management.

The need for mental health services is no longer seen as a Western phenomenon. This disaster has opened the gate for an awareness of the existence of emotional impacts and the need for healing. The Ago Shu Buddhist Association, for example, hosted an open forum for the citizens of Kobe on March 7, 1996. Over 450 people attended and participated in an educational debriefing on how to help neighbors and family members deal with earthquake-related emotional problems.

A new type of service provision in Japan has appeared—volunteers—to fill the gap between the needs of the devastated citizenry and the systemic governmental provision of services. Building upon the cultural concept of putting the needs of others first, persons are being trained in the techniques of listening skills, emotional responses to disaster, and provision of assistance to refugees. Prior to the use of volunteers in this disaster, there was no history of volunteerism or "volunteer culture" to guide the Japanese. No one had a sense of the status of a volunteer. It was the responsibility of teachers and master teachers to house and care for people in their neighborhood. They volunteered their services day and night.

Tatsuki and other Swansei Gakuin University professors created the Relief Volunteer Center to organize relief efforts for the first 3 months following the earthquake with 7,277 volunteers at 14 temporary shelters and other locations. Phases of emergency, development, and endings each lasted approximately 1 month. During the emergency phase, student relief volunteers mobilized in high numbers to move, sort, and store relief food and materials, prepare hot soup for victims, and build temporary toilets. Some volunteers patrolled shelters to ensure the safety of evacuees and increase external coping resources. The center encouraged volunteers to return to the same shelter and become acquainted with children, elderly, and handicapped individuals who were more vulnerable to stress.

During the development phase, the relief work began to empower individual citizens to form their own governance procedures. Asking for psychological help was seen as a sign of weakness and vulnerability; however, talking to a social worker or student volunteer (female) while the volunteer peeled an apple for the elderly individual was acceptable. Over time, the number of relief volunteers decreased. In certain centers, power struggles occurred as centers could not decide when to stop operation.

Many persons who survived the Kobe earthquake exhibited no symptoms of acute or posttraumatic stress (11% had no symptoms). What symptoms did appear? The primary symptom was one of reexperiencing through flashbacks and arousal (muscle tension, irritability, sleep disturbance). Second were symptoms of burn-out. Survivors tended to express their pain more physiologically than psychologically, through somatization that enabled them to ask nurses and other healthcare workers for help.

A PERSONAL RESPONSE TO KOBE

Dr. Robert Baker, coauthor of this chapter, provided the following commentary about the impact of the quake on him, personally.

As I walked through one neighborhood on my first day in Kobe, there were cars flattened and homes crushed. I saw children's toys smashed by heavy timbers that were once main supports of their homes, now gone. It looked and smelled much like a combat zone. Visions of a war from my adolescent past intruded into the disaster area where children played, just weeks ago. I looked at one large apartment building from a distance of two blocks and wasn't sure at first why it looked surreal to me. . . . Closer, I could see why. The third floor had collapsed into the second floor and the first floor had collapsed into the underground garage.

I also remember the Sports Club where all 10,000 teddy bears were housed for us at no charge. Outside the large building was the sports field (on which) the rubble of the City was being dumped about 15–20 feet high. . . . There were skyscrapers tilted to one side or . . . just a little shorter than before the quake.

I remember the horrible smell and sights of the neighborhood that lost 2,500 of its residents to the quake: the fire that burned so hot that only gnarled steel girders remained, as well as the smell of fire-burned ground, wood, plastic, and people. . . . I could not believe the smell was so strong after 2 months. . . . (Yet) the primary school in the same area had . . . new flowers and some greenery and . . . fresh paint . . . to help the children in the postearthquake environment to remember that a new day was unveiling itself to them. . . . The smell of fresh paint and the smell of smoke and dust mixed in the air to present a battlefield smell and feel. (Baker, 1996)

CONCLUSIONS

The Great Hanshin Earthquake was devastating in the loss of human life, the loss of property, and the dislocation incurred by many after its occurrence. Many survivors experienced acute stress disorder symptoms of shock and trauma. Persons who had lost loved ones suffered more intensely than those who had lost property alone. Speakers at a presentation at the 13th Annual Meeting of the International Society for Traumatic Stress Studies noted that the long-term effects of the earthquake were many. Among them were a decrease in population, reduction of industrial production due to closed and/or damaged factories; unemployment; change in physical community and dislocations of residents from their home neighborhoods; increase in school phobia and divorce; and increase in alcohol consumption.

A major problem area was that of temporary housing. By November 1997, 50,000 persons still remained in temporary housing. Frequently these units, assigned by lottery, are far from the original community of the inhabitants. Thus these individuals, many of them aged and/or sick, are now located far from their relatives, their communities, hospitals, stores, and resources. Their new neighborhoods have become concentrations of urban poverty. Cultural practices that reinforce the sanctity of the neighborhood and provide care for elderly who remained in their home now undermine adjustment of individuals who had been torn from their original locales.

This chapter began with a story, a story of a teddy bear. The chapter ends with a story, the story of the creator of "Teddycare," when he met the children of Kobe.

In his reflections of his experiences in Kobe, Dr. Baker describes the following to the senior chapter author (March, 1998):

The children I met on my first visit were hollow-eyed but cleanly dressed. When entertained by the teddy-bear story, they seemed to brighten up, smile, and laugh as they learned that teddy bears of all types (fire fighters, police officers) worked together to rebuild their city. During the story of the teddy bear that saved San Francisco, as I presented bears to individual children, that child thought of the bear as his or her gift.

No country is immune from disaster and no country that experiences a disaster is immune from its short-term acute impacts and long-term traumatic responses. The extent and nature of those responses vary with the number of stressors, community support, and cultural factors. As we have seen, cultural factors influenced the response to the quake and the responses of community after the quake, particularly, as noted here, in treatment of the dead. Response to community disasters varies. In the case of Kobe, individuals stepped in to serve as focal points for community interventions. Whether delivering teddy bears, leading workshops, or organizing volunteers, these individuals fostered community grief resolution and healing. Perhaps the lesson learned most from Kobe is that no government or city can function totally alone or in isolation when faced with a crisis of this magnitude. If the occurrence of this earthquake has taught countries of the world that they must work together to protect the populace either prior to a disaster or postdisaster, then some meaning has been found in an otherwise horrific event.

REFERENCES

Baker, G. R. (1995). *A teddy bear's story*. Palo Alto, CA: Department of Veterans Affairs and Bearapy.

Baker, G. R. (1996, February). *Bearapy in Kobe: Therapeutic use of teddy bears with traumatized children*. Paper presented at the Fifth Annual Meeting of the International Association of Trauma Counseling, San Francisco, CA.

Counselors due in Kobe. (1995, February 4). *Japan Times*.

Great Hanshin Earthquake statistics. Kobe, Japan (1996, August 13). Report [On-line]. Available: http://www.Kobe-cufs.ac.jp/kobe-city/quake/report.html.

Haberstein, R. W. (1963). *Funeral customs the world over*. Milwaukee, WI: Buffin Printers.

International Psycho-Oncology Society. (1995, October 19–20). *Special Symposium on the Great Hanshin Earthquake and psychological care of the victims*, International Psycho-Oncology Society Second International Congress, Kobe, Japan.

Japanese gangsters stand to profit from quake repair. (1995, February 11). Associated Press Wire Report. *Rocky Mountain News*, p. 2.

Japan Meterological Association. (1995). Sixty second readings from 05:45:1995/01/17. Seismograph from the Kobe JMA-87 Site.

Japanese Organization for Crisis Response (1996, March 6–8). *Proceedings of the comprehensive seminar for disaster mental health responders*. Kobe, Japan: Author.

Kastenbaum, R. (1969). Death and bereavement in later life. In A. H. Kutscher (Ed.), *Death and bereavement*. Springfield, IL: Charles C. Thomas.

National Organization for Victim Assistance (1994). *Community crisis response training manual*. Washington, DC: Author.

Next step dealing with trauma. (1995, February 7). *Manichi Daily News*.

Pikin, S. D. B. (1989). *Japan's spiritual roots*. Tokyo, Japan: Kodansha Press.

Tatsuki, S., (1997a, November). *A life-modeled social work practitioner's view of relief volunteer management: Phase specific responses to earthquake victims.* Paper presentation at the 13th Annual Meeting of the International Society for Traumatic Stress Studies, Montreal, Canada..

Tatsuki, S. (1997b). *Family centered eco-system model of traumatic stress and coping: Structural equation modeling and their clinical/policy implications.* Unpublished manuscript, School of Sociology, Kwansei Gakuin University, Nishinomiya, Japan.

The quake. (1995, January 30). *Time.*

Up from the ashes. (1995, February 3). *Asiaweek Magazine,* 18.

Part Two

The Loss of Leaders and Heroes

This section of the book turns from massive death and destruction and the impact of those events on the communities in which they occur to the death of an individual. Eliezer Witztum and Ruth Malkinson, Israeli mental health professionals and researchers, begin the section with their social analysis of the assassination of Israeli Prime Minister Rabin, in late fall, 1995. Their chapter recounts collective bereavement events and patterns, the idealization of a fallen leader, and the cultural construction of social grief as reflected in Israeli society. Numerous and large-scale memorializations are seen as an outgrowth of Israel's felt obligation to the dead prime minister. As in other modern tragedies, television played a central role by repeatedly presenting the details of the assassination, the funeral ceremony, and the bereavement responses within and outside the country.

The death of Mickey Mantle was primarily an American tragedy. Lynda Harrell, employing a narrative style that reflects her status as a professional writer, tells of the life, tribulations, illness, and death of a baseball hero. Harrell is also the mother of an organ donor and thus became immersed in the furor surrounding the effort to save Mantle's life. Mantle contracted hepatitis C, but the primary conditions that led to his death were alcohol-induced cirrhosis and cancer. The saga of this former baseball Most Valuable Player becomes the saga of the quest to stay alive; his story replicates that of countless thousands of others who need organ transplants to survive. The speedy acquisition of a liver for Mantle led to attack, controversy, public education about transplantation, and the creation of the Mickey Mantle Foundation and the sports figure donor card. While Mantle's death signified the end of an era for baseball fans, it also served as the impetus for increased awareness about organ donation. In this, Mantle became a true role model. He took the threat to his own life and turned it into something of public worth.

Figure 7.1 Rabin's coffin carried by eight officers, all of whom have served or is serving as chief of staff. (Personal copy of the author; photo taken by Government Press Office, State of Israel.)

Chapter 7

Death of a Leader: The Social Construction of Bereavement

Eliezer Witztum and Ruth Malkinson

The concept of trauma has been widely studied, both in the short- and long-term effects of adversities on individuals, families, and communities (Figley, 1988; Kleber & Brom, 1992). Trauma involving an entire nation has been little explored. A national trauma is defined as a singular catastrophic event that has a pervasive effect on the whole nation. Compared to adversities that befall individuals or families, national catastrophes have been less examined because:

1   Individual and family traumatic events by and large outnumber national traumatic events.

2   By definition, a national trauma implies a crisis situation that calls for immediate interventions rather than objective study.

3   During a national trauma, the professional person who is an observer of an event is also more than likely to be a "wounded" eyewitness (participant).

Personal accounts of those who experienced a trauma, however, are increasingly recognized as valuable documents for research purposes for gaining greater understanding and insights into the phenomena of national trauma. This chapter will offer an integration of an existing model of individual bereavement following a death event with the subjective observations of the authors as wounded professionals (Alexander & Lavie, 1993; Samuels, 1985), through an examination of the traumatic death of Israeli Prime Minister Yitzhak Rabin on November 4, 1995.

Three perspectives will be employed to analyze the assassination of Israeli Prime Minister Yitzhak Rabin and the reactions that followed his death. First, the individual bereavement model will be applied and compared to social collective grief. Second, a linking object model (Volkan, 1983) related to the spontaneous rituals and behaviors that took place will be used incorporating Winnicott's (1971) transitional object. Lastly, a contextual perspective will be offered to analyze the psychosocial and cultural constructions of bereavement in traumatic loss, with a comparison to reactions that followed the death of former Prime Minister Menachem Begin and the first Israeli President, Chaim Weitzman.

BACKGROUND: BEFORE THE ASSASSINATION

The peace rally on Saturday evening, November 4, 1995, took place amidst a feeling of an unmended split within the nation over the signing of the Oslo Peace Agreement between Israeli Prime Minister Rabin and the Palestinian leader, Yasser Arafat. An atmosphere of instigation against Rabin preceded the rally, with increased agitation aimed at the delegitimization of the democratic political system. This reached its peak in a crowded demonstration of the parties of the political right, accompanied by posters depicting Rabin dressed in a Nazi SS uniform.

The peace rally itself was organized to demonstrate that a large part of the nation still supported the peace process, and it was planned as an evening of peace songs, with many artists performing and few speeches scheduled. A central place in the city of Tel Aviv was chosen: the Square of Kings of Israel. Thousands of people from all over the country gathered for what was seen as a successful event, both in its large turnout and in the atmosphere of people joined in singing. One of the central songs was the *Song of Peace,* by Ya'akov Rotblit:

> Let the bright sun rise again
> to light the breaking dawn
> Purity in pious prayers
> won't bring back those who've gone.
> He whose candle guttered out
>
> who's lying in the dust:
> bitter tears won't wake him up,
> won't bring him back to us.
> No one can now raise us from
> the deep and dismal pit—
> salvation will not
> come from victory parades
> and not from psalms of praise.
>
> So only sing out a song of peace
> and not a whispered prayer.
> It's best to sing out a song for peace,
> Proclaim peace everywhere.

Let the sunshine pierce the ground
through flowers on the graves.
Don't look back, don't turn around
for those who've gone away.
Do lift up your eyes in hope
not through the sights of guns.
Do not sing song of war—
but sing a song of love.
Do not say the day will come,
just make that day exist.
It is no dream and
now in all the city squares
blow trumpet blasts for peace.

So only sing out a song for peace
and not a whispered prayer.
It's best to sing out a song for peace.
Proclaim peace everywhere. (Rotblit, 1970)

The climax of the rally came when the two present architects of peace and past political rivals—Yitzhak Rabin and Shimon Peres—hugged each other. Rabin, known as a restrained person and an introvert, was shyly smiling and joined in the singing of the *Song of Peace,* reading the words from a piece of paper. The rally ended with a feeling of euphoria and with the impression that peace would continue.

THE ASSASSINATION

Rabin folded the paper with the words of the *Song of Peace,* put it in his pocket as a memento, shook hands with the artists, and made his way from the back stage entrance to his car. There, an assassin made his way towards the Prime Minister, bypassed the securityman who unsuccessfully tried to shield Rabin, and shot Rabin three times in the back. Rabin fell down and, supported by his driver and securityman, was pushed into the car and rushed to the nearest hospital.

Confusion and tumult arose as soon as shots were heard. Rumors spread, and initial bulletins on the radio and television reported that there had been shots at the peace rally and that it was likely that Rabin had been wounded. Eyewitnesses interviewed gave contradictory descriptions of what had happened. Even at this early stage, there were reactions of shock and disbelief. The crowd that minutes earlier had been singing spontaneously gathered near the hospital; many remained in the square where the rally took place.

Rabin died at the hospital during surgery. He had been critically wounded and could not have been saved. The shock of those around him was total; all were at a loss. The director of Rabin's office, a person close to him, took the initiative and wrote a few words on a piece of paper, went out to the crowd and read it repeatedly, as if not believing himself what he was reading: "In shock and sadness, the Government of Israel announces the death of its Prime Minister, Yitzhak Rabin."

BEREAVEMENT: THE STAGES MODEL

Trauma refers to changes of internal constructions following an external, sudden, unexpected, and unwanted event. The process that follows is that of reorganizing one's "assumptive" world (Janoff-Bulman, 1992; Parkes, 1972). Reorganization of internal turmoil, shock, and disbelief, and the external world that has changed forever are all part of the process of bereavement that the individual may experience following the traumatic death of a significant person. The more traumatic the circumstances of the death, the more intense the bereaved person's experience is known to be, with possible difficulties in the future, especially in coming to terms with the loss. Stages, phases, or components signify the course that the bereaved person goes through, referring to its time-related dynamic: very intense emotions immediately following the loss, which decrease over time, accompanied by an increased awareness of the finality of the loss (Bowlby, 1961; Bowlby, 1980; Parkes, 1972; Ramsay, 1979; Sanders, 1982; Worden, 1991).

Although the process is universal with identified stereotyped reactions, bereavement is recognized as an idiosyncratic experience affected by, among other variables, its sociocultural context (Sanders, 1989; Stroebe, Stroebe, & Hansson, 1993; Worden, 1991). The most observable components of the process include the following:

1   Shock and disbelief that death has occurred.
2   Denial of the death and the pain and grief that follow its acknowledgment.
3   Disorientation (changes in eating and sleeping habits, social withdrawal).
4   Despair and feelings of anger and guilt over the death event.
5   Reorganization of the relationship with the deceased, from a reality-based relationship to one based on memories. Also, reorganization of one's life, which excludes the deceased.
6   Learning new behavioral patterns adapted to life with the pain and grief associated with absence of the person who died (Bowlby, 1961; 1980).

As noted earlier, we intend to use the above model as an analogy between the individual bereavement process and the social one and as a framework within which a national trauma and the social and cultural construction of bereavement can be understood. We will refer to the first 100 days following Rabin's assassination to examine similarities and differences between individual and collective bereavement processes.

FOLLOWING THE ASSASSINATION

The Funeral: Shock and Disbelief

The announcement of the assassination was followed by an intense shock reaction. Disbelief combined with a general feeling of depersonalization and derealization as to the occurrence of the event: "It couldn't have happened!" "Such a terrible thing can't happen to us!" It was almost midnight on Saturday night when the horrible news was announced and, from that moment onward, all television and radio networks canceled their scheduled programs and repeatedly broadcast the news of the assassination, describing over and over again the rally, especially the singing of the *Song of Peace* and Rabin's last moments as he made his way towards his car. The media's coverage also included people's expressions of shock, disbelief, and crying. The flow of thousands of people towards the square where the assassination occurred, Rabin's residence, and the Knesset Square where the coffin rested before the funeral was broadcast continuously, depicting a nation in grief.

Also observed was the disorientation of a nation on hearing the news of the assassination of its Prime Minister. A common reaction among individuals experiencing a sudden loss of a loved one is to search for similar events so as to comprehend the event and its circumstances. A comparable pattern was observed at the national level. For example, the media compared Rabin's assassinations with that of President Kennedy, 32 years earlier.

Explanations and descriptions of the event by experts such as historians, sociologists, and psychologists are in themselves part of a coping mechanism for overcoming the shock of the news during the acute phase. The timing of the analysis (during the acute crisis) was extremely helpful because it helped to cognitively reconstruct what Janoff-Bulman (1992) calls "shattered assumptions." In other words, it offered a logical explanation and some understanding of an otherwise incomprehensible behavioral phenomenon that created uncertainty. It is an identified mechanism of coping with the emotional flooding associated with uncertainty and the breaking of former assumptions.

The first few days after the assassination were dominated by expressions of shock and disbelief regarding the assassination, combined with the idealization of the Prime Minister as a martyr, in that the event of his death occurred during a proclamation for peace. A flow of youngsters filled the city square where the assassination occurred, singing and lighting candles, crying, grieving, writing songs and letters, and refusing to leave the site, in a way detached from the experts' efforts to understand and explain the tragic death. Ironically, by doing so, the youngsters became yet another subject for analysis.

Intense shock and disbelief were also indications of the event being so sudden and unexpected, resulting in a reaction pattern that had never before been experienced in Israeli society: collective bereavement, in which the media played a crucial role. Not only did the media provide immediacy in information and offer experts' interpretations, but it also brought the news in real time, enabling viewers to become involved in the event in a very immediate and personal way. This phenomenon was later referred to as "a live broadcast of bereavement." Later, it became evident that all the radio and television stations acted spontaneously and intuitively, having no guidelines for such circumstances. Scheduled programs were canceled, and, instead, the assassination, the pilgrimage to the Knesset Square in Jerusalem where the coffin was laid, and the details about the funeral were broadcast nonstop, reaching a peak with the live broadcast of the funeral.

There was a sense of a momentarily harmonious community, united in its grief. Undoubtedly, the media played a central role in shaping the national bereavement pattern. Moreover, the direct and immediate reports became a bridge between the individual grief and that of the nation, giving permission to experience privately the reported and publicly observed grief, in a catharsis-like experience.

The acute phase of grief was characterized by confusion and disorientation reactions among many people whose reality perception temporarily collapsed. One example of this was the frequently repeated statement of Rabin's office director: "I lost my country." The words *shalom chaver* ("farewell, friend"), coined by President Clinton in his eulogy at the White House upon hearing the news of the assassination, best expressed these feelings and were printed as a sticker and posted everywhere.

The Funeral and the First 7 Days

The funeral was preceded by placing the coffin in the Knesset Square, holding a military ceremony, and opening the gates to those who wanted to pay a last tribute to Rabin. Tens of thousands poured into the Square throughout the day and night. The presence of dignitaries and leaders from all over the world strengthened the sense of tragic loss, reflecting that it was also felt by people outside Israel. In Israel, the nation as a whole, via the media, participated in the funeral and mourning.

Thus, shock, disbelief, and anger were the identified initial responses. These were directed by now not only towards the assassin and his family but also towards the collective "self" for its negligence in not reading early warning signs and not taking the necessary precautions to prevent the assassination. These feelings were also combined with intense sadness, pain, and a sense of togetherness which reached a peak with the funeral.

That sense of togetherness lasted only a short time, until after the *shiva* (according to Jewish tradition, the first 7 days of mourning). At this time, a mass assembly was held at The Kings of Israel Square, renamed as Rabin Plaza. At the same time, books, albums, and discs with songs heard at the peace rally prior to the assassination started to appear, as did massive memorial ceremonies.

The First 30 Days of Mourning:
Denial and Disorientation

Though there was no question of whether to hold memorial ceremonies, it was argued, particularly by political commentators, that these were too numerous and too early in the process of a nation reorganizing itself following the traumatic event. We would like to propose that the large number of ceremonies in some way served as a sublimation for guilt feelings, as is often the case in an individual's grief. It was also felt that the many memorial ceremonies were, in a way, the leaders' expression of sympathy and condolence to Rabin's family, especially to his widow, Lea. But in actual fact, by holding numerous ceremonies, the opposite effect occurred, especially as perceived by the public and the media. Combined with anger and guilt, too many ceremonies were seen as an idealization of the leader.

Articles were published describing in detail Rabin's personality as a leader and a strategist, and, most of all, as a person representing the "beautiful and noble Israeli sabra" whose life symbolized the birth and growth of the nation. At the same time, articles, reports, and interviews in the press and on TV included accusations directed at the leaders of the opposition and the security forces for creating an atmosphere of hatred around political issues of national security and peace which had led to the strengthening of extremists who opposed the peace process. An accusatory finger was pointed at all those who kept quiet. In other words, all were guilty. Accusation and counteraccusation were additional characteristics of the nation in mourning as it debated issues concerning the failed security arrangements as well as the most appropriate ways of commemorating and remembering the Prime Minister. This was the process of sociocultural reconstruction.

The initial spontaneous responses of bringing flowers to the grave and other sites, lighting candles, writing letters and graffiti (Azaryahu & Witztum, 1996), and visiting or even remaining at the site of the assassination were turning the grave and other sites into memorial spaces (Azaryahu, 1995). Rabin Plaza, including the adjacent site of the assassination, and the front of Rabin's residence both became spontaneous mourning sites or "emotional grounds" (Azaryahu & Witztum, 1996). There appeared to be a fundamental difference between the immediate and spontaneous responses of grief exhibited by the majority and the organized (institutionalized) public ceremonies of renaming streets and buildings in honor of Rabin that took place in later days (Azaryahu, 1995; Shamir, 1996). These rededications, such as the renaming of Beilinson Medical Center to The Rabin Medical Center, became a source of criticism for developing new myths and secular rituals in place of existing national ones.

There was also a focus on the "negative outcomes" for a grieving nation that had never before in its history experienced the assassination of its prime minister. One such example was the failure of the government to stop the massive commemoration ceremonies as well as its refraining from publicly criticizing Rabin's widow, whose request for an office and a chauffeur brought enormous response, some in support and some against. Supporters of the government who felt guilty for not actively standing behind the assassinated Prime Minister believed that the honoring of the widow's request was appropriate and the least the nation could do for the family. But opponents of the government felt the action to be improper. Sadness combined with anger resulted in ironical humor depicting a security mishap.

Some writers compared Rabin's assassination to the death of yet another contemporary "mythological" Zionist figure, Joseph Trumpeldor, saying that "like Trumpeldor, Rabin, at his death and within a single moment of crystallization of historical symbols, turned into a martyr of the democratic belief" (Almog, 1995).

Three months after the assassination, commemorative activities accelerated and intensified with the publication of more books, albums, and musical recordings, and the inauguration of the Rabin Trauma Center at the hospital where Rabin was treated on the night of the assassination and from where his death was announced. Of note during this time period was the devaluation, anger, and guilt reactions that developed in parallel with the idealization process that had begun between the first and second week after the assassination.

A Year Later: The First Anniversary

In the individual model of bereavement, the end of the first year marks the symbolic end of a multidimensional process that the bereaved have gone through cognitively, emotionally, physiologically, and socially. Although we know that at this phase there is a continued preoccupation with the deceased, its intensity and quality have changed as compared to the initial response. The period that follows the process does not always signify grief resolution but is certainly an indication of the dynamic nature of the process. What are the processes that take place at the national level of grief? Are there any characteristic patterns for collective grief? Is the role of time similar to or different from that of the individual process? It probably is too early to conclude as far as Israeli society is concerned, but some comments can be made concerning the various reactions a year later.

The first anniversary was marked by a religious ceremony at Rabin's grave. Endless discussions over the way the nation should remember and commemorate its leader took place. The word most frequently used to describe the national reaction a year later was denial. Not denial of the event itself, but denial of the circumstances of the assassination to the point of suggesting that there had been a conspiracy to kill the Prime Minister. There was also denial of the consequences of the assassination, specifically with regard to the continued increase in verbal violence as well as in the numbers of extremist groups. Some people took the rise to power of Binyamin Netanyahu and the Likud party, which were opposed to Rabin's peace policies, in the elections following the assassination as further evidence of this denial. Overall, there seemed to be ambivalence and indecisiveness toward anything connected to the late Prime Minister.

At the same time, a year later, many were still preoccupied with the traumatic killing, visiting Rabin's grave and the site of the assassination. The continued mourning process varied in its intensity and stage among different individuals. This diversity expressed itself in public surveys, interviews in the media, and letters to the editors of the daily newspapers. For some, refusing to accept the new reality and to reconcile with it, the grief remained acute and the pain, sharp. For others, grief had not only been for Rabin as a person and for his political way, but for the loss of an illusion as well. As one Israeli wrote in a letter to the editor, "We mourn not only for Rabin the leader, but also for ourselves and the end of an era—the era of naiveté and the break in our society, a split that may have existed before, but emerged in all its ugliness, with the shots of the assassin, and continues to follow us from that day to the present" (Michtavim Lámarechet, 1996).

STAGES OF INDIVIDUAL AND SOCIAL GRIEF: A COMPARISON

By using the stage model, a symbolic analogy can be drawn between the individual process of bereavement and the reactions that took place socially: shock, disbelief, idealization and devaluation, accusation and counteraccusation, and the controversy over memorial activities and their timing, intertwined with efforts to return to a routine at the public level. All are reactions frequently identified in a somewhat different form among grieving individuals. Although there exists a resemblance in the components, there are differences with the sequelae. Whereas in the individual process, these reactions characterize the first three stages, in the collective one, they appear as one, with shock, disbelief, grief, and pain being the most dominant during the first week of the acute phase, followed by disorientation and denial.

A possible source for the analogy as well as the blending of the individual and social levels is the fact that many individuals were experiencing the assassination of Rabin as a personal trauma or loss. Crying, confusion, and dysphoria were reactions noticed and reported not only by the family and close friends but also among individuals from various social groups. Kushnir and Malkinson's (1996) survey revealed intense emotional impact (4.4 on a 5-point scale) experienced for the week following the assassination by fully employed interviewees ($n = 199$). The negative mood lasted for an average of 6.8 days, and lasted significantly longer among respondents who had experienced a painful loss in their families.

Perhaps the most profound difference between the individual and the collective processes of grief is the timing and function of memorialization. For the individual mourner, the mere act of commemoration has a healing effect, marking the end to a phase in one's life and the beginning of a new one: life without the deceased. Unlike individual memorialization, the collective one reflects, more than anything else, society's obligation to its deceased members as well as to their survivors. Hence, commemoration ceremonies can take place at any time appropriate for the purpose of preserving the complementary relationship between society and its members.

If we relate the individual and collective grief models, the massive commemoration can be seen as an indication of denial more then anything else. Commemoration ceremonies that followed the assassination of Rabin were the subject of criticism for both their timing and their range, reflecting the guilt experienced mainly by supporters of the peace process, a process that was seen as the cause of the assassination. Also, guilt was attached to the perceived negligence in not reading the situation correctly and before it was too late. Though the need to remember was unquestionable, it was felt that more time and planning would be appropriate to commemorate the memory of the leader who, more than any other, was identified with the birth of the nation. Rabin's name had became synonymous with Israeli society. As often is the case in the individual grief process, it is likely that excessive and, at times, cynical criticism was an expression of ambivalent feelings towards the situation, the circumstances, and most of all the tragic outcome that befell the society.

As time went by, it became evident that criticism had increased and involvement with the character of the Prime Minister per se diminished, although visits to his grave continued to be massive. Based on the pattern described, an additional difference between the individual process and the collective one can be identified: not only do the pace and intensity differ, but returning to full life routine seems to be a less intense process on the collective level. Recuperating from national trauma appears to be less painful when compared to the vacuum created by the loss, never to be filled at the individual level.

CREATION AND CONSTRUCTION OF RITUALS

So far we have examined the collective expressions following a trauma from the perspective of a stage model of bereavement. Another comparison between the individual and collective levels takes us away from the temporal dimension to one related to the creation of ritualistic and symbolic mechanisms which are used to reconstruct the letting go of the dead (Turner, 1969). This approach is based on a conceptualization of transitional objects and transitional phenomena as developed by Winnicott (1971). He introduced the concept of "potential space," which refers to an intermediate area of experiencing what lies between fantasy and reality. Specific forms of potential space include the play space, the area of the transitional object and the phenomena, the analytic space, the area of cultural experience, and the area of creativity (Ogden, 1985).

According to Winnicott, potential space is "the hypothetical area that exists between the baby and the object (mother or part of mother) during the phase of repudiation of the object as a not-me, that is, at the end of being merged in with the object" (1971, p. 107). Thus, potential space lies between the subjective object and the object objectively perceived between me-extension and not-me. The intermediate area of the potential space is the transitional area which originates in infancy, then develops to the child play space, and, in adulthood, takes the forms of cultural experience as artistic and philosophical transitional objects.

Volkan (1983) applied the concept of past phenomena and transitional objects to the area of loss and bereavement to explain the behavioral expressions of grieving people and coined the term *linking object*. Volkan, a psychoanalyst and a research pioneer in the field of grief and bereavement, defined a linking object as an object that becomes a source for a continuing (imagined) relationship with the deceased. Such linking objects can include real memorabilia (a watch, key, or clothes) or can be symbolic (a musical tune, a smell). All belong or are related to the deceased and, because of their relatedness, turn into precious objects for the survivor. We believe that this conceptualization can highlight and better explain the meaning of the ritualistic components that were observed during the collective bereavement process following Rabin's death, particularly in the first few days.

Volkan (1988) is also a pioneer in bringing forth his understanding of the relationship that exists between individual and group (social) mourning processes. He described them as parallel processes, though indicating that, in the collective mourning (the group level), linking objects (real and imagined) become central in a much more dramatic way. Indeed, that was the case following Rabin's death, where the linking objects identified were highly emotional, dramatic, and attracted much attention: lighting candles, writing songs, leaving personal belongings at the site of the assassination, and passing by his coffin. The coffin turned out to play a central role as a psychological linking object, connecting the mourning nation and the representation of its lost leader. The funeral procession to Mount Herzl (where national leaders are buried) passed through Sha'ar Ha'gay ("the gate of the valley"), an historical passage linked to the War of Independence, where many soldiers were killed in a battle over Jerusalem and where Rabin was a commander of one of the famous fighting units (Harel Division). Thus, there was an added dimension to the old tanks restored as monuments at the side of the road leading to Jerusalem. As linking objects, they became "a hot container," a term signifying the intensity of emotions associated with its representation (the emotions provoked by the object).

The *Song for Peace*, which was sung on the eve of the assassination (with Rabin joining in the singing), is yet another example of a linking object. The blood-stained paper with the words of the *Song for Peace* printed on it, found in Rabin's pocket on the night of the assassination, is a hot container, absorbing emotions of sadness. While some of the linking objects, like songs, candles, and graffiti, are more personal in character, others, like the Sha'ar Ha'gay passage or the grave, are more public. Some linking objects are timeless and more permanent (e.g., the grave), whereas others are transitional (e.g., the candles). All linking objects facilitate a continuing relationship with the dead person.

SOCIOPSYCHOLOGICAL PERSPECTIVE: COLLECTIVE GRIEF IN ISRAELI SOCIETY

The death on April 2, 1791, of Mirabeau, the admired French politician and orator who played a central role in the early phases of French Revolution, was deeply grieved by the French, and he was given a magnificent funeral. The following is a description of the crowd awaiting the written bulletin of Mirabeau's condition and the announcement of his death:

> The people spontaneously keep silence; no carriage shall enter with noise; there is crowding pressure; but the sister of Mirabeau is reverently recognized, and has free way made for her. The people stand mute, heart-stricken; to all it seems as if a great calamity were nigh; as if the last man of France who could have swayed these coming troubles, lay there at hand-grips with the unhealthy power. The silence of a whole People, the wakeful toil of Cabanis, Friend and Physician, skills not: On Saturday, the second day of April, Mirabeau feels that the last of the Days has risen for him, that on this day he has to depart and be no more. His death is titanic as his life has been! . . . At half-past eight in the morning, the Doctor Petit, standing at the foot of the bed, says, " 'Il ne souffre plus." His suffering and his working are now ended. Even so, ye silent Patriot, all ye man of France; this man is rapt away (from you. . . . His word you shall hear no more, his guidance follow no more. . . . All theaters, public amusement close; no joyful meeting can be held in these nights, joy is not for them. . . . The gloom is universal, never in this city was such sorrow for one death, never since that old night when Louis XII departed. . . . The good King Louis, Father of the People is dead! King Mirabeau is now the lost King; and one may say with little exaggeration, all the People mourn for him. (Carlyle, 1934/ 1837, pp. 341–342)

Clearly, there is an authentic sense of expression of deep sorrow and grief following the death of the leader. This description suggests that there exists a similar and perhaps universal pattern of response to a death of a leader, especially during the initial phase of mourning. Note, too, a resemblance to the individual pattern of reactions following a death of a significant person.

A people's response to a death of a leader could also be viewed from a sociohistorical perspective. The construction of collective bereavement processes that took place in Israel following the assassination of Rabin are related to the sociohistorical reality in Israel. Over the years, the complementary relationship between loss as experienced by the individual and by society has changed following the various wars that have taken place in Israel. Typically, mourning patterns are determined on the collective level, and it is individuals who adopt their behavior accordingly. With societies undergoing transitions from traditional structures to more contemporary ones, individual mourning rituals are less likely to be culturally (religiously) determined, and hence it is less clear what is socially acceptable and what is not.

Elsewhere (Malkinson & Witztum, 1996; Witztum & Malkinson, 1993) we have described the place of heroism as expressed in myth-making in Israeli society. The interweaving of the personal and national response to losses in wars as reflected in memorialization vis-à-vis personal grief is interesting to observe, especially in Israel. Stages of personal grief were used as an analogy for explaining trends and changes in the development of a "national bereavement culture" involving memorialization and commemoration after the four Arab–Israeli wars.

Death of Israeli Leaders

Rabin's assassination was compared to other critical events in Israel: the Yom Kippur War in 1973 and the assassination of the Zionist leader Arlozerov, and, especially, the death of Israel's first president, Chaim Weitzman. Not only was Weitzman admired as a person, but his role reflected, more then anything else, the rebirth of the state of Israel, with the presidency being one of its first and obvious symbols. Yet never before in the history of the nation had a prime minister been shot to death by one of his people.

In retrospect, it seems that in order to understand the mourning patterns that developed following the assassination of Rabin, it is also necessary to examine intracontextual cultural trends concerning the evolvement of collective mourning patterns following the death of other national leaders.

A more recent example is the death of former Prime Minister Menachem Begin. Bilu and Levy (1993), in their analysis of the nation's mourning pattern, describe the initial response among Israelis following the announcement of Begin's death and analyze the efforts to turn Begin's figure into a myth (efforts which, according to them, were still not accomplished a year after his death at the time they published their observations). There is no question as to the different circumstances of the death of the two leaders. Begin's death was the result of a long-standing heart ailment while Rabin's death was the result of a traumatic assassination. Yet, when Begin's death was announced, masses of people paid their last tribute to a beloved leader, coming to the funeral, lighting candles, and visiting his grave in what seemed like a pilgrimage to the grave of a saint. Television played a central role in bringing the event to everyone's home by broadcasting interviews and reports about the late Prime Minister. It could be said that, in a way, television played the part of constructing the story of a leader, emphasizing his popularity as a person and a leader.

This description resembles in many ways that of the nation's reactions when the assassination of Rabin was initially announced, despite the fundamental difference between the two leaders and the circumstances of their deaths. There were those who felt that the circumstances of Rabin's death explained the massive reactions. Had his death been a natural one, some observers claimed, these responses would have been different, and he would not have become a myth. In both cases, however, people had a tremendous need to identify with the two leaders and to visit their graves in a ritualistic manner. Bilu and Levy (1993) describe this phenomenon as a new form of secular religion, characterized by turning the grave into a shrine: a meaningful place to visit, pray, cry, or find solitude.

As previously described, television played a central role in people's experience of Rabin's death, providing coverage that continued all day and throughout the night, repeating details of the assassination over and over again, coming back to the square and to the Prime Minister's residence, and reviewing and rerunning pictures from the funeral ceremony. This was, in many ways, similar to the rumination during the acute phase of individual grief. Rumination is an identified act known to assist the person in grasping the new reality. It is the very beginning of a cognitive understanding of this new reality. Rumination also has a cathartic effect emerging from the repetitious pattern of going through the details of the death event.

The massive television coverage also resembled the one following the assassination of President Kennedy, which was watched by almost all of the United States. The media coverage of Kennedy's assassination is viewed by many as the origin of the media as a collective authority (Zelitzer, 1992); it ushered in a new era in which the media not only delivers information in real time but also shapes the "here and now" and has a significant impact on its viewers and readers.

In all descriptions, the tendency to personify the event was evident. In many ways the expressions of sorrow, sadness, and anger at the assassin were similar to feelings experienced by individuals who have lost a close relative or a friend. A death of a leader, even from natural causes (President Roosevelt or Prime Minister Begin), seems to evoke emotional reactions of grief; but seemingly, when assassination is the cause, the initial collective emotional response appears to be intensely experienced by almost all members of society, regardless of their political affiliation. Also evident is the use of formal language conveying similar responses following the death of the leaders. A detailed report of the results of a U.S. national survey on the public reactions and behaviors following Kennedy's assassination said that the President's assassination seemed "to have engaged the 'gut feeling' of virtually every American. . . . [E]ven political opponents of the late President shared the general grief. Shock and disbelief were experienced by supporters as well as by opponents, a sense of loss, sorrow, anger and shame" (Sheatsley & Feldman, 1965, p. 167). Almost the exact pattern was observed in Israel following the assassination of Prime Minister Rabin, especially during the first week (Kushnir & Malkinson, 1996).

Children's Reactions: Observed and Reported

What is the impact of a national trauma on children? It seems natural to assume that their responses would be similar to those of adults. In the assassinations of both President Kennedy and Prime Minister Rabin, the responses of children and adolescents drew attention and were the subject of studies. Following Kennedy's assassination, children's reactions were observed and studied particularly in relation to their political socialization (Sigel, 1965). An analysis of the responses revealed a deep involvement with the presidency in general and with the assassination in particular.

Also, a comparison of reactions of children from different age groups to those of adults indicated similar patterns of emotional and behavioral mourning reactions. The general pattern was similar to that of adults, especially among teenagers: disbelief, shock, sadness, and anger, with disbelief persisting longer among adolescents. It was suggested that disbelief could partly be related to their unreadiness at this phase of development but also to the fact that they had lost someone to whom they felt so close, an ideal parent (Wolfenstein, 1965).

Although only a few empirical studies were carried out and reported in Israel, some observations are possible. The assassination shocked people within and outside of Israel, regardless of their political affiliation. Because Prime Minister Rabin was involved in promoting the peace process, he signified for many individuals the prospect of transformation of the future to one where there would be no more wars. Thus, the mourning of the "candle children" drew special attention, not necessarily as a representative sample of Israeli youth but mainly as a group that, more than others, identified with Rabin's efforts to promote peace. Rapoport (1996) argues that the public discussion about Israeli youth reflects first and foremost the adult expectation of the youth, an expectation that goes back historically to the myth of the "sabra."[1]

Prior to the assassination, criticism had been leveled at the youngsters' narcissistic behavior in everyday life, exhibiting lack of motivation and involvement on the national level. In contrast, after the assassination, they were praised as being sensitive youth mourning the death of their leader. Rapoport's interviews with various nonreligious groups of young students revealed differences in attitudes among them, representing the wide range of political attitudes of the general population: Whereas some were grieving the tragic loss of Prime Minister Rabin, others were indifferent; and yet others expressed relief because they identified him as a leader who endangered Israel's future security and even its existence by planning to give back territories. Certainly, Rapoport concludes, there were many voices among Israeli youth interpreting the assassination. The concern and fear expressed just after the assassination that the "candle children" phenomenon would eventually turn into a cult proved to be false.

---

[1]Sabra is the Hebrew name for prickly pear and is used to characterize the first generation of Israeli-born children following World War II and the War of Independence in 1948. It refers metaphorically to a personality with a prickly exterior and a tender interior.

THE "WOUNDED OBSERVERS":
A PERSONAL ACCOUNT

Our attempt to offer an analysis of the mourning patterns that emerged following Rabin's assassination cannot exclude our subjective experience as wounded
observers whose initial reaction was similar to that of the majority of people in
Israel: one of shock and refusal to believe that the traumatic event had indeed
occurred. We, too, were involved in offering explanations—a cognitive reaction
to one's shattered assumptions—as a way to make sense of a traumatic and
senseless event.

Ruth Malkinson (coauthor of this chapter), in her role as the President of
the Israeli Association of Marital and Family Therapy, was involved in an additional drama concerning the upcoming annual conference of the association,
which was to start on the same day as Rabin's funeral. The conference's theme,
which had been determined months earlier, was "Individuals, families and communities living in uncertainty resulting from illness, loss, unemployment and
political changes," a theme which unexpectedly turned into a timely reality
following the assassination. A decision had to be made to hold or cancel the
conference. This was a painful dilemma. On one hand, many other events were
canceled, and, on the other, the participants in the conference could become a
mini-community sharing pain and uncertainty—the very theme of the conference. The initial response favored cancellation, but at the same time Malkinson
knew that many presentations dealt with the very issue of the reality that had
traumatically befallen. Talks with her colleague Eliezer Witztum (coauthor of
this chapter) as well as with others revealed a strong opinion in favor of holding
the conference, especially given the general theme and a special session that had
been planned on collective mourning, which could become a lever for legitimizing the expression of grief.

After a sleepless night as the President of the Association, Malkinson decided to recommend that the conference be held as a scientific meeting, omit-
ting scheduled social events and allowing each person to decide whether to
come or cancel. This recommendation was approved, and it was announced that
the conference would take place. Interestingly, the majority of registrants came,
and only about 10% requested their money back.

The first day of the conference was the day of the funeral. At the time of
the funeral, all conference attendees gathered in the auditorium to watch the live
broadcast of the ceremony. There we were "a weeping professional community"
who had chosen to participate in the conference. There was a sense of sadness
and grief, blended with closeness and a feeling of unspoken togetherness among
people who represented a diverse political range. Shortly after the end of the
broadcast, the scientific program resumed, and both authors took part in a sym-
posia session entitled "Cultural Constructions of Death and Life and Its Impact
on the Israeli Family," where panelists presented their model of collective mourning in Israeli society from a psychosocial perspective. The room was full, and

there was a sense of sadness and pain as people listened attentively to the presentations which not only reflected the "here and now" experience but also legitimized it. It had a cathartic quality, and people remained seated afterwards and continued to discuss the similarity between the presentation and the actual feelings they were experiencing. These strong affects lasted long after the conference ended.

CONCLUDING REMARKS AND IMPLICATIONS

We have described the collective mourning patterns following the trauma using three forms of conceptualizations: two individual-based models (the bereavement stage model and the linking object) and a third model focusing on the contextual perspective to analyze the social and cultural construction of bereavement in traumatic loss. We have indicated similarities and differences between individual and collective mourning and have proposed that the components of collective mourning are a combination of the three first phases identified in the individual process.

Also, we have compared the national reactions to the deaths of two other prominent Israeli leaders, Prime Minister Menahem Begin and President Chaim Weitzman. The initial response in all three cases was that of deep grief and sorrow. We suggested that while in the three events there was a fundamental need to identify and express grief for the loss of a leader (some compare it to the loss of a father figure), the shock, disbelief, anger, and disorientation were markedly more intense following the death of Rabin. Also, in both the deaths of Begin and Rabin, television played a central role in connecting the viewers to the event and shaping the social and cultural construction of bereavement. Central in coverage of Begin's death was the construction of his life story, his personality. This was also true in Rabin's coverage, but there was an added element characteristic of traumatic events, that of repetitively reviewing the details of the assassination. Repeating and continually broadcasting the details of the assassination had an effect and an impact on shaping the collective responses, normalizing them, and, in a way, legitimizing expressions of pain and grief. Although these are common reactions in the individual process, in the case of Israeli society, they were viewed for many years as an antonym of heroism.

What has been the role of mental health professionals during this social tragedy? Comparing the traumatic circumstances following the death of a leader to yet another crisis in Israeli society in the past few decades reveals that there have been noticeable differences in the role of mental health professionals. During the Yom Kippur War in 1973, their voice was hardly heard. After 1973, the beginning of a process of "psychologization" of Israeli society and its military had begun. The Persian Gulf War in 1990 extended this process; during this war, there was a serious crisis of leadership. The national leaders, who were at first ambivalent, vanished from the media. Mental health professionals were sucked into the vacuum that was created. Similar phenomena of less magnitude happened in the crisis after Rabin's assassination, when psychologists, clinicians, and "bereavement specialists" were asked to explain in the media the intensity of the grief behavior, especially in children and youngsters.

The lessons regarding the duty of mental health professionals in such a national disaster should be the same as in the Gulf War (Witztum & Cohen, 1994). In addition to supplying the need for organization and early planning, they should assist by giving the public clear and authoritative information (e.g., about stress reaction and the normal grief process), explaining and providing legitimization for the anxieties, fears, sadness, pain, and strong negative feelings concerning the specific catastrophe. Nevertheless, when implementing these recommendations, it should also be noted that such legitimization must have limits and be accompanied by explicit instruction on how to maintain routine daily activities (Witztum & Cohen).

We would like, based on our observations, to conclude by referring to two otherwise contradictory components that in the case of collective mourning, may coexist. We refer to the emotional-behavioral responses of individuals following the national trauma of the assassination, which included expressions of sorrow, sadness, anger, and even crying. In contrast was the formal institutionalized response which, through massive premature commemoration ceremonies, might have reinforced a dominant pattern of denial. These may have represented and created the denial of the many complex and sensitive elements that are part of a functional process of grief. Unquestionably, more research will be needed to evaluate the short- and long-term outcomes of the assassination on Israeli society.

REFERENCES

Alexander, A., & Lavie, Y. (1993). The "wounded healer:" Group co-therapy with bereaved parents. In R. Malkinson, S. Rubin, & E. Witztum (Eds.), *Loss and bereavement in Jewish society in Israel* (pp. 139–154). Jerusalem: Ministry of Defense Publishing House & Cana Publishing House.

Almog, O. (1995, December). Ha'Admorim Hachiloniyim. *Ha'Aretz.*

Azariyahu, M. (1995). Katot Le'iemiyot: Hanzchet Hanoflim Be Israel 1948–1956. *State cults: Celebrating independence and commiserating the fallen in Israel 1948–1956.* Beer Sheva: The Ben Gurion Research Center.

Azariyahu, M., & Witztum, E. (1996). Haunia Spontanit Shel Merhav Zikaron: Hamikre Shel Kikar Rabin. *The spontaneous formation of memorial space: The case of kikar Rabin.* Unpublished manuscript.

Bilu, Y., & Levy, A. (1993). The elusive sanctification of Menachem Begin. *International Journal of Politics. Culture and Society, 7*(2), 297–328.

Bowlby, J. (1961). The processes of mourning. *International Journal of Psycho-Analysis, 42,* 317–340.

Bowlby, J. (1980). *Loss: Sadness and depression.* London: The Hegarth Press.

Carlyle, T. (1934). Extracts from Carlyle's comments on the French Revolution, originally written 1837. *The Modern Library* (pp. 339–350). New York: Publisher.

Figley, C. R. (1988). Towards a field of traumatic stress. *Journal of Traumatic Stress, 1,* 3–6.

Janoff-Bulman, R. (1992). *Shattered assumptions: Towards a new psychology of trauma.* New York: The Free Press.

Kleber, R. J., & Brom, D. (1992). *Coping with trauma: Therapy, prevention and treatment.* Amsterdam: Swets & Zietlinger.

Kushnir, T., & Malkinson, R. (1996, June). *A national level trauma: Behavioral and emotional reactions to Prime Minister Rabin's assassination.* Paper presented at the meeting of the International Studies for Stress and Trauma, Jerusalem, Israel.

Michtavim Lámaiechet, M. (1996, November). Letter to the Editor. *Ha'Aretz.*

Malkinson, R., & Witztum, E. (1996). Mimaash Itakasel Ve'ad. And who shall remember the dead: Psychological perspective of social and cultural analysis of bereavement. *Alpayim, 12,* 211–239.

Ogden, T. H. (1985). On potential space. *International Journal of Psychoanalysis, 66,* 129–141.

Parkes, C. M. (1972). *Bereavement: Studies of grief in adult life.* New York: International Universities Press.

Ramsay, R. W. (1979). Bereavement: A behavioral treatment of pathological grief. In P. O. Sjodeh, S. Bates, & W. S. Dochens (Eds.), *Trends in behavior therapy* (pp. 217–247). New York: Academic Press.

Rapoport, T. (1996). *The many voices of Israeli youth: Multiple interpretation of Rabin's assassination.* Unpublished manuscript.

Rotblit, Y. (1970). *Song of Peace.* Israel: Association of Musicians and Song Writers.

Shamir, I. (1996). Zikaron ve Hanzacha. *Commemoration and remembrance: Israel's way of molding its collective memory patterns.* Tel Aviv: Oved Publishers.

Sheatsley P. B., & Feldman J. F. (1965). A national survey on public reactions and behaviors. In B. S. Greenberg & E. B. Parker (Eds.), *The Kennedy assassination and the American public* (pp. 149–176). Stanford, CA: Stanford University Press.

Samuels, A. (1985). *Jung and the post-Jungians.* London: Tavistok and Routledge.

Sigel, R. S. (1965). An exploration into some aspects of political socialization: School children's reactions to the death of a President. In M. Wolfenstein & G. Kliman (Eds.), *Children and the death of a President* (pp. 199–219). New York: Doubleday.

Stroebe, M. S., Stroebe, W., & Hansson, R. O. (1993). *Handbook of bereavement: Theory, research and intervention.* Cambridge: University Press.

Turner, V. (1969). *The ritual processes: Structure and anti-structure.* Chicago: Aldine.

Volkan, V. D. (1983). *Linking objects and linking phenomena.* New York: International Universities Press.

Volkan, V. D. (1988). *The need to have enemies and allies.* London: Jason Aronson.

Winnicott, D. W. (1971). *Playing and reality.* London: Tavistock Publication.

Witztum, E., & Malkinson, R. (1993). Bereavement and commemoration: The dual face of the national myth. In R. Malkinson, S. Rubin, & E. Witztum (Eds.), *Loss and bereavement in Jewish society in Israel* (pp. 231–258). Tel Aviv: Ministry of Defense Publishing House & Cana Publishing House (Hebrew).

Witztum, E., & Cohen, A. A. (1994). Uses and abuses of mental health professionals on Israeli radio during the Persian Gulf War. *Professional Psychology: Research and Practice, 25*(3), 259–267.

Wolfenstein, M. (1965). Death of a parent and death of an president: Children's reaction to two kinds of a loss. In M. Wolfenstein & G. Kliman (Eds.), *Children and the death of a president* (pp. 62–70). New York: Doubleday.

Worden, J. W. (1991). *Grief counseling and grief therapy: A handbook for the mental health practitioner.* New York: Springer.

Zelitzer, B. (1992). *Covering the body.* Chicago: Chicago University Press.

Mickey Charles Mantle

The best gift I ever got was on June 8, 1995 when an organ donor gave me and five other patients at Baylor University Medical Center in Dallas the organs we needed to live. I guess you could say I got another time at bat.

Now I want to give something back. I can do that first by telling kids and parents to take care of their bodies. Don't drink or do drugs. Your health is the main thing you've got, so don't blow it.

Second, think hard about being an organ and tissue donor if the time ever comes. Sign this card, carry it with you, and let your family know how you feel.

Thanks for your prayers and kindness. I'll never be able to make up all I owe God and the American people. But if you will join me in supporting the cause of organ and tissue donation, it would be a great start.

Mickey Mantle

THE MICKEY MANTLE FOUNDATION · 1931 · MICKEY'S TEAM · 1995 · 7

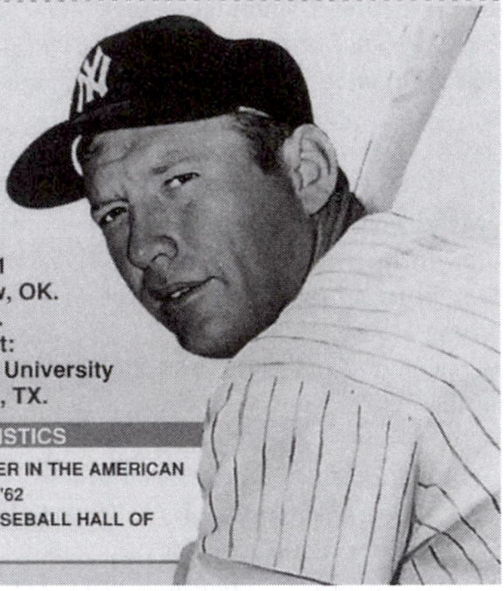

Born: October 20, 1931
Home Town: Spavinaw, OK.
Resident of Dallas, TX.
Organ Donor Recipient:
June 8, 1995 at Baylor University Medical Center, Dallas, TX.

STATISTICS

- MOST VALUABLE PLAYER IN THE AMERICAN LEAGUE: 1956, '57, AND '62
- INDUCTED INTO THE BASEBALL HALL OF FAME IN 1974

Figure 8.1 The Mickey Mantle Organ Donor Baseball Card (obverse) contains Mantle's message of thanks to the American public. (Used with permission of The Mickey Mantle Foundation.)

Chapter 8

The Death and Rebirth of a Hero: Mickey Mantle's Legacy

Lynda Harrell

On July 11, 1995, the baseball world revolved around Dallas, Texas. The All Star Game was about to occur 20 miles down the highway at The Ballpark in Arlington, showcasing the sport's current luminaries. But first, the assembled national media gathered at Baylor University Medical Center for an appearance by a legendary star.

Mickey Mantle shuffled and steadied himself on furniture as he entered the press conference. He looked gaunt at 40 pounds under his usual weight, his skin and eyes yellowed. His love of a good joke, however, proved unimpaired when he spotted Barry Halper in the audience.

Reputedly the world's greatest collector of sports memorabilia, Halper's stash includes items that border on the macabre. He bought Babe Ruth's will. He owns a set of Ty Cobb's dentures.

"Barry," Mantle called, grinning ear to ear. "Did you buy my liver?" (Wrolstad, 1995, p. 25A).

Forty years before, almost to the day, Mickey Mantle smashed a home run during one of his 16 All Star Game appearances. But, on this All Star day, a month out from his controversial liver transplant, the Bronx Bomber would slug no homers, and the grim words he uttered later in the conference would belie his record-setting career. "This is a role model," he barked, tapping his chest with self-contempt. "Don't be like me" (Wrolstad, 1995, p. 25A).

For 4 decades, Mickey Mantle amused and confused millions of fans. But he left his most meaningful mark on the American culture when he died. The final days of his life provide a study in collective grief. They illustrate the nature of heroes in American culture, how people respond when heroes struggle, and how the lives of tangential groups are affected. In the end, Mantle's legacy demonstrates an effective model to help groups recover by taking action to restore balance after a loss.

AN AMERICAN HERO

From 1951 to 1969, Mickey Mantle played center field for the New York Yankees. His 18 seasons included 12 World Series. Selected the American League's Most Valuable Player three times, he won the coveted Triple Crown in 1956, leading the League in batting average, home runs, and runs batted in ("Mickey Mantle," 1995). Mantle hit with enormous power from both sides of the plate. His career home runs rank him eighth on the all-time list, first among switch hitters ("Mickey Mantle Defined," 1995). "Go around the American League," said teammate and, later, writer Tony Kubek, "and the longest home runs in about half the parks were hit by Mickey Mantle" (Rogers & Sherrington, 1995, p. 1A).

To many baseball buffs, Mantle's skills remain unequaled. Author Roger Kahn claims that "people are bigger and stronger today, and nobody hits the ball the way Mantle did. He was . . . the most powerful hitter after Babe Ruth in the history of baseball" ("Mickey Mantle," 1995).

Plus, he had speed. Mantle confounded opponents with occasional bunts which he beat down the first base line. "Some scouts timed him at 2.9 seconds," Kubek remembered. "Today they talk about Willie Wilson and Vince Coleman getting down to first at 3.1, and they think that's amazing. Even Willie Mays didn't have Mickey's combination of speed and power" (Sherrington & Rogers, 1995, p. 1A).

Best of all, he delivered the big hit when his team needed it most. For the Yankees, that usually meant October. Mickey Mantle holds the record for World Series home runs with 18. In addition, he tops the list of all-time World Series performers in runs scored (42) and runs batted in (40). He ranks second for World Series hits at 59, behind teammate Yogi Berra ("Mickey Mantle," 1995).

Within a few months of Mantle's transplant, a riding accident paralyzed "Superman" star Christopher Reeve. One California fan summed up why he admired both men. "One was faster than a speeding bullet, more powerful than a locomotive, and a real American hero," he wrote. "And the other is a fine actor" (Thompson, 1995, p. 17).

THE AMERICAN DREAM

As impressive as his numbers were, Mantle's aura exceeded them. He played terrific ball, but others, less popular, compiled more important statistics. During 1961, he and fellow Yankee Roger Maris paced each other to break Babe Ruth's single-season home run record. When Mickey succumbed to a September injury, fans sighed with disappointment. Maris went on to make history, but America had rooted for Mantle (Lipsyte, 1995).

Hank Aaron broke Ruth's record for career homers. Yet, Mantle's autograph—not Aaron's—was still one of the two most requested in sports 27 years after he retired (Sherrington & Rogers, 1995). In 1995, a well-preserved Mantle rookie baseball card drew $23,000 in the memorabilia market (Hopper, 1995).

Mickey Mantle was more than a great player. Mickey Mantle embodied the mythological American dream. According to newspaper headlines, Mickey Mantle "defined the word 'hero'" ("Mickey Mantle Defined," 1995). Tom Sorensen represented a generation when he wrote that Mantle "was more than a baseball star. He was fast and strong and handsome. He was who we wanted to be" (Sorensen, 1995, p. 18).

He certainly looked the hero's part: blond and beefy with a wide, frequent smile, modest while still sporting a mischievous twinkle in sparkling blue eyes. He rose from humble circumstances in America's heartland, like millions of other sons trying to play out their fathers' dreams. "Mutt" Mantle, Mickey's father, had two jobs in Commerce, Oklahoma. The first, working in the zinc mines all day, supported a growing family. When he came home, his second job started: teaching Mickey to play ball. From the time the boy could hold a bat, Mutt taught him to hit from both sides of the plate. He wanted a better life for his boy. Baseball would be Mickey's ticket out of the shafts ("Courage at the End," 1995).

Like heroes should, Mickey Mantle overcame obstacles. A football injury during his high school sophomore year revealed osteomyelitis, a bone disease, and almost led to amputation of one leg. Later, Mantle suffered from arthritis and multiple knee injuries ("Mickey Mantle Defined," 1995). Still, the man delivered, playing through pain. Kubek wrote, "I'd look at the scars on his knees and wondered how he ever stood up, much less played" (Sherrington & Rogers, 1995, p. 1A).

Signed at age 17, Mantle played in the World Series 2 years later. He had worked hard to develop his talent. Everyone liked him. He got the job done for his team, even if it meant sacrificing himself. The American Dream never worked better. So, why was Mickey Mantle, legitimate legend in his own time, fresh from an apparent triumph over liver disease, facing a wall of cameras on All Star Game day in Dallas and saying, "Don't be like me"?

THE DIAGNOSIS

Mickey Mantle entered Baylor University Medical Center on May 28, 1995, complaining of abdominal pain. Doctors diagnosed a failing liver, plagued by hepatitis C contracted during one of his many surgeries. They also found cirrhosis and cancer (Wrolstad, 1995). Without a successful liver transplant, Mickey would not leave the hospital.

Dr. Goran Klintmalm, head of the transplant program, had no idea who he was treating. "Baseball doesn't exist outside the United States," according to the native of Sweden. "They told me he was a baseball player, but I thought, 'Who cares?'" (personal communication, February 29, 1996).

Mantle's name was placed on the regional waiting list for potential liver recipients on June 6, 1995. For reasons Klintmalm did not fully understand, a press conference was called to announce the patient's status. Amazed, the head surgeon entered the hospital auditorium and tried to absorb the implications of the assembled mass of journalists and cameras. "I began to comprehend that this was going to be something quite extraordinary" (personal communication, February 29, 1996).

In the auditorium, Klintmalm got only an inkling of how much his life would be complicated by this baseball player. Wisely, as his first act when he left the press conference, he contacted UNOS, the United Network for Organ Sharing. He asked the agency, which maintains the computerized organ allocation system, to review Mantle's whole certification process, making sure every decision met standard protocol (personal communication, February 29, 1996).

REALITY AND THE DREAM

Mickey Mantle received a new liver June 8, exactly 26 years after 60,000 adoring fans watched the Yankees retire his uniform ("Operation Goes 'Well,'" 1995). But, not everyone cheered this time. During those 2½ decades, Mantle had disappointed his fans. The American Dream does not include rewards for weaknesses, and Mickey Mantle had turned out to be an alcoholic.

As is often the case, the very speed of his success acted to turn Mantle's American Dream into a nightmare. The Oklahoman hit New York not yet out of his teens. "We were still using crank telephones," said his long-suffering bride, Merlyn. "We didn't have anything and suddenly Mick was the toast of New York. It scared us both to death" (Matthews, 1995, p. 5).

The same humble roots that propelled Mantle's popularity failed to prepare him for the pressure. He said that after the final out in each World Series, he couldn't wait to go home. "It was as if a big boulder had been lifted off my shoulders" ("Mantle's Wife," 1995, p. 75).

The culture shock was compounded by a death never fully mourned. While Mickey played his first Series, Mutt entered the hospital and emerged with a fatal diagnosis. He died the next year of Hodgkin's disease. The same killer took Mickey's grandfather and two of his uncles, all before they turned 40 (Hoffer, 1995).

"I never saw Mickey drunk, never even saw him take a drink, all the time we were dating," Merlyn remembered. "Not until after his dad died" (Matthews, 1995, p. 5). Mutt never saw the boy's bat boom, and Mantle spent his adult life feeling he'd failed to live up to his father's expectations (Mantle, 1994). Alcohol eased the pressure, deadened both physical and emotional pain, loosened him up to face the public, and helped him have fun.

He also assumed his life would be short. Hodgkin's controlled the fate of Mantle men. If he didn't have much time, he might as well have a good time. Mantle practiced a fatalistic hedonism: live fast, die young, and leave a good-looking corpse.

But Hodgkin's skipped him. Shortly after he surprised himself by turning 50, Mantle uttered his most famous, oft-repeated words: "If I'd known I was going to live this long, I'd have taken better care of myself" (Anderson, 1995, p. 1).

At home, Mantle ignored his four sons during their childhood. Once the boys were old enough, he made them his drinking buddies, and they got to know their father through the bottom of a bottle (Mantle, 1994; Myerson, 1995). Merlyn checked out of their home and into a 12-step program in the late 1980s. Danny and David share Betty Ford Clinic alumni status. Billy died at 36 from a heart attack suffered while a patient in a Texas rehab center (Matthews, 1995).

Heroes are lost not only when they die. Heroes are lost when they fail to live up to their billing. Mantle appeared at baseball card shows and charity auctions completely inebriated. Some fans became disillusioned. "You don't want to see him," they told their friends (Hansen, 1995, p. 1C). Others practiced denial, ignoring his escapades and talking only of his glory days, as if nothing had changed. During the 1970s and 1980s, Mantle's fans mourned the psychic loss of a hero, some more effectively than others.

REDEMPTION

A series of events in 1993 changed Mantle's life. He was spending much of his time playing golf at the Harbor Club in Greensboro, Georgia, and on October 20, his birthday, he hosted the Mickey Mantle Golf Classic. Proceeds benefited a local Christmas fund for underprivileged children.

For Mantle, the 1993 Classic was a typical day. He drank before he left home, on the course, and at the memorabilia auction. By the time he got to dinner—loud, obnoxious, and crude—he couldn't remember the name of the minister in charge of the fund. So, he called him, over the loud speaker, "the _____ preacher" (Mantle, 1994, p. 67). The next day, Mantle remembered none of the evening's events, also a typical occurrence. His friends urged him to get help (Lieber, 1995).

In fact, Danny Mantle had entered the Betty Ford Clinic that same month. When he came out, his father asked tentative questions about the place. Danny urged him to go (Myerson, 1995). So did his long-time friend, Fox broadcaster Pat Summerall, who had also attended the Ford program ("Courage at the End," 1995).

His doctor gave him the same advice. He told Mantle that his liver had healed itself over so many times, it was one giant scab (Mantle, 1994). He said Mick would eventually need a new liver and, in the meantime, the next drink he took could be his last (Anderson, 1995).

Mickey Mantle, tarnished American hero, signed into the Betty Ford Clinic. He came out a different man.

Every alcoholic recovering under a 12-step program enumerates past misdeeds and tries to make amends. Few do it as publicly as Mickey Mantle. Six months after rehab, _Sports Illustrated_ carried Mantle's confessional, "Time in a Bottle" (Mantle, 1994). In it, Mickey blamed his bad habits for shortening his career. He called himself a bad husband and a worse father, condemning himself for his son's death. "If I hadn't been drinking, I might have been able to get

[Billy] to stop doing drugs" (Mantle, 1994, p. 76). He believed he had cost Mickey Jr. a major league career by not pushing and encouraging the boy, as Mutt had done for him. "My kids have never blamed me for not being there," he said. "They don't have to. I blame myself" (Mantle, p. 75).

Through the ensuing months, friends confirmed his sincere regret and intense resolve to make up for what he'd done (Anderson, 1995; "Courage at the End," 1995; Herskowitz, 1995; Lieber, 1995). "Maybe I can truly be a role model now—because I admitted I had a problem, got treatment and am staying sober—and maybe I can help more people than I ever helped when I was a famous ballplayer," he declared (Mantle, 1994, p. 70). Burnished and refurbished, this new Mickey Mantle wanted to be a new kind of hero.

THE TRANSPLANT

The computer at Southwest Organ Bank spat out a name, a match for the liver of an East Texas donor. "Last name: Mantle. First initial: M." At Baylor, Dr. Klintmalm took the call notifying him of the match. His team had a chance to save the life of an American icon. His reaction was immediate. "Oh, no," he said (LeBreton, 1995, p. 1). It had been less than 2 days since Mantle's name went on the waiting list.

At 4:30 a.m. on June 8, transplant surgeon Robert Goldstein picked up a scalpel and began cutting the anesthetized body of Mickey Mantle. "Everything went well," he told the press that afternoon. "He now has an excellent chance for recovery" ("Operation Goes 'Well,'" 1995, p. 7).

But Mantle's recovery chances were not the hottest topic of the day. Everyone really wanted to know how he got a donor organ so quickly. Phone lines to organ banks burned as outraged callers expressed certainty that Mickey got special treatment, cutting in front of the sicker and less famous (Burke, 1995; Lacy, 1995; Poirot, 1995). Mantle's new liver made every talk radio show from coast to coast (Duskey, 1995; Stein, 1995). A Dallas TV station questioned why Mantle got his liver within 36 hours while a local patient had waited more than 2 years for a heart-lung transplant, as if livers, hearts, and lungs were interchangeable (Matthews, 1995). The world overflowed with experts, steamed by the thought that Mickey batted out of order.

Klintmalm had seen other noted surgeons take criticism on high-profile cases. He immediately asked UNOS to rerun the list "to make sure there would be no grounds for allegations of special treatment. I was thinking whether I should turn it down, wait for the next one," he admitted in an interview recently. But, he knew Mantle was on the verge of moving to the intensive care unit and the next step of criticality. "Had we turned this donor down for the sake of press relations, he may not have survived. Mantle was the issue. We'd have to deal with the press later" (personal communication, February 29, 1996).

Then, the learned doctor made a totally nonmedical decision, potentially of more widespread impact than any other he had made that day. He decided to use the public's cynicism as an opportunity to educate.

THE SYSTEM

People do not get transplants because they are "next in line," like getting groceries at the supermarket. In fact, there is no position in line until there is a donor. The unique characteristics of each opportunity make the waiting list print out differently each time. The selection system is very complex, very computerized, and very closed to human manipulation.

First, the patient must match the donor in blood and antigen (tissue) type to stay in contention. Age, sex, and body type can determine continued eligibility: doctors can't put a big man's liver into a small child; a 95-pound woman's heart probably won't power a 200-pound man (Kochik, 1995).

Other factors apply. To prevent the unconscionable practice of selling scarce organs to the highest bidder, The National Organ Transplant Act of 1984 banned commerce in organs and set up a network of 69 local organizations to procure and distribute organs. Within each organ procurement organization (OPO), potential recipients gain priority status as their conditions worsen. Some patients, diagnosed early, spend years on waiting lists before their conditions become life-threatening. Others go undiagnosed until their condition is critical. Waiting the longest doesn't put someone up front on the list. Being sickest does (Klintmalm, personal communication, February 29, 1996).

Geography, the most controversial factor, plays a decisive role. Each OPO grants top priority to patients registered within its own service area. There were no Status 1 patients who matched Mantle's donor within Southwest Organ Bank's region. By standard procedure, the computer moved to search for Status 2 matches within the territory rather than search for Status 1 matches in other regions. So, some patients may have existed who were sicker than Mickey and who might have matched his donor. But, if they existed, they were registered in other regions. Mickey got the organ because that is how the system is set up (Kochik, 1995).

Typical waiting times vary tremendously among regions, depending on rates of donation and number of patients registered in covered programs. Southwest Organ Bank announced its region's 3.3-day average in finding organs for patients with Mantle's medical status. There was nothing terribly unusual about his 2-day wait (Brown, 1995).

But the public, with virtually no knowledge of how the system works, just could not believe there was no chicanery. Everyone had heard of someone's Aunt Mabel who had been waiting for 3 years in Poughkeepsie where she still ran a little B&B but she might have to quit soon because her liver seemed to be getting worse. Obviously, they concluded, Mantle pushed ahead of Mabel just because he was famous.

Furthermore, Mabel's lips never touched whiskey in her life. Many in the public questioned a system that let alcoholics get on the list at all. They chose to destroy their own bodies, the theory went. And what if they started drinking again and wasted another good liver?

From Mantle's own restaurant in New York to the state of Washington and points in between, skeptics questioned the use of a scarce liver for an alcoholic (Goodstein, 1995; LeBreton, 1995; "Mickey Mantle's Liver," 1995). "What message does Mantle's transplant send those who are being told to be responsible for their own lifestyle and health decisions?" writer Stephen Bray editorialized (Bray, 1995), and many others echoed his thought.

EDUCATION

Klintmalm committed himself. His high-profile client offered a real opportunity to educate a generally uninterested public on the issues of transplantation. He spent hours with the press explaining the process and demonstrating how Baylor had applied it to Mickey. UNOS confirmed the pristine handling of the case. Klintmalm announced that another transplant occurred June 11 at Baylor on a patient Mantle's age with cirrhosis and hepatitis C. "This patient, just like Mr. Mantle, waited two days," the doctor said ("Mantle to Promote," 1995, p. 13A). Others followed Klintmalm's lead. Across the country, physicians and OPO personnel blitzed the press with explanations of the system and testimony to Mantle's fair treatment (Brown, 1995; "Experts," 1995; Gregg, 1995; Kochik, 1995; "Liver Patients," 1995).

Suddenly, a previously unnoticed community found itself the focus of national attention. The community included rabid baseball fans and people who, like Klintmalm, had never heard of Mickey Mantle. They all, however, had one thing in common with him: They had received a transplanted organ. They knew the system firsthand.

Robert Zanten, an ordinary Pennsylvanian, told of waiting only 6 hours for his liver transplant (Kochik, 1995). Martin Smith, a transplant survivor who waited 6 weeks, told Boston he certainly didn't question the handling of Mantle's case. "Some people get a transplant in two hours. It's all luck and being in the right place at the right time," he said ("Experts," 1995). Illinois resident Alice Willard, who had already logged 2 years on the list with an incurable (but not yet critical) liver disease, knew why Mickey got the liver and she didn't. "Once you get hospitalized you move up on the list, famous or not." Furthermore, she endorsed his getting first shot despite his short wait. "He is fighting for his life. I'm glad he got it" ("Liver Patients," 1995, p. A1).

Regarding the alcohol issue, doctors assured the press that confirmed absti-nence was required for transplant qualification. Experts said the recidivism rate for transplanted alcoholics was much lower than that of recovering alcoholics in general ("Lifelong Drinkers," 1995; "Mantle's Speedy Transplant," 1995). Klintmalm affirmed that Mickey would not have been considered had he not been sober. "This is a man who abused alcohol, understood what went wrong and took care of it," he reminded the critics (Sherrington, 1995, p. 5B).

Others pointed out that if people with vices were disqualified from trans-plant consideration, many of those complaining would find themselves ineli-gible. "If you're going to deny transplants and hold people responsible for their health, why single out alcoholics?" asked Martin Benjamin of the University of Michigan ("Mantle's Speedy Transplant," 1995, p. 3C). What about people who don't take their blood pressure medication? Don't exercise? Smoke? Eat too much? Practice unsafe sex? Fail to buckle up?

Shortage, not celebrity or morality, emerged as the real culprit when deciding who lives and who dies. At any given time, more than 40,000 Americans wait for organs. Each donor contributes an average of three to four organs. About 12,000 brain deaths occur per year which could result in organ donation (Manning, 1995). Looking just at the numbers, there seems to be no reason to quibble over who deserves an organ and who doesn't. There should be enough for everyone in need.

So why do some people die waiting for organs? Only about a third of the potential cases actually become donors; that percentage substantially reduces the odds of finding a match for any given patient (Manning, 1995). The low donation rate means there aren't enough matching organs for those who need them, famous or not. Everyone in the transplant community wanted that set of facts emphasized instead of Mantle's presumed special treatment.

Klintmalm and his supporters gained considerable clout explaining and re-explaining the system to an impressed media. Unfortunately, even as the doctor spoke, he knew events were taking shape that would again test the credibility he so carefully nurtured. The entire medical team would grieve not only a lost patient, but also their damaged professional egos and the disappointing reversal of their efforts to educate.

THE DOUBLE BIND

When Goldstein and his assistants began surgery, they knew Mantle's liver contained a cancerous tumor. If they discovered it had spread beyond the organ, they would abort the transplant. Another patient and another team of surgeons would receive the donor's precious gift. Goldstein would sew Mantle up and return him to whatever life he had left (Klintmalm, personal communication, February 29, 1996).

The team ran multiple tests to determine the cancer's status. Every test said proceed, so the surgeons removed the sick liver and stitched in the new one. A final pathology report showed microscopic cancer cells at the bile duct. They could not remove it. Following an experimental approach which had shown promise in transplanted liver cancer patients at Baylor, the doctors administered chemotherapy both during and after the procedure. They hoped it would overcome the inoperable site as well as any undetected cells that had spread through Mantle's system (Coleman & Spaeth, 1996).

Four days after surgery, Klintmalm described "an ordinary, normal recovery" ("Mantle to Promote," 1995, p. 13A). In, at the worst, a sin of omission, he emphasized how well the new liver was working, diverting attention from the cancer question (Klintmalm, personal communication, February 29, 1996).

Discussions in the patient's room, however, exhibited less optimism. By July 13, tumors showed up in Mantle's lungs, demonstrating that the treatment plan had not worked. Mantle insisted the information remain confidential. "Up on 14, we had a patient demanding absolute discretion," Klintmalm described the situation. "In the lobby, we had the clamoring press and the sort of hysteria they provide. That put us in an extraordinary bind" (Klintmalm, personal communication, February 29, 1996).

On July 6, *The Dallas Morning News* followed Dr. David Mulligan to his home. Mulligan, who had just completed 2 years of transplant training at Baylor, assisted during Mantle's surgery. He told a reporter that some unremovable tumor was left behind, posing risk to successful recovery ("Mantle's Surgeon," 1995).

Goldstein denied Mulligan's report, dismissing the excessive pessimism of "junior people." He stuck by his previous 85% prediction for survival after 1 year ("Mantle's Surgeon,"1995). Omission now distinctly resembled a lie.

"That's where things went wrong," Klintmalm believes. "We really had two options—to say 'no comment,' or to confirm the leak. You cannot lie to the press. That was bad judgment" (Klintmalm, personal communication, February 29, 1996).

By August 1, rumors forced Mantle to disclose his condition via videotape, and all hell broke loose. The press felt betrayed by the medical team they had come to trust. Klintmalm regretted the damaged alliance. Annoying as they were, journalists were powerful and necessary partners in educating the public.

Medical ethicists unanimously endorse respect for the patient's wishes regarding dissemination of private medical information. "There would have been a backlash if doctors were too honest," said John Burnside, associate dean and ethics instructor at the University of Texas Southwestern Medical Center ("Doctors Say," 1995, p. 6). At every turn of events during the 9-week Mantle saga, medical and ancillary staff faced the age-old dilemma: damned if you do, damned if you don't.

GIVING SOMETHING BACK

When Mickey Mantle regained consciousness after his transplant, he experienced what Klintmalm called "as close to a religious experience as he ever went through" (Klintmalm, personal communication, February 29, 1996). Mantle's lawyer and 30-year friend, Roy True, sat with him 4 days after surgery. "Mickey was really in awe of the whole situation," True remembered. Throughout his life, Mantle remained skeptical of strangers. They always seemed to want something from him. Yet, this total stranger, and the family who mourned him, gave Mickey part of himself, saved Mickey's life, and expected nothing in return. "He felt a gigantic responsibility for having a second opportunity, and a burning desire to give something back" (True, personal communication, March 8, 1996).

Mantle asked his friend, "'What do you know about this [organ donation]?' I told him I knew very little. He was thirsty for information. He said, 'Let's go find out about it. Find out what we can do to help.'" True got a quick course in organ donor basics and reported what he'd learned. "Mickey's first thought was to help people pay for transplants. But I told him the biggest problem is the shortage" (True, personal communication, March 8, 1996).

Mantle confirmed that assessment with Klintmalm. "Doc, what can I do? I'll give you anything you want," he said.

"I didn't ask him for his autograph," the doctor recalled. "I asked him to help promote awareness of the need for organ donation" (Klintmalm, personal communication, February 29, 1996).

So by the time Mantle shuffled into his July 11 press conference, his first public appearance since the surgery, he had three things to say:

He was grateful to be alive and particularly grateful to his anonymous donor.

He deeply regretted the way he had spent his first chance at life.

This second chance would be different; he intended to spend the rest of his life promoting donor awareness ("Mantle Is Weaker," 1995).

He thought it might be a long life, but the treacherous cancer had other plans. It roared through his system, faster than Mantle running the baseline. In the combined 150 years of experience shared by the Baylor treatment team, none had seen a more aggressive cancer. Klintmalm shook his head, looking back months later, both awed and disgusted by the enemy's power. "You could literally see it grow day to day, just by examining him" (Klintmalm, personal communication, February 29, 1996).

The doctors told Mantle they'd lost the battle. The blue eyes saddened, turned away, and a very sober American hero simply said, "Thank you." He had limited time left to give something back. He wanted to get it done. "What's taking so long?" he demanded of True, almost daily (True, personal communication, March 8, 1996).

THE WRAP UP

Mickey Charles Mantle died August 13, 1995. On August 15, 2,000 people overflowed the sanctuary, chapel, and hall of Lovers Lane United Methodist Church in Dallas to bid goodbye to "Number 7." Men, mostly in their 40s and 50s, made up three quarters of the crowd. But boys in baseball caps, reminded by their mothers to remove them in respect, also shared seats with the likes of Reggie Jackson and George Steinbrenner ("Goodbye," 1995).

NBC Sports broadcaster Bob Costas, who had carried Mantle's baseball card in his wallet since he was 12, eulogized his flawed idol. Country singer Roy Clark sang, as Mickey had requested, words expressive of Mantle's acceptance of responsibility for his own errors:

Yesterday when I was young. . .
I teased at life as if it were some foolish game . . .
I used my magic age as if it were a wand
And never saw the waste and emptiness beyond . . .
The time has come for me to pay for yesterday
When I was young."

It was the largest requiem for a sports hero since the death of another Yankee, Babe Ruth, 47 years before ("Goodbye," 1995). Almost every newspaper in the country carried the story; major broadcast media carried the funeral live. Hundreds of affiliates and all network evening newscasts included tape.

Millions mourned a hero, coming to terms with his flaws much as Costas did in his eulogy. "None of us, Mickey included," he said, "would want to be held accountable for every moment of our lives. But how many of us could say that our best moments were as magnificent as his?" ("Nation Mourns," 1995, p. 1).

Sometimes, words and actions from the famous bespeak the emotions of the common man. After the funeral, Stan "The Man" Musial, himself the hero of many St. Louis Cardinals seasons, talked to the press. He said he had once been advised to tell people what they mean to you. "The last time I saw him, I told Mickey I loved him," Musial said. Then, tears burst from the Hall of Famer's eyes. He abruptly turned and walked away, sobbing ("Goodbye," 1995, p. 1A).

"BE A HERO"

It took only 2 days for Mickey Mantle to make news again. The Mantle family, True, and Baylor officials announced formation of the Mickey Mantle Foundation. "The only goal we have is one Mickey would have set, and that's an absolute home run," True told the assembled press. "Mickey's Team" would recruit members until they could "end the waiting list for donated organs" (Weiss, 1995, p. 27A).

The Foundation's inaugural effort was a special organ donor card. On it, Mantle posed in classic baseball card stance. The back of the card contained a donor declaration and signature form. Before he died, Mickey approved the design of the card and the slogan for the Foundation: "Be a hero. Be a donor." He also wrote the message on the card.

> The best gift I ever got was on June 8, 1995 when an organ donor gave me and five other patients . . . the organs we needed to live. I guess you could say I got another time at bat.
>
> Now I want to give something back. I can do that first by telling kids and parents to take care of their bodies. Don't drink or do drugs. . . .
>
> Second, think hard about being an organ and tissue donor if the time ever comes. Sign this card, carry it with you, and let your family know how you feel. . . . I'll never be able to make up all I owe God and the American people. But if you will join me in supporting. . . organ and tissue donation, it would be a great start.

Volunteers, including transplant recipients and donor survivors, distributed the cards at ballparks throughout the nation over the Labor Day weekend. The Texas Rangers led the distribution by staging a 4-night promotion beginning September 1. The Mantles then flew from Dallas to New York for a similar September 5 event in Yankee Stadium ("Mantle Foundation," 1995).

CREATING GOOD FROM GRIEF

Grief counselor Larry Yeagley defines grief as "the attempt of the person to bring about equilibrium" (Yeagley, 1994). Balance is restored when one stops resisting the end of life as it was and moves on into life as it is. Carl Lewis, winner of nine Olympic gold medals in track and field whose own "Mickey's Team" card was distributed during the 1996 Olympic Games in Atlanta, spoke of one way to restore balance after loss by "taking an unspeakable negative and doing whatever possible to turn it into something positive" (Lewis, 1995, p. 5J).

The controversy surrounding Mickey Mantle's transplant, his subsequent death, and establishment of The Mantle Foundation offered to various groups—fans, medical team, and those with lives directly touched by organ donation—many opportunities to restore balance by turning their own unique grief into positive action. How was each group affected by Mantle's struggle? How did each respond? How did each response contribute to each group's restoration of balance?

The Fans

As a symbol, Mantle's death sealed the death of an era for lifelong fans of the game, providing final closure to the "better time" they had long mourned and enabling them to move on, to deal with the new realities. When Mickey played, baseball was America's sport and America's soul. The NFL provided secondary entertainment, and the NBA barely registered. By the time Mickey died, both he and baseball had lost their innocence. The innocence of a country boy disappeared in the city. The innocence of the game turned sophisticated and sour.

Mickey played for a team and for a game. Getting paid well was incredible good fortune, not an entitlement. He played baseball in that time before "free agency, investigative sports reporting, stratospheric salaries and the accompanying fan cynicism. In such a way, Mantle takes with him an irretrievable piece of history" (Strauss, 1995, p. 2B).

"He was Baseball's flag-bearer at a time when money wasn't the issue and loyalty was," said one writer (Hansen, 1995, p. 1C). By August of 1995, those times were dead. Fans buried them with Mickey and faced the reality of the new game: zillionaire players and strikes and a canceled World Series. "Baseball wanted to be treated like a business, so that's what we've done," wrote Tim Wood, a fan in Texas. "But Mickey Mantle reminded us of what the game once meant to the nation" (Wood, 1995, p. 3).

On a personal level, life as a Mantle fan had long been a roller-coaster ride. Many lost their hero for the second time when he died. Disillusionment hurts. Few Americans had room in their concept of "hero" for a vision of Mantle, a golf club in one hand and a tumbler of vodka in the other, tossing crude suggestions to female spectators. "The first great disappointment in joining the sports staff here in 1967," wrote columnist John Anders in *The Dallas Morning News,* "was learning that my boyhood idol, Mickey Mantle, was a big drunk" (Anders, 1995, p. 1C).

Then Mantle repented and, suddenly, he deserved admiration again. Fans had new reasons to justify their hero-worship. The "American Dream" looked a whole lot more like their own life than they had ever imagined, and they truly appreciated what it took to overcome such human frailty. "Courage is not playing baseball with bad knees," declared writer Bill Reynolds. "Courage is announcing to the world you're an alcoholic, especially when you are Mickey Mantle and you are supposed to be an American hero, however personally flawed you may be" (Reynolds, 1995, p. 26). "He's more of a hero for being brave in the face of that than for the great and entertaining things he did on the ballfield," wrote another fan (Vecsey, 1995, p. D1).

Then, when critics questioned Mickey's right to that liver, any still-wavering worshiper found his faith restored. Among baseball's faithful, Mantle's stock rebounded to previous heights. Fans had someone to cheer for again, and a few folks to cheer against. "I know all the arguments you're going to make," Art Lawler, among others, blasted. "Transplants shouldn't be dispensed based on fame. Moral judgment, OK, but not fame. Alcoholics, you say, should get less consideration....What you're saying is people should be responsible and without vices, as you've always been" (Lawler, 1995, p. 1C).

Bill Lyon administered more than a tongue-lashing to the self-righteous. He issued a call to action. "Why not use your energy and passion for something far more constructive instead? Why not take the time to fill out an organ donor agreement? Why not make something good out of this?" (Lyon, 1995).

Like the hero they knew him to be, Mickey Mantle left his fans a way to make something good happen, a way to restore equilibrium. Initially, the Foundation printed 3 million Mantle donor cards. By September 8, the enormous response demanded a second printing. Potentially, a month after Mickey Mantle's death, 3 million more people carried organ donor cards than did the month before: fans taking positive action to restore balance after a loss.

The Medical Team

Mantle brought his medical team into the world's most unforgiving spotlight. His doctors found their integrity under attack at every turn. Some critics accused Baylor of taking the case just to make a name for itself, but doctors scoffed at that charge. No one who had experienced the media would take a high profile case for the sake of publicity. "It's very unpleasant," Klintmalm complained, "to work these situations, with so many unknowns, with the press breathing down your neck" (Klintmalm, personal communication, February 29, 1996).

When Mantle died, the doctors grieved the loss of a patient, one they had come to admire and care about personally. They also grieved their own failure, now exposed to the world. Repeatedly, and with varying success, they defended their professional reputations and integrity. The public scrutiny only heightened their personal loss. "His death intensified all the attacks on us for what we had done," charged a tight-lipped Klintmalm. "And everyone's so darn smart in retrospect" (Klintmalm, personal communication, February 29, 1996).

The team worked exceptionally hard to bring something good out of Mantle's situation. They had established a working relationship with the press, a key to allaying persistent public doubts about the fairness of organ allocation. But, just when their integrity seemed accepted, the leak about Mantle's cancer occurred, and the headlines said they had lied. The good they had accomplished seemed to be dying along with their patient.

"I don't think the press has ever forgiven us for not telling them everything," Klintmalm said 8 months after Mantle's death, still sounding weary and just a little bitter. The media had trusted the Baylor program. He now thought they would never do it again. With a public relations nightmare on his hands, Klintmalm committed his emotional and physical being to bringing something good out of the tragedy. He does not feel he succeeded (Klintmalm, personal communication, February 29, 1996).

But the doctor clings fiercely to the one victory he feels he can claim. The Mantle episode brought the issue of organ transplantation to the large segment of the American population that reads nothing but the sports pages. "Mickey gave us the opportunity to speak to them," said the doctor. "I guarantee you, it was the first time ESPN reported on organ donation" (Klintmalm, personal communication, February 29, 1996). Because of the controversy, millions first learned about the process, and millions more carry donor cards.

Nevertheless, very little worked to ease the medical staff's pain. With the spotlights on and the accusations flying, they had to search for quiet moments alone to deal with their grief. Public acknowledgment was not an option. As they talk, their emotional scars lurk just beneath the professional surface, visible with very little prodding.

The Transplant Community

The transplant community, as used here, includes all those personally affected by the organ donation/organ transplant process: recipients who live today with transplanted organs, potential recipients who wait for the chance for a life-saving match, and surviving families who approved organ donation when a loved one died. Of course, not all of them were baseball fans. Still, in the summer of 1995, they all shared a very special bond with Mickey Mantle and the organ transplant system he then represented.

Recipients   After transplant, survivor guilt plagues virtually every transplant recipient. For example, Susan Reid, heart and double lung recipient, grieved for her donor as deeply as if she were a relative and asked herself all the "survivor guilt" questions: Did someone die so I could live? Am I worthy? What if I fail? (Reid, personal communication, September 25, 1995). Her guilt is irrational, but real nonetheless.

The Mantle controversy added heat to every recipient's cauldron of doubts. If the system was corrupt, were they tainted as well? Did people who thought Mickey Mantle was undeserving think the same of them? The approximately 20% of all liver recipients whose organ damage resulted from alcohol problems (Bavley, 1995) had to take the attacks on Mantle's worthiness personally. If people questioned giving an American hero a transplant because of his problem, what must people think of the recipient's own ordinary, flawed life?

"You wouldn't believe how many people called me," said Sandy Sanders who received a liver transplant several years earlier. Alcohol played no role in Sandy's illness. Nevertheless, attacks on the system upset her. "I got so angry with people talking about things they knew nothing about, as if they were experts. And, I don't understand people who think they should get to decide who gets a chance to live" (Sanders, personal communication, February 25, 1996).

The last thing Sandy needed was the hint, even indirectly through Mickey, that someone else should have gotten her liver. She vociferously defended the system's integrity. "There is nothing rich or special about me. I had the same doctors, in the same hospital, and I waited 2 days" (Sanders, personal communication, February 25, 1996).

Sandy and others needed the public to understand that a short wait for an organ just means the recipient is really, really sick. As detailed earlier, many recipients took the opportunity to act during the Mantle controversy, a time-honored tool for emotional recovery. They spoke about their experiences in print and broadcast media all over the country, contradicting accusations of special treatment. They staffed tables at baseball games after Mickey's death, whether they liked baseball or not, to distribute donor cards and answer questions from anyone who asked. Speaking out and participating helped justify their good fortune in living, providing them a way, as Mickey said, to give something back.

(Alcoholics who had received transplants may not have felt as free to use community action as an aid to recovery. Extensive research for this chapter, reviewing hundreds of pages of editorial content from across the nation, uncovered not one example of a recovering alcoholic—or even a friend or a relative—willing to offer living proof that those with Mickey's problem deserved a second chance. While there surely were some such examples, they must have been few and far between to be so blatantly absent from this review.)

Potential Recipients   For those waiting for organ transplants, criticism of the system's fairness hurt even worse, for it meant losing faith in their future. Suddenly, accusations flew concerning the grossest disregard for human life, accusations hurled at the very people who held the lifeline of hope. Could potential recipients trust the people they had to trust with their lives? Was it possible they would die waiting for an organ because someone famous, like Mickey, was considered more valuable?

Those who waited also knew that they needed as many chances for a match as possible. So, every time a talk radio caller declared he'd torn up his donor card because he was sick of seeing organs go to rich drunks, a listener on the waiting list winced. Each torn-up card became, literally, a lost opportunity for life.

But the combined forces of Mantle's fame, press interest, and the medical community's educational commitment gave individuals like Cindy Jensen opportunities to help restore balance. Doctors had diagnosed Jensen's incurable liver disease 5 years before, but, because the demand for organs so exceeds the supply, her condition had to worsen significantly before she could get on the transplant list. She spoke out on donation during the Mantle fracas. "Being able to do this makes me feel there is a reason and a purpose to my situation. I'm doing what I'm supposed to be doing while I'm waiting" (Emerson, 1995, p. B1). Taking action to increase public awareness of the need for organ donation helped potential recipients deal constructively with the uncertainty of their lives. Mantle's fame provided them opportunities.

Donor Survivors   Mickey Mantle's situation provoked a painful deja vu for those whose loved ones became organ donors when they died. The survivors re-lived their own tragedy every time they flipped on the car radio or opened the paper. Rich Bender, for example, lost his 48-year-old wife in 1991. Still, each time he hears about a transplant, "I relive everything," he says. "I am in the emergency room, holding Mary's hand" (Bender, personal communication, February 14, 1996).

The controversy surrounding Mantle made the pain even worse. The deci-sion to donate a loved one's organs can aid in grief recovery. Survivors take comfort from the good they have done. Friends and relatives reinforce and praise them for the honor they brought to their loved one. It all helps balance senseless tragedy (Lynda Harrell, donor mother, personal experience; communi-cations with multiple donor survivors).

But, as donor survivors relived their own tragedy during the Mantle cover-age, the pain returned, this time without the reward. Large parts of the public condemned the donation process. Bender took it personally when people at-tacked the organ donor system. "I made that decision. I am part of that system," he said (Bender, personal communication, February 14, 1996).

Then one night, in the midst of the controversy, Mickey Mantle talked to his friend, Roy True. Mantle never considered himself a proper hero. He spoke of the awe he felt for his donor, a man who had saved six lives, and for the donor's family. "Those are the real heroes, Roy," Mantle exclaimed. "Some-body ought to know that!"

"That's where we came up with the slogan," True explained. "Be a hero. Be a donor" (True, personal communication, March 8, 1996). Publicly, offi-cially, and for all time to come, Mickey Mantle sanctioned the selfless courage of the act. An American hero restored Rich and Mary Bender, and thousands like them, to their rightful places of honor.

Activity, too, can aid the healing process. The increased discussion gave donor families chances to speak out positively for donor awareness, whether it was in private conversations, as part of educational efforts, or by staffing volunteer tables at distribution events such as those at the ballparks. To Ardell Richardson, a mother whose son touched the lives of over 100 people through organ and tissue donation, Mantle "gave us all more opportunity to promote the good we made come from our tragedy" (Richardson, personal communication, February 17, 1996).

CONCLUSION

Bob Costas distinguished between Mickey Mantle, the role model, and Mickey Mantle, the hero. "The first, he often was not," he said in his eulogy. "The second he will always be" ("Courage at the End," 1995, p. 79).

In spite of his accomplishments, his fame, his fortune, Mantle's life remained that of a humble, flawed man. He managed to achieve true role model status in death. Mantle demonstrated how to take a grievous loss—his own life—and produce something good: his legacy. He gave something back, in a way that restored balance to what came before. When "donors" are "heroes," they move from passive resource to active contributor. When "donors" are "heroes," more people are likely to declare their wishes before tragedy strikes, more lives are saved, and more survivors are able to balance their grief.

Mickey Mantle saved his best for his ninth inning. He died a model of action in the face of adversity, leaving those who mourn a way to recover.

REFERENCES

Anders, J. (1995, August 16). In the end, Mickey Mantle was a real hero. *The Dallas Morning News*, p. 1C.

Anderson, D. (1995, June 8). Hard-fought sobriety late in life couldn't cure Mantle. *American Statesman* (Austin, TX), p. 1.

Bavley, A. (1995, June 8). No "playing God" with transplants. *Kansas City Star*, p. A-1.

Bray, S. (1995, June 18). Did Mantle deserve his transplant? *The Olympian* (Seattle, WA).

Brown, D. (1995, June 9). Mantle gets liver transplant. *Review Journal* (Las Vegas, NV).

Burke, C. (1995, June 9). "Blame" luck, not celebrity. *New York Post*, p. 8.

Coleman, J., & Spaeth, M. (1996, Spring). Transplanting the Mick's liver. *The Public Relations Strategist, 2*(1), 53.

Courage at the end of the road. (1995, August 28). *People*, 79.

Doctors say misleading media about Mantle justified. (1995, August 20). *Daily Progress* (Jacksonville, TX), p. 6.

Duskey, G. (1995, June 10). Who are we to say no to living? *Alexandria Daily Town Talk* (Alexandria, VA).

Emerson, J. (1995, June 9). While Mantle gets new liver, Jensen waits. *Register Star* (Rockford, IL), p. B1.

Experts: No favoritism for Yankee great's transplant. (1995, June 12). *Boston Herald*.

Goodbye to no. 7. (1995, August 16). *The Dallas Morning News*, p.1A.

Goodstein, L. (1995, June 10). Mantle: One strike & you're out? *Washington Post*, D1, D4.

Gregg, B. G. (1995, June 9). Mantle gets liver—but no favoritism. *Cincinnati Enquirer*.

Hansen, G. (1995, June 9). Yanks' no. 7 will always be a hero. *Arizona Daily Star* (Tucson, AZ), p. 1C.

Herskowitz, M. (1995, August 15). All my Octobers. *Reporter News* (Abilene, TX).

Hoffer, R. (1995, August 21). Mickey Mantle. *Sports Illustrated, 83*(8), 25ff.

Hopper, K. (1995, August 15). "The Mick" mementos. *Star-Telegram* (Fort Worth, Texas), p. 1, Business Section.

Kochik, R. (1995, June 24). Mantle would have had the same wait for a liver here. *Philadelphia Inquirer*.

Lacy, T. (1995, June 9). Mantle transplant angers donors. *Nevada Sun* (Las Vegas), p. 3A.

Lawler, A. (1995, June 11). And now for Mick's leverage. *Idaho Statesman* (Boise, ID), p. 1C.

LeBreton, G. (1995, June 9). Protest over Mantle getting liver transplant unfounded. *Star-Telegram* (Fort Worth, TX), p. 1.

Levy, D. (1995, October 20). Transplant decisions are based on need, not celebrity. *USA Today*, p. 3D.

Lewis, C. (1995, August 27). Be a superstar in the game of life and join Mickey's team. *The Dallas Morning News*, p. 5J.

Lieber, J. (1995, October 18). Mick's friends mourn with fond memories. *USA Today*, p. 1C.

Lifelong drinkers must meet the test to get liver. (1995, July 8). *The Tennessean* (Nashville, TN).

Lipsyte, R. (1995, June 9). Commentary. *Daily News*, p. 1.

Liver patients express gladness, concern about Mantle's short wait for a transplant. (1995, June 9). *The Courier-News* (Elgin, IL), pp. A1, A6.

Lyon, B. (1995, June 9). Body and spirit, a salvage job. *Philadelphia Inquirer*.

Manning, A. (1995, October 20). Mantle's family sets up organ donor program. *USA Today*, p. 3D.

Mantle foundation says 3 million donor cards distributed to date. (1995, September 8). *Transplant News*, p. 2.

Mantle is weaker but wiser. (1995, July 12). *The Dallas Morning News*, p. 1B.

Mantle lucky to get on list. (1995, June 9). *Tampa Tribune*, p. 10, Nation World Section.

Mantle, M. (1994, April 18). Time in a bottle. *Sports Illustrated*, 80, 66-76.

Mantle to promote organ donations. (1995, June 12).*The Dallas Morning News*, p. 13A.

Mantle's speedy transplant raises ethical points. (1995, June 9). *USA Today*, p. 3C.

Mantle's surgeon discounts assistant's gloomy comment. (1995, July 9). *Star-Telegram* (Fort Worth, TX), p. 19, Metro Section.

Mantle's wife bares agony over life with Mick and the bottle. (1995, June 9). *New York Post*, p. 75.

Matthews, W. (1995, June 11). It's sick when a doctor has to say "sorry" for saving a life. *New York Post*, p. 5.

Mickey Mantle: 1931–1995. (1995, August 14). *The Dallas Morning News*, p. 1A.

Mickey Mantle defined the word "hero" for a generation. (1995, August 14). *Gazette* (Texarkana, TX).

Mickey Mantle's liver is on readers' minds. (1995, July 7). *Free Press* (Detroit, MI), p. 7F.

Myerson, A. R. (1995, June 13). Reality strikes home for Mantle family. *Arizona Republic* (Phoenix, AZ).

Nation mourns death of baseball hero Mickey Mantle. (1995, August 15). *Transplant News*, *5*(15), p. 1.

Operation goes "well," docs say. (1995, June 9). *New York Daily News*, p. 7.

Poirot, C. (1995, June 13). Mantle transplant spotlights donation. *Fort Worth Star Telegram*, p. 3.

Reynolds, B. (1995, June 11). As Mantle knows now, alcohol abuse leaves no prisoners. *Journal* (Providence, RI), p. 26.

Sherrington, K. (1995, June 20). Family pulls together around Mantle during ordeal. *The Dallas Morning News*, p. B5.

Sherrington, K., & Rogers, P. (1995, August 14). Baseball great Mickey Mantle dead at 63. *The Dallas Morning News*, p. 1A.

Some exploit edge in organ "shopping." (1995, June 9). *Atlanta Constitution*.

Sorensen, T. (1995, June 8). Mantle was life in 1950s *American* (Odessa, TX), p. 18.

Thompson, J. (1995, June 17). Viewpoint letters. *Los Angeles Times*, p. 17.

Stein, G. (1995, June 9). Everyone's an expert on Mantle's liver. *Sun-Sentinel* (Fort Lauderdale, FL), p. C2.

Strauss, J. (1995, August 14). Mantle carried Yankees, heavy burden of personal tragedy. *The Lufkin Daily News*, p. 2B.

Vecsey, L. (1995, June 9). Mantle still can be hero. *The Phoenix Gazette*, p. D1.

Weiss, J. (1995, August 18). "Mickey's team": A ballplayer's legacy. (1995, August 18). *The Dallas Morning News*, p. 27A.

Wood, T. (1995, August 18). Weatherford watch. *Democrat* (Weatherford, TX), p. 3.

Wrolstad, M. (1995, July 12). Give and take situation. *The Dallas Morning News*, p. 25A.

Yeagley, L. (1994). *Grief Recovery*, Charlotte, MI: Author. (5201 N. Stine Road, Charlotte, MI 48813).

Part Three

Terrorism and Political Action

The third section of the book examines the special impact of terrorist acts and politically instigated deaths upon the communities which fall victim to intentional destruction.

When the Murrah Building in Oklahoma City exploded on Wednesday, April 19, 1995, taking 168 lives, Americans suddenly were forced to acknowledge that terrorism was not a misfortune that happened only outside its borders. When Americans sought a perpetrator among international terrorists, they found none. Instead, the perpetrator(s) were fellow citizens. The heinousness of the crime, reflected in the number of children murdered while playing at their daycare center, is well documented in Chapter 9. Karen Sitterle and Robin Gurwitch, who continue to be involved in intervention efforts in Oklahoma City, paint a picture of bereavement and overwhelming grief tempered by the outreach efforts of thousands of professionals, volunteers, and rescue workers. The description of memorialization and rituals is a moving and significant part of their account.

The Remembrance Day Bombing in Enniskillen, Northern Ireland, killed 11 people and injured over 60 in November 1987. David Bolton, an Enniskillen social worker, depicts the background of disaster in the context of conflict in Northern Ireland. He introduces several important concepts related to community recovery, including belonging, communality, resilience, and competency in coping. During this tragedy, the most significant source of support was the churches themselves. Bolton illustrates the concept of "emergent leaders" with the story of a bereaved father whose speech to all of Northern Ireland's citizens set the tone for subsequent communal response. This bombing occurred within the context of historical intercommunity strife; healing occurred within a cultural context that relied on the use of group ritual and the desire for belongingness.

The final chapter in this section fits less comfortably under the heading of terrorism and political actions; it is about a single death in an isolated community whose very existence is threatened by government actions and politics largely outside of its control. The unforeseen natural death of a 30-year-old member of an Israeli kibbutz in the Jordan Valley in the spring of 1994 becomes a symbol of the confusion and uncertainty of the existence of kibbutz members. Amia Lieblich, a well-known Israeli mental health researcher and author, describes the culture of the Kibbutz Gilgal as well as the meaning of the death of its member, Mali, for her group survivors. Her death shook the growing sense of impassivity within the kibbutz and motivated its members to reorganize their lives at the very same time that they were forced to deal with a future reality that differed dramatically from their original hopes and expectations. Mali's death has significance in the context of ongoing personal, communal, and national processes. In this chapter, Lieblich concentrates on the role of death as a catalyst for change of a communal vision of the future—a future that is transient, uncertain, and fluid.

Figure 9.1 Gifts of stuffed animals, flowers, and flags are laid against a fallen slab of concrete from the Alfred P. Murrah Federal Building in Oklahoma City a few days after the April 19, 1995 bombing. Written upon the concrete are the words, "Bless the Children + the Innocent." (Personal photo of the author.)

Chapter 9

The Terrorist Bombing in Oklahoma City

Karen A. Sitterle and Robin H. Gurwitch

It was the most deadly terrorist bombing in American history. On Wednesday, April 19, 1995, a blast from thousands of pounds of fuel oil and fertilizer ripped through the nine-story Alfred P. Murrah Federal Building in Oklahoma City in an instant, tearing a huge crater from the street to the roof. A red-orange fireball lit the sky as the north side of the building dissolved. What remained of the building looked monstrous, spitting cable and concrete onto the plaza below while gas, smoke, and dust filled the sky. Layer after layer of the building collapsed and pancaked one onto the other as ceilings crashed onto the floors below. Desks, chairs, file cabinets, refrigerators, and potted plants were thrown into the street in a tangle of wires, steel, and concrete. Toys from the children's daycare center located on the second floor scattered everywhere. Reverberations from the blast shattered windows throughout the city; and glass fell like sharp rain over whole sections of the city, literally covering the streets for blocks and blocks throughout the downtown area. Parking meters were ripped from the ground, roofs collapsed, and metal doors twisted around themselves. Cars parked on the street crumbled, flipped, and burst into flames. Hundreds of frantic people streamed out of nearby office buildings, with blood-matted hair, cut faces, and clothes in bloody shreds. There was no screaming; just quiet terror showed in their faces.

All over Oklahoma City, people felt the force of a blast. Some thought it was a sonic boom; others, a gas explosion. Those who were trained to respond to an emergency—doctors, nurses, police, firefighters—dropped whatever they were doing and rushed to the scene. As police and firefighters located the site of the explosion, the scale of the devastation astounded them. Gradually, there was the sickening recognition that a daycare center was located in the building.

"Hundreds of individual acts of heroism and initiative—dealing with grim life-or-death decisions—were carried out in the first hour" (Irving, 1995, p. 34). Scores of untrained individuals swarmed to the building in an attempt to help while hundreds of people mobilized at the bomb site in search of family members and friends. About 90 minutes after the blast, an alarm sounded that there was a second bomb, and everyone was ordered to leave the building. Some rescuers, in the middle of extricating victims, at first refused to retreat. They agonized over leaving trapped victims, many of whom pleaded with them not to go; but they were ordered to get out a second time. This hiatus in the search lasted for about 45 minutes before rescuers could return to the victims they felt they had abandoned. Several had died.

Out of the chaos emerged an organized rescue effort. For example, a makeshift triage site was quickly set up at the building, and victims were tagged as minor, moderate, critical, or dead. The firemen brought out so many dead that a temporary morgue was established. Rescuers reported that they kept laying one dead child beside the next. Within 30 minutes of the explosion, local hospitals activated their emergency plans and began receiving hundreds of casualties. As the first wave of victims arrived in a fleet of ambulances, police cars, and vans, and personal cars driven by victims themselves, more staff were called in because a second wave of victims seemed inevitable. By the end of the day, four local hospitals had received 282 victims. Meanwhile, families who had members working in the Murrah building began trying to locate them. Soon, hospitals found themselves handling not only casualties but also desperate relatives.

At 7:00 p.m. that first night, a 15-year-old girl was also found alive and freed from the rubble. She was to be the last survivor removed from the building. By evening, there was no accurate count of the missing, and the worst estimates put the number in the hundreds. In desperation, families of the missing began to gather at designated centers combing lists of those hospitalized in the hope of finding loved ones. As it became increasingly clear that an organized way to account for the missing was needed, a family assistance center to collect information about the missing was established by the medical examiner's office.

On the second day, teams of rescue specialists from other parts of the country arrived and began to work alongside local firemen and law enforcement. Rescuers, using K-9 search dogs and high-tech optical and listening devices, worked down through the layers of pancaked floors trying to detect signs of life. Literally thousands of firefighters from 57 fire departments around the country worked with Oklahoma firefighters in the tedious and painstaking search and body recovery process. Working around the clock, a cadre of 60 firefighters eventually increased to 250 individuals per shift. Searching for survivors was a dangerous and increasingly heartbreaking job. Much of the digging was done by hand for fear of upsetting the building's precarious balance atop layers of crushed debris. Rescuers also had to contend with lightning, heavy rains, strong winds, bomb scares, and concern about building movement. Forty-eight hours later, as search crews kept working, optimism was fading. By the end of this period, there was a change in the task at hand: the search for survivors became a drawn-out search for bodies. The rescuers, however, never gave up hope of locating someone alive. The frustration of not finding any more survivors, however, was offset by the fact that the professional rescuers performed their operations without any loss of life or serious injury.

On days 3–5, debris removal became extremely slow-going. Cranes were used to lift the massive pieces of shattered concrete gingerly to avoid crushing any victims and to shore up the structure of the building to make it more safe to conduct recovery work. For the next 10 days, buckets of rubble were carried out by firefighters at a rate of 100–350 tons a day. By the 16th day of the search, the operation began to slow down. Although rescuers knew that victims remained buried near the blast crater, they had to halt their search because removal of the bodies became too dangerous.

Disaster experts had predicted that, due to the nature of the injuries sustained in the blast, no more than 80% of the victims would be identified. In fact, all were. Remains were taken first to a temporary morgue at the site. Twenty-four people, including 16 specialists from the U.S. Army, worked in this morgue. They used fingerprints, dental charts, and full-body X rays to identify bodies. DNA testing proved crucial in some of the most difficult cases (Irving, 1995).

Sixteen days after the blast, when the search effort concluded, the workers had removed 450 tons of debris. Every piece had been sifted for evidence of remains and criminal evidence. At that time, it was thought that two bodies remained in the core. These could not be extricated without endangering the entire building. It turned out, however, that there were three bodies remaining which could not be removed until after the implosion.

The Breath of Disaster

The magnitude and horror of this act of terrorism was unprecedented in America's history. A total of 842 persons were injured or killed as a direct result of the bombing. Of these 842, 168 persons were killed, including 19 children, most from a daycare center located in the heart of the Murrah Federal Building. Ninety-eight (59%) of those killed in the blast and 140 (21%) of those injured were federal government employees. Three (2%) of those killed and 126 (19%) of those injured in the blast were state government employees. Four hundred and forty-two persons were treated in area hospitals: 83 were admitted and 359 were treated and released from emergency rooms. An additional 233 individuals were treated in private physicians' offices. Four hundred and sixty-two people were left homeless (Oklahoma State Department of Health (OSDH),

1996). The bomb also damaged 312 buildings and businesses in a one-square-mile area. Damage estimates were expected to exceed $510 million due to damage to the federal building, adjacent businesses, and loss of life.

Nineteen children died in the explosion (15 children in the daycare center and 4 children visiting the building with relatives). Only five children in the daycare center survived the blast; all five were injured and hospitalized. A YMCA daycare center adjacent to the Murrah building was also severely damaged, injuring 52 children and 9 of the daycare staff (OSDH, 1996). Thirty children were orphaned and 219 children lost one parent. Many more children, both locally and across the nation, were also indirectly affected by this event due to the extensive live coverage by the media. All over America, children asked questions and reported fears and difficulty sleeping. These staggering statistics do not even begin to document how many lives were ripped apart and scarred forever by this tragedy.

RISK FACTORS IN POSTTRAUMA RESPONSES

It has been well documented that there are risk factors that place survivors and survivor groups at higher probability of experiencing posttraumatic stress, complicated bereavement reactions, and chronic trauma-related psychological problems (Smith & North, 1993). In using the Oklahoma City bombing as the point of reference for community survivorship, several risk factors emerge as important dimensions to determine the full extent and severity of the victims' emotional reaction and the course of their emotional recovery. These factors include the nature of the act, severity of exposure, the length and success of rescue efforts, and involvement in the criminal justice system (Lord, 1996; Rando, 1993; Redmond, 1996; Weisaeth, 1994).

The literature examining the role of traumatic exposure is definitive. That is, regardless of the traumatic stressor, whether it stems from war, physical or sexual assault, or a natural disaster, it has been shown conclusively that dose-response is the strongest predictor of who will likely be most affected (Young, Ford, Ruzek, Friedman, & Gusman, 1997). People directly exposed to danger and life-threatening situations are at greatest risk for emotional impact. Thus, the greater the perceived life threat and the greater the sensory exposure (i.e., the more one sees distressing sights, smells distressing odors, hears distressing sounds, or is physically injured), the more likely that posttraumatic stress will be manifest and the more profound the experienced losses will be. In terms of group survivorship, the severity of exposure includes not only an overwhelming threat to one's own life but also the extent to which the event touched the lives of family members. For example, if a child's life is threatened by a traumatic event, the parents are similarly affected, as though they were also victims of the threat (Rando, 1993). Additionally, if a family member is killed or injured in a traumatic incident, other family members are likely to be at increased risk for psychological distress. They respond as if the injury has been to themselves, and they face complicated bereavement issues associated with traumatic loss.

A community-wide traumatic incident, such as this terrorist bombing, is by its very nature sudden, unexpected, and violent. It occurs suddenly and without warning, producing violent injury and death. Victims are unable to grasp the full implications of the loss or come to terms with the reality of the situation: it is inexplicable, unbelievable, and incomprehensible. Feelings of control, predictability, and security, and the assumptions, expectations, and beliefs upon which the mourner has based his or her life are violated in an instant (Rando, 1993).

The nature and severity of the psychological impact of the Oklahoma City bombing involve a complex interaction of the above factors that combine uniquely for each individual or survivor group. However, an understanding of these factors can serve as a useful guide for mental health professionals in understanding the nature and severity of the survivors' reactions and in addressing the emotional needs of survivor groups. Each of these factors contributed to the increased risk of emotional difficulties that were seen in survivors, the families of those who died, and other victim or survivorship groups.

The Oklahoma City bombing involved a massive loss of life, including that of many young children. These traumatic deaths further involved violence, mutilation, and destruction on a level unprecedented in the United States. Sudden death arouses intense feelings of horror, shock, helplessness, and vulnerability. It has also been noted that the greater the violence, destruction, or brutality, the greater the survivor's/mourner's anxiety, fear, violation, and powerlessness as well as feelings of anger, guilt, self-blame, and shattered assumptions are likely to be (Rando, 1993). Mutilation, in particular, appears to distress survivors by conjuring up images of the suffering the victims presumably experienced; this results in more complicated bereavement and mourning (Rando, 1993).

The rescue and recovery effort at the bombing, as previously described, was long and painstaking. No more survivors were found after the first day of the bombing, yet the recovery and identification of bodies went on for over 2 weeks. Thus, the task of body recovery, identification, and transport involved prolonged contact with mass death and was a gruesome process. This exposure to traumatic death presents a significant psychological stress that can make victims of rescuers (Ursano, Fullerton, & McCaughey, 1994). Viewing, smelling, touching, and experiencing the grotesque over days and weeks resulted in particular difficulties for this survivor group of rescue workers. Repeatedly, rescuers expressed tremendous guilt about victims they were unable to save because they were unable to reach them in time.

The prolonged process of recovery and identification kept the families whose loved ones were unaccounted for in a state of emotional limbo. Waiting compounded the trauma and distress as families were left to contemplate their worst fears and fantasies. Without the closure of having the death confirmed, families were unable to begin grieving. When bodies are not recovered, this closure is never quite complete.

The bombing of the Oklahoma City federal building was an act of terrorism and violent crime, not a natural disaster or an accident. It was a calculated, premeditated act of mass murder and injury of hundreds of individuals. Its traumatic impact was greatly magnified by the fact that it occurred by human design. It was sudden and unpredictable and aimed at people who are in a defenseless position. Such willful and malicious acts of violence or murder are associated with more profound emotional wounds in addition to the physical wounds suffered (Bard & Sangrey, 1996). Additionally, victims often find themselves involved in an ongoing and prolonged manner with the criminal justice system. Their involvement can further aggravate and exacerbate emotional reactions and can lengthen the recovery process. Lengthy preparations interfere with the natural process of healing by keeping the traumatic event and associated losses in the forefront and by continually re-evoking the memories and feelings of the bombing. Thus, involvement in the legal system carries with it a large degree of additional stress and secondary traumatization for survivors and for family members.

THE VICTIM AND SURVIVOR GROUPS IN OKLAHOMA CITY

In a split second, thousands of individuals, the Oklahoma City community, and the nation became victims of the terrorist bombing in Oklahoma City. The effects of the bombing were widespread and devastating, creating a ripple effect that directly damaged the lives of thousands of individuals. For example, although Oklahoma City and its surrounding communities number close to 400,000 citizens, a survey of schoolchildren found that almost all of the children knew at least one person who was killed or injured in the explosion. The effects of such community-wide traumatic events extend well beyond immediate victims to include their families, their communities, and those who have responded as helpers. When there are few degrees of separation in the community, the mental health needs are intensified, and there is a collective sense of loss, associated reactions related to trauma, and disruption of routine. All become part of the "trauma and disaster community" (Ursano, Fullerton, & McCaughey, 1994).

Following the Oklahoma City bombing, different victim or survivor groups slowly emerged to form the traumatized community. These included: (a) individuals who were directly involved in the blast and survived; (b) individuals who lost a loved one in the blast, but were not directly involved in the blast itself; (c) children who survived, whose parents were victims, or who were affected as members of the community; (d) families and co-workers of those involved in the blast; (e) rescue workers, volunteers, and mental health professionals; (f) the Oklahoma City community; and (g) the nation as a whole.

The Oklahoma City bombing represented a direct attack against the federal government and, in essence, an attack against the nation. Also, with the capabilities of mass communication, the eyes of the nation were focused on the horror of the bombing; many watched it unfold live in front of their eyes. Thus, the bombing not only affected those directly involved and the stricken Oklahoma City community but reverberated throughout the country. Each survivor group had unique needs due to its particular experience of loss and trauma.

INTERVENTIONS WITH SURVIVOR GROUPS

Help for survivor groups is best understood in the context of when, where, and with whom interventions take place (Young et al., 1997). These dimensions can be used to guide effective clinical interventions following disaster. The temporal dimension of "when" may be broken down into the emergency phase, the postimpact phase, and the restoration or recovery phase. It is important to consider the point in time at which the intervention is done, where it is done, as well as the particular survivor group served. Mental health interventions need to provide phase-appropriate mental health services to survivor groups. Thus, it is important to reevaluate constantly the changing and unique needs of survivor groups and communities over time in the months and years of postdisaster recovery.

Support for Families with Missing Loved Ones:
The Compassion Center

In the hours following the blast, families of the 300 people thought to be missing silently gathered in a state of anguish and shock at the First Christian Church. They were searching for answers and information. As rescue workers attempted to formulate lists of those reported to have been in the federal building, family members faced grim requests for detailed descriptions, photographs, and medical/dental records of their missing loved ones. Although chaos initially permeated the church, a multiagency effort was quickly organized to provide accurate information about the rescue effort, to facilitate the efforts of the medical examiner's office, and to provide emotional support and assistance. This site became known as the Compassion Center (Sitterle, 1995). For 16 days, until nearly all of the death notifications of the 116 missing could be completed, the Compassion Center provided sanctuary for those keeping vigil and was the site for eventual communication of the heartbreaking news when a body was recovered and positively identified. Day by day, families waited in hope. Unfortunately, all came to the same grim end: their loved one had not survived.

As a highly complex operation, the Compassion Center involved numerous emergency and community organizations working together to respond to the overwhelming physical and psychological trauma for those with a missing loved one(s). During the days following the bombing, literally thousands of volunteers and hundreds of family members passed through the center. The medical examiner's office, the National Guard, the military, police, clergy, the

American Red Cross, the Department of Veterans Affairs Oklahoma Medical Center, the Department of Veterans Affairs Emergency Management Preparedness Office, the Department of Veteran's Affairs National Center for PTSD, and the Salvation Army integrated and worked in a coordinated fashion to deliver immediate services. Mental health services were provided by volunteer mental health professionals with the American Red Cross. Nearly 400 mental health professionals a day worked at the multifaceted and anguishing task of providing support and solace as well as assisting with death notification to the families.

Mental health operations were guided by a number of principles (Myers, 1994). First, it was important to provide a safe and protective environment for families to share their pain with people who cared. Second, a sense of order, predictability, and structure were provided through leadership and communication at a time of overwhelming chaos and helplessness. Third, every effort was made to empower families by providing information in a truthful, respectful, and nonintrusive manner. The third principle also involved treating family members as normal people experiencing an abnormal event (Myers, 1994). Fourth, an understanding of the emotional climate and how it differed from the experience of an outsider watching on television was at the heart of the crisis intervention response at the Compassion Center. As optimism waned outside the center and the rest of the country began slowly realizing that there was virtually no hope for more survivors, the family members continued to hold vigil under what appeared to be a blanket of denial against the realization of their worst fear. It seemed critical for families to remain hopeful, to be vigilant, and not to abandon or betray their loved one until the death notification was confirmed.

Mental health services were organized into four primary functions: support services, family services, death notification, and stress management. Each mental health function was headed by a coordinator, who reported to an overall mental health supervisor overseeing the mental health services at the Compassion Center. All coordinating staff had cellular phones to facilitate communication and quick decision making.

Support Services   The convergence of volunteers, motivated but often untrained or unsuited to the job at hand, is a universal phenomenon in disasters (Myers, 1994). Thousands of individuals called or simply arrived at the Compassion Center to offer assistance, creating an overwhelming logistical problem. Support services were developed to devise a system to ensure that qualified professionals were selected, to prevent unauthorized persons from entering the center, and to handle many of the pragmatic aspects that arose. This tragedy brought together volunteers who had never before worked together, had varying skill levels, and were unfamiliar with the procedures of the many organizations and agencies working at the Compassion Center. Mental health professionals were thus screened for ability and experience before they were placed in any position.

Given the stressful nature of providing death notifications, professionals with Ph.D.'s and M.D.'s, or those with extensive counseling experience with death, grief, and bereavement were selected to participate as members of the death notification teams. Individuals with debriefing experience, particularly training in critical incident stress debriefing (CISD) techniques, were recruited to staff the stress management/debriefing services. An attempt was also made to use mental health professionals from the Oklahoma City community and to place them in key coordinator positions. An extensive database was also created using information about each professional's areas of specialty, expertise, address, hours available to volunteer, and phone numbers. A schedule was then created each day to provide coverage for all mental health functions for what was often an 18-hour day. Such coverage usually involved 200–350 mental health professionals daily.

In order to ensure that only authorized persons were entering the center, a complex identification process was developed. All Compassion Center staff and family members wore identification with color-coded name tags. Each service or organization (e.g., clergy, mental health, medical, medical examiner, and media) was identified by a different color. Similarly, family members were designated with a blue dot for next-of-kin or a yellow dot for extended or immediate family members. This identification system allowed both staff and families to locate each other easily when needed. To ensure privacy and safety, the building was secured by the National Guard, the police, and the military. At no time was the media allowed into the building to meet with families; however, a separate area was arranged for the media where regular briefings were made by the medical examiner and other center staff. In this way, families could meet with the media only if and when they chose, outside the center to protect the privacy of other families.

Services in the Family Room   Upon arrival at the Compassion Center, each family was assigned a mental health professional whose function it was to provide an information link between the medical examiner's office and that family. The professional's job was to be aware of the family's whereabouts in case information was needed or became available. These mental health professionals worked 4-hour shifts and up to 2 shifts per day. A 2-hour break between shifts was mandatory. Mental health professionals were briefed prior to a shift as to current developments, problems, and available resources.

A family room was created to provide a meeting area for families to obtain information and support. The goal was to create a safe, protective environment to meet the physical and emotional needs of the families and to prevent intrusions from the press and outside world. An attempt was made to keep families together in a single location where they could provide support to each other and be with families who truly understood their situation. The emotional climate, particularly in the family room, was dominated by a mood of anguished waiting, emotional limbo, rapid change, and, at times, conflicting information. Attempts were made to organize and structure the family room to be responsive to the ever-changing needs of families.

As the days progressed, it became clear that the families used the Compassion Center not only as a place to wait for information but also as a place to gain emotional support and to offer support to others. Families often checked in with each other. They tended to sit in the same areas of the room each day, placing photos and mementos on the tables provided. Families became somewhat agitated if someone inadvertently moved their belongings or if their space was intruded upon in some way. Their tables seemed to provide a small degree of security in their immediate world of chaos and powerlessness. Families in the Compassion Center appeared to develop their own sense of community as they struggled to cope with and comprehend the horror that had befallen them.

The center also became a place for communities around the country to express their support and grief surrounding the bombing. Cards and posters from schoolchildren and individuals from all over the country wallpapered the room with loving support. Flowers sent from strangers decorated the tables set up as a gathering place for the families. Inside this huge room, an area was set up to provide three daily hot meals for workers and family members. A constant supply of donated sandwiches, snacks, sodas, and baked goods were also available to families and staff. An area was established for families to make private phone calls using donated long distance service. Additionally, a cellular phone company donated hundreds of portable phones to families so they could be reached quickly if they left the center to go home or to work.

One corner of the room was set aside as a Children's Corner, filled with stuffed animals, crayons, paints, toys, videotapes, and floor mats. This separate area was also a visible part of the room, allowing children to venture into their own activities but still remain physically close to their caretakers. It allowed parents to take needed time away from their children to deal with their own feelings or to provide assistance to the medical examiner's office. The children's corner was always staffed by a mental health professional with expertise in working with children.

As the days of waiting increased, activities were developed to provide structure, distraction, and opportunities to be physically active for the children. Animals were a part of these healing activities. Local mental health professionals with certified pet therapy animals, including rabbits, a sheltie, a Dalmatian, and an infant spider monkey named "Charlie," staffed the room. Many of the children at the center were withdrawn or hyperactive, feeling as vulnerable as their parents. The opportunity to care for and play with pet therapy animals helped them engage and focus and engendered their sense of control.

Another invaluable intervention for the families was the help of victim advocate, Victoria Cummock, whose husband was murdered in the 1988 terrorist bombing of Pan Am Flight 103. She met with families, offering comfort, support, and her personal experience. She visited homes, read stories to the children, and provided advice to both the mental health staff and rescue officials (Cummock, 1995).

Use of Briefings   A critical feature of family services was the establishment of an ongoing information link with the official rescue effort at the federal building to dispel rumors and provide accurate information. Regular briefings were conducted by the medical examiner's office two or three times a day to provide updates and to answer questions. Additionally, the governor designated a state trooper to address any and all questions from the families. This uniformed representative met frequently with the families to share up-to-date information about the rescue effort. This constant link to the rescue scene had a calming effect on the families and reassured them that every effort was being made to recover their missing loved ones, to address their needs, and to keep them informed.

The Death Notification Process   The notification staff was briefed on specific guidelines before participating in death notifications. One of the most devastating moments for any family is receiving notification of their loved one's death. In an attempt to make this horrific moment more tolerable, systematic death notification procedures using trained staff were established. Proper death notification can be an important tool to support surviving family members and to facilitate the grieving process (Lord, 1996; Young, 1985).

The death notification process was clearly one of the most difficult jobs facing staff, particularly when it involved the loss of a child. The death notification team was headed by two representatives from the medical examiner's office and included a mental health professional and a member of the clergy. All mental health professionals involved in this process were licensed psychologists and psychiatrists trained to identify problems within the notification and to respond appropriately to family members. Another component that was quickly added to each team was the presence of a mental health professional (again, a licensed psychologist/psychiatrist) with specialized training in working with children. As many families had issues related to talking or dealing with their children about the death of their loved one, this team member was a critical addition.

Once a body was recovered and positively identified by the medical examiner's office, the file was transferred to the Compassion Center and protected by the National Guard. The family was then located and discreetly escorted to a quiet, secluded area on a separate floor in the Center. The medical examiner's representative identified himself/herself and the next-of-kin before informing the family that their loved one had been positively identified as dead. After being notified, family members inevitably asked questions such as, "Are you sure?" "How do you know?" and "Did they suffer?" Families responded to the news differently. Many seemed relieved that the wait was finally over; others were stunned; some became hysterical.

The medical examiner's representative responded by explaining how identifications were made and that, in most cases, the deceased had died immediately. Questions about the condition of the body and whether they could view the body were referred to funeral home representatives. The clergy member then offered a brief prayer if requested. Families were then asked to make a number of decisions about funeral home arrangements, when information could be released to the media, and whether they needed assistance in contacting other family members. Finally, the team inquired if the family needed assistance or wished to be left alone. Many families had formed a relationship with a mental health professional who had assisted them in the family room and asked for the individual to be present at the death notification. Several family members later returned to the family room to help other families with the wait and with what was to come.

Stress Management Services for Workers

The scope of human suffering at the Compassion Center was often unimaginable, creating a highly stressful and emotionally charged environment. Given the unique stresses at the center, it was critical to provide stress management services for staff members as a separate function of the overall mental health operation. Noone is immune; mental health professionals can be adversely affected by the stress of their work (Myers, 1994; Mitchell & Dyregrov, 1993). They are also normal people reacting to abnormal events. No one is ever fully prepared for the anguishing tasks and heartbreaking exposure to human suffering that were experienced during those weeks. This service was staffed by a coordinator and other mental health professionals experienced in disaster mental health and critical incident stress debriefing/management (CISD/CISM) techniques (Mitchell & Bray, 1990).

Defusings were frequently employed by staff working at the center. Lasting 20–25 minutes, these sessions are short versions of the more formal debriefing process and are intended for a small group (Young et al., 1997). All mental health and volunteer staff at the center were required to participate in a defusing after serving their shift each day. Defusings were held every hour so that staff could attend when convenient. Structured as a conversation about a particularly distressing event, the defusing contained three main components: introduction of the process, description of each person's role and his/her reactions, and suggestions to protect staff from further harmful effects (Mitchell, 1983). Pamphlets and handouts on stress reduction exercises, coping strategies, and stress management were also provided to staff. Members of the stress management team were also available to address staff difficulties on an individual basis.

Additionally, members of each death notification team had a mandatory defusing immediately following each notification. To further protect these individuals from the extreme stress involved in this duty, no team member was allowed to participate in more than two notifications a day or more than four notifications overall.

Interaction Between Families and Rescue Workers

Another helpful intervention that evolved over time was the interaction between the families and the rescue workers at the federal building. Images of a ribbon held together by a guardian angel pin, a fireman hugging a family member, a child petting a search and rescue dog, and a fire chief searching the building site to find rubble for family members capture the special relationships that developed between families and rescue workers. The courage of the bereaved and the heroism of the rescuers bonded these two groups.

Clearly, one of the most difficult tasks for waiting families was not only having to wait but not being able to help directly with the rescue effort at the federal building. The bomb site was heavily secured by the military and the FBI; only authorized personnel were allowed inside the perimeter at "ground zero." Families were therefore totally dependent upon the efforts of the rescue workers and reports from outside the center on the status of the search. To express their appreciation for the rescue workers, several of the families requested a machine to make ribbons for the firefighters and rescue workers. These families worked long hours fashioning thousands of ribbons held together by guardian angel pins. The purpose of the ribbons was to recognize workers' valor and courage, to provide guidance and support, and to symbolize care and concern for workers' safety and welfare during the dangerous search for bodies. The firefighters were grateful and, in fact, insisted on wearing the ribbons before entering the bombing site. One firefighter was known to have become so upset when he was unable to find his pin that he tore apart his hotel room until he found it.

Several days into the search, families made a formal request to the mental health staff to have some of the firefighters meet personally with them at the center. During the briefing before meeting with the families, the firefighters expressed concerns that the families would be angry and disappointed with them for not having rescued any survivors. Much to their surprise, the families were deeply grateful and gave them a standing ovation when they entered the room. Family members waited to touch the rescue workers, to hug them, to talk with them, and to put a face to those engaged in the search. While deeply emotional, the meeting seemed to be helpful for both the families and the firefighters.

This bond became particularly important when, 14 days into the search and recovery effort, newspapers were delivered one morning with large headline announcing, "All Hope is Gone: The Search is Over." The firefighters were reportedly discontinuing their search, and large machinery was reportedly going to be used to search through the rubble. This news spread like a shock wave through the family room. At this point, many families had still not been notified and became hysterical that the bodies of their missing loved ones would never be recovered. To add to the turmoil, many families visualized the building site as a tomb; the thought of the remains of their loved ones being shoveled by machinery was very disturbing. To address these concerns, mental health staff arranged an emergency briefing for families to meet with the governor, the fire chief, and the police commissioner to discuss how important decisions were being made about the direction of the rescue effort. Mental health professionals consulted with officials prior to their meeting with the families and encouraged them to share information in a straightforward, truthful fashion, even though to do so was quite difficult (Cummock, 1996).

For rescue workers from around the country, the search for casualties, not survivors, became increasingly more disturbing. Even rescue dogs were reported to be "depressed" and had adverse reactions to finding so many dead bodies. What appeared to make their efforts all the more difficult was the loss of so many children. In addition to the supportive work and the defusings at the Compassion Center, many of the rescue squads made visits to the relocated YMCA daycare center. Here they were able to interact with injured children. The children needed to interact with the rescue workers, the firefighters, and their dogs as much as the adults and animals needed the contact with them. Many of the men left with tears in their eyes. They stated that the visits helped them to feel rejuvenated and better able to handle the emotional roller-coaster they had been experiencing.

Mental health professionals learned an important lesson from these experiences. Although the survivors and victims of a terrorist act may be one of the more obvious groups in need of services, those working at the scene are deeply affected as well. The need for contact with survivors, the families of the dead, and young children seems as important to the grieving process for rescue workers as is their contact with mental health professionals. Furthermore, the contact with these heroes of the hour appeared to aid in the grieving and coping process of those directly affected by a sudden traumatic incident of this magnitude.

Services for Children

The loss of so many children and their families' anguish brought home most vividly the horror of the Oklahoma City terrorist bombing. The darkest part of the Oklahoma tragedy lies in the wreckage of the Federal building day care center. If the random and senseless destruction of a government building shows a nation how vulnerable it is, the random murder of so many innocent children at one time and in one place reveals how deep the pain can be.

If there were to be a bright side to the horror of the bombing, it was the survival of the children in the YMCA daycare center next door to the Alfred P. Murrah Federal building. With the force of the blast, all the windows in the adjacent building were shattered, metal doors came unhinged and crumpled, and the ceiling rained down on the children below. Staff quickly evacuated the infants and young children in their care. Both the staff and children suffered multiple cuts and bruises, many needing attention at area hospitals. Fortunately, no one died or suffered serious or life-threatening injuries.

The children, parents, and staff of the YMCA quickly became their own survivors group, bonded together by their shared experiences following the bombing of the Murrah building. Mental health professionals from the University of

Oklahoma Health Sciences Center contacted the Oklahoma Office of Child Care to see if any services were needed. Within a few days of the disaster, mental health professionals were at the new location for the daycare facility at a YMCA several miles from the bomb site. Although still within Oklahoma City, the center was relatively isolated from other buildings and was surrounded by trees.

Despite the move to a more ideal environment, symptoms associated with trauma were evident in all these children. The age of each child appeared to affect how each child reacted to the trauma. Specifically, the parents of infants and infant care staff reported more sleep difficulties, more clingy behavior, and more difficulty with soothing and consoling a crying infant. In the toddler room, children also showed these behaviors as well as a heightened response to loud noises and more irritability. The increased startle response was particularly problematic for these very young children. Moreover, their new room in the YMCA was located directly below the YMCA weight room, and each time a member dropped weights in the room above, it produced a loud noise in the toddler room below. Mental health professionals noted a startle followed by a brief freeze response in both the children and the staff. Many of the children cried following the pounding noise from above. Parents also reported a change in affect in some of the children, particularly a more restricted emotional demeanor. One parent, for example, described her toddler by stating, "the sunshine has gone out of her eyes." These characteristics are consistent with posttraumatic stress responses and symptomatology in young children following exposure to a traumatic event (Pynoos & Nader, 1990).

In children between 3 and 5 years of age, other behaviors consistent with posttraumatic stress difficulties were also observed. Regressive behaviors such as a return to a pacifier and toileting accidents were noted. These young victims also displayed more separation anxiety and sleep disturbances. Parents reported that many of the children no longer slept in their own beds, preferring to sleep with their parents instead. At the daycare center, many children were unable to rest and had problems napping. Others would only lie down if a staff member remained near their cot. Staff also reported increased clinging behaviors. Posttraumatic play was evident in almost all children in this age group. Examples included repeated play with police, fire, and rescue hats and riding on toy motorcycles.

Startle responses were similarly observed in the older children. As the Oklahoma City community and the nation grieved over the smallest victims of the bombing, older children appeared to find solace and comfort in the fact that the children from the adjacent YMCA escaped with relatively minor physical injuries. Gifts for the daycare center as well as individual gifts for the children began pouring into the YMCA. Along with the gifts came "famous" visitors, TV cameras, and photographers. The bright lights and flashes of the media distressed many children. On the advice of the mental health professionals, much media attention was discontinued. In addition, unfortunately, the bombing was followed by a series of severe thunderstorms in the Oklahoma City area. Many of the parents reported startle reactions and emotional upset in their older children during the storms.

Children in the 3 to 5 year age group had fairly well developed verbal skills On several occasions, the children were seen and heard discussing the bombing and comparing their scars and injuries. They voiced questions about what happened, but often supplied erroneous information such as, "I got hurt; the bad man shot me." Similarly, some children expressed concerns that the blast would reoccur. Children had to be reassured that the walls of the new YMCA center were strong and would not fall and that their new room did not have lots of windows and glass (many of the children's injuries were due to shattered glass). However, this reassurance did not allay all the children's fears; noted one child: "the room still has a ceiling that can fall."

Staff members also were not immune to the effects of the bombing. Although they responded with courage and caring to their young charges at the time of the blast, they were also emotionally distressed by the terrorism. Staff reported difficulties sleeping, traumatic dreams, lability of emotions, irritability, trouble concentrating, and rumination about the bombing. Many reported a lack of interest in pleasurable activities and difficulty focusing on their work for extended periods of time.

To address the needs of the YMCA staff and children, mental health professionals from Oklahoma University Health Services Center were present on a daily basis for several months following the bombing. They held debriefings for parents of the children to allow parents to discuss their concerns and provided information about children's and parents' responses to trauma. Parents were also given information and practical suggestions about how to help their children and themselves cope with the immediate aftermath of this disaster. Therapists were also present in each of the children's daycare rooms. They played with the children, aided the staff, and provided support for each area of the YMCA. They held debriefing sessions with the older children. They gave children many opportunities to talk (and to play) about what happened and what they thought about the events. They led children on walks through the YMCA and had them hit the walls and feel how strong they were. If a child became extremely upset during the day, therapists helped the child and staff.

Additionally, debriefing sessions (both individual and group) were held for the YMCA staff. These sessions enabled staff to voice their thoughts and feelings, including those they were unable to share with their family. Staff members were given individual "minisessions" throughout the day to support their efforts to cope.

An interesting group dynamic evolved during the first few weeks after the bombing. Several staff members were not at the downtown site at the time of the blast. Thus, a sense of "we" and "they" appeared to develop between the two groups. Staff involved in the bombing did not want to share their experiences with staff not involved and stated that only those directly affected could "understand." They developed their own support group that became extremely important to several families. They looked to each other for support and confirmation of their feelings and ideas, but felt somewhat isolated from those who had not experienced the disaster.

Their group identification was also separate from those families who lost children in the federal building. In the first few months following the disaster, many of these families expressed frustration and anger that only the children from the federal building daycare center were receiving attention, monies, and gifts. They believed that their families also were entitled to all that was bestowed on families from the federal building. The families of children from the YMCA daycare center formed a close group. By the first anniversary of the bombing, many of the children had relocated their daycare arrangements. However, at the reunion of the YMCA families, the majority of the families attended the event. These shared beliefs and the shared bombing experience created a close-knit survivors group that had continued to function, albeit on an informal level, for 2 years after the bombing.

Group Support From Outside Oklahoma

Not only in Oklahoma, but all over the United States, schoolchildren reacted to the tragedy in what seemed to be an exercise in national compassion and support for the victims and the rescue workers. Children were encouraged to send messages to Oklahoma and hundreds of thousands of letters and drawings poured in to show their support. For example, one wrote: "Dear Governor Keating, I am five years old and this is my favorite stuffed animal. I thought you might know a little boy or girl who needs it more than I do. I send it with love" (Irving, 1995, p. 128). Locally, many schoolchildren also sent their support to victims and rescue workers. One eighth grade class in Oklahoma City, for example, sent lunch sacks to the rescuers, filled with snacks and messages, and a banner. Several days later, four ATF agents walked into their classroom to express their thanks. They told the children they had been encouraged by the cards and had come to say thank you. The children jumped to their feet and burst into cheers.

Their letters and drawings offering support and comfort, placed on rescuers' pillows between shifts and at the bombing site, inspired the firefighters, police officers, and civilian volunteers throughout the toughest days of the rescue operation. Jon Hansen, the assistant fire chief of Oklahoma City, expressed the coming together of our nation's children:

Possibly the brightest spot of all was the support offered by America's children. Their cards, buttons, candy, and letters poured in. We placed these treasures at the disaster site, in the rest areas, and in meeting places. When we felt down or started losing hope, we had only to look around and the spirit of the nation's children would be with us. (Ross & Myers, 1996)

RITUALS FOR SURVIVORS AND FAMILIES
OF THE DECEASED

Rituals are at the core of human experience. Many universal forms of ritual allow emotions associated with grief and terror to be directed into activities that unify survivors, reaffirm life, and promote a sense of faith in the healing process. Ceremonies, vigils, celebrations, and other forms of ritual give people an opportunity to connect at a time when they feel disconnected by affirming identity, relatedness, and the social values of goodness and justice (Young, Sitterle, & Myers, 1996). Because these have an important healing power for survivors of a disaster and the grieving survivors of those that died (Myers, 1994; Rando, 1993), mental health professionals can play an important role in providing leadership and consultation to individuals, groups, and public entities regarding appropriate ritual or anniversary activities. The following rituals, some organized and others spontaneous, occurred in response to the Oklahoma City bombing.

Informal Memorial at the Bombing Site

Early in the rescue operation, someone spraypainted the words, "Bless the Children + the Innocent" on a jagged piece of concrete at the bomb site. Spontaneously, toys, flowers, sympathy cards, and notes of thanks were left by Oklahomans at street corners near the site as a tribute to victims, volunteers, and rescue workers. Later, a picture of one of the daycare victims with a card "in loving memory" came from a relative who wished it to be placed where the rescue workers could see it. These items were placed next to the concrete memorial. The memorial became a symbol to rescue personnel of all those they had hoped to save. It was later the focal point for the memorial service held for rescue workers at the close of the rescue operation.

Memorial at the Bomb Site for Families of Victims

On May 6, 1995, after the recovery effort was officially ended, a private ceremony and tour of the federal building blast site was organized for the families who had lost a loved one(s). Mental health professionals consulted with government officials and those in charge of the rescue effort and helped with the logistics of how to best meet the emotional needs of this survivor group. Immediate and extended families, close friends, and coworkers were allowed to walk close to the building and to view what happened there. Many of the families had only seen the bombing site on television and in press photos while they were waiting for news from the site. Twenty-two city buses transported families to the site, and the procession took the entire day in order to allow all to visit. There were two mental health professionals on each bus who prepared families and answered questions before they arrived at the site.

A double line of orange barricades marked the path to the concrete memorial and allowed the families to come face-to-face with the jagged, torn, and battered building and its festoons of flags representing each of the agencies and states involved in the rescue effort. Mental health professionals, American Red Cross volunteers, and chaplains lined the short route to assure privacy and support. As they moved down the path, family members stopped to stare, to point, or to weep. Faces tilted upward to scan the height of the building. Many talked in hushed voices; others took photographs. Many of the families brought flowers, wreaths, framed photos, mementos, framed prayers, and toys and stuffed animals to place at the concrete shrine in remembrance of those who had died. Local police, Oklahoma Highway Patrol officers, and members of several military branches who formed an honor guard were joined by some 70 officers representing 27 police agencies. When someone requested a piece of the rubble from the building, the fire chief himself waded into the bombing site to find chunks of the building to give to families. The Governor of Oklahoma and his wife also met with each family to offer their condolences and present them with an Oklahoma flag. It seemed important for families to return to the site and to see where their loved ones had perished. Such ritual activities appeared to help the surviving family members begin to confront the reality of the death of their loved ones and, perhaps, facilitated an important initial step in the grieving process (Rando, 1993).

The Fence and Survivor Tree

Following the bombing, visitors to the blast site left memorials, tokens of remembrance, flowers, stuffed animals, pictures, and poems on the cyclone fence erected around the ruins. After the implosion of the building, the fence remained as a beacon for the thousands who wanted to show their support and continued remembrance of the victims and families. It has also become a sacred gathering place for the community and for survivors of the bombing to remember and to mourn those who died. At the first- and second-year anniversaries, gatherings were held at the fence. (Later, hundreds would await the trial verdict of Timothy McVeigh at the fence, holding hands and each other.) The fence has become a place where ethnic, cultural, and class differences cease to matter. It has also become a symbol of healing to the community, a place where family members and members of the national community can literally hang their hopes and prayers for the victims and for the future.

Close to the fence is an elm tree disfigured from the blast that has been named the "survivor tree," as it survived the blast while all the surrounding buildings were destroyed. Like the fence, family members, survivors, and visitors gather around this symbol of survival and hope. It was in front of this survivor tree that President Clinton spoke to survivors and rescue workers at the first anniversary of the bombing. (Similarly, following the guilty verdict at the McVeigh trial in June 1997, approximately 150 survivors and family members gathered at the tree with the Governor of Oklahoma and his wife to pour water onto the tree in a symbolic gesture of growth and healing.) In Oklahoma City, the fence with its memorabilia and the surviving elm tree, symbols of remembrance, survival, and hope, facilitate the grieving process, provide opportunities for survivor groups to gather and share their grief and support for each other, and provide avenues through which the community affirms its existence in the face of the devastating adversity and horror of the bombing.

THE 1-YEAR ANNIVERSARY

The 1-year anniversary is an important time for individuals and communities following any traumatic event. The anniversary of a disaster can reawaken a wide range of feelings and reactions in the survivor population (Myers, 1994). The 1-year anniversary ceremonies of the Oklahoma City bombing were designed specifically for victims and survivors to be allowed onto the building site for the first time. These survivor groups actively participated in the planning process. As part of the ceremony, 168 seconds, one for each of the victims who perished in the blast, were set aside for a period of silence as thousands of people crowded into the few blocks around the Alfred P. Murrah Federal Building site. The whole nation paused while the names of those murdered were read. One by one, name by name, for 20 minutes, a roll call of 168 people was recited. With each name, family members stepped into the fenced, grassy area and placed flowers, wreaths, or mementos on the site. A bugler played taps, and military salutes snapped to foreheads. Four F-14s flew overhead in the missing man formation and Oklahoma police helicopters flew by. This survivor group then left the site and walked a lined street to the convention center for a program closed to the public. Sympathetic onlookers along the sidewalks were kept at a distance from the marchers. The program included prayers from a number of local clergy and chaplains, music, and a video depicting the victims. Both the governor and the mayor spoke, as did Vice President Al Gore. Afterwards, rescue workers and family members reunited and visited with each other at a reception closed to the public.

For some, it was their first visit to the site. One woman who lost her husband in the blast remarked: "I'm so very proud to be an American. The experience of being at the site and being able to touch the ground where he died. . . . It was tough." Another man who lost his daughter said, "It was important to me—I knew the spot where her body was found. It was really important to us to leave the flowers." Another survivor commented, "It brought back old memories, but I loved it. I'm very glad I came."

Signs of remembrance of the Oklahoma City bombing reverberated around the country as well. Many motorists pulled off roadways at 9:02 a.m. to observe the 168 seconds of silence in memory of those murdered in the blast. Church bells rang across the nation and the buzz of activity at the stock market came to a halt.

REFLECTIONS AND CONCLUSIONS

Over the past decade, Americans have become increasingly aware of terrorism. It no longer happens in far-away places to people who seem foreign and unfamiliar. American lives have been touched by the bombings of Pan Am Flight 103, the World Trade Center in New York City, and more recently the A. P. Murrah Federal Building in Oklahoma City. Terrorism has a presence in our lives that is unprecedented, and Americans are no longer insulated from such destructive, devastating events. Our sense of security and our view of the world are indelibly altered by acts of terrorism. Our fearfulness and vigilance have increased with our awareness of our nation's vulnerability.

The terrible reality of acts of terrorism such as the Oklahoma City bombing is that, unlike accidents and natural disasters, they are humanmade. They are vicious and calculated acts of murder designed to intimidate and control a group or a nation through the killing of innocent people. Terrorism involves crimes that are committed for social and political reasons against innocent people. For these reasons, careful attention must be paid to the psychological impact of terrorism.

Moreover, when compared to natural disasters, the magnitude and severity of emotional difficulties are likely to be far greater in response to terrorist incidents. This is especially true of terrorist incidents that involve large numbers of fatalities, including the deaths of many children, are the result of deliberate acts of violence, and involve a protracted rescue and recovery effort. Broad community reaction is also common in the aftermath of terrorist incidents. Incidents involving massive traumatic death are likely to lead to more prevalent immediate and long-term traumatic stress reactions and to place individuals at risk for complicated mourning. The traumatic aspects of sudden death can also add an overlay of posttraumatic symptoms that intensify the mourning experience. In situations such as Oklahoma City, there is a greater need for mental health professionals skilled in intervening with posttraumatic stress reactions as well as bereavement, and these clinicians must comprehend the complex interplay between both processes and be prepared to identify the wide range of survivor groups in need.

General Lessons Learned

The mental health response to the Oklahoma City bombing was the most extensive response to a terrorist event in the United States to date. During the emergency phase (first 2–4 weeks) of this disaster, mental health services to survivors and families of the victims were swift, efficient, and impressive. In many ways, the response could serve as a standard or model for future mass casualty or terrorist incidents. The state of Oklahoma had a mental health response team in place with preexisting relationships and experience with other local emergency response and law enforcement agencies, the American Red Cross, and the state Critical Incident Stress Management team. Additional mental health professionals with considerable experience and expertise in disaster mental health, response to mass casualty events, CISM, and trauma and loss were recruited from around the nation. These professionals augmented and provided guidance to the efforts of the local mental health community. The combination of the local and national mental health professionals helped to assure a smooth delivery of services. In addition, the placement of local experts in key leadership positions facilitated the transition of services to local individuals and agencies after the national experts departed.

The need for large numbers of trained volunteer mental health professionals in the immediate aftermath of a mass casualty incident was an important lesson learned from the tragedy in Oklahoma City. These professionals require specialized training and experience in disaster mental health, CISM, death notification, traumatic stress, and grief as well as familiarity with emergency response protocols prior to the occurrence of an incident. Similarly, it is essential that stress management services be provided to all volunteer staff, including mental health professionals, who provide services to victims and their families. There is probably a greater need for mental health professionals trained in CISM following a mass casualty incident or terrorist event than in some other critical incidents or natural disasters because of the increased level of traumatic stress and associated clinical symptomatology.

Lastly, in mass casualty incidents, there is a need for mental health professional staff with specialized training in death notification procedures and protocols. Although mental health professionals rarely, if ever, provide the actual death notification in such situations, they are often asked to participate on death notification teams or provide consultation, education, and training to other team members. Having a team member knowledgeable about child trauma-related issues also seems critical. It is the authors' experience that few mental health professionals have had prior experience or training for this difficult and intensely emotional position. As volunteers are identified, training in this aspect of mental health services should be provided (Lord, 1996).

Interventions Focused on Survivor Groups

In the immediate aftermath of the Oklahoma City bombing, a number of interventions helped to address the emotional needs of the different survivor groups. With regards to the needs of the next-of-kin awaiting official death notification, there were a number of approaches that appeared to facilitate grief and early stages of recovery. The Compassion Center was designed to provide a safe, protective environment to meet the physical and emotional needs of next-of-kin, to provide information, and to prevent intrusions from the press or outsiders. The need for safety and protection were foremost, and security provided by the military and law enforcement maintained the semipermeable membrane around this community of survivors. The families' need for truth and official information was also a priority. Next-of-kin were provided with a direct link to the medical examiner, the rescue and recovery team members, and other key officials in charge. Briefings were held regularly and questions were answered truthfully at all points. This seemed crucial to the families, who struggled with how to make sense of this tragedy. It was imperative that families were given firsthand official information before it was released to the media, thus allowing them private time to cope with the facts prior to public consumption (Cummock, 1996). For the families to have interaction and access to those directly involved in the rescue/recovery effort also proved to be empowering to them in a chaotic situation.

Over time, the families at the Compassion Center developed their own sense of community, forming bonds with other survivors sharing their situation; some developed friendships that continue to the present. However, not all of the families found it helpful to be surrounded by others who shared the same sense of loss and grief. They preferred to wait in the privacy of their own homes for news of their missing relative. For these families and individuals who wanted to be able to move back and forth from the center, pagers and cellular phones were provided so that they could maintain contact with the Center. Mental health professionals recognized that individuals had different ways to respond to traumatic loss and were flexible in providing for these individual differences.

Another crucial element in facilitating the grief of these families was sensitivity to their protective need for denial in the early days and weeks following the bombing (Redmond, 1996). As family members waited for news on the status of a missing relative, their initial reactions were disbelief, shock, numbness, and the inability to make sense or comprehend what had happened. Given the suddenness of the bombing, they had no time to anticipate and prepare for the loss. It seemed literally too much to absorb at one time. The observed reaction in this group of survivors was consistent with what Raphael (1983) has called the "shock effect" of sudden death. For example, families talked initially of the hope of rescue. However, as the days progressed into weeks, their conversations evolved "from hope of survival to hope of recovering a body" (Cummock, 1996). Slowly, the degree of denial changed as they gradually absorbed the reality that loved ones had been murdered. The rate at which this process took place varied dramatically from one person to another, depending on the ability to deal with the degree of horror, anguish, and pain that came with the acceptance of reality (Cummock, 1996). It is essential for mental health professionals to recognize, respect, and be sensitive to the psychological protection of this denial mechanism and not to rush this process.

For the families of the deceased, the prolonged process of recovery, identification, and official death notification kept them in a state of emotional limbo. The waiting compounded the trauma and created its own form of torture as families contemplated their worst fears and fantasies. Nearly all of the families wanted to know if their loved ones had physically suffered, They also struggled with terrifying and intrusive images of the fantasies they developed from the bits and pieces of information they had about the building collapse and the difficulties that the medical examiner had in identifying bodies grossly disfigured and mutilated. As Lord (1996) points out, "people are intimately attached to the bodies of their loved ones . . . and they significantly mourn what happened to his or her body" (p. 30). Without the closure of having a death confirmed, the grieving process cannot easily begin. If bodies are not recovered, this closure is never quite complete and it is difficult for the mourner to take the first step of acknowledging the loss in the mourning process.

Intrusive influences such as tremendous public interest and mass media also can greatly complicate the grieving process. The surviving families of the Oklahoma City bombing were forced to face their loss and grief in public. The eyes of the entire nation and world were on them as the media provided live, unedited footage, which began to ease only after the first 3 weeks. In fact, the coverage of the first-year anniversary of the bombing was estimated to have exceeded the audience of the preceding Superbowl (American Psychological Association (APA), 1997).

It is important to honor the families' needs for privacy and to minimize unnecessary outside intrusions to avoid compounding their loss. Also, as Cummock (1996, p. 2) points out, "once the deceased becomes a public persona entering the public domain, families have lost yet another part of that person during a time that they have not learned how to cope with their initial loss." While some individuals wanted protection from the media, others found talking with reporters to be a helpful expression of their loss. Those in charge of coordinating mental health efforts provided for these contradictory and opposing needs. In Oklahoma City, the provision of regular briefings by the medical examiner and the accessibility of mental health "experts" helped to reduce the media's intrusive efforts to meet deadlines and educated the media about respecting the families' need for privacy.

Children dealing with the aftermath of sudden trauma have some unique needs (Saylor, 1993). A child's age and level of exposure, and the coping skills of significant adults can effect a child's experience and future adjustment to trauma and loss (Pynoos, 1993). Furthermore, children are not affected in a vacuum. Consequently, interventions must be conducted and understood within the context of families, peer groups, school groups, and communities (Eth & Pynoos, 1985; Pynoos & Nader, 1990). These systems are important points of contact for intervention with children, can strengthen the ties of group membership, and can offer support to the adults in charge as well. For children injured in a terrorist action, issues of safety, security, and routine must be quickly addressed. As parents/caretakers may also be affected directly by the traumatic event, guidance for helping them to help their children is essential.

At the Compassion Center, children remained in physical proximity to their caretakers while, at the same time, being offered a place of their own where they could engage in age-appropriate activities. Interventions with children were crisis oriented and provided practical assistance and guidance to families on how to answer questions and deal appropriately with the needs of their children. It was not advisable to provide intensive intervention to these young victims until their families had been able to adjust to their new situation.

As observed in other postimpact disaster communities, repeated acknowledgment of the common experience of grief and loss involving the community as a whole promotes and strengthens the bonds among survivor group members (Raphael, 1986; Tierney & Braisden, 1979). Similarly, key public leaders influenced the positive transformation seen within the Oklahoma City community following the bombing. These leaders focused the community on shared values and common goals, uniting them in the significance of their mutual experience of loss and bereavement. To accomplish this goal, meaningful public rituals, such as the memorial service for rescue workers, the national memorial service attended by the President, and the 1-year anniversary commemoration helped to foster a sense of hope and coming together. It has been suggested that this type of transformation within the community as a whole provides a backdrop for supporting the bereaved and helps to reconstruct the psychological life (Wright & Bartone, 1994).

Role of Community Leaders

The importance of key community leaders assuming a role of "grief leadership" in the mourning process cannot be overemphasized (Wright & Bartone, 1994). As these authors point out, "in the early period of shock and disbelief, community leaders reassure families and survivors by conveying accurate information, dispelling rumors, and providing a calm and controlled role model for others to follow." Several key figures in Oklahoma City, including the Governor, the fire chief, and the chief medical examiner, assumed such roles and met regularly with the bereaved families at the Compassion Center. All of these key leaders actively sought out consultation with mental health professionals and worked closely with them to address the needs of surviving family members. Public acknowledgment of the loss by national leaders such as the President of the United States furthered the community's comfort with the knowledge that the nation was grieving with them.

It is critical that school personnel and the mental health community work together to determine and provide for the emotional needs of children following a community-wide traumatic incident, as children do not have a voice to express their needs. Otherwise, this often silent group of survivors may not receive the services they need and have a more complicated and prolonged healing process than is necessary.

Following the bombing, efforts were also made to provide crisis intervention services to hundreds of schoolchildren within the Oklahoma City community through federally funded programs. Of importance in school-based interventions following a traumatic incident or disaster is the attitude of key adults in the school environment. Some of the local school principals relied on their own coping styles and ideas as yardsticks to evaluate and make decisions regarding the emotional needs of the young children in their schools. The end result was that some school leaders refused mental health services for their student population, believing that their students were not in need. This decision was made in opposition to the advice of mental health professionals who had been working with the children and in spite of the results of a survey clearly indicating that there were large numbers of children experiencing emotional difficulties (Krug et al., 1995).

SYNOPSIS

At present, the federal laws designed to provide funding for the long-term emotional needs of victim groups are not adequate (APA, 1997). The conditions under which these federal funds are released for crisis intervention grants are rather narrow and seldom apply to focused mass casualty events, particularly of human design. Moreover, the intervention model supported by these grants is a brief crisis intervention model, depending largely on paraprofessionals and mental health professionals with little training in disaster, trauma, or grief counseling. While such a model can work well for most of the emotional needs arising from a natural disaster, a different model is needed to serve the long-term emotional needs that present themselves in most mass casualty or terrorist acts of the magnitude of the Oklahoma City bombing. For example, 2 years following the bombing, many of the survivors of the blast and the families of the bereaved still struggled with intense difficulties associated with traumatic stress and complicated mourning. Research on sudden, violent death describes a 4- to 7-year recovery period and acknowledges that recovery is never complete (Lehman & Wortman, 1987; Mercer, 1993). Thus, it is critical to recognize the magnitude and severity of emotional difficulties that will present following such incidents and that are likely to require specialized clinical interventions.

Therapeutic rituals also seemed to facilitate the grief and mourning of survivor groups. As Rando (1993) points out,

> Therapeutic bereavement rituals provide a structured way to affirm the death; recall the loved one; or explore, clarify, express, integrate, and subsequently make statements about the mourner's diverse feelings and thoughts about the loved one. They can assist the mourner in saying good-bye to the deceased and in encouraging the necessary formulation of a healthy new relationship with that person. Finally, they can symbolize the transition back into the new world. (p. 314)

Many of the rituals (e.g., the mementos left at the fence surrounding the bomb site, ceremonies at the survivor tree, the one-year anniversary memorial service) were significant events that helped unify the Oklahoma City community in its mourning process. These rituals emphasized the community experience of loss and reinforced emotional bonds among survivors, the Oklahoma City community, and the nation. The memorial services showed respect for the dead, affirmed the loss to the community, and acknowledged the need to grieve. Particularly helpful was allowing the next-of-kin to visit the blast site. This ritual was planned with considerable input of and consultation with mental health professionals who had a preexisting relationship with the families and therefore were part of the trauma membrane that had formed around this group of survivors from the beginning.

The first-year anniversary commemoration furthered the recovery process due to several factors. Members of the various survivor groups actively helped to plan the ceremony, to select symbolic activities that were meaningful to them (e.g., the roll call of the victims, the 168 seconds of silence), and to select speakers. Additionally, only members of the various survivor groups and the mental health professionals who had actively worked with them were permitted into the perimeter around the bombing site where the ceremony was held.

Finally, when a community-wide terrorist incident involves legal proceedings, the recovery process is further complicated as families of homicide victims contend with the criminal justice system. While this chapter has not focused on the impact of the trial and verdict of Timothy McVeigh, it is important to emphasis that the intrusion of the judicial system into personal lives can be overwhelming and confusing, preventing families from regaining a sense of balance and control over their lives. Often, it interferes with or postpones survivors' mourning the loss of victims and life as they knew it before the traumatic death of their loved ones. The legal proceedings serve as a constant reminder to the survivor community of the events which destroyed its previous way of functioning. The citizens are forced to relive the events at each step in the criminal case. In many instances, a trial can take several years to complete, derailing this phase of healing and preventing closure.

From a mental health perspective, it is important to prepare the community for the impact of court proceedings. In Oklahoma City, most citizens welcomed the trial of Timothy McVeigh as an important step towards closure for the survivors and the Oklahoma City community. However, few survivors were prepared for the emotional toll the trial took, as intense, gruesome stories about the bombing unfolded and were broadcast in the media daily. By the end of the trial, the community reexperienced the tragedy with the same intensity as when it occurred and reexperienced all the symptoms associated with the original trauma and its complicated bereavement. Involvement in the legal system can produce a secondary traumatization for victims for years after the actual incident (Redmond, 1989). On the other hand, the legal system also offers the possibility of returning a sense of power and justice to those victimized. For some victims, the opportunity and experience of testifying may help restore a sense of power and give closure to this traumatic experience.

Mental health professionals can normalize the emotional rollercoaster that the next-of-kin and survivors frequently experience as they seek to find closure through the pursuit of "justice." During the McVeigh trial, crisis counseling services and safe havens were available to survivors and families of victims attending the proceedings in Denver and the closed circuit broadcast of the trial in Oklahoma City. These innovative counseling services were coordinated through the U.S. Attorney's Office. The availability of mental health experts who worked closely with victim assistance advocates before, during, and after legal proceedings further aided survivors in their grief, coping, and adjustment.

However great the individual sense of grief following traumatic loss, it is clear that the whole of a community's grief is indeed different and somehow greater than the sum of its parts. When traumatic loss strikes an entire community, the evolution of survivor groups and the formulation of interventions for these various groups become important parts of the healing process. Group kinship facilitates recovery and helps to fill the terrible gap that is left by widespread-traumatic loss. A new connection and sense of community develop that is lifeaffirming. Hope and comfort can be found in the coming together of people with common threads of mourning. At a time when feelings of being alone and isolated are particularly intense, new bonds may form and mutual support may grow. There is a synergy that arises from the survivor group process which makes it easier to find meaning in the face of great tragedy and loss. In this way, many individual lights have combined to dispel darkness from the community of Oklahoma City and have cast a new light on the hope for its future.

REFERENCES

American Psychological Association. (1997). *Final report: Task force on the mental health response to the Oklahoma City bombing.* Washington, DC: Author.

Bard, M., & Sangrey, D. (1996). *The crime victim's book.* New York: Brunner/Mazel.

Cummock, M. V. (1995). The necessity of denial in grieving murder: Observations of the victims' families following the bombing in Oklahoma City. *National Center for PTSD Clinical Quarterly, 5*(2–3), 17–18.

Cummock, M. V. (1996). Journey of a young widow. In K. J. Doka (Ed.), *Living with grief after sudden loss* (pp. 1–9). Washington, DC: Taylor & Francis.

Eth, S., & Pynoos, R. (1985). *Post-traumatic stress disorder in children.* Washington, DC: American Psychiatric Press.

Injury Prevention Service. (1996, April). Injury update: Investigation of physical injuries directly associated with the Oklahoma City bombing. A report to Oklahoma injury surveillance participants. Oklahoma State Department of Health, Oklahoma City, Oklahoma.

Irving, C. (1995). *In their name.* New York: Random House.

Krug, R. S., Pfefferbaum, B., Gurwitch, R., Nixon, S., Foy, D., & Pynoos, R. S. (1995, November). *The Oklahoma City bombing: A public mental health response.* Paper presented at the annual meeting of the International Society for Traumatic Stress Studies, Boston.

Lehman, D., & Wortman, C. (1987). Long-term effects of losing a spouse or a child in a motor vehicle crash. *Journal of Personality and Social Psychology, 52*(1), 218–231.

Lord, J. H. (1996). America's number one killer: Vehicular crashes. In K. J. Doka (Ed.), *Living with grief after sudden loss* (pp. 25–40). Washington, DC: Taylor & Francis.

Mercer, D. (1993, October). *Drunk driving victimization or non-victimization effects on volunteer victim advocates.* Paper presented at the annual meeting of the International Society for Traumatic Stress Studies, San Antonio.

Mitchell, J. T. (1983). When disaster strikes: The critical incident stress debriefing. *Journal of Medical Emergency Services, 8,* 36–39.

Mitchell, J. T., & Bray, C. (1990). *Emergency services stress: Guidelines for preserving the health and careers of emergency services personnel.* Englewood-Cliffs, NJ: Prentice-Hall.

Mitchell, J. T., & Dyregrov, A. (1993). Traumatic stress in disaster workers and emergency personnel: Prevention and intervention. In J. P. Wilson & B. Raphael (Eds.), *International handbook of traumatic stress syndromes,* 905–914. New York: Plenum Press.

Myers, D. (1994). *Disaster response and recovery: A handbook for mental health professionals.* Publication No. (SMA) 94-3010. Washington, DC: U.S. Department of Health and Human Services.

Pynoos, R. S., & Nader, K. (1993). Issues in the treatment of posttraumatic stress in children and adolescents. In J. P. Wilson & B. Raphael (Eds.), *International handbook of traumatic stress syndromes,* 535–549. New York: Plenum Press.

Pynoos, R., & Nader, K. (1990). Children's exposure to violence and traumatic death.*Psychiatric Annuals, 20*(6), 334–344.

Rando, T. A. (1993). *Treatment of complicated mourning.* Champaign, IL: Research Press.

Raphael, B. (1983). *The anatomy of bereavement.* New York: Basic Books.

Raphael, B. (1986). *When disaster strikes: How individuals and communities cope with catastrophe.* New York: Basic Books.

Redmond, L. (1989). *Surviving: When someone you love was murdered.* Clearwater, FL: Psychological Consultation and Education Services.

Redmond, L. (1996). Sudden violent death. In K. J. Doka (Ed.), *Living with grief after sudden loss* (pp. 53–71). Washington, DC: Taylor & Francis.

Ross, J., & Myers, P. (1996). *Dear Oklahoma City. Get well soon.* New York: Walker and Company.

Sitterle, K. A. (1995). Mental health services at the Compassion Center: The Oklahoma City bombing. *National Center for PTSD Clinical Quarterly, 5*(4) 20–23.

Smith, E. M., & North, C. S. (1993). Posttraumatic stress disorder in natural disasters and technological accidents. In J. P. Wilson & B. Raphael (Eds.), *International handbook of traumatic stress syndromes* (pp. 405–419). New York: Plenum Press.

Tierney, K. J., & Braisden, B. (1979). *Crisis intervention programs for disaster victims: A sourcebook and manual for small communities.* DHHS Publication No. (ADM) 83-675. Rockville, MD: National Institute of Mental Health.

Ursano, R. J., Fullerton, C. S., & McCaughey, B. G. (1994). Trauma and disaster. In R. J. Ursano, B. G. McCaughey, & C. S. Fullerton (Eds.), *Individual and community responses to trauma and disaster: The structure of human chaos* (pp. 3–27). Cambridge, England: Cambridge University Press.

Weisaeth, L. (1994). Psychological and psychiatric aspects of technological disasters. In R. J. Ursano, B. G. McCaughey, & C. S. Fullerton (Eds.), *Individual and community responses to trauma and disaster: The structure of chaos* (pp. 72–102). Cambridge, England: Cambridge University Press.

Wright, K. M., & Bartone, P. T. (1994). Community responses to disaster: The Gander plane crash. In R. J. Ursano, B. G. McCaughey, & C. S. Fullerton (Eds.), *Individual and community responses to trauma and disaster: The structure of human chaos* (pp. 267–284). Cambridge, England: Cambridge University Press.

Young, B. H., Ford, J., Ruzek, J. I., Friedman, M. J., & Gusman, F. D. (1997). *Disaster mental health services: A guidebook for clinicians and administrators.* The National Center for Post-Traumatic Stress Disorder, Education and Executive Divisions. Palo Alto, CA: Department of Veterans Affairs.

Young, B. H., Sitterle, K. A., & Myers, D. (1996). *The use of ritual following traumatic loss: A community, group, and individual perspective.* Workshop presented at the annual meeting of the International Society for Traumatic Stress Studies, San Francisco, CA.

Young, M. (1985). Survivors of homicide victims. *National Organization for Victim Assistance Network Information Bulletin 2,* 3.

Figure 10.1 The funeral of one of the 11 people killed in the Remembrance Day bombing in Enniskillen, Sunday, November 8, 1987. The procession is shown passing the bombing scene in the background. Photographed by Raymond Humphreys, Impartial Reporter, Enniskillen, Northern Ireland. (Used by permission of the photographer.)

Chapter 10

The Threat to Belonging in Enniskillen: Reflections on the Remembrance Day Bombing

David Bolton

On Sunday morning, November 8, 1987, a bomb exploded in a building adjacent to the War Memorial in the market town of Enniskillen, Northern Ireland. Eleven people were killed and over 60 were injured, some very seriously. Over 400 people, it is estimated, who had gathered for the annual Remembrance ceremony were in close proximity to the explosion. Apart from the terrible consequences for those directly affected, the bombing and its aftermath was one of the most dangerous episodes in the recent political strife in Northern Ireland and threatened to lead to a cycle of greater violence. Locally, it threatened to undermine the well-being of the total community as the attack was perceived to be a sectarian attack on the Protestant and Unionist community, leading in turn to fears of reprisals within the Catholic and Nationalist community.

The building in which the bomb had been placed was immediately adjacent to the footpath on which bystanders stood every year to watch and participate in the ceremony. The building collapsed, sending up a huge cloud of dust and debris, and falling down on top of those who were standing around. Many people were trapped under the wall of the building as it fell, pinned against the railings, which protected pedestrians from the road. The time was just about 10:40 a.m. The parade of the Ballyreagh Silver Band and the service and ex-service personnel had not yet departed from its assembly location at the College of Further Education, about 200 yards away. At the sound of the explosion, many ran towards the scene, fearful for friends and relatives. Others ran away in terror. The accounts of people's experiences in these moments are chilling and deeply moving: the man who wandered around looking for his mother, whom he found out some hours later had been killed; the woman who ran towards the scene in terror and concern for her mother, whom, unknowingly, she had passed on the way as her mother fled from the scene. She then searched through the debris and the dying for her mother and now lives with powerful and unforgettable memories of that dreadful day. One young man, standing between his parents, survived with relatively minor injuries, while both his parents were killed.

Many came to the rescue, and a process of removing the dead and injured began—a scene captured on video by an amateur cameraman and shown around the world on news bulletins. Within a few hours after collating the information from the scene, the temporary mortuary, and the nearby Erne Hospital, the extent of the tragedy was established. Most of the injured were brought to the Erne Hospital, about half of a mile away. As it was a Sunday, the outpatients and operating theatres were all but empty, leaving them free, along with the radiography, laboratory, and CSSD (Central Sterile Service Departments) departments, to spring into action. Hospital staff were called in or came to the hospital of their own initiative on hearing of the explosion.

The present writer was at church less than half a mile away when the bomb exploded. A short time later, I went to the hospital and was met with a scene of utter mayhem. What struck me was the powerful sense of unreality in seeing the familiar hospital environment filled with so many disheveled and distressed people. People were arriving all the time and, within minutes, the accident and emergency department was inundated.

Together with another social worker, I was at the hospital for a number of hours until after the situation returned to some degree of order. The primary task involved linking people with others or facilitating contact between families, their injured relatives, and medical or nursing staff. Also, I and other staff responded to inquiries from the media, which were seeking regular updates for newsflashes and regular bulletins. It was a fast-moving few hours, with very distressed people seeking information about lost relatives, a high level of uncertainty about who was where and how many had been killed, and helicopters landing outside the front door of the hospital to take seriously injured to regional hospitals. A few hours later, it all seemed strangely quiet.

A History of Conflict

Before exploring the implications for the community of the bombing, some background to the conflict in Northern Ireland will place what is to follow in context. At the time of this chapter's writing, the constitutional position of Northern Ireland is in dispute. Six out of the 32 counties that make up the whole island of Ireland continued to be governed from Britain after the political settlement between the British Government and the Irish Nationalists in 1921. The other 26 counties then formed the new Irish Free State. In the years that followed, nationalists have aspired to a united Ireland, independent from Britain.

With matching vigor, the unionists (those supporting union between Britain and Northern Ireland) have sought to retain the constitutional link.

At times in the years since the 1920s, the aspiration of nationalists has been expressed in violence, particularly by extreme nationalists who pursue a republican ideal for Ireland. This violence has at times been directed at institutions and interests closely associated with Britain, including attacks on economic, constitutional, and security targets. On other occasions, it has been directed at the unionist population.

Two other points are important to note. First, the violence of republicans has been matched by the violence of extreme unionists (often referred to as loyalists, viz. loyal to the British crown). Second, an understanding of the various interests in the constitutional conflict is bedeviled by the use of various terms, which are often used interchangeably but actually have precise meanings. To simplify, the Roman Catholic community is, generally speaking, nationalist in its political aspirations and identity, and republicans (extreme nationalists) are generally taken to be from the Catholic community. Conversely, the Protestant community is, again generally speaking, unionist in its aspirations and identity. Loyalist is a term used to identify those with pronounced unionist views and is usually applied to those who use or support violence to defend the link with Britain. The Protestant and Catholic (or Roman Catholic) labels, when used in political or community contexts, have less to do with one's religious practice and more to do with one's political identity and sometimes may mean something about where one lives, since in parts of Northern Ireland (though not everywhere) members of the two religious groups live in highly segregated areas.

The term "community" will be used in several ways, including to denote one or other of the politicoreligious communities, the total community of Enniskillen and the surrounding areas, and the wider community of Northern Ireland. It will also be used in its generic and academic senses. The context should determine which meaning is appropriate.

THE ESSENTIAL ATTRIBUTES OF A COMMUNITY

It goes without saying that no two communities are alike, and therefore it is important to note that no two disasters are alike. It is remarkable, however, how traumatic experiences in different places happening to different people have a high degree of similarity when it comes to the impact on individual people. This reminds us that even though disasters and communities are different, people and people's needs have a considerable degree of commonality (always remembering, of course, that we need to consider and regard people caught up in such events as individuals and to recognize that the needs and perceptions of the individual change over time).

To understand the impact of a disaster on a community, it is necessary to have some means of judging how well it can endure the impact and consequences

of a major traumatic experience, and, specifically, to enumerate those characteristics of community that are inherently supportive and which, if threatened or
overwhelmed, can lead to serious consequences for the community as a whole and
for individuals within it. A number of concepts can provide a framework for
describing and assessing the robustness of a community.

Belonging

The concept of *belonging* (what Simone Weil refers to as *enracinement*)[1] is
fundamental to the experience of individuals within their community. A community could be held to exist when, for reasons of geography, shared interests
or values, or for some other reason, individuals believe they "belong." In practice, we all have many belongings, such as our friendship groups, leisure and
interest groups, school, religious groups, family, and our workplace. There are
also the belongings of place such as the street and home in which one lives or
the school or church one attends. These various belongings contribute to our
overall identity with the community in which we live and are the source of
meanings in our lives that affirm and give us our own identity. If one of those
belongings is threatened, then we can often gain support from the others. This
is very apparent when a family disintegrates through death or legal separation,
and the school or workplace then becomes the constant belonging which sees
us through. If, on the other hand, within the context of a major tragic experience, several or all of our belongings are disrupted or destroyed, then we
become like refugees in our own community. We feel that to which we belong
has been taken away (or possibly has rejected us), and we feel we are no longer
part of the whole. In particularly devastating circumstances, perhaps the whole
itself (i.e., the community) has disintegrated or ceased to exist in a meaningful
way.

Communality

Also of relevance is the idea of "communality," which Erikson wrote about in his
study of the Buffalo Creek disaster (Erikson, 1976). Communality is the cohesive
threads which positively bind a community together to create a certain, safe,

---

[1]Simone Weil was a French mystic and philosopher (1872–1943) who wrote a book, *The
Need for Roots*, at the request of General de Gaulle towards the end of the World War II. Her
work addressed the duties and privileges of the French nation at peace. She was particularly
concerned about "uprootedness" or, in her terms, *deracinement*. The original title of her work
was *L'enracinement: Prelude a use declaration des devoirs envers l'etre humain* (1949, Paris:
Gallimard). It has been translated into English under the title, *The need for Roots: Prelude to á
Declaration of Duties Toward Mankind*, by A. Wills (New York: Putnam, 1952). I have chosen
the word "belonging" to encapsulate a similar theme and because of its appropriateness to the
experience of a community in adversity. "Belonging" is not a literal translation; *enracinement*, in
this context, could best be translated "rootedness," or "the experience of being rooted." The text
used here was published by Ark, London, 1987.

and wholesome environment in which individuals can lead effective, enriching, and safe lives. Erikson points to the experience of collective trauma where "'I' continues to exist, although damaged and maybe even permanently changed. 'You' continues to exist, although distant and hard to relate to. But 'we' no longer exists as a connected pair or as linked cells in a larger communal body" (Erikson, p. 302). Where such links are disrupted or destroyed, then certainty and predictability are removed from the experience of the individual, leading to adverse social, emotional, and psychological consequences.

Segregating and Integrating Choices

Where communities within a community are in conflict or have divergent or conflicting values or aspirations, then the degree of integration can be gauged from the extent to which the communities or groups integrate in key areas of life. Such indicators of integration can be applied to formal arrangements that separate the communities (e.g., in Northern Ireland, the separate arrangements for education of children) and to informal choices (e.g., intermarriage; see Figure 10.1).

While some of these are institutionalized (e.g., structures and funding for education) and others have a long "lead-in" time (e.g., patterns of intermarriage probably do not change rapidly in light of significant positive social and political events and changes), others may be very sensitive indicators (e.g., participa-

---

1. **FORMAL SEGREGATING STRUCTURE**
   - Education
   - Religious structures

2. **COMMUNITY-DEFINED SEGREGATING STRUCTURES**
   - Choices and opportunities about where one lives
   - Choices and opportunities about where one works

3. **INFORMAL SEGREGATING AND INTEGRATING CHOICES**
   - Intermarriage
   - Transfer of property between communities
   - Use of services and professionals from same/different backgrounds (e.g., family doctor, solicitor, etc.)
   - Banking and shopping choices
   - Choices about participating in religious and other activities identified with the other community
   - The adoption of symbols associated with the other community
   - Participation in leisure and social events associated with the other community
   - Choices about going into areas associated with the other community
   - Choices and behavior associated with the sense of threat from the other community

Figure 10.1

tion in activities associated with the other community). These could be taken as clues to the mind of a community in the wake of a major tragic and divisive event and could help to determine in what direction a community is responding (i.e., integration or segregation).

In Northern Ireland, these patterns of behavior are probably more likely to retrench in response to negative political and violent events than to move in the direction of integration in response to positive developments. This means that painstaking work aimed at achieving integration or mutual acceptance can be rapidly undone by relatively short-lived but negative political or violent events. Conversely, it takes a lot of time to achieve little progress. Therefore, disasters that directly arise from the conflict in a divided community can have very significant negative consequences, which can take a long time to overcome. In some circumstances, the negative responses can emerge in the form of retaliation, running the risk of a cycle of violence (or other negative social or political outcomes).

These indicators of integration can be viewed as a "zip fastener" barometer of integration and acceptance on one hand or division on the other (see Figure 10.2). This obviously has implications for the perception of belonging and communality within a community.

In Northern Ireland, probably like most societies where more than one distinct cultural group shares the same space, clearly distinguishing cultural practices are maintained and practiced to sustain and assert each culture. The issue of parades by the Protestant (and unionist) Orange Order has led to conflict, most notably in recent times in 1995 and 1996. The assumed right to parade has clashed with the right asserted by Catholic (and mainly nationalist) neighborhoods not to have what they see as triumphalist and "coat trailing" demonstrations of Protestant culture. This led to the setting up of an Independent Review of Parades and Marches, led by Dr. Peter North, an Oxford professor invited by the British government in 1996 to chair the commission. The outcome of the review's deliberations were published in January 1997 (*Independent Review of Parades and Marches,* 1997). The controversy over parades subsequently led to the establishment of a Parades Commission to reach decisions on contentious parades.

Another important feature of communities in conflict (and certainly a feature of Northern Ireland) is the politeness which masks conflict. In a report on sectarianism in Northern Ireland (The Report of the Working Party on Sectarianism, 1993), the following observation is made:

> Polite relationships in divided societies are often uncertain and ambivalent relationships because there is usually fear and anxiety around. Polite relationships should, therefore, not be confused with trusting relationships. Relationships of trust and openness are ones in which deep disagreement and hurt can be aired, as well as positive feelings expressed. Needless to say, trusting relationships are comparatively rare across the communities in divided societies.

AREAS OF COMMUNITY LIFE	TIME SPAN FOR CHANGE	PRESENT STATUS	CHANGE TO POSITIVE EVENTS	CHANGE TO NEGATIVE EVENTS
Transfer of property	long term	low integration	slow change	further retrenches
Intermarriage	long term	low integration (increasing)	slow change	resistant
Shared cultural activity	long term	low integration (some areas)	slow change	retrenches
Shared religious activity	long term	low integration	some changes	resistant
Integrated housing	medium term	higher in rural areas	slow change	further retrenches
Commerce & trading	medium–short term	some highly segregated	fairly sensitive	likely to rapidly segregate
Leisure & social activity	short term	fairly integrated	fairly–quite sensitive	likely to rapidly segregate

Figure 10.2 Chart illustrating ways of testing level of intercommunity integration and sensitivity of each area of community life to change, in response to positive and negative events.

The silence or acquiescence of a community or group of people should not be taken to mean satisfaction or contentment, particularly in communities that have been divided or where a tragedy leads to or has highlighted division. This politeness sometimes makes invisible the differences and prejudices which exist in a divided community. Gebler (1991), recording the words of someone with whom he had spoken, notes: "There's a glass curtain here. When you first arrive you can't see it, and many people who live here can't see it either, or won't. But it's there all right, separating the two communities, only you don't find out about it until you walk into it—bang!—and break your nose" (p. 54).

Preparation, Resilience & Competency In Coping

Three other concepts are relevant. First, there is the degree to which a community is prepared for a disaster. *Preparation* can take two forms. In passive preparedness, the infrastructure and reserves of a community can see it though a disaster. In active preparedness, specific preparation is made (e.g., to build defenses, store up reserves, develop contingencies, and plan for the disaster). Expectedness, where tragedy is in some way anticipated even if its precise timing and circumstances are unclear, will also be an important element of preparedness.

Second, the concept of *resilience* is the degree to which a community can absorb tragedy and the challenge to its practical and emotional resources. A community overwhelmed by two consecutive disasters within a short time span may not be able to regroup after the first catastrophe in time to reestablish its resilience. Likewise, communities facing a major disastrous event for the first time may not be prepared enough to cope (or to prepare for coping) when such challenges arise. Conversely, a community that has learned how to cope through preparation and experience may be very resilient in the face of threats to its existence and well-being.

Linked to the concepts of preparedness and resilience is that of *competency in coping*. How competently will the community and its agencies and leaders cope with the changing and unpredictable variables which accompany a disaster? How well will it deal with the threats it faces? How sensitively will the various parts of the community (e.g., statutory bodies, churches, etc.) address the implications of the disaster, and, specifically, the needs of those individuals, groups, and communities that have suffered directly?

THE IMPLICATIONS OF THE REMEMBRANCE DAY BOMBING: HOW THE COMMUNITY RESPONDED

Multiple Loss

Many of those injured and killed came from the churches in the town. The Presbyterian church located a few yards from the scene of the explosion lost five members and another individual who often frequented the church. The nearby Methodist church lost three members, and two local Church of Ireland churches lost one member each. To have a number of one's church members killed in such a dramatic and public way was quite a terrible and chilling experience, and it placed quite a strain on the churches and especially their clergy. To have multiple funerals from your church, including those from the same family (three of which were double funerals, as three married couples were killed) also marked the seriousness and heightened the distress of it all. The funerals were deeply moving and powerful events. Thousands of people attended and walked in silence behind the hearses as they moved through the town to the graveyards. It was here that the sorrow and outrage of the community was seen and expressed. This was a community in grief. Its tears were on the solemn faces of its people.

Hierarchies of Suffering

It was perhaps in the belonging that the greatest support was derived from the churches themselves. Everyone knew what everyone else was feeling and, through the liturgy and the pastoral care, support was provided. Churches have their weaknesses, however. Sometimes people felt they should be coping better because they were Christians, and so they did not seek help. Likewise, for the very reason that everyone thought they knew what everyone else was going through, they themselves felt it was inappropriate to ask for help, as it would be asserting their needs over the needs of others. In this way, hierarchies of suffering evolved, with the bereaved deemed to be the most affected, then the injured, and then the rest. Close personal and church friends deferred their grief because they thought the grief of the families of those who had been killed must be greater.

In some of the meetings of bereaved and injured which took place within the months following the bombing, those involved in providing support sought to legitimize that suppressed suffering through acknowledgment and the giving of information about suffering, trauma, etc., with some effect. Also, the media were used to heighten awareness of the continuing grief and the pressures people were under.

The Threat to Communality

The bombing was an unexpected incident (even within Northern Ireland), but as an incident, it constituted a relatively short-lived experience of uncertainty during the few hours of the rescue and recovery. However, greater concerns emerged within hours and days as to the political and security implications of what had happened. This was linked to the context in which the bombing had taken place, namely, the political violence of the previous 19 years. This rolling disaster, where one event was superseded by the next, created a climate of expectation of further violence. Fears of reprisals were very strong in the Catholic community because of the identity of the Irish Republican Army (IRA) with that community. Within the context of civil conflict, these fears symbolized the grave dangers to communality at two levels. First, on the local level, the bombing was seen as very divisive and had the potential to disengage the Catholic community whose members would unselfconsciously have come forward to support their Protestant neighbors if the deaths and injuries had been caused by a nonpolitical cause. In fact, the distinctions between the communities would hardly have been visible in such circumstances. The second risk was the very serious danger of retaliatory attacks; and it is now known that such were planned (Bardon, 1992). Some reprisal attacks and killings were carried out, chiefly in and around Belfast, but mass murder was averted, and no reprisals were carried out locally.

With regard to integrating and segregating choices, the outcome is difficult to gauge accurately, as choices following divisive events such as the bombing are often private or masked. Nonetheless, some interesting things happened. In Northern Ireland, the education of children up to the age of 16 years (and sometimes 18 years) is highly segregated, with two parallel school systems. Since the early 1980s, attempts have been made to provide integrated schooling. Following the Remembrance Day bombing, an integrated primary school (for children up to the age of 11 years) opened in Enniskillen, followed later by an integrated college for older children. Second, a local interchurch and intercommunity body was established, called Enniskillen Together. This did not receive widespread support but has continued to exist, providing opportunities for people from different backgrounds to meet and discuss some of the sensitive religious and political matters that divide the two politicoreligious communities. It has played a part in mediating circumstances that could lead to violence (such as the contentious parades, referred to above). Less visible were the subtle changes that led to a hardening of the divisions, with an increase in mistrust. This must ultimately have influenced many individual choices, particularly those informal choices referred to earlier.

Responses That Reduced the Threat to Communality

What enabled the Catholic community to reengage in its supportive role at a local level, and what constrained the feared serious reprisals? The response of the Enniskillen total community was significant. The inherent strengths, attachments, and commitments between personal acquaintances within both communities and the more general sense of obligation and commitment from each community to the other played a key role in maintaining stability. Also, people responded in a way that transcended this terrible event, a response that was amplified by people all over Ireland and Britain and further afield. The condemnation of the bombing by the USSR was in itself significant, and many in faraway places saw and understood the violation of the Remembrance Day ceremony. There were many kind and generous responses to what had happened, and the people of Enniskillen felt very much the concern of the wider world.

This was felt as an extension of the experience of belonging, and the cards, letters, and other gestures that flooded into Enniskillen were received warmly.

Of considerable significance was the response of the father of a 22-year-old nurse who was killed in the bombing. Gordon Wilson, within hours of his daughter Marie's death, spoke to the British Broadcasting Corporation (BBC), and, in words which revealed in starkest horror the awfulness of what had happened, he spoke with tolerance and charity.

He said of his daughter's killers: "I bear no ill-will. I bear no grudge. Dirty sort of talk is not going to bring her back to life. . . . Don't ask me, please, for a purpose. I don't have a purpose. I don't have an answer. . . . It's part of a greater plan, and God is good. And we shall meet again" (Wilson, 1990, pp. 46–47). These words and his account of the last few moments with his daughter as they lay entombed under the rubble following the explosion moved most who heard them. Significantly, as Bardon records in his *History of Ulster* (1991, p. 777), "loyalist paramilitaries admitted later that they were planning retaliation within hours of the Enniskillen bombing, but were halted by [Mr. Wilson's] broadcast." There was a tremendous response to the tragedy and to Mr. Wilson's words. (Later Mr. Wilson was appointed to the position of Senator in the Senate, or upper house, of the Irish Parliament.)

Raphael in her book *When Disaster Strikes* (1986), speaks of emergent leaders who are thrown up unexpectedly in the midst of disasters to provide leadership. Mr. Wilson, while his contribution was primarily one of inspiration, established a way of responding to this terrible event at a time when many people did not know what to think and others clearly had malevolent responses in mind. This caused some problems for those most closely affected, many of whom had little time to determine their own response before the interview with Mr. Wilson was broadcast. Nonetheless, at a community and international level, his contribution was very significant. McCreary (1996) wrote in his biography of Senator Wilson (who died in June 1995) that "[His] contribution was both timely and untimely. It was timely because at a political level it reduced the risks of terrible reprisals. . . . On the other hand, at an emotional level his words were untimely and it was for this reason he attracted criticism" (p. 60).

The informal and "natural" responses of the communities were of considerable importance. These were particularly exemplified in the very large and solemn funerals. The churches were filled to capacity and many thousands joined in to walk behind the eight separate funerals. The Catholic community held a special evening Mass a few days after the bombing. The Chapel, also, was filled to capacity with Protestants as well as Catholics. Vigils were held at the War Memorial where the bomb had exploded. A week after the bombing, a special church service was held in St. Patrick's Cathedral, Dublin. Later, Wilson (1990) wrote,

> It was as if the whole land was mourning with the families of the dead and with the injured and their families, and at the same time mourning for all the terrible tragedies, for all the hurts and heartaches, and the misunderstandings and divisions

among all the peoples of this island, North and South. It was truly a nation-wide day of mourning. (pp. 63–64)

These and many other less public, personal gestures of practical and emotional support played a key part in acknowledging the losses and injuries that had been experienced and sent a clear signal of identification and support to those directly affected. These were very important responses.

The Absence of a Shared View

In spite of the widespread abhorrence of the Enniskillen bombing, there was (and remains) the problem of the absence of a shared view of the significance of the event. Some apologists for the bombing indicated that the ceremony of Remembrance Day was a paramilitary occasion and therefore a legitimate target. This was difficult to accept for those bereaved and injured and by many in the wider community, and such a view caused hurt and distress. At the other end of the politicoreligious spectrum, some conservative Protestants and extreme unionists felt that the generous responses of some of the people who had been affected by the bombing were naive and amounted to capitulation to those who were responsible for the bombing. The absence of a shared understanding of events, especially tragic events, is characteristic of divided communities. The same events are perceived differently by different participants. Even in communities not so markedly divided, when a community is challenged by a major catastrophic event, differences and tensions can emerge to create problems, and motives and actions can be misconstrued.

The Implications of Political Violence

The implications of violent experiences within the context of political strife brings with it complicating and additional features for the individual. These include:

- the sense of being used as a pawn in a political game orchestrated by fellow human beings which is over and beyond one's control;
- the loss of a sense of trust and well-being with the world in general or with certain groups of people or places;
- the experience of betrayal, accentuated when people or their families have been targeted or set up;
- the failure of the state to protect and/or the state being the source of the afflicting violence;
- the additional and ensuing experiences that accentuate the unnaturalness of the experience of the loss (for example, the interest of the media; the politicization of the person's experiences; the additional rituals of the churches);
- the constant reminders evoked by other incidents, especially those seen to be similar in some way;

- the rational fear of it happening again; especially, in a place as small as Northern Ireland, the limited possibilities of moving to an area considered safe results in people continuing to live in uncertainty or fear, or actually leaving the province;
- the absence of a shared view of what has happened and the distress caused by a member of one's community being equivocal about one's loss or injury (Bolton, 1996).

PROVIDING SUPPORT AND RESPONDING TO A COMMUNITY DISASTER

Assessing the Disaster and Its Impact on the Community

The most important element of a response to major tragic events is that of assessment. This is central to an initial and dynamic understanding of what has happened and what people's needs are. Assessment should be iterative and carried out on a number of levels, from the informal gathering of intelligence to the strategic determination of what people's immediate wants are and what responses are required to meet them. Some of the key areas and risk factors are summarized in Figure 10.3.

Intervention

Having gained a picture of what has happened and the needs that have arisen as a result, it is then necessary to determine what action is required. Importantly, health and social services agencies and, indeed, all emergency and disaster response agencies should be extremely sensitive to the fact that they function

POSITIVE INDICATORS		NEGATIVE INDICATORS
Expectedness	↔	Unexpected
Contained	↔	Extensive
Low horror	↔	Intense horror
Few losses	↔	Multiple loss
No displacement	↔	Extensive displacement
No disruption	↔	Extensive disruption
Control maintained	↔	High loss of control
Minimal uncertainty	↔	Sustained uncertainty
A shared & common view	↔	Conflicting understanding
Accidental or natural	↔	Afflicted

Figure 10.3 Assessing the impact of a disaster.

within an environment where people already have their own support mechanisms and that other organizations and structures, which may not have a direct role in disaster management, will automatically be responding to peoples' needs (e.g., schools and churches). However, the responses of these organizations will be variable, and the role of the health and social services agencies is to raise awareness and empower such organizations to respond appropriately (see Figure 10.4).

There is also the danger that these natural support mechanisms will not respond or will themselves be disengaged (as exemplified in the initial response of the Catholic community following the Enniskillen bombing). Assessment is the key. Action should be based on a determination of how the agencies charged with providing support can assist or compensate for the inadequacies of the natural support systems. Also, there needs to be a readiness to recognize, accept, and utilize the unexpected support, whether it be demonstrated through leadership, inspiration, or practical responses.

Supporting Those Affected by the Bombing

The support provided by the local health and social services department and others involved in aiding those bereaved, injured, and traumatized by the bombing was shaped to dovetail with those wider community responses. It was agreed that the initial response of the social services department should be to reinforce the existing networks and mechanisms of support within the community, such as the churches and schools. Training was arranged for teachers and others, and this was led by CRUSE Bereavement Care Northern Ireland (a voluntary organization providing bereavement counseling and support), which played a very important and supportive role in the early days. That approach, of supporting

- Low impact: informational responses required
- High impact: trauma services required
- Anticipating needs through assessment and listening
- Catalyst: stimulating responses
- Linking and coordination of responses
- Ameliorating harmful responses
- Facilitating acknowledgment of loss
- Off-setting additional stresses
- Keeping people together (avoiding displacement)
- Preparing victims & wider community for grief and other reactions, and for new stressors
- Sensitizing wider community to the needs and experiences of those most directly affected
- Trauma services available in the immediate, short, & long term

Figure 4   Tasks of intervention for helping agencies.

existing mechanisms, was an important strategic response that recognized the capacity of the community to care for itself, while simultaneously recognizing that it may have some weaknesses or that people may require additional support. This approach enabled control to remain within the community and its important institutions and mechanisms and did not undermine even further the community's belief in itself. Such decisions are always finely balanced, and one can err on the side of failing to spot and respond to need or overreacting and responding too early or inappropriately, thereby robbing the community of its belief in itself to provide support and concurrently devaluing the contribution and skills of its helpers.

Another important task was to anticipate and head-off additional stresses. Clues were picked up as to what sorts of things were causing distress or anxiety, and steps were taken to address them. Information was provided to victims over several months through letters. The media were briefed, sometimes off-the-record, to bring them up to date and sensitize them, especially as the first anniversary approached. Attempts were made to address anxieties about the proposed memorial, by speaking with members of the Trust that had been established to manage the fund set up in response to public donations. Clergy were asked to arrange a special service on two occasions for those most directly involved. This was found to be helpful. The laying of a wreath by representatives of the bereaved (on behalf of all the bereaved families) on the anniversary date (November 8) was facilitated and coordinated for the families for the first 5 years after the bombing. A meeting with the clerk of the coroner's court took place as proceedings were being arranged for the inquest to prepare the court and the coroner for people's concerns. Central to all of these actions was the consultation with those affected by the bombing to determine how their concerns could be addressed. Writing on this subject, Aileen Quinton (1996), whose mother died in the Remembrance Day bombing, comments, "What can be very useful from those with appropriate skills and experience, as early a point as it can be provided, is facilitation; that is, supporting and helping local communities, including the directly affected victims, to help themselves and each other" (p. 7).

On some occasions, those who were bereaved and injured spoke out for themselves, especially through media interviews. However, in relation to some issues, for example the tensions over the form the memorial should take, some felt uncomfortable in asserting their views if they were at variance with the views of others. Such issues were mediated by others, including the present writer. This mediation of concerns, disappointments, anger, etc., can be an important task for those involved in the effort of providing support and pastoral care.

Children

The bombing was especially significant because of its impact on children. Many were present at the scene because they were laying wreaths on behalf of youth organizations or schools. Also, some children from the nearby Presbyterian Church had gone to the War Memorial as a matter of course. Then there were children who were there with their parents. In one case, the headmaster of a secondary school was very badly injured and remained in a coma long after the bombing. His school was very directly affected by the bombing.

Some excellent work was carried out by teachers to support children, and other work was done with families. Some children had profound traumatic responses and needed a great deal of support over a lengthy period of time. Examples of support included letter and essay writing, which was used as a form of debriefing for some of the children. One teacher wrote the following:

> So on Wednesday (3 days after the bombing), we collected up all the little victims, these sad children whose heads were filled with horror and whose ears were ringing with the sound of screaming and of silence. We gave them paper and simply asked them to write. . . . They wrote fast and with great concentration . . . without much punctuation but with great perception. One small boy gave a sigh as he finished and pushed his paper away from him, as though he had unloaded it all. (Doherty, 1991, pp. 29–30)

Teachers also provided some counseling for some of the children. Kate Doherty, deputy principal of a local school, recalls her own work with one student. She writes,

> One pupil who seemed to have recovered well from a minor injury . . . was to experience her worst reactions some months after the event. . . . When I spoke at length to this young girl it was so clear that while she had not 'lost' anyone in the bombing, her own sense of loss was very great. What she had lost above all was her sense of safety and security. (Doherty, 1991, p. 31)

A wide variety of interventions were used, with the most appropriate forms being identified after careful consideration of the children's needs.

The Contribution of the Media

When the bomb exploded in Enniskillen, the media descended upon the town from across the world. Their interest was so intense and immediate that local people were following events that were literally happening outside their front doors through television and radio (for example, live broadcasts from the town on various public events that happened in the wake of the bombing). Two remote satellite stations were set up close to the bomb site by the BBC and ITN (Independent Television News), a technological novelty in 1987.

In the early days, the story of the bombing had such power and richness that it seemed that all reporters had to do was report what was happening (although I am aware of the personal difficulties and costs to some reporters of their own particular contribution). By contrast, there were some quite intrusive examples of coverage, including the entry of photographers dressed as hospital staff onto hospital wards.

Reflecting on the involvement of the media, a number of observations and lessons can be identified. First, some coverage by the media can be very intrusive, cause distress and alarm, or be inaccurate. Second, while the media are often subject to much criticism, people and communities have come to rely on newspapers, television, radio, and other media for information about their environment. Indeed, it would be difficult to consider contemporary society without the media. The media can play a very important role in providing information about important events in the life of the community (and about important events happening elsewhere). Specifically, in relation to major tragic events, the media can act as a vehicle for the transmission of experiences and feelings and can facilitate the acknowledgment of major tragic experiences and losses. Third, reflecting on the earlier discussion on hierarchies of suffering, the media can overlook people who have a story to tell or whose experiences are also worthy of acknowledgment, reinforcing experiences of victimization and powerlessness and amplifying feelings of anger and resentment. Fourth, as happened with Enniskillen, the media can convey a simplistic and stylized image of a community. In this situation, the image portrayed was of a community that was forgiving and tolerant (particularly potent images within the context of political violence). While there were a great number who felt and sometimes portrayed generous responses to their experiences, the media coverage somehow failed to deal with the anger and outrage that was (quite properly) felt by many people.

The local newspapers were able to address this much better. The national and international media, however, which had participated in the creation of an image of a forgiving community, seemed as though they were afraid to deal with other issues. This fear was understandable for two reasons. First, the response of the Enniskillen community was intrinsically dignified and generous, and to introduce what might be regarded by some as negative issues (such as anger) might have reflected badly on the media and been regarded as churlish. Second, the threats and risks were finely balanced. Any intemperate coverage by the media could have tipped the wider community into greater levels of violence. Perhaps there was a third reason. I was struck by the powerful emotional impact the bombing had on journalists, reporters, and producers. The intense drama and emotional power of the bombing and its consequences seemed to overwhelm those on whom we expect or rely on to hold up a mirror to those events which shape our lives, to an extent where their normal approach was altered.

Reflecting on these events and experiences, there is the danger, as Lahad (1988) notes, that individuals and perhaps even whole communities can become locked into a media role and image that inhibit adjustment to the tragic experience. "Survivors who become 'familiar' may be trapped in their newly formed public image and feel coerced to hold on to this image. Such pressures interfere with the therapeutic intervention and may postpone the necessary working-through of the mourning process" (Lahad, p. 118).

Finally, it is important to note that helping agencies and the media can collaborate to provide much needed information and support to communities and to furnish the wider society with information about what has happened and how it can and cannot support the affected community. The exercise of a proactive and collaborative relationship with key media organizations (and the clear exclusion from such arrangements of those that ignore or breach such understandings) can bring complimentary benefits to those who suffer, to the community, and to those who are seeking to provide support.

The Community Helping Itself

It is important to understand how the community can help itself. Communities *can* help themselves. The natural caring processes can mobilize even in the greatest adversity. These responses can be nurtured through legitimization by key people, organizations, and interests through facilitation and mediation. The care provided by the teachers quoted earlier is such an example of spontaneous and altruistic concern. Many neighbors and friends responded in similar ways. However, circumstances can conspire against such caring responses. For example, the beliefs that talking is unhelpful or that it amplifies or sustains suffering can dampen caring responses. [For an excellent exploration of organizational resistance to help, see Capewell (1996).]

Quinton (1996) comments:

> The issue of control in communities is a very difficult one. . . . The important thing for victims is to regain some control over events relating to the disaster. What can happen is that control is assumed by community "leaders," (e.g., clergy and priests, councilors, social services and fund trustees) and they hang on to it. This can be because they do not realize the importance of giving control to the people who have been most adversely affected. They may believe that they are relieving those suffering the most of an unnecessary burden and they honestly believe they know what the victims want or need. . . . There are of course, some local "leaders" who do take the trouble to check out their assumptions and to tailor their responses in line with the actual needs of the victims and to whom . . . it is actually a great relief that they do not have to come up with all the answers. (pp. 7–8)

Two points arise from Quinton's observations. First, her final remark affirms the importance of helpers (clergy, local politicians, social workers, etc.) adopting roles that involve partnership with those who have suffered. Asking the question, "how can we help you?" is one of the most empowering for victim and helper alike. It involves and values the victim, while acknowledging and legitimizing the helper's skills and their proper mobilization. Through this act of partnership, control is being returned to those who have been disempowered and disabled by their experiences. Second, Quinton's comments raise the question, "whose is the disaster?" The disaster is a tragedy for the victims and the wider community, but in different and often conflicting ways. The implications for a town or community are predominantly social, economic, and political, and are more dispersed. The implications for victims are much more immediate, physically and emotionally, and intensely personal. These two perspectives need to be held together with due regard for both, and, in particular, for how the interests of a community can trample on the needs and interests of victims.

The natural ritual forms of expression are also important. Bolton writes (1995):

> [Rituals] are engaged in to mark endings and beginnings; to honor, commemorate, remember and celebrate. They can impart meanings of significance, criticism and hope. They can express constant and essential elements, which are external to the self, but which can become internalized to give direction, perspective and consolation at a time of change and transition. . . . They must be authentic, relevant and timely. (p. 1)

The use of ritual, sensitive to the occasion and the needs of those involved, can be a very positive mechanism for retaining a sense of belonging and identity with the community. However, ritual can be suppressed or misused, with unhelpful outcomes. Those placed in the position of helping a community to respond to a major traumatic event can affirm the natural helping, supportive, and ritualistic mechanisms and processes within a community. Further, these mechanisms can be directed, maximized, influenced, and nudged to enable the community to begin to respond to its own needs and to facilitate the involvement of people who may not feel their needs are as great as others (Bolton, 1995).

Sometimes, however, a disaster will be so overwhelming that a community will have great difficulty helping itself. Communities and individuals may be destroyed or displaced, and the destruction of their sense of belonging may be so great that they are unable to link with each other and provide the necessary interconnections for effective support. In such circumstances, external intervention will be required to begin to rebuild a substitute sense of community and to provide the necessary initial and medium- to long-term support to enable individuals and communities to play their interacting roles with each other. To some extent, the process of peace building is about reconstructing a society which may not necessarily have had its sense of belonging destroyed but, because of the depths of its inner conflicts, has a defective mechanism and experience of belonging.

Community Maintenance and Development

On a wider front, the ability to adjust following a disaster is also about community self-confidence and its ability to transform what has been a tragedy into an opportunity for growth. Enniskillen has shown much evidence of this, with the town itself being the subject of many new commercial and architectural developments. Local people have a sense of self-confidence that was not there before. Having been in the eye of a media storm, they have become very used to visitors to the town, and many good things have been done among young people, enabling mutual understanding. Not everyone has been part of these developments, however, nor does everyone wish to be, and it is important to ensure that such improvements are at least open to everyone, even if not everyone wishes to be part of them. In the early days, the efforts were put into maintaining the community as it ran perilously close to disintegration. The efforts have now become focused on development, and the local health and social services, along with the District Council, central government, and other statutory bodies, have played an important part in this process.

FINAL REMARKS

Returning to one of the key words mentioned earlier, this paper concludes with some reflections on the notion of belonging and some consideration as to how it can help in the assessment of need and in determining what the appropriate responses to disaster should be. The Remembrance Day bombing challenged the belongingness of one community because of an attack perceived to come from the other. That community, in turn, felt a challenge to its belongingness as it feared a backlash. In assessing the impact of disaster, we do well to ask, "How has this event interfered with or challenged the sense of belonging that this individual, this family, this group, or this community has with its environment and with the community or context in which it lives or exists?" In determining our response to disasters, our approach should be aimed at minimizing the risks to people's sense of belonging, rebuilding a sense of belonging that has been impaired, and, in extreme circumstances, helping to create a new sense of belonging. Finally, interventions should be shaped to ensure that an individual's, family's, group's, or community's sense of belonging is not further challenged by the manner in which we provide help and support.

Postscript: The Gift of Belonging

As I was preparing to write this chapter, Northern Ireland was once again experiencing intense political tensions and violence with the end of the IRA ceasefire in February 1996. In the months that followed, the political and intercommunity tensions grew, culminating in serious tensions and street violence surrounding a stand-off between loyalist Orange (Protestant) marchers and the police (the Royal Ulster Constabulary) at Drumcree, near Portadown, in County Armagh. The Orange marchers wanted to parade along a road adjacent to which live mainly Roman Catholic residents, some of whom objected to the march. The police blocked the march, resulting in a stand-off which lasted over 4 days and nights and which ended when the police ultimately permitted the march to go along the road, to the strong objections of the local residents. The stand-off became a matter of principle for the Orange Order, and members across Northern Ireland became involved. During the stand-off, Orange Order members set up road blocks and held demonstrations across Northern Ireland, creating havoc, disruption, and fear. People had to move from their homes following intimidation and threats. Following the march of the Orange Order members, there was rioting in some nationalist areas over a number of days in outrage at the decision to allow the march along the contested route. In the days, weeks, and months that have followed, many Roman Catholic people have withdrawn their support from Protestant businesses, resulting in financial threats to businesses and further tensions.

Looked at from the perspective of belonging, these events demonstrated clearly that the experience of belonging is as much a "gift" of the wider or other community or communities, as it is a natural phenomenon or natural consequence of community living. The gift of making a community feel it belongs can be withdrawn and is not to be presumed. In a conflict situation, especially where there is a majority community and one or more minority communities, the withdrawal of the gift of belonging can be perceived as a threat, engendering a sense of exclusion for a minority and causing destabilization for a majority.

The withdrawal of the gift by political or social forces is likely to be more profound in its consequences for relationships than the loss of a sense of belonging arising from a natural disaster, for instance. The politeness that holds communities with competing objectives together is easily eroded in such circumstances. The risk of intercommunity tensions and strife are greatly increased and the reestablishment of trust will take a long time and require much evidence to occur.

REFERENCES

Bardon, J. (1992). *A history of Ulster*. Belfast, Northern Ireland: Blackstaff.

Bolton, D. (1995). The role of ritual, symbols, and meanings in psychological and community adjustment following civil conflict. In *Grief & Bereavement: Proceedings from the Fourth International Conference on Grief & Bereavement* (pp. 1–8). Stockholm, Sweden: Swedish National Association for Mental Health.

Bolton, D. (1996). When a community grieves; the Remembrance Day bombing, Enniskillen. In C. Mead (Ed.), *Journeys of discovery*. London: National Institute of Social Work.

Capewell, A. (1996). Planning an organizational response. In J. Elsegood (Ed.), *Working with children in grief and loss* (pp. 73–96). London: Bailliere Tindall.

Doherty, K. (1991). The Enniskillen Remembrance day bomb, 8 November, 1987. *Pastoral Care, 8*, 29-33.

Erikson, K. T. (1976). Everything in its path: Loss of communality at Buffalo Creek. *American Journal of Psychiatry, 133*(3), 302–305.

Gebler, C. (1991). *The glass curtain*. London: Abacus.

Independent review of parades and marches. (1997, January). Belfast, Northern Ireland: The Stationery Office.

Lahad, M. (1988). *Community stress prevention*. Kiriat Shmona, Israel: The Community Stress Prevention Centre.

McCreary, A. (1996). *Gordon Wilson: An ordinary hero*. London: Marshall Pickering.

Quinton, A. (1996). After the disaster. *Welfare World, 1*, 5–9.

Raphael, B. (1986). *When disaster strikes*. London: Hutchinson.

The Report of the Working Party on Sectarianism. (1993). *Sectarianism: A discussion document for presentation to the Irish Inter-Church Meeting*. Unpublished manuscript.

Weil, S. (1987). *The need for roots*. London: Ark.

Wilson, G. (with McCreary, A.). (1990). *Marie: A story from Enniskillen*. London: Marshall Pickering.

Figure 11.1 The children of Kibbutz Gilgal, shown with their caretakers. From a picture postcard, used with permission of the secretary of Kibbutz Gilgal, a settlement in the Jordan Valley.

Chapter 11

The Significance of Unforeseen Death in a Community on the Brink

Amia Lieblich

In the spring of 1994, some 6 months after the "Declaration of Principles" regarding peace between Israel and the Palestinians had been signed (and before an agreement had been reached with Jordan), I was approached by two members of Kibbutz Gilgal, a settlement in the Jordan Valley. As they talked to me that day at the university, a proposal began to take shape to document events in the region from a personal and community perspective by interviewing members of the kibbutz about their lives and their prognoses for the future. After a number of discussions, I received permission to conduct my study about a kibbutz's experience of the transition from a state of war to one of peace, or, as it came to be referred to in many of our preliminary meetings, "the price paid for peace" in the lives of the kibbutz members. During the following year, I conducted and taped individual meetings with any members willing to talk to me, using models developed in some of my previous research (Lieblich, 1978, 1981, 1989, 1993, 1994).

Gilgal, an Israeli kibbutz, is situated in the Jordan Valley, 15 kilometers north of Jericho and 6 kilometers north of the present autonomy lines. (These facts are valid as of September 1995.) The kibbutz was founded in 1973 as part of a governmental policy for settling the eastern boundary of the state. Its first residents were young second-generation members of other established kibbutzim. They were joined on the kibbutz by members of Nahal[1] units who had

The author wishes to thank the members of Kibbutz Gilgal for their confidence and sincerity, the Eshkol Institute and the Truman Institute of the Hebrew University for their financial support of the study, and Yael Oberman for her translation and editorial work.

[1]Refers to a branch of the army whose members complete part of their military service either on an already established kibbutz or in the establishment of new kibbutz settlements. Members of such units are referred to by a term meaning "kernel" in Hebrew, and their service on the kibbutz is in a group context.

served on Gilgal and had settled there after their term of military service was completed. Presently, Gilgal is the only kibbutz among 16 moshavim[2] in the northern part of the Jordan Valley. It includes 65 adult members and a similar number of children. The economy is based primarily on agriculture: the production of sod and ornamental trees, milk, chicken-farming, dates, and a vineyard.

The Jordan Valley was captured by the Israelis from Jordan in June 1967 during the Six Day War. Its continued status as Israeli territory has been uncertain since the inception of the political process towards peace in the Middle East. Arab settlement in the Jordan Valley, with the exception of an urban center in Jericho, is extremely limited. Many view the Jordan river and the Jordan Valley highway, running to the east of Gilgal, as a necessary security zone for the state. The politicians, however, have made few pronouncements on the future plans for the area, and speculations are rampant. Residents of the area, therefore, remain in a state of particularly difficult psychological uncertainty.

I began to visit Gilgal weekly in the fall of 1994. By the summer of 1995, I had spoken once or twice with most of the permanent adult members of the kibbutz, which had 56 members: 26 women and 30 men. The interviews followed a chronological format and attempted to elicit the speakers' perceptions of their past, present, and future lives in the place.

Throughout the interviews, several events or key periods in the history of the kibbutz seemed to acquire particular significance, serving as touchstones for the more individual and personal recollections. The initial period—bachelorhood, intensive agricultural labor, and the creation of a communality and friendship among the young pioneers—was painted in nostalgic colors by the more long-standing members of the kibbutz. Many referred to the 10th anniversary of the kibbutz, in 1983, and the preparations for its celebration as a high point. The kibbutz had then numbered almost 100 adults.

Internal power struggles began to unsettle the community in the 2 years that followed, particularly in 1985 when almost half of the members left the kibbutz. The following years were marked by slow but certain recovery, as well as increasing isolation in the wake of the Intifada.[3] This continued until the recent dramatic events which featured so prominently in the stories of the members: the sudden death of a young adult member of the kibbutz in 1993 and then, 3 months later, the Declaration of Principles between Israel and the Palestinians along with the declaration of autonomy specified by the Jericho-Gaza accords.

Mali, a member of the kibbutz since 1980, had worked primarily in education and the dairy. She was married to Uri Yaacobi, manager of the sod production industry on the kibbutz (and, at the time of her death, the secretary of the

---

[2]A moshav (moshavim is the plural) is a semicooperative settlement in which families support themselves individually; but various aspects of the village economy are cooperative.

[3]Meaning uprising; it refers to the Palestinian uprising in the occupied territories, 1987–1994.

kibbutz) and had two small children, Guy and Adi. One summer afternoon, about a year and a half before the beginning of this research project, Mali died in her sleep at the age of 30. She had been napping and was found in bed by her husband on his return from work that day. Although Mali had fainted several times in the year before her death, there were no indications that she suffered from any particular illness; the reasons for her heart failure are unclear. She was buried in Herzliya (north of Tel-Aviv) next to the grave of her father. All the members of the kibbutz participated in the shiva,[4] the month of mourning, and the 1-year memorial service; these events were portrayed vividly and emotionally in many of the stories offered to me by the kibbuzniks.

Accidental and terrorist deaths are, unfortunately, part of the fabric of Israeli reality. They are never anticipated but never completely a surprise. Mali's quiet death at such a young age, however, was totally unforeseen and a shock to the community of the kibbutz.

This chapter concentrates on Mali's death as a key to understanding the plight of Gilgal and its inhabitants as they confronted the confusion and uncertainty of their existence. One of the principal questions is why Mali's death assumed such a large proportion in the stories of members who had never been either her close friends or her admirers. The significance of her death to the members of the kibbutz appears to go beyond her and her husband's personal and social contributions to the community. In their grief over Mali and in their construction of their stories of bereavement and pain a year and a half after her death, the members of the kibbutz coped with and internalized their experiences of impermanence and mortality in both the personal and communal spheres. Through their reconstructions of this unforeseen tragedy, the narrators anticipate the pain of separating and mourning of a kibbutz whose future is shrouded in mystery and whose days (many of them believe) are numbered.

THE BODY, THE SUSTENANCE, AND THE HOME: CENTRAL DEVELOPMENTAL PROCESSES

As one sifts through the stories of the members of Kibbutz Gilgal, the simultaneous occurrence of three developmental processes emerges in the accounts of their lives. These are: the approach of middle-age, the dissolution of the collective fabric of the kibbutz, and coming to terms with the threat of evacuation from the area as a consequence of the ongoing political process. Mali's death sharpened the kibbutz members' awareness of these processes on the one hand, while, on the other, the very natural, social, and historical essence of these processes heightened and deepened their experience of the tragedy of her death. The analysis of the experience of Mali's death in the lives of Gilgal members follows a description of these three developmental processes.

[4]Meaning seven, it refers to a traditional 7-day mourning period in which the bereaved sit at home while friends and relatives gather in the bereaved's home to share their grief.

The Body. Midlife Crisis: Maturation of the Individual

The adult members of Gilgal are a fairly homogeneous group, all of them between the ages of 30 and 40, and they are experiencing the processes of growing older as a group. The population has recently been quite stable. Integration
of new members ceased almost completely during the last 5 years and, since the
signing of the peace agreement with the Palestinians, has acquired the status of
firm policy. Most of the children on the kibbutz are under the age of 12, and, as
there are almost no adolescents or young adults, the age gap between parents
and children is felt keenly. Likewise, there is a noticeable absence of older
adults or senior citizens in the community, or even of transient residents such as
parents of members.

The adult group shares a number of characteristic life-cycle traits. They
describe thoughts and feelings generally found in individuals approaching mid-
life in a manner particularly typical of the autonomous and isolated kibbutz
community, which is colored, too, by the looming threats to their future. They
are busy balancing accounts, evaluating the gains and losses of their personal
and collective lives and their choices of living in a kibbutz in this particular
region.

Their words prominently feature an awareness of advancing age. Of particular concern is a diminished capacity to labor intensively in the fields under
the desert sun, on the one hand, and anxiety about starting another kind of
lifestyle on the other. Alongside the physical exhaustion, several of the interviewees
describe a sense of social and organizational burnout. The more talented of the
members have, for many years, assumed public roles which require organizational and leadership skills, exchanging among themselves over and over the
jobs of kibbutz secretary, treasurer, kibbutz coordinator, and directors of the
various branches of the kibbutz. Their sense of exhaustion and burnout are
related to the absence of "a new generation" who could take on some of the
burden, gradually assume responsibility for the kibbutz and its social structure,
and, one day, when they are old, care for them. Their descriptions of the kibbutz
as a dying community failing to renew are particularly powerful:

> We're very small, there is no new generation . . . and people aren't getting any
> younger. It's as if there is no future. This kibbutz could really die. There's no new
> blood in the Jordan Valley. (Gad)

The impression given by the narrators' descriptions of themselves are of a
population much older than their actual chronological age suggests, and at times
they seem to be aware of this in describing themselves:

> I'm 38, an age at which I see people [outside the kibbutz] at a peak of renewal and
> activity . . . and I will have to experience the feeling of a person who has exhausted
> themselves, and it's all over. Sometimes I feel as if I've come to the end of the road
> in a sense. (Dalia)

The words they use most often to describe their lives, notwithstanding their relative youth (under the age of 40!), reflect processes of decline: tiredness, exhaustion, missing out on opportunities, waste, paralysis, entrapment, concessions, aging, last boat, loss of blood, extinction, and death. Expressions of life, growth, and development are few.

Thus, although most of them are currently studying to acquire new professional skills (as a consequence of the political situation) and are parents of young children, they sound as if their lives are behind them. It may be that, given the effort, challenge, and pride associated with their past—with their establishment of the kibbutz, rejuvenation of the community after the crisis, acceptance from a young age of the extensive responsibilities associated with key positions on the kibbutz, intense physical labor, and lonely confrontation with the elements—the members of Gilgal have reached the fourth decade of their lives with a sense of age beyond their years. Also it may be that the uncertainty of the future prevents them from looking forward optimistically. Many of them seemed to be trying to evaluate whether, in the event of evacuation, they will be able to summon the necessary strength to uproot and resettle in a different place, with different people and different work.

Thus it seems that Mali's death simultaneously symbolized and accelerated the experience of getting older among the members of Kibbutz Gilgal. In terms of the dimension of personal maturation, her premature, sudden, and unexplainable heart failure served as a reminder that life is all too short. For many, her death symbolized their own acknowledged mortality. For others, perhaps, it served as an injunction to do everything in their power to make the most of whatever time is left to them.

Sustenance. The Ideological Crisis on the Kibbutz

Over the last decade, there have been extreme changes in the social structure of the Israeli kibbutz. The process has culminated in the decollectivization of several of the kibbutzim (Harel, 1993). One by one the principles of equality, communality, and mutual responsibility (Bettelheim, 1969; Blasi, 1980; Lieblich, 1981) have come under question. Kibbutzim are experiencing economic and social crises. On the one hand, they face multiple debts and financial deficit. On the other, membership rates are diminishing and the quality of communal life is deteriorating. Many members of the kibbutz movement are suffering from severe conflicts over the validity of their choice of kibbutz life, guilt over missed opportunities and past mistakes, and doubts about the continued existence of their life's work. In sum, it seems that kibbutz members presently experience the death of their dream.

As a kibbutz, Gilgal is also experiencing important changes, which featured centrally in the stories of the members. The most pronounced effects are felt in the economic sphere, particularly in the transformation of the kibbutz member from a "social person" to an "economic person." This is reflected in, among other things, the allocation of more responsibility to individuals for their own lives (e.g., privatization of various expenses) and greater autonomy to the economic branches of the kibbutz society. During the year of my interviews, members were requested, for the first time, to pay their own electricity bills as assessed by meters installed in their homes. Food distribution was also privatized, collective food budgets were transferred to the private accounts of members or families, and the community dining room and free mini-market were closed. Community meals were served only at lunch time and two evenings a week. These had to be paid for in vouchers. Members must now buy food at the kibbutz supermarket and prepare meals by themselves.

At Gilgal, as in other kibbutzim around the country, free food and the community dining room—symbols of the collective life—seem to be gone forever. The significance of this change far exceeds the importance it assumes in the daily lives of the members of the community. Some feel threatened by the prospect of hunger or lack of food. For many others, the new regulations reawaken memories of an earlier step in decollectivization, when, 12 years ago, a decision was made to close the children's houses[5] at night and bring the children home to sleep. Then, too, an essential element, indeed a central symbol of the kibbutz during its founding years, met its demise. As a result, young parents were no longer free to leave their homes in order to participate in public social activities, leading to their withdrawal into the more intimate circle of family and close friends.

This process of drawing inward has intensified in recent years. This is so much the case that, in some of the life stories, a sense of a community with a shared social fabric was hardly discernible. One of the interviewees referred to this as a process of internal leave taking: "The members of Gilgal are on the kibbutz in body but, in the lives they have adopted, their minds and hearts are absent from the kibbutz community."

In stark contrast to these dark descriptions are the reminiscences of the longer-standing members of Gilgal, full of nostalgic descriptions of the wonderful times back then, when the "togetherness" was so strong and there was complete sharing and equality among members. Agricultural work was always done together. Everyone worked long hours, 7 days a week, and there was an almost mystical collective experience. After work, they would spend hours on the grass, talking and eating together or joyously celebrating various events on the kibbutz. Such memories went hand in hand with comparisons to the present and were filled with a sense of loss for what had been but was no longer.

The members' stories, moreover, were rife with references to the end of the kibbutz age. While some, however, felt pained by the loss, others saw it as a positive turning point. For example:

I feel like pioneering is dying out . . . and soon there will be no more kibbutz. (Orit)

[5]Dormitories in which all kubbutz children used to sleep, separate from their parents.

> I think that the kibbutz is finished. Today, the kibbutz, the cooperative community, has exhausted it's utility. It's dead. (Asaf)

While the following demonstrates a positive attitude:

> I think this is a good beginning. . . . It is a process, and people will get used to the new state of affairs. . . . It's the way of progress. (Itamar)

The current evolution of the kibbutz idea is, then, a second issue in the development of the kibbutz and assumes a central place in the minds of kibbutz members today. For, congruent to the maturation and evolution of the concept of kibbutz is a sense of pain and loss no weaker and, perhaps, far stronger than the hope for rebirth as a different kind of community. In this context, the death of Mali also acquires multiple significances. Many members described the funeral and the shiva as a peak moment in the life of the community. The fact that the rituals of mourning took place and were experienced in a manner so particular to the kibbutz renewed, if only temporarily, the sense of extended family and community on Gilgal. At the level of the kibbutz, then, Mali's death symbolizes the victory of the kibbutz over mortality. This was a victory won by virtue of the spirit of the kibbutz community, notwithstanding the major changes that are infiltrating its life at every level.

The Home. Implications of the Peace Process.

The third change to affect the members of Gilgal is occurring at the national level. It hinges on the question of the borders that will be established in the region, among Israel and her future neighbors, in the wake of negotiations among Israel, the Palestinians, and perhaps the State of Jordan.

The members of Gilgal are fairly heterogeneous in their political views and attitudes towards the peace process. While the kibbutz movement is affiliated with the Labor Party, there exists a small, but not inadmissible minority whose members, with varying intensity, claim allegiance to the nationalist right-wing camp and express reservations about the peace process. There are even wide attitudinal gaps within some of the families. Most of the members of Gilgal, however, support the peace process, notwithstanding its high cost to themselves. In response to explicit questioning, almost all the interviewees said that, if the government decides to evacuate the place, they have no intention of repeating the physical resistance demonstrated in the evacuation of Yamit.[6]

At this point, the political process has had a dual effect on the residents of Gilgal, both shaking their sense of security and motivating them to reorganize

---

[6]A Jewish town in Gaza Strip which was evacuated in 1982 as a result of the peace agreement with Egypt, leading to violent resistance among the residents (Cohen, 1987; Wolfsfeld, 1987).

their lives towards a different direction in the future. There are many unanswered questions haunting the residents of Gilgal: Will the Jordan Valley be handed over to the Palestinians? Will the government implement evacuation in an organized manner, with requisite compensation? Is the Jordan Valley going to become an Israeli enclave in a Palestinian corridor, and if so, what kind of access will Israelis have to it? Will the Israeli government continue to invest in the Jordan Valley, or will it, rather, cut its losses and simply let the valley dry up and die? These questions have become a looming threat in the lives of the residents and fill them with uncertainty. Indeed the lack of certainty was the subject raised most often in discussions of their present lives. While some claim to have learned to live with uncertainty and even to ignore it, only a very few see it as a blessing, an opening for new alternatives in life.

Currently, then, the members of Gilgal are striving to deal with the possibility of a future reality that differs from the one they now know. This is reflected in the choice, by many, to study towards a higher degree or professional diploma. When news of the peace agreement first aired, Uri, secretary of the kibbutz, formulated a circular in which he urged Gilgal members to take up studies which would give them the training and credentials to be able to compete in the work market outside the kibbutz. His letter fell on fertile ground, and, in 1994/1995, there were 24 students in Gilgal, some 40% of its permanent residents.

Other consequences are, of course, the mental, emotional, and intrapersonal processes that are related to the situation of stress and uncertainty. Everyone spoke about separating from Gilgal, wondering what would happen to the kibbutz without them and to them without the kibbutz. They spoke feelingly about their deep ties to Gilgal: to the place, to the community, the people, the scenery, the vegetation, the agricultural branches. Each speaker had his or her own personal link to Gilgal. It seemed as if these reflections not only referred to the past but also represented a kind of preparation for the future, a rehearsal of anticipated separation and grief. There are references to separation in all the interviews, and most were communicated in tones of sadness and pain. A striking example is the following:

> When I imagine myself being evacuated, and I ask myself what I will leave for them, then there is only one thing I want to take, and that is the trees. Because I know how important a tree is for an Arab (silence). For me too. So I'll leave them all the houses. What's a wall, what is a house after all? A house is important when you are in it. You are what's important, not the wall. But a tree is something else . . . you uproot it and take it with you. That is what I'll try to do. I'm serious. I'll take all the date trees. If I have a say in how to leave the settlement, I want to leave Gilgal without trees. A tree has roots. A tree is a statement. The trees change everything. . . . The people and the trees. (Uri)

It is tempting to speculate that Uri, still in the process of coming to terms with his wife's loss, makes a keen differentiation between living and inanimate objects in talking about his separation from Gilgal. But, for all members of Gilgal as well, there is a close association between the looming threat of evacuation and the death of Mali.

COMING TO TERMS WITH TRAUMA: MALI'S DEATH AT GILGAL

Mali's death, as reflected on by Gilgal members, acquires special significance in the context of the personal, communal, and national processes described above. On one hand, her death both represents and legitimizes the workings of those processes; on the other, the processes themselves influence the kibbutz members' perception of her death and help clarify why they were so deeply shaken by it. It was in the context of the national issues discussed above that the following question arose:

Where Should Mali Be Buried?

Mali died 3 months before the national agreement. Confronted with the question of where to bury his wife, Uri rejected the obvious option of the kibbutz cemetery which then, as now, consisted of the single grave of P., a member who had been accidentally electrocuted on the kibbutz many years ago. The family of the deceased had long left the kibbutz, and Gilgal members have little to say about this death, which occurred when they were young or before they had joined the kibbutz. Gideon, one of the old-timers, is an exception. He says the following about the first death, the construction of the cemetery, and his sense of its importance for Gilgal:[7]

> As I see it, P.'s death was more important because then we had to build a graveyard. . . . I see a graveyard as something very important. To me it signifies that people live here all their lives, until they die. It's not a temporary place. It's a place for living in for many generations. It's a shame that it's so run down. I remember once making the comparison between homes that you build with 12 meter foundations that can be torn down and forgotten (like in Yamit). But a grave for a kibbutz member next to your home is forever, an everlasting emotional link, and it really ties us to this place. It really completes the picture [of life and death in one place]. (Gideon)

With regard to the place of the graveyard in the life of the community, a less senior member comments:

> In older kibbutzim the cemetery is the history of the place, a calm place that makes you feel that this is it, this is *the* place. Here we don't have that and that says a lot.

[7]Since the remaining part of this chapter deals directly with the community experience of Mali's death, quotations from the interviews will be frequently presented. These, as all other quotes from the interviews, are verbatim translations from Hebrew.

Someone once said that Gilgal is like a train station. A lot of people were here and left. (Naomi)

Uri and Mali's mother decided to bury her beside her father in Herzliya. Most of the members either justify this decision or see it as a private matter on which their own feelings are not relevant. Those who justify the decision point out the uncertainty and impermanence of the kibbutz and claim that Uri was right not to bury his wife in a site whose future is unclear. When asked how he could have thought about this before the agreement was signed, their responses seemed to me a backwards reconstruction of events in which private sentiments about abandonment and withdrawal, locked in their hearts throughout that whole period, have seeped into their understanding of the earlier events.

I think it's easier for Uri that she isn't buried in Gilgal . . . this way it's most honorable if I think ahead a few years. (Itamar)

When I heard where she was going to be buried I was really happy. I thought to myself, "good." So we needn't move her later on. I think that says a lot. (Naomi)

It would have made me crazy if we had to leave her here with the Arabs. It would have been a crime. (Orit)

The following passage reflects the combination of grief and understanding which underlies another member's painful thoughts about where he himself would wish to be buried:

I had mixed feelings about the burial. There was the enlightened, the modern acceptance that this is what the family wanted, and this is what was done. But I think there was also some sorrow. . . . I imagine my own self lying there under the date trees in Gilgal's cemetery, and nowhere else. (Rafi)

It is hardly coincidental that the one person to grieve about Uri's decision is Gideon, the only remaining member of the original settlers of Gilgal. Gideon felt a particular kinship with the lands of Gilgal and vehemently resisted the prospect of withdrawal. He said:

I was very unhappy that they decided not to bury her at Gilgal. Maybe it was out of fear that one day we might not be here, that we might have to perform memorial services on Palestinian territory. (Gideon)

It is clear, therefore, that the fact that Mali, a prominent kibbutz member, was buried in the "heart of the country," rather than its periphery, reflects the temporariness of life at Gilgal. Indeed, the location of her grave emphasizes just how intertwined are responses to the death and to the political events, with the increasingly insistent doubts of the kibbutzniks about the future of the region.

Family Communality and a Sense of Finality:
The Kibbutz Members' Narratives of Grief

Mentioning Mali's death (whether the subject was raised in response to questions or by the speakers themselves) seemed to elicit, in most of the narrators, participation in a communal discourse, a shared recitation of a well-rehearsed chapter in the collective narrative of Gilgal. This is history that requires no reconstruction, a memory that has not yet gone dim. In interviews that took place a year and a half after the death, many of the members say they haven't yet recovered. These are some of the voices of the collective experience:

> It was summertime. The heat was oppressive and all this was going on. . . . It was like a whole year of grief at Gilgal. I think we were more preoccupied with all that than with the peace process. I don't know how to explain it. (Hagai)

Mali's death at the height of the day staggered Gilgal.

> It was so sudden. The unexpectedness made it even more of a shock. That it should happen just like that in the middle of the day, not an accident, not an illness. A woman goes to sleep and suddenly she's gone. You can't be prepared for something like that. People were at home, the kids were starting to come home from the children's houses . . . and suddenly there was silence, an incredible trauma. (Miriam)

> Everyone was stunned. No one slept that night. There was total hysteria. (Tami)

The unexpectedness of the death is brought to bear on the community's solidity in the face of the tragedy:

> This sudden death raised difficult questions. We're still young. We're supposed to be busy with weddings and births, and suddenly there we all were in a cemetery . . . with children. . . . We didn't expect this to happen for a long time. The death hit us much too soon and strengthened the ties among us. We literally reunited. (Hagit)

In these recollections, the shock is more pronounced than the grief, perhaps because the grief is assumed to be obvious and yet difficult to describe in words. Or perhaps the element of surprise was, at first, stronger than the pain, which took much longer to register. The few that expressed their sorrow and longing directly said, for example:

> For me it was terrible. I am aware of her absence in everything I do. I miss her constantly. As if she had been my sister. It was much worse than when my mother died (Orit).

The language of the speakers emphasizes the powerfulness of the experience: words about shock, trauma, disaster, drama, and tragedy. But what emerges most strongly is how the community rallied together, rising to the task of coping with this terrible period together. It is this that is clearly expressed in so many of their stories:

> When Mali died it was the greatest trauma we had ever known. We had never tested ourselves, never encountered a tough period, a transition. And it turned out that there was so much strength here. They helped so much, they were so much together that it was just . . . it was good to know that you belong here, that if something happens, you aren't alone. . . . How we got through the week of mourning, all that support, we were always together. We would stay up all night, the whole kibbutz. Uri didn't really want to be alone and we were with him, all of his friends. And a lot of the time we were helping one another, and if someone wanted to cry, he could cry in front of everyone . . . it made it so much easier. When it was all over, when you thought about it you could say "now I know that I can—[die]. If I need someone, they'll be there." That's a great thing. It's easy to be a friend when everything is OK. What's hard is being a friend when things are rough, when he needs you and you have to help. And it wasn't just close friends . . . everyone was in this. Everyone, even the kids came and wanted to help. (Tami)

> Actually I think it brought us closer. Suddenly it turned out that there was strength here in all of us together. Before we weren't so sure. People came together. (Dalia)

> We have no family here. No grandfathers and grandmothers, just members of the kibbutz. It goes beyond neighbors, it's a real family. We couldn't just turn off at night. We would put the kids to bed quickly and sit together outside for 3–4 hours, talking, remembering, telling stories, looking at photos. The kids thought Guy was having one long party. They wanted to go there too. (Dafna)

> It was like a carnival. I was there all the time of course. Everyone was in it together, taking turns at the dishes, baking cakes. . . . In times like these, the whole kibbutz rallies. We are very united during disasters. You see it too when people's parents die. People come in droves, visiting, bringing things, worrying, calling, taking part. Everyone, not just close friends. (Gila)

Not all the members are surprised by the solidarity or see it as worthy of mention:

> I don't see it as a test. There are no alternatives in such situations. Just like the country unites during war-time. I think it happens out of instinct, it's automatic. It has nothing to do with the individual. A group of monkeys would also need to be together during a period of distress. (Itamar)

> I don't think the community's reactions were surprising. Everyone was involved, everyone was shocked, everyone tried to do their utmost for the family. That is one of the advantages of being on a kibbutz, especially one so small. (Yoram)

The extent of the solidarity was demonstrated in the responses of Naomi, who had been angry with Uri at the time. It was as if the community could not withstand disharmony at such a time and forced her to participate in the shared sorrow.

> I wasn't a friend of hers, and I'd just argued with Uri, who was secretary of the kibbutz, about a number of things. When the panic started outside, Rafi insisted I come out and join Uri and everyone. There were nights that no one slept, and when we finally dozed off, we dreamed of her. It was a dreadful summer. (Naomi)

It seems strange to speak of collective sleeplessness and common dreams. Yet, many of the women recounted detailed dreams which had clearly been shared and discussed together before. And, of course, there were others, close friends of Uri and his family, who spoke of a link that had remained strong up until the time of the interviews:

> The truth is I felt I had to take some of the burden off of Uri and the kids. That's what we did all year long, taking on a lot of the physical and emotional tasks. We just stayed with him, made sure he was never alone. . . . And anything with the kids, if they were sick, their cupboards had to be straightened. It became my second home. (Tamar)

> Her kids still come here, mine go there, as always. This is like their second home. I hear them through the wall, in the shower, and I wonder: "For how long can we go on without her. How could she do it?" I feel longing and anger all at once. (Dafna)

Some of the members referred to the solidarity as transient, a phenomenon which perhaps threw into relief the general tendency to withdraw into oneself.

> It influenced the community very powerfully. Everyone had been through the death of a family member, of a friend, but this event, in terms of the community was enormous. It brought us together, at least for a time. At first we felt like a family. But life goes on, and other things came up. And then we felt even more isolated. Eventually people withdrew even more, and this damaged the sense of togetherness here. (Eli)

Out of a sense of shame, the closeness had dissipated:

> I feel a little uncomfortable with Uri, with the whole situation. We stayed with him through entire nights, and, little by little, it's winding down. That's natural, but there's an uneasy feeling that we aren't doing enough. (Yoram)

The extent to which the sense of solidarity on the kibbutz was linked to Mali's death and allowed the community to come to terms with the tragedy is evident in the responses of members who were not on the kibbutz just after she died:

> I wasn't here at all [when Mali died]. They decided to keep me in the hospital until I gave birth . . . and for me it's like she's still here, like I just can't accept that she's

died, that she's gone. Because I wasn't here, I wasn't at the funeral; I didn't participate in the mourning. I didn't share the experience that everyone else shared here
together. For me it's like she went away and is coming back soon. When we sit
shiva all that stuff about "God made the world in seven days," it's to let you get
used to a new world without that person in it . . . and I wasn't at that part, and it's
as if I'm not in that new world without her. (Yasmin)

The deep sense of participation is a central element of the members' mechanisms for coping with the sudden death. Such an experience is typical, said
some of the kibbutz members, of the communal structure of a kibbutz society
and is quite different from the pattern of events which follow a death in the city.
The kibbutz community is very close and many aspects of the lives of the
individuals within it are shared: their social lives, employment, place of residence, schools attended by the children, etc. Thus, members of the kibbutz are
in many sense dependent on one another. Such a community, like an extended
family, can give maximal support to a bereaved family. The flip side of the
coin, however, is the inescapability of the tragedy in such a close-knit environment. (See also an account of war widows, in Lieblich, 1981, pp. 221–230.) The
constant visibility of the members of the bereaved family in a community made
up of young families serves as a continuous reminder of death and of Mali's
absence from the community. This is evident in fears of death that have since
sprung up in the kibbutz. The speakers reflect on the transience of life:

It shakes your confidence. Because if, at the age of 30, someone doesn't wake up
. . . you never believe that such a thing can happen to you! Suddenly it happens.
People can't cope. Death is difficult to deal with and especially so at such an age,
and in such circumstances. (Tami)

Suddenly I was afraid to sleep alone at night, and Amir was in the reserves—these
are things I'd never felt before. It's not as if I were a child. (Naomi)

The adults told of even greater fears among the children. In such a kibbutz
community, where children are all neighbors, where they all play, study, and
spend their free time together, it's impossible to evade reality by telling stories.
The children's presence and their questions threw the adults, themselves victims
of fear, into the role of the soothers:

The children started with all kinds of questions: Mummy, do all mothers die when
they are 30? Are you going to go to sleep and never wake up? Am I going to die
in my sleep? It was one big uncomfortable mess. (Dafna)

And what do you do about the children? You have to explain to them. . . . Disaster
also strengthens you. It's not a nice thing to say, but it's part of life. (Tami)

It raises questions about everything, all those questions and doubts, because after
all how could such a thing happen. . . . And because of the kids, we had to get on
with our lives. (Itamar)

And from the school-counselor's point of view:

> The kids, too, were thunderstruck. We did a lot of work with the metaplot[8] and the parents so they would know how to work with the kids. Although the medical diagnosis was unclear, we decided to explain it in terms of Mali's strange tendency to faint at loud noises and to say it was a kind of illness. That was the story for the kids, anyway. It may not be the whole truth, but we had to do it because there were children waking up at night to check if their mothers were breathing. (Alona)

Of course, a major issue was the bereaved children. The intimacy of the kibbutz community is once again in evidence: the woman who looks after the children in the children's house is your neighbor; your teacher is also your mother's friend; and everyone sees each other at meals or, on the grass, everyone sees everything. The social worker took it upon herself as a professional obligation to advise the father about his children, but several women on the kibbutz more or less consciously played the role of mother substitutes. It seems that the children, especially the little girl, Adi, remind the members of Mali's absence and are a source of collective anxiety.

> I was Adi's *metapelet* in the children's house at the time. When it happened, I thought more about Adi than Mali. I wondered how not to make her seem pitiful, not to treat her differently then the others. . . . When she cried and only wanted her mother, I had to tell her she had no mother, and it was so hard. . . . And Uri said to me "you've also lost your mother, maybe it's harder for you to look after Adi now." (Smadar)

> Everybody wanted to help Adi, and they didn't know how. They spoiled her. . . . The kibbutz didn't know what to do. Now things have straightened out a little. (Adi)

> It's hard for the kids, and you see them all the time. The little girl looks just like Mali. (Miriam)

> It used to break my heart . . . it still does . . . to see Adi . . . well maybe not as much. We'd be on the grass, some mothers and children, and I'd say, "How are you Adi?" And she'd say, "My mother's in the cemetery and she's not coming back." (Jasmine)

One of the women who was particularly close to the children and was herself an orphan from a young age says:

> I try to make sure that Mali remains part of their lives, of our lives . . . to talk about her, to wear a sweater that she knit, and to say "it's the sweater that Mummy knit." Mali as I knew her with her kids was a full-blooded person. She could be funny or

---

[8]Plural of metapelet, the title used to refer to a nonmaternal caregiver of children of all ages in the kibbutz who works in the children's houses.

irritating, good or bad. She was many things. She was your mother, and it's natural to talk about her. . . . It's very natural to say to Adi, "You're a little Mali, you act just like your mother did. . . ." In that way, she is still with us. For the kids it mustn't be something frightening or terrible or taboo, that they have no mother. (Hagit)

Some introspective members realized how their responses to the tragedy had assumed certain patterns. Some noted a growing sense of attachment to the community (as will be seen with regard to the friendship between Rafi and Uri). Others expressed a need for personal fulfillment, given the brevity of life. Many of them grew philosophical about questions of life and death.

Mali's death made us more mature. It's a part of life. Death is part of life. (Gideon)

Mali's death made us more aware that we are mortals and have to use the time that's at our disposal. Of course that is always true, but something very strong and unique happened here. It seems like since then no one has any patience: I want to get my degree now. I want it all now. I don't want to wait. Life is short, and I want to have time for everything. Her death really crystallized those feelings. (Eli)

It did a lot. Since then things have certainly begun to change. Life is short and you've got to make the most of it, drink it up to the last drop. (Naomi)

Mali's death—it seems to be one of the things that ties me to this place. (Orit)

Since her death, people are much more altruistic on the kibbutz, more of a collective concern for one another, that has continued to this day . . . when anyone goes away, or doesn't feel well. . . . It suddenly felt as if everyone was looking after everyone else, not just their close friends. There are more heart to heart talks. (Dafna)

A more complex response follows:

It's somehow settled me. I don't know if I'll ever get over it. . . . Maybe it brought me closer to my home, to my work, made me fight less, act less crazy, push myself less. I tell you, it settled me . . . stopped me short. You say to yourself, "what am I going to fight if one day something like this happens?" It minimizes things. I think altogether I am more lenient because of it in my relations with people, not just with her family. It's sapped me of my strength, my will, my ability to stand and fight. (Merav)

Within the tapestry of responses to Mali's death, Rafi and Uri's interpretations of events stand out in particular. Rafi and Uri are key characters at Gilgal, central symbols of the kibbutz. Like two focal points in an ellipse, they are figures of authority and inspiration. Rafi represents the spirit and the community, and Uri, the land of the kibbutz, the economic dimension. They both claim that the friendship between them developed only after Mali's death. As Uri sees it, Rafi's loyalty and intelligence (wanting to help and doing so wisely) reflects the position of the community as a whole towards him and his family in their moment of tragedy. For Rafi, the increasing closeness to Uri is inseparable from his renewed and refortified connection to the kibbutz as a whole. Their narrative of loss and of the powerful friendship that sprung up in its wake reflects the blurring of boundaries between self and collective in the consciousness of these two central figures of the kibbutz. At the same time, it reflects the firm belief at Gilgal that death and rebirth are inherent in life: a loved one dies and the link to her is severed; but, out of the ashes of the old union, a new relationship is born.

It must be explained that, in the years before the tragedy, Rafi had begun to distance himself from the kibbutz. He had spent much of his time studying in Jerusalem, looking for a fulfilling career that would allow him to escape the identity he had previously established for himself as a date-farmer at Gilgal. He had contemplated leaving the kibbutz with his wife and three children. Meanwhile, at the time of his wife's death, Uri was serving as kibbutz secretary, having assumed the obligation of seeing the kibbutz through the changes involved in privatizing the kibbutz economy, while simultaneously studying business administration in college. When Rafi heard of Mali's death, he took it upon himself to help fill Uri's position as kibbutz secretary, assuming those duties related to the internal social functioning of the kibbutz community (and resigning from this role, approximately 12 months later, as the official year of mourning for Mali was coming to a close).

In my 4 hours of conversations with Uri about his wife's death, he shared the following:

> Rafi is my friend. . . . When Mali died, I think that his presence here and the fact that he took upon himself the role of kibbutz secretary meant so much. . . . I wonder, if he or someone like him hadn't been here, whether we wouldn't have fallen apart altogether. After her death the kibbutz would have gone to pieces. No one ever dreamed we would have to absorb such a blow. You can imagine someone having a road accident. But you never dream that someone will go to sleep in the afternoon and never get up again. A young girl. A woman. A prominent family in the kibbutz. It was a difficult blow for everyone. Of course, for us most of all, that's natural. People were completely crushed. No one could function. No one could work. They didn't know how to be with me, how to look at me. They were careful of how they talked to me.

> And suddenly there was Rafi . . . for years he'd been thought of as someone with no . . . only studying, doing nothing on the kibbutz, and he just said "I'll be your secretary. Come to me, with your problems, I'll take care of them." And he started to move things.

> There were people here for me: Tami, Eli, Dina, Merav, and others who were close to me. That was my closest circle of friends. They surrounded me all the time. I felt it just when Mali died, how close we were. Rafi and Tamar became friends only after Mali died. In fact they only "returned" to Gilgal after she died. When something like this happens on a large scale, in a kibbutz, it's easier. One of the things

that happened immediately, and that is what is so special, is that everyone who had ever felt close to me gathered round. . . . You know then that there are people who will be your friends forever. They all care about you.

The shiva was a very special time here. . . . This is the real Gilgal, the real spirit of the place came out. . . . As if in honor of Mali, we stopped everything for a week. Ironically, there was a period of blossoming on Gilgal after her death.

At first, the kibbutz offices just stopped functioning. Afterwards we started to hold meetings so that things would get back on track, so that people would see that, little by little, you pretend that life is going back to normal. It helped us cope . . . and somewhere along the line Gilgal calmed down. . . . Today, socially, Gilgal has gone back to how it was before Mali died. We've come full circle.

What stands out in these reflections is the multiplicity of associations to loss and renewal: the references to the period of mourning as a time of ascent for the kibbutz, as a period in which the community could reunite, Uri's circle of friends could draw close, and Rafi and his family could be rewelcomed to the fold. Likewise, there is a pronounced blurring of boundaries between Uri and the kibbutz. Who is falling apart, who is going to pieces? Who is functioning and who is recovering? The narrative creates an almost total identification of hero and collective. Running throughout are the themes of friendship with and gratitude to Rafi.

From Rafi's point of view,

Mali's death was the only event in the recent history of Gilgal to take me back-wards [to the togetherness that we had and was lost]. It also roused something basic in me. In the last few years I felt I had been trying to find myself on the outside. This event shook me deeply in that respect.

Rafi talked at length about how he heard of Mali's death in a telephone call to his wife, Tamar, from a bus stop, while returning home from an interview for a job that would have allowed the family to leave Gilgal. He recalls how he burst into tears and refused to accept the terrible news.

[When I got to the kibbutz] what I remember most that there was a feeling even in the air. Even the air felt her death [sobbing]. I couldn't accept that she'd died, not even until today. Then I felt as if life couldn't go on. [I felt] there is no reason to act now. Now we need to have a dialogue with someone, with God, with ourselves. . . . I felt as if I was interfering with the plans for the funeral, for the shiva, for all that with family members all arriving . . . and Uri was the kibbutz secretary!

Rafi described how, during the customary thrice-daily prayers that accom-pany the period of mourning according to Jewish law, he refused to open a prayer book, refused to acknowledge the God who had taken a young woman, and hurt his beloved Gilgal. And then this chain of events:

Two days later, Doris, I think it was, went off to give birth and came back with her newborn child during the shiva. And suddenly I saw the whole complicated mosaic: the same one who sends Mali to sleep at two in the afternoon, so that she doesn't wake up at four, brings a new child to the kibbutz 2 days later. The whole thing woke up in me long dormant feelings about Gilgal, about the community here. I believe these were fine hours at Gilgal . . . there was a feeling of family, of real pain. No one who hasn't experienced the family-community could understand. It was something that restored the togetherness of Gilgal and brought me back here. I don't believe many kibbutzim have experienced such a thing.

I felt as if there were something that only I could do now for the kibbutz. I had to somehow take care of Uri, help him to go on, allow him to return to the community, while confronting his grief. I felt that it was my job to somehow preserve him whole. When I volunteered to join him as secretary of the kibbutz, I understood that only I had the key to allowing Uri to remain both inside and outside. . . . I could handle the daily drudgery and leave him to deal with the larger issues that had drawn him to the position of secretary . . . even though, given how I was constructing my life at that point, all this was a long way from how I'd pictured myself those days.

Rafi's words also express the dissolution of boundaries between individuals in the face of the kibbutz tragedy. As he speaks of steps taken to care for Uri, it is clear that he includes, in these aspirations, the preservation of the entire community. And, even more than those of Uri, his words reflect a faith in a cycle of life which compensates death with rebirth.

This death represented, then, an at least temporary catalyst for solidarity and reunification on Gilgal at the same time that historical trends concerning the kibbutz and the peace process were driving the community apart. This temporary closeness allowed the kibbutz to shelter the bereaved and create a protective circle of close and distant friends around them. It permitted the community to ensure the survival of the family while reasserting, for itself, its own strength and value. Yet, in the context of the historical events that were occurring in the background, it is vital to view the narrative of the death (as opposed to the real events to which we have no access) from an interpretive viewpoint (e.g., Neisser & Fivush, 1994; Widdershoven, 1993). It is necessary, in other words, to place it in the context of the three processes of maturation and transition that are now occurring in Gilgal: the aging of its members, the structure of the kibbutz, and the peace process.

On Impermanence: Amplification
of the Tale of Mali's Death

At the end of that summer, when the Gaza-Jericho accord was signed, the members of Kibbutz Gilgal, still traumatized by Mali's death, were forced, as they put it, "to absorb yet another blow." In the collective narrative of the kibbutz, there is an almost mystical juxtaposition between the two sets of events, both of them related to grief and death in the community. Mali's death seemed, after the fact, to grow in significance in the members' structuring of their recent lives, while simultaneously accentuating the ephemeral quality of their existence, whether in terms of their mortality, their continuity as a kibbutz community at Gilgal, or their political situation in the Jordan valley.

The kibbutz members' sense of the transitoriness of life and of the impermanence in their situation was expressed in varying contexts. Many recalled that in the early days of its establishment, Gilgal bore the air of a transit station. People were constantly either leaving the kibbutz or joining it, and good-bye parties were held on a weekly basis. Later, during the "crisis," there was a great exodus of families, a "trauma," in the words of the narrators, which further shook their trust in the continuity of relationships at Gilgal. Several years of respite followed, a period of calm and stabilization on the kibbutz. But then Mali's death and the peace agreements brought home, with even more force, the fragility of their individual and collective existence. Examples of some of the spontaneous expressions of these sentiments follow:

> Gilgal is so small and so changeable when it comes to people. I mean they come and go, or live or die. At the moment there is only one grave, but everyone is mortal here. And these hills, this wonderful scenery, they were here before us and will remain when we leave. (Itai)

> The peace agreement is a catalyst, a sort of a slap in the face that rouses us from a kind of dream and says: Wake up, look around you, this is what life is really like. It's a kind of alarm clock telling you if there is time, and it passes, and nothing is certain. . . . This is your life. It doesn't feel so great when you are told the truth straight out. (Amir)

> I don't hear anyone dreaming about a future together . . . or saying "we'll see what these girls are up to when they're teenagers." If you have any kind of dream for the future, somebody immediately comes and squashes it . . . because we don't know what will become of us. All in all, we know we won't be here forever. (Dafna)

> Even before the peace agreement, I don't remember anyone at Gilgal talking about forever. That's the way Gilgal has always been. . . . I don't remember anyone ever saying, we'll get old here. . . . I don't think anyone ever imagined Gilgal in another 20, another 50 years. The peace talks have sharpened that feeling, but really, Gilgal has always been that way. (Jasmine)

> This peace process made us anxious, because there is a difference between living here and making the decision to leave in another 10 years, and someone else deciding you have to leave in 5 years. (Hagit)

The existential quality of their situation is best described by Rafi, who discusses the conflict between wanting to believe in an eternal claim to Gilgal and the necessity of confronting the possibility that tomorrow will bring evacuation. This is, however, but a paradigm for the all too human paradox of existence. One expects to die but is surprised when death hits at the unexpected age of 30. Yet one continues to hope and believe in an eternally peaceful existence.

> We are being asked to do the impossible: to act as if this present situation will continue forever, on one hand, and, on the other, to act as if we expect it to end tomorrow. It's impossible. It's inhuman. (Rafi)

Perhaps it is not surprising to hear the uncertainty so deeply ingrained in these words. It was Rafi, cited above, who saw himself one day being buried under the date trees he had planted at Gilgal. Thus, it is he who reflects on the existential dilemma of living in full knowledge of one's mortality.

It seems, therefore, that both Mali's death and the autonomy agreements pushed awareness of the transitory quality of life on Gilgal to the foreground for these narrators, even before they had begun to speak of either of these events. Some members who have been living on Gilgal for over 15 years claim that they perceive it as a temporary way-station in their lives. They recall a decision to stay "for now," which has dragged on into the present. Others admit, even today, plans to "go home," meaning to the homes of their parents where they were raised.

Still others recall their lives throughout the period of conflict and describe several failed attempts to leave the kibbutz. Many of them, mostly women, say cynically that "Arafat will redeem them" because he will force their families to leave the kibbutz, which they had in any case hoped to do. Only a few responded affirmatively when asked if they could imagine themselves at a ripe old age with their children and grandchildren on Kibbutz Gilgal, in this part of the country. Many could not even imagine their child's Bar Mitzvah on the lawns of the kibbutz. They emphasize that this uncertainty had been part of their lives before the recent events and that the peace agreements, like Mali's death, gave them a pretext for thoughts they had always secretly harbored, even about the death of Gilgal.

It could be argued that, as humans, we all share knowledge of the transience of life, given our finality in the face of death. This sensibility was particularly salient at Gilgal, in the light of the circumstances described up to this point: the aging of the body, the loss of the security that the old kibbutz had granted as symbolized by the cessation of free food, and the threat of losing a home. Depictions of Mali's death, her burial, and the grief that emerges in the narratives of the kibbutz members are symbols and represent a culmination of these three processes. No wonder that the strongest impressions from these narratives are of loss and grief, of descent from the heights to the depths. Only a small few view the chain of events as an opportunity for growth and renewal, in terms of greater responsibility of individuals for their own lives. The foregrounding of transience in the events described in this chapter culminates in the intense responses of the members to Mali's sudden death. Life, then, wavers between the two poles: impermanence and permanence, the certainty of the end, and the illusion of eternity.

REFERENCES

Bettleheim, B. (1969). *The Children of a dream: Communal childrearing and its implications for society.* New York: Macmillan.

Blasi, J. (1978). *The communal future: The kibbutz and the Utopian dilemma.* Norwood, PA: Norwood.

Cohen, E. (1987). The removal of the Israeli settlements in Sinai: An ambiguous resolution of an existential conflict. *Applied Behavioral Science, 23,* 139–149.

Harel, Y. (1993). *Hakibbutz hechadash.* Jerusalem: Keter Publishing. (Hebrew)

Lieblich, A. (1978). *Tin soldiers on Jerusalem Beach.* New York: Pantheon.

Lieblich, A. (1981). *Kibbutz Makom.* New York: Pantheon.

Lieblich, A. (1989). *Transition to adulthood during military service—The case of Israel.* New York: State University of New York Press.

Lieblich, A. (1993). Looking at change. Natasha, 21: New immigrant from Russia to Israel. *The Narrative Study of Lives, 1,* 92–129.

Lieblich, A. (1994). *Seasons of captivity: The experience of POWs in the Middle East.* New York: New York University Press.

Neisser, U., & Fivush, R. (Eds.) (1994). *The remembering self.* Cambridge, England: Cambridge University Press.

Widdershoven, G. A. M. (1993). The story of life: Hermeneutic perspectives on the relationship between narrative and life history. *The Narrative Study of Lives, 1,* 1–20.

Wolfsfeld, G. (1987). Protest and the removal of Yamit: Ostentatious political action. *Applied Behavioral Science, 23,* 103–116.

Synopsis

Chapter 12

Summary and Incorporation: A Reference Frame for Community Recovery and Restoration

Ellen S. Zinner and Mary Beth Williams

It is many, many months after the start of this book that the coeditors have sat down together to review the wealth of information and insights offered by the chapter authors. The cause of the crash of TWA Flight 800, an immense tragedy which had just occurred as we began the introductory chapter, has only recently been determined; family and friends of the victims of that flight have already acknowledged the first-year anniversary of that disaster with private and public ceremony. If we have learned anything over the last decade, it is how to mourn together our separate tragedies. This was demonstrated in the collective demonstrations of grief and public condolences for mourners following the Oklahoma City bombing, the TWA 800 downing, and, most recently, the very distinct deaths of Princess Diana and Mother Theresa. Worldwide, it has become more acceptable and more common to talk about and show grief in the public arena.

Such acceptance should encourage grief and trauma professionals to guide this growing public willingness in ways that promote individual and community recovery following crisis and loss. This book was designed to be a series of real life examples, presented and assessed by professionals, which would ultimately yield a model or template to serve as a guide for intervenors and trained community leaders during a future community ordeal. At the end of the introductory chapter, a list of questions was laid out for readers to reflect upon as they examined each chapter because the "secrets to group recovery" would be there for all to discover and decipher.

Despite the highly readable and intrinsically interesting nature of these case studies, and perhaps because of their diversity over time, place, and type of crisis, a neat model held together with arrows and dotted lines eludes us for a number of reasons. The first of these is that each of the case studies lacks some degree of scientific validity in the views presented, despite the good attempts by some authors (e.g., Nurmi, Watts, & Wilson) to examine certain aspects of the postcrisis situation more quantitatively. This is not to condemn the authors but to acknowledge that questions of what helps or what hurts a community confronted by crisis and loss have rarely if ever been assessed adequately. We simply haven't been in the position to take advantage of our investigative abilities to do quantitative or qualitative research regarding victims' or responders' views of the efficacy of interventions either in a short- or long-term perspective. What is offered here, primarily, are viewpoints, albeit from impressive and knowledgeable professionals, that may (or may not) give strong hints as to what factors may propel a group toward more rapid or more satisfactory recovery. (Even the clarity of that outcome point is hard to establish.)

It is interesting to note the personal involvement of these narrators of the case studies. There are as many ways to perceive and conceptualize these events as there are reporters. In most of the crises presented, the authors were part of the response to and part of the effect of the trauma. Their personal experiences and emotional responses, in fact, color the data they offer. The impact of crisis intervention on intervenors, whether professionally trained or ad hoc, is well known. It may be called vicarious traumatization, compassion fatigue, or event countertransference. Ron Watts and Marise Wilson, in their chapter on the bus crash in Kempsey, New South Wales, aptly call it the "ripple effect of trauma."

The factors involved in understanding the phenomenon of community trauma are, additionally, too numerous, too subtle, and too time-linked to put together into one circumscribed model. Chapters here have described, variously, both micro- and macro-level interventions ranging from accounts of the death overload of rescue workers handling bodies on the military island of Uto, Finland, to the nationally televised funeral of U.S. shuttle crew members; from the Compassion Center for family survivors in Oklahoma City to the community-wide vigils at the War Memorial in Enniskillen, Northern Ireland. The significance of time posttrauma is also apparent as authors recount the initial attempts of communities, groups, and nations to regain safety and restore basic needs, in contrast to later efforts to memorialize and signify the dead and/or event(s). These activities are not distinct phases but, rather, are linked aspects of the crisis response; actions taken in the first stage actually may produce additional survivor groups, spreading the breadth of the disaster, or may reduce tensions, hastening a return to more normal functioning.

David Bolton raises the question of *whose disaster is it*? While this book focuses on the impact of a crisis on the community, any loss involving destruction and death is, without doubt, a profoundly significant event for the immediate survivors. While both the community and immediate survivors share the tragedy, they do so with differing levels of intensity and needs. The community needs to restore order and move on using a different timetable than the timetable utilized by individuals most closely affected by the trauma. In this attempt to restore order, the physical, political, and social implications of disaster which are of central importance to the group may conflict with the highly personal needs of any one person or family or neighborhood. Interventions that may serve one side may not support the other.

The issue of community or group healing raises a thorny dilemma of how to assess community devastation and recovery without becoming anthropomorphic, projecting upon a community a life and identity of its own. A community consists of individuals. Buildings may crumble, laws may be broken, but it is individuals alone who feel the weight of these assaults. Group survivorship has meaning only if we accept the premise that the feelings and behaviors of individuals are influenced, positively or negatively, by the recognition and acceptance of shared meaning. The power of mental health professionals, of group leaders, and of the conveyors of mass communication lies in how those individuals and groups affect the way a community gains that meaning and copes with the crisis at hand. In this manner, the process of responding to any disaster becomes part of the story of the disaster. Indeed, salutogenic interventions coupled with responsible journalism may dilute the horror of the disaster by providing uplifting, heroic chapters for the community to share.

The broad goal of crisis intervention with any group of individuals is to offer immediate help to establish a sense of control and safety, with an eye to how each move, each aspect, each activity contributes to the later trauma narrative. If we, as traumatologists and grief professionals, are able to make the story "good," then we will have done the work we need to do.

While we concede our inability to present an all-encompassing model that would show what percentage of intervention at what point of time would lead to what outcome, we do believe that these case studies yield insights into and direction for facilitating group survivorship that can be extended to new disasters and events. Harvesting these insights across the nine case studies has led to the development of a Reference Frame for Community Recovery and Restoration (see Table 12.1). This framework for contextual analysis of nodal traumatic events identifies, along a trauma timeline, the multiple issues and sensitizing concepts that influence communal reactions to trauma. The reference frame alerts crisis responders and leaders to important aspects of assistance across time. In addition, these issues and concepts describe the factors that ultimately lead groups toward recovery and resilience or toward prolonged personal and social grief and weakened community ties. While many will agree with the significance of the variables listed, still others may add important additional sensitizing concepts to help guide intervenors. Ultimately, however, the value of this reference frame will be evident when researchers in the field of trauma and grief demonstrate the power of these factors through postevent investigations.

What follows this rather lengthy apologia is a discussion of the issues and sensitizing concepts identified by chapter authors in their case studies and organized in the Reference Frame for Community Recovery and Restoration.

Table 12.1   Summary and Synthesis of Group Survivorship Approaches: A Reference Frame for Community Recovery and Restoration

A framework for contextual analysis of nodal traumatic events that identifies, along a trauma timeline, the multiple issues and sensitizing concepts that influence communal reactions to trauma and ultimately lead groups toward recovery and resiliency or toward prolonged personal and social grief and weakened community ties.

Timeline	Issues	Sensitizing Concepts
Pretrauma period	1. Sociocultural history of community/group	Cultural narrative
	2. Connectivity of group	Belongingness
	3. Community resiliency	Preexisting group functioning level Preplanning Competency in coping Resistance to change Accumulation of losses Unresolved past traumas
Trauma period	4. Magnifying/minimizing factors	Risk factors Degree of social offensiveness Dislocation of community Dose response Controllability
	5. Duration of trauma	Emotional limbo Interim homeostasis Rolling disaster
	6. Significance of trauma	Nodal event Communal perception of stressor
Primary intervention period	7. Response of leadership	Grief leadership Emergent leaders Models of recovery Symbolic representation of control Group denial
	8. Response of intervenors	CIS Stress management intervention Death overload Trauma assessment Ripple effect of trauma

(Table continues on next page)

Table 12.1 Summary and Synthesis of Group Survivorship Approaches: A Reference Frame for Community Recovery and Restoration (*Continued*)

Timeline	Issues	Sensitizing Concepts
	9. Intra- and intercommunity communications	Narrative of event Shared view Surrogate grief processing group
Secondary adjustment period	10. Intermediate intervention approaches	Multilevel assessment Phase-appropriate mental health services Logotherapy
	11. Survivorship groups	Levels of survivorship Hierarchies of suffering Social rights/social obligations Vulnerable groups Silent survivor groups Acknowledgment of gaps
	12. Ritualization/ memorialization	Shared mourning Symbolic communal responses Emotional grounds Survivor group identification Reframing Collective fabric Myth making Negative outcomes
Posttrauma period	13. Recovery and restoration	Positive transformation Community's narrative record Timeline of the community Nodal event Homeostasis, permanent Academic autopsy

PRETRAUMA PERIOD

Sociocultural History of Community/Group

Trauma does not occur against a blank slate but to individuals and groups who bring their own histories of assumptions and self-beliefs to that crisis. Anie Kalayjian addresses this directly in her proposal to put any disaster within its cultural context. She outlines how religion, language, and a history of genocide and survival contributed greatly to the coping skills of many Armenians after the devastating 1988 earthquake. Conversely, the delicate balance between religious groups in Ireland, as described by David Bolton, had much to do with the explosive posttrauma situation in Enniskillen following a terrorist bombing. We can also ask whether the relatively nondramatic death of a young woman in her sleep would have had as much effect as it did in Kibbutz Gilgal were it not for its group history in time and place. Thus the *cultural narrative*, the life story of a group before a disaster strikes, plays heavily into the drama of response and adjustment.

The cultural narrative is also relevant to the endpoint of the reference frame as well. Ultimately, how well a group copes with adversity will be measured and passed on, accurately or not, in how the story of the trauma is told in the months and years following its occurrence. Beyond the impact of individual lives lost and mourned by immediate survivors is the group's incorporation of the trauma episode into its history and cultural view.

Connectivity of the Group

Bolton, in his chapter on a divided Enniskillen, poignantly depicts the issue of *belongingness* as one that characterizes and influences a community's response to tragedy and that ultimately becomes the goal or measure of positive recovery. Indeed, for Bolton, the essence of community lies in the shared belief that a group of people "belong." A cohesive community affords "a certain, safe, and wholesome environment in which individuals can lead effective, enriching and safe lives."

The power of this preexisting sense of belonging is more enduring in united communities than in communities in which divergent values and norms present a weaker front in the face of challenging events. It is clear, for example, that in the crisis generated by the sudden death of a kibbutz member, the bonds within this tightly knit community strengthened. However, the lack of shared perspective on the meaning and consequence of events, especially with regard to community crises, is common in estranged communities where differing interpretations of the same event are almost inevitable. Bolton predicted that, in Enniskillen, Northern Ireland, with its history of divided groups, a community tragedy was more likely to lead to retrenchment than to cooperation and increased integration across groups. Echoes of this conclusion also appear in the description offered by Kalayjian of the politically tense climate of Armenia following the earthquake. Writes Bolton, "in determining our response to disasters, our approach should be aimed at minimizing the risks to people's sense of belonging, rebuilding a sense of belonging that has been impaired, and, in extreme circumstances, helping to create a new sense of belonging."

Community Resiliency

Aligned with this sense of belongingness are a number of other pretrauma variables that might suggest how and how successfully a group manages a crisis. These variables might be subsumed under the general heading of community resiliency. Bolton defines *resilience* as the degree to which a community can absorb tragedy and the challenge to its practical and emotional resources.

The *preexisting group functioning level* yields abundant clues to the general resiliency of a community. Watts and Wilson speak of the helpfulness of natural support systems already in place prior to a tragedy. Indeed, intervention by external intervenors may undermine the power and confidence of natural systems of support and do damage in the long run to the community's perspective of self-reliance. Such uninvited help is of more danger in today's world where the number of outside experts, organized in numerous groups or individually, are ready and willing to descend upon a besieged community. For instance, an overabundance of helpers was known to have occurred in Oklahoma City following the bombing, and some of these so-called helpers argued over their "right" to be working at the scene.

The extent to which natural support systems have exercised *preplanning* for an emergency dictates, in part, what outside help, if any, will be needed. Watts and Wilson describe two forms of preparation. *Passive* preparedness describes the resources, economic and human, that a community has to draw upon; *active* preparedness illustrates the conscious planning and specific arrangements set up for anticipated emergencies. International and national intervention organizations, such as the Red Cross and the National Organization for Victim Assistance (NOVA); national professional organizations, such as the International Society for Traumatic Stress Studies, the Green Cross, the Association of Traumatic Stress Specialists, and the Association for Death Education and Counseling; and government agencies on the national and local level, through training offered and responses provided to disasters, make it more likely that communities will be involved in active crisis preparation. On the other hand, even readied communities may find themselves faced with unanticipated emergencies. The latter situation is well illustrated by Lassi Nurmi in his description of the travails of the Disaster Victim Identification Team's response to the totally unexpected sinking of the *Estonia*.

Community resiliency is also related to a general *competency in coping*. The flexibility and openness of a community, especially among its leadership, determines how well the unpredictability of trauma can be met. Communities that are historically resistant to change and cautious of assistance from outside of known channels find adaptation more difficult. Competency in coping can be overwhelmed and weakened in groups that have experienced an *accumulation of losses* and are still dealing with *unresolved past traumas*. Bereavement overload, often observed in individuals who have suffered many losses within a circumscribed period of time, can numb a community and interfere with efforts to respond to a current crisis.

TRAUMA PERIOD

Magnifying/Minimizing Factors

Grief professionals continue to debate what constitutes the concept of complicated bereavement (a.k.a. prolonged bereavement, abnormal bereavement, atypical
bereavement) as a pattern of unusual, nonstandard grief. They question if
complicated bereavement occurs because of the character of the griever or because of a situation of loss that is extreme in its number, mode, or circumstance
of death. Groups or communities of survivors present factors that contribute to
more serious consequences of and challenges to coping with trauma. We have
already noted, above, the significance of the character of the group. Additionally, there are numerous *risk factors* directly related to the nature of the crisis
that may maximize or minimize a group's ability to endure.

Long talked about in the field of traumatology is the differential impact of
human versus natural disasters. Those events which are often called "acts of
God"—hurricanes, earthquakes, volcanic eruptions, etc.—prove to be more readily
accepted; human caused traumatic events bring with them the disturbing sense
of intentionality of harm and preventability. Contrast the focus of anger among
the Armenian earthquake survivors described by Kalayjian with the shock and
fury of family survivors of the Oklahoma City bombing tragedy depicted by
Karen Sitterle and Robin Gurwitch. Ellen Zinner's description of public reaction
to the *Challenger*'s failing emphasizes widespread concern over human error.
Even Lynda Harrell's account of the public reaction to baseball hero Mickey
Mantle's transplant and subsequent death includes the ire of those who felt that
his death due to kidney failure was self-induced.

Other risk factors that complicate or intensify the nature of a tragedy
include the number of deaths involved, the mode of death (murder/suicide/
accidental/disease), the breadth of physical destruction, and the degree of physical mutilation to both the dead and survivors. These and similar factors might
be subsumed under the heading of *degree of social offensiveness*. The impact of
terrorism, particularly, goes beyond the body count of any single act to a broader
assault upon the safety and security of the community itself. Nurmi's account of
the effects of the circumstances of rescue for responders and Watts and Wilson's
research on the rescuers involved in the Kempsey bus crash illustrate also the
issue of *dose response,* the degree of personal exposure to trauma, as a corollary
to the social offensiveness of an event. Sitterle and Gurwitch assert that dose
response is closely related to who, among survivors and rescuers, is most likely
to be negatively affected in the long term by a crisis.

Another risk domain is *controllability*, not in preventing the trauma but in
preparing for its imminent coming and in effectively responding to the emergency situation it creates. In none of the case studies presented in this book,
save in Mantle's death, was there any public warning of events to come; in the
latter case, some argued that the public should have been informed sooner of

Mantle's pending death. But in situations where there is some knowledge of impending destruction from hurricanes, tornadoes, and such, both physical and psychological steeling is possible. Controllability also speaks to the degree of effective response that is mustered following trauma and the minimizing of a sense of social chaos. Geographic and political factors limited the immediacy of response in Armenia and maximized it in Oklahoma City. On the other hand, the limited "success" in finding survivors in the rubble of the Murrah Building in Oklahoma City seemed to diminish the distinction of the rescue efforts, at least in the minds of the first responders involved.

The extent of *dislocation of the community* also contributes to general trauma impact. The greater the number of social support systems, both community and individual, left intact following a crisis, the more resources exist for rescue and respite to move the group forward beyond the crisis. Kalayjian describes the difficulties in Armenia that resulted, not only from the widespread destruction sustained, but by the relocation of family units and the resulting breakdown of local neighborhood support. Mary Beth Williams, Robert Baker, and Tom Williams describe similar responses in Kobe, Japan, particularly among the elderly who were most frequently relocated away from their home environments. However, for many tragedies, the destruction is symbolic, not physical, and dislocation occurs only in terms of changed political circumstances and social assumptions, as was the case for NASA after the *Challenger* explosion.

Addressed only circumspectly in the chapter on the bombing in Oklahoma City and in Eliezer Witztum and Ruth Malkinson's account of the assassination of Yitzhak Rabin was the public controllability realized through the criminal or civil justice systems. The positive impact of those systems to identify and punish those responsible for community tragedies and to create a public perception of lawfulness and social order can be great. Responsibility for the rupture of the shuttle *Challenger,* for example, was a major concern for both the public and NASA, though for different reasons. The public wanted and needed some sense of accountability. Responsibility for an emergency event or for the unsatisfactory response to an emergency event is often sought to bring about some sense of justice following loss.

Duration of Trauma

It stands to reason that the prolongation of a trauma results in greater emotional cost to individuals and groups. Bolton describes the benefits of having only a minimal time period between the bombing and rescue efforts in Enniskillen, whereas Watts and Wilson describe the torturously long efforts throughout the night to cut away victims and survivors from the frames of collided buses. Longer still were the futile rescue efforts in Oklahoma City. Some emergencies, like the Mississippi and Missouri River flooding of the summer of 1994, continued for weeks, testing the usual definition of an emergency situation. To continue to endure within a life-and-property-threatening situation magnifies vulnerability and helplessness. Moreover, when the process of recovery is also prolonged, communities enter an *emotional limbo* that increases the extent of victimization and delays the initiation of the grieving and recovery process.

Crises that occur over a prolonged time frame or are repetitive emergencies hamper any possibility of establishing an *interim homeostasis*, a symbolic but crucial breathing period when groups can take stock of the situation and direct efforts toward restoration of a genuine homeostasis. Bolton introduces the concept of *rolling disaster* to describe one event followed by another, creating a fearful expectancy of continued threats to community order and safety.

Significance of Trauma

Some events become markers in the history of a community or nation. Members easily recall where they were when the event took place or when they first learned about its occurrence. Community history may be conceptualized in terms of before and after a particularly norm-changing trauma. Such *nodal events* reflect the significance with which the group defines that particular situation. What makes an event so "earthshaking" in the life of a group is the combination and interplay of all the characteristics of the trauma period described in this section of the summary. Thus, the preexisting cultural narrative of a group merged with the particular nature of the trauma, its duration, and the degree of group dislocation contribute to the significance of an event. It is in this vein that Watts and Wilson describe the designation of a "bus crash person" for those responders who are distinguished and set apart from others by their involvement in a particular trauma.

Of overarching importance is the *communal perception of the stressor* and its characteristics. Communal perception is more than the total sum of all risk factors and prior history; it includes the additional interpretation of moment placed by the group at every point in the trauma and posttrauma recovery periods. For all of the staggering implications of the disasters encountered in the bombing in Oklahoma City, the earthquake in Armenia, and the sinking of the *Estonia*, shock and pain is also echoed in the survivors' reactions to Mali's singular death, as described by Amia Lieblich in her chapter on Kibbutz Gilgal. Zinner's description of the nodality of the *Challenger* disaster for the American public also portrays an event of great cultural weight despite its circumscribed consequences.

PRIMARY INTERVENTION PERIOD

Response of Leadership

Timely support during crises is offered best by those who are able to provide a sense of control by reducing both physical and cognitive uncertainty. These people become the event "leaders"; it is the pretrauma leadership to whom we look first to bring the community back to its feet following shared loss. Ronald Reagan's response to the *Challenger* disaster and his eulogy at the funeral for the astronauts both identified and directed the grief of the U.S. citizenry. The Governor of Oklahoma gracefully represented his state to the survivors and families of those lost in the federal building bombing. Bolton identified, in the aftermath of the terrorist bombing in Ireland, the enormous significance of key public leaders stimulating positive transformation by conveying accurate and up-to-date information, dispelling rumors, acknowledging loss, and modeling rationality. *Grief leadership* is important because recognized authority figures, whose influence in the community is enhanced during times of communal vulnerability and need, can so readily and appropriately guide members in ways of coping, even when the immediate effects of the disaster are still occurring and the ground is still shaking. Leaders have the opportunity to be *symbolic representations of control.* Writes Kalayjian, "exposure to a common threat can, with the right leadership, pull people together, and the recollection of cooperation and support can also promote individual and group maturity."

Why would leaders *not* respond effectively, when to do so is so important to group recovery? Lack of knowledge and experience are perhaps the greatest restraints to adaptive response by those in authority. Training leaders to be prepared in the event of disaster means more than simply ensuring that sufficient emergency supplies are on hand. It means providing leaders with a full understanding and appreciation of the psychological impact of loss and threat of loss on individuals and on the community as a whole. Many of today's leaders are being trained vicariously by well-publicized examples of executive action such as that shown in Oklahoma City. At the same time, the general public has come to *expect* direction and understanding from their leaders. This was clearly demonstrated in the public frustration directed toward the monarchy following Princess Diana's death. Today's public may be disappointed and angry when salutary grief leadership is not forthcoming.

Leaders may fail to respond appropriately because the dimensions of the tragedy have left them genuinely without the physical resources to respond in an adequate way. Some leaders may become personally incapacitated by the crisis, just as some responders do, while still others may choose to minimize the extent of group loss either for self-serving reasons or as part of general *group denial.* Although denial may allow the group time to get its bearing, ultimately, denial will not and cannot lead to recovery. Finally, some leaders may simply lack the personal philosophic perspective to find or create meaning in adversity that is sufficient to guide, support, and sustain community members in time of loss.

Bolton acknowledges Beverly Raphael's pioneering work and her conceptualization of the role of *emergent leaders* who may arise in the absence of any authorized management. This was the role of Mr. Wilson, the father of one of the slain Irish in Enniskillen, who served as a *model of recovery* for others caught up in the confusion following the bombing. Emergent leaders who themselves are direct survivors of the crisis bring with them their own cachet of authority.

Response of Intervenors

Traumatology as a profession has grown significantly over the last decade. Various national and international organizations, including the International Society for Traumatic Stress Studies, now exist wherein traumatologists may share their experiences, research, insights, and training models. Certification responding to set standards of education and experience now exists for trauma counselors, emergency workers, and agencies offering response and training in crisis intervention through the Association of Traumatic Stress Specialists. The ability to carry out appropriate *trauma assessment* as quickly as possible and continuously over the various phases of a community crisis is becoming more defined and refined as traumatologists expand and elevate their profession. Nurmi adds to this need for accurate situational assessment the importance of having preexisting relationships and experiences among team members; of having broader resources of trained professionals available; and of having training specifically for the challenges of death notification.

The very presence of a crisis team is an important statement to first responders of the emotional and physical difficulty they may have faced, without making the statement that they are impaired. *Critical incident stress debriefing, critical incident stress management,* and other *stress management interventions* aimed at crisis responders have become accepted and widely used in the growing professional world of traumatologists. The well-executed research of Watts and Wilson on the long-term emotional consequences for responders of the Kempsey bus crash demonstrates what has long been recognized by those in the trauma field: first responders often become disaster victims of the very trauma that they manage.

This is one of the dimensions of the *ripple effect of trauma,* expanding the impact of tragedies to those not touched by the first blow. Rescuers are an often forgotten survivor group whose need to be acknowledged, both for their heroic acts and for their suffering, parallel those of other groups more readily identified by those using Zinner's model of group survivorship. Baker, who created "bearapy" after the San Francisco earthquake, reports that his visits to Kobe significantly affected him by bringing him back to scenes of early combat experiences in Vietnam. Watts and Wilson detail the distressing intrusive phenomena experienced by intervention team members in Kempsey. Nurmi points out the feeling of *death overload,* of being overwhelmed and mentally engulfed by the experience, as expressed by himself and responders to the *Estonia* sinking. These feelings were exacerbated, he notes, by the enormity of the loss, the numbers of victims, extreme rescue conditions, faulty rescue equipment, and time pressure for rescue. Moreover, the impact of confronting trauma for the intervenors may well be underestimated in research and anecdotal reports due to the need for trained intervenors to appear strong and invulnerable. Not all rescue efforts are or can be handled by trained professionals. Individuals who come upon the scene or who have been caught in the crisis itself often become first responders. These incidental rescuers may be overlooked when outreach efforts to intervenors are offered.

Rescuers look for meaning, too, in the event and in the outcome of their professional interventions. Sitterle and Gurwitch poignantly describe the spontaneous acknowledgments of the efforts of rescue workers in Oklahoma City and how helpful it was for rescue team members to interact with families of the victims at the Compassion Center and, later, to visit surviving children at relocated daycare centers. Nurmi notes the positive effect that rituals designed for the family and communities of victims had for many of the *Estonia* rescue team members and, conversely, the missed opportunity for support for rescuers who were not able to participate in the debriefings that took place at other locations. At the same time, Nurmi openly describes some of the negative changes in personal life perspective that the sinking and subsequent rescue efforts had on him.

Intra- and Intercommunity Communications

Communication is an essential aspect of community; it is within the *shared view* of life and living that the foundation of belongingness and community are to be found. We have already noted how important the leadership is in providing factual information and supportive direction to members. Survivors themselves, given the ability to share experiences and assistance, will form spontaneous support groups for one another that help in the process of psychological recovery. The media have also come to play an especially important role in disseminating information and in offering an instant analysis of the significance and/or meaning of the event, both within and outside the community in crisis. This is demonstrated in the immediate and extensive press coverage of Rabin's assassination and in the *Estonia* disaster, where information on what had occurred helped to dispel rumors. Conversely, the delay in obtaining and reporting facts about the *Challenger* explosion led to questions about the veracity of the government agency in charge of the space project. In the Oklahoma City bombing, Sitterle and Gurwitch write that description of rescue efforts broadcasted by the media provided a sense of order and proactivity that supported waiting families. In cooperation with mental health professionals and volunteers, press reporting of emotional consequences to be anticipated in survivors and in children exposed to crises helps to lay the groundwork for mental health interventions. The media also provided the stage for the expression of loss by survivors and of concern by outsiders. Individual stories of death, escape, bravery, and good fortune all become part of the *narrative of the event*. A community tragedy is less about buildings falling than it is about the people of the community. How the people tell the story of the event colors recovery, and communal events today are more widely shared via the media, shaping and reshaping a shared perspective.

In taking a broad view perspective, the chapters in this text are less anecdotal in focus. However, it is the individual story or single photo that brings an event down to understandable proportions and symbolically represents the larger crisis. Such is the impact of the now-famous photograph of the fireman carrying the limp body of a dead child in his arms in Oklahoma City. In Israel, the photos and TV coverage of the children's parade and candlelighting symbolized the mourning of a nation. Conversely, Bolton points out that the press can overlook or choose to ignore the experiences of some individuals and groups and thereby reinforce their sense of vulnerability and victimization.

The coverage of funerals and memorial ceremonies by the press invites a broader audience to these events today, and newspeople themselves often become the *surrogate grief processing group*. Thus, we were all invited to the funeral of the *Challenger* astronauts when Reagan spoke on behalf of the American nation. We all took part in the funeral of Mickey Mantle and heard the moving eulogy by Bob Costas. Often shown is the moment on television when Walter Cronkite, the premier news anchorman of his day, announced to the public the death of John Kennedy in 1963 and paused to wipe a tear from his eye—a moment remembered over the intervening 35 years.

SECONDARY ADJUSTMENT PERIOD

Intermediate Intervention Approaches

Multilevel assessment, repeated over time, is the hallmark of professional intervention during a community crisis. The unexpectedness of a traumatic event often necessitates an immediate response more directed by necessity than by plan. However, subsequent interventions following the initial crisis should reflect the changing needs of both individuals and groups of individuals within the community. Kalayjian writes that "expeditious, careful, and comprehensive assessment of several layers of the community is essential to diagnose and meet the bereaved community's needs." She cautions, however, that it is more difficult to assess the needs of a community, given the complexity of membership, deficiencies, and expectations, than it is of individual survivors.

Related to this is what Sitterle and Gurwitch label as "phase-appropriate mental health services." The Compassion Center in Oklahoma City is one example of an intervention that worked well in the initial aftermath of the bombing. Bolton describes how helpful the trained volunteers from CRUSE Bereavement Care were in assisting (as opposed to supplanting) existing support mechanisms within Enniskillen following the explosion. Central to that success was consultation with those directly affected by the trauma in order to assess the best course of action.

Few of the chapters describe more formal therapeutic approaches to bereavement intervention postcrisis. Kalayjian notes, in passing. the growing acceptance of EMDR (eye movement desensitization and reprogramming) and describes more fully the theory and value of logotherapy. Frankl's long-respected therapy model is one tool therapists may use to help trauma survivors find meaning and resolution from loss. Whether and how this can work on a large scale has yet to be demonstrated. *Sociotherapists*, professionals expert in analyzing and creating treatment plans for the community, are at this writing more of a concept than a reality.

Survivorship Groups

Zinner presents an extended examination and model of group survivorship. She writes that "the idea of group survivorship permits the examination of the impact of a death on aggregates of individuals beyond the family and friends of the deceased and promotes the exploration of ways to help groups respond positively to the death." The power of the group survivorship concept lies in directing intervenors to identify all groups affected by the tragedy, to assess their *level of survivorship* or relationship to the loss, and to shape responses appropriately to the needs and norms of each group. Bolton refers to *hierarchies of suffering* in an attempt to distinguish between those who may merit our immediate and most focused support versus those who are less affected. When victims close to a crisis (for example, the children in the daycare center near the Murrah building) are helped, then other groups less directly affected by the crisis often feel supported vicariously.

Vulnerable *groups*, such as children, adolescents, and elderly, whose life stage makes them especially sensitive to loss and change, have often been disregarded or ignored in postcrisis disaster plans. As Williams, Baker, and Williams wrote in describing the aftermath of the Kobe earthquake, the elderly became the "lost souls" and frequently died from isolation and loneliness. Another group whose needs are less often identified are those individuals who bear responsibility for leadership and support giving during a crisis, such as government leaders, clergy, mental health personnel, and volunteers. Sitterle and Gurwitch label these *"silent survivor groups"* because they are so rarely heard from or attended to in otherwise exemplary intervention efforts.

Zinner's description of the *social rights and social obligation* of survivor groups provides another sensitizing framework to direct and evaluate responses. The importance of *acknowledgment of survivor groups* cannot be underemphasized. Communal support of those who are suffering depends upon a mutual interplay of survivor groups recognizing their own connection to the disaster and those outside the group affirming the hardship that has been endured. As we have noted, Bolton raises a difficult issue when he asks the question, "whose disaster is it?" He argues that "the implications for a town or community are predominantly social, economic, political, and more dispersed. The implications for victims are much more immediate, physically and emotionally, and intensely personal. These two perspectives need to be held together with due regard for both."

Ritualization/Memorialization

Rituals have great power and have been a part of communal interactions from time immemorial. They may be traditional and at the ready (e.g., the Catholic mass in Enniskillen); arise spontaneously out of circumstances and capture the urgency and imagination of the moment (i.e., the singing of the peace song in Jerusalem; leaving teddy bears at the fence surrounding the Murrah building; the spontaneous religious ceremony when the bodies of the *Estonia* victims came to the Finnish mainland); or may be planned to serve an identified need (*Challenger* learning centers; Mickie Mantle's organ donor/baseball card). In each of the crises and losses described in this text, rituals play a healing role as *symbolic communal responses* to an event that goes beyond any one individual or family in its impact and consequence.

One function met by the use of ceremonies is that of *survivor group identification*. The distinguishing of those who have suffered from those who have not and who would/should serve the role of consolers reflects the very essence of group survivorship. Group identification through ritual emblems or behaviors also operationalizes the concept of hierarchies of suffering, denoting those most burdened by trauma. Families who had lost a loved one or loved ones in the Oklahoma City bombing were consistently treated with deference; they were protected from the press in the first days following the explosion and were included in the efforts to set up a memorial many months later.

The wearing of armbands or ribbons, the lowering of flags, the coming together in group demonstration of grief and loss all serve as evidence of *shared mourning*. Frequently, this coming together occurs literally when *emotional grounds* are spontaneously (e.g., the perimeter of the fence around the Murrah building) or intentionally (e.g., the Vietnam Veteran's Memorial in DC) created. The support offered to families at the funeral of a single family member is multiplied and extended to a community when funerals are opened and broadcast to a nation. Such was true for the funerals of the astronauts as well as that of Rabin and Mantle. In many instances, funerals and later memorial ceremonies not only give evidence to communal grief but give direction in how to act out grief publicly. The children's candlelighting vigils at the site of Rabin's assassination, for example, provided an avenue to demonstrate grief. Rituals give people a structured opportunity to "connect when they feel disconnected."

Such was not the case, however, in Kobe, where mass funerals necessitated by environmental circumstances were not experienced as a way to bring the group together; instead, they were culturally unacceptable and did not allow for the spirits of the deceased to enter the afterlife in a socially acceptable manner. If the culture does not allow for mass grief or emotional outpouring, as was the case in Kobe, then mass funerals and other communal demonstration will not provide for emotional release and comfort.

Rituals and memorializations provide means to establish remembrance and bring closure. It is important to families that the dead be remembered, which is the function of tombstones and personal shrines. It is important to communities that major communal events are recalled and commemorated as significant threads in the total *collective fabric* or unique history of the community or group, which is the function of statues and plaques and renamed streets and buildings to honor the deceased. Remembrance and closure are different sides of the same coin. One focuses on the loss, the other on the recovery. Both are needed but may be required at different stages in the crisis. Similarly, permanent memorials and markers may be designed and used to commemorate the event, the loss, the rescue, or the recovery. It is the latter focus that provides material for *myth making* that interweaves the trauma into the *community's collective fabric.*

Perhaps the most important aspect is that rituals are a tool for creating meaning. The impact of an event is measured more by its interpretation than its consequence. Even death, a seemingly all or nothing situation, can be judged heroic and contributory or debased and senseless. *Reframing* events as evidence of the strength of a community, the humanity of a nation, or the existence of divine providence through the use of rituals and memorializations does much to promote individual healing and communal recovery. This is what Sitterle and Gurwitch mean when they write about "taking an unspeakable negative and doing whatever possible to turn it into something positive." Bolton notes that less helpful outcomes may be realized, however, when symbols are misused or suppressed or when the recovery rate of one group is at a different level than that of others. Sensitivity to timing is significant, too, as Witztum and Malkinson point out in their discussion of the possibly excessive number of memorial ceremonies held in the initial wake of the Rabin assassination which led, in the authors' eyes, to *negative outcomes* for Israeli society.

POSTTRAUMA PERIOD

Recovery and Restoration

Kalayjian writes:

> Massive traumatic losses not only create a crisis in the community, they create opportunities for survivors to understand their obligations to one another and to the earth, and also help the community feel such obligation. . . . It may well be a paradox that traumatic disasters which disrupt the way of life of a community may lead to spiritual evolution as long as the community can learn from and find positive meaning in a communal crisis.

The existential meaning of life and death, responsibility, and human significance are challenged and sharpened in times of personal and community crisis.

Nodal events, those that are and will always be of significance as markers in the *timeline of the community* and as "a pivotal event in the world view of the community" (Kalayjian), must undergo a *positive transformation* in order to be of immediate and long-term value to the group. This is part of the task of community response to trauma. A community must respond to the immediate emergency; must restore homeostasis by regaining stability and/or establishing a new stability and "new normal state," and, finally, must offer a renewed and strengthened community identity based on the community's ability to transform the crisis into a triumph of survival and growth. Professional intervention and guidance can and should be a force in this transformation effort.

The posttrauma period is, theoretically, an indefinite period following the disaster because it is part of the *community's narrative record* for the life of the community. Witness the 10th-anniversary commemorations of the *Challenger* disaster described in Zinner's chapter. Some events (birth of nations, wars, major political events) may always be remembered by a community. Other events, of seeming importance today, may fade in the intervening decades (e.g., "Remember the Alamo") but their importance in the tapestry of a community should not be devalued. Community lessons inform the generations to come.

How best to reduce the negative consequences of trauma and to promote individual and community recovery and health is, in essence, the quest and purpose of this book. The authors of these chapters have told the stories of particular events in such a way that the reader can understand the power and influence of the crisis on the peoples affected, often including the authors themselves. The value of bringing these historical narratives into one collection is to provide a forum in which to see the themes that reoccur and to judge the effectiveness of interventions taken and opportunities missed. The framework described in this summary chapter merely highlights what these previous chapters have brought so vividly to light. What is still needed, however, are *academic autopsies,* concerted focus efforts to determine not only what took place following a significant crisis but how interventions were received by those for which they were designed, both in the immediate aftermath and in the longer term.

When a community weeps symbolically, it does so for the social fabric torn by tragedy and for the suffering of its members. We deal perhaps only metaphorically when we speak of such tears at a communal level; yet the recovery of the community and its return to a renewed stability are crucial for the well-being of each and every group member. This is the goal of group survivorship.

Index